MYSTERY READER'S WALKING GUIDE:
NEW YORK

MYSTERY READER'S WALKING GUIDE:
NEW YORK

ALZINA STONE DALE

INTERIOR MAPS BY KENNETH HERRICK DALE

PASSPORT BOOKS
a division of *NTC Publishing Group*
Lincolnwood, Illinois USA

Cover illustration and map by John Babcock.

Published by Passport Books, a division of NTC Publishing Group,
4255 West Touhy Avenue,
Lincolnwood (Chicago), Illinois 60646-1975 U.S.A.
© 1993 by Alzina Stone Dale.
Interior maps by Kenneth Herrick Dale, © Alzina Stone Dale.
Manufactured in the United States of America.
Library of Congress Catalog Card Number: 92-60398

2 3 4 5 6 7 8 9 BC 9 8 7 6 5 4 3 2 1

Dedication

For Marshall,
   who loves New York City, and without whom, as the saying
   goes, this book would never have been written.

M.A.D.

CONTENTS

Maps

Acknowledgments

I would like to thank the following people for aid and comfort far beyond the call of either friendship or duty!

Mystery organizations:

The Wolfe Pack, P.O. Box 822, New York, NY 10023, who shared their expertise and enthusiasm for Nero Wolfe's NYC with me and allowed me to make use of both. Special thanks to the Werowance herself and to Margaret Goodman, who told me about them.

Mystery Writers of America, both the NYC and Midwest Chapters, where Executive Secretary Priscilla Ridgeway and *Third Degree/Clues* editor Betty Nicholas chased down facts and people for me.

Jeffrey Wexler, Director of Editorial Services, New York Convention and Visitors Bureau, for a tremendous amount of useful information and maps.

Christina Zeniou, Manager, and Danny Reggio, Oak Room Maitre d' at The Algonquin Hotel, who patiently and pleasantly answered my questions and let us eat lunch at the Round Table.

Dr. Jack Kenney, D.D.S., Chief Forensic Dentist for the Office of the Medical Examiner of Cook County, and his friend, Dr. Jeff Burkes, D.D.S., Chief Forensic Dentist for the Office of the Medical Examiner of New York City, who between them made clear the history and location of New York's Medical Examiner's Office (known to mystery buffs simply as the Morgue).

Friends and authors who gave or loaned me treasured books or read and commented on the walks in progress:

Barbara Sloan Hendershott, Louise Howe, Susan Hoelschen, Harriet Rylaarsdam, Susy Lackner, Margaret Maron, Barbara Damato, Stefanie Matteson, Trella Crespi, Bill Love, Marshall Patner, and Fred Blum.

Writers who answered questions about their books:

Isabelle Holland, Charlotte MacLeod, Elizabeth Peters, Aaron Elkins, Mary Higgins Clark, Carolyn G. Hart, Annette

Meyers, P. M. Carlson, and Margaret Maron (again, for double credit).

Bookstores and libraries who helped me try to cover the field:

Bridgman Public Library, Bridgman, MI; The Book Rack, Sawyer, MI; Scotland Yard Books, Winnetka, IL; and Fifty-Seventh Street Books, Chicago.

My Newberry Library Lyceum class who contributed NYC authors and helped identify NYC locations:

Pamela Davis, Phyllis Dix, Karen Fredrickson, Nancy Goodman, Katherine Hart, Susan Hopkinson, Maureen Liebenson, Mary Prenta, Betty Rotman, Barbara Shaffer, Ferle Terry, Mary Thompson, and Mary Vacula.

Finally, this guide was a family affair:

From Chuck, who walked the walks and learned the new computer to teach me; to Betsy, who contributed mysteries and coped with the new system when neither of us could manage; to Alec, our "immigrant" New Yorker, who shared his expertise on foot and by phone; to our artist, Ken, who drew the maps; and April, our dog, who sat by the window and kept me company. All of their work was a true labor of love.

INTRODUCTION

How to Use This Guide

New York City has been the center of the mystery novel since its inventor, Edgar Allan Poe, borrowed a NYC crime for his chilling tale, *The Mystery of Marie Roget*, published in 1841. A generation later, in 1878, New Yorker Anna Katherine Green's *The Leavenworth Case* was the first detective story written by a woman. From then on, Manhattan's central role as the scene of the crime has been acknowledged by such different writers as Britisher Leslie Charteris, whose Saint declared the city to be "the wonder island of the West, a modern Baghdad . . . where civilization and savagery had climbed on each other's shoulders," to Craig Rice, whose Chicago criminal lawyer, John J. Malone, compared everything in the Big Apple, from City Hall to the Public Library lions, to their counterparts in his beloved Second City.

New York City's many different neighborhoods give it a strong sense of place. Mystery writers from Ellery Queen and Rex Stout—called America's "answer" to Agatha Christie—to George Chesbro and Mary Higgins Clark make good use of its specific settings to give their stories "reality." New York's sense of neighborhood is so strong that characters from one world, like Broadway, are rarely found murdered in Wall Street. As Margaret Maron wrote in *Past Imperfect*, "New York is a collection of parallel villages and the inhabitants . . . rarely venture outside the parameters defined by work and home . . . this is why in a city of seven million inhabitants, New Yorkers . . . walk down a teeming Manhattan street and greet . . . familiar faces."

There is a superabundance of guides to Manhattan's art, architecture, history, literature, shopping, and theaters, but none of them tell the mystery tourist where to find Nero Wolfe's brownstone, or locate Philo Vance's sumptuous Murray Hill duplex, or pick a university for Kate Fansler to teach Victorian literature. This book hopes to fill that gap. It will let you explore Manhattan by following in the footsteps of your favorite New York mystery characters from Ed McBain or Jerome Charyn's cops and robbers, Isabelle Holland's unbalanced clergy, Annette Meyers's unprincipled brokers, and Donald Westlake's engaging burglars, to amateur sleuths like Emma Lathen's urbane banker, John Putnam Thatcher and Haughton Murphy's sardonic lawyer, Reuben Frost.

Since there are literally hundreds of mysteries set in NYC, I first chose two or three books by each of the "classic" authors like S. S. Van Dine, Rex Stout, Ellery Queen, Mary Roberts Rinehart, Dorothy B. Hughes, and Dashiell Hammett. Next, I added books by my special favorites like Emma Lathen and Amanda Cross, then tried—with the help of friends, relatives, libraries, and mystery bookstores—to include at least one mystery by as many more writers as possible. There is an impression that the mystery story is moving out of NYC, but I would echo NYC literary critic Alfred Kazin, who said, "I'm sure New York is the single most important factor in American [mystery] writing today."

Still, every reader may find mysteries and authors he loves that are not mentioned. I tried to be as eclectic as possible, ranging from a thriller by Helen MacInnes to cozies by the Lockridges to the horror stories of William Katz; to have as many women as men, both as writers and sleuths; and to reflect Manhattan's diverse populations by having as many native New Yorkers, like Philo Vance, as representatives of NYC's immigrant groups, like Montenegrin Nero Wolfe or Jonathan Gash's British Lovejoy.

In addition, to keep the book a usable size, it proved to be impossible to include mysteries set in the other four boroughs or exurbia. Their fans will have to wait for a Greater New York mystery guide. Then we can explore together the 1939 World's

Fair with Phoebe Atwood Taylor in *Murder at the World's Fair*, investigate the New Jersey kidnapping of the Lindbergh baby with Max Allan Collins in *Stolen Away*, visit the Bronx Zoo with George Chesbro in *Second Horseman Out of Eden*, or help P. M. Carlson's Maggie and Nick O'Connor buy their Brooklyn brownstone in *Murder Unrenovated*.

Like its sister crime city, London, walking is the best way to see Manhattan. Each walk covers one neighborhood, like the Lower East Side or Central Park, but some walks are divided into two or three parts because there was so much material. The walks are two to three miles long, but they are not timed because, like the mysterious characters he is tracking, the mystery tourist should feel free to stop to visit the Natural History Museum, or shop at Saks, or have a drink at the Plaza Hotel.

Each walk begins with a brief historical introduction, followed by Places of Interest and Places to Eat, and a map of the walk. The walk itself has a step-by-step description of where you are and what happened there. They are neighborhood-oriented, not author- or book-oriented, so if you are only interested in Nick and Nora Charles or the Norths, you should look them up in the index, or check the lists of mysteries covered. Most Places of Interest are on the "must see" list of NYC's Convention and Visitors Bureau, sights like the Empire State Building or Grand Central Station. Most of them also appear in mysteries. Places to Eat mainly lists restaurants or hotels visited in detective stories, like the Plaza Hotel's Palm Court or the Carnegie Deli.

Restaurants mentioned range from the very expensive to the very cheap. Many require reservations, so plan ahead. They are listed because some mystery character went there; if you have an Archie Goodwin pocketbook, look for the museum cafeterias and diners; if you feel like John Putnam Thatcher, try some of the elegant places. Since all New Yorkers seem to eat out, there are always alternatives nearby.

The walks begin and end at easy to find locations, like Grand Central Station or Columbus Circle, that are handy to public transportation. If you use the subway, it is a good idea to go with someone else, use only the middle cars, and avoid the time of day when schools let out. Buses give you scenic views but are often caught in traffic and can be very slow.

As many mystery writers tell you, the NYC cabby is a special breed. Taking a cab, it helps to have a map or know how to get where you want to go, and to check to see if the cabby understands English. But remember, as the manager at the Algonquin pointed out, Midtown Manhattan cabs are plentiful and cheap. (In taking cabs it also helps to say your rock musician son drives a cab. The drivers not only take good care of you but explain—at length—why he should find a better job.)

Remember also: No cab driver has been a murderer in any mystery I have read—yet. On the contrary, there are many delightful cabby characters, from the savvy immigrant who saved the crusading Saint's bacon in Charteris's *The Saint in New York* to Judy Blue, who wore a Mets cap and gave Leslie Wetzon aid and comfort in Meyers's *Tender Death*.

Restrooms can be a real problem when walking in NYC. The old standbys like train stations are few and far between, and many hotels have closed their lobbies to nonguests. The best bets are department stores, restaurants and—sometimes—McDonald's and Burger Kings (though some lock up their facilities).

This guide is meant to be handy and portable, one you can easily carry about NYC as you explore, or can enjoy at home with a cup of coffee and a slice of NYC's famous cheesecake. Mysterious Manhattan is a Wonder Island. Enjoy your trip!

MYSTERY READER'S WALKING GUIDE:
NEW YORK

1

WALL STREET WALK

Historic New York

BACKGROUND

This walk takes you through historic New York's original settlement, now the home of high finance, city government, and police department headquarters. It begins at the southern tip of Manhattan Island, an area once covered with forest and filled with bears, mountain lions, bobcats, foxes, wolves, and wild turkeys. Manhattan was also occupied by James Fenimore Cooper's noble Algonquin Indians, who hunted and fished, wore deerskin and copper ornaments, and used wampum or strings of shells for money. The name "Manhattan" comes from an Indian phrase, *Minna-atn*, which means "island of hills." Built on solid rock with two deep rivers and the best natural harbor in America, Manhattan really began to grow when it was linked to the Great Lakes by the Erie Canal in the 1820s.

Its origins pointed to its future history as a city of immigrants from many cultures. In 1524 Giovanni da Verrazano anchored at New York, and the modern Verrazano Narrows Bridge between Staten Island and Brooklyn is named for him. In 1609 Henry Hudson, seeking a Northwest Passage to India for the Dutch East India Company, sailed the *Half-Moon* up the Hudson River to Albany, and brought home a cargo of furs. By 1621 the Dutch West India Company had been granted a

1

twenty-four-year trading monopoly and the first permanent settlement of Nieuw Amsterdam had begun.

The first Director-General, Peter Minuit, bought Manhattan Island from the Indians for sixty Dutch guilders (about twenty-four dollars), but war broke out because he paid the wrong tribe. In 1647 another Director-General, peg-legged Peter Stuyvesant, built a wooden Wall (Street) to protect his settlers. These early Dutch colonists lived along the East River in "water lots," extended with landfill, an old Dutch custom still being followed. The British captured the settlement in 1667 and renamed it for the king's brother, James, Duke of York and Albany. By 1700 New York had almost 5,000 inhabitants.

Today, almost no buildings in Lower Manhattan remain from those early days, only narrow streets and alleys and place names. These were often "translated," like the Dutch "Jan Quese," or "John Cheese," which later turned into "Yankee," typifying the native breed of sharp trader.

New York always was and always will be a market, not a do-gooding New England "city on a hill." Its founding families were lampooned by a brash young journalist, Washington Irving, in his *Knickerbocker's History of New-York*; most of the famous New York fortunes were made in trade, and the very names—the Vanderbilts, Astors, Roosevelts, and Rockefellers—stir memories of the original trading post and the first merchants who cornered the market in wampum.

Today, however, New York City's power axis not only includes "Wall Street," but "City Hall" and "Centre Street," the city's names for high finance, government, and the police.

LENGTH OF WALK: 3 miles

It is about one mile from the World Trade Center to Peter Minuit Plaza, one mile to South Street Seaport, and one mile to Centre Street and the Tombs. You can cover the entire walk in a day, but you should stop for refreshment and/or lunch. Like all the walks in this guide, you can also reverse the directions to begin at "Centre Street" and walk downtown and west around the tip of the island to end up at the World Trade Center.

As you do this walk, remember that despite new residential development along the lower Hudson River, Wall Street is a work week neighborhood that closes down over the weekend.

See map on page 6 for exact boundaries of this walk and page 287 for a list of books and detectives mentioned.

PLACES OF INTEREST*

New York Stock Exchange, 11 Wall Street. Visitors' Gallery open Mon.–Fri., 10:00 A.M.–3:30 P.M. Admission free.

Trinity Church (1846), Broadway and Wall Street. Open daily for services. Tours at 2:00 P.M. Call 602-0800.

Battery Park, Ticket Office for Ferry to Statue of Liberty/Ellis Island. Open daily, except Christmas, 9:30 A.M.–5:30 P.M. Admission fee. Call 269-5755.

Castle Clinton, Battery Park. Open Mon.–Fri., 9:00 A.M.–5:00 P.M., Sept.–Dec., Mar.–May; daily, June–Aug. Free. Call 344-7220.

Peter Minuit Park.

South Street Seaport, Fulton Fish Market, Schermerhorn Row, and South Street Seaport Museum, FDR Drive and South Street, Peck-Burling Slips. Call 669-9424. Admission fee. Seaport Harbor Line 90-minute cruises. Call 385-0791. Admission fee.

World Trade Center, Church and Liberty Streets, Building 2, 107th Observation Deck. Open daily 9:30 A.M.–9:30 P.M. Admission fee.

Federal Hall National Memorial, Broad and Wall Streets. Open Mon.–Fri., 9:00 A.M.–5:00 P.M. Admission free.

City Hall–Tweed Courthouse, City Hall Park at Park Row and Broadway.

Woolworth Building, 233 Broadway. 1913 "Cathedral of Commerce."

"Centre Street": One Police Plaza (police headquarters).

*Just a reminder, the area code for Manhattan is 212.

The Tombs, Centre Street and Hogan.

Brooklyn Bridge (1883).

1907 U.S. Customs House, Bowling Green.

Sidetrips

Statue of Liberty, Ellis Island (see Castle Clinton).

Staten Island, take either Staten Island Ferry or Verrazano Narrows Bridge.

PLACES TO EAT

Fraunces Tavern Restaurant, 54 Pearl Street. Open Mon.–Fri., 7:30–10:30 A.M., 11:30 A.M.–4:00 P.M., 5:00–9:30 P.M. Closed Saturday and Sunday. Expensive. Call 269-0144.

South Street Seaport and *Pier 17.* Numerous options: fast food and sit-down. Open daily. Call 406-1111.

Delmonico's, 56 Beaver Street. Restaurant dates to 1838. Old-fashioned decor. Very Expensive. Call 422-4747.

World Trade Center. Windows on the World, Cellar in the Sky, others. Call 938-1111.

Harry's at Hanover Square, between Pearl and Stone Streets. Meat and potatoes restaurant; pop. Wall Street bar.

Street venders: all over.

Chinatown.

Little Italy.

———— WALL STREET WALK ————

Begin your walk on New York's West Side on the Hudson River at the World Trade Center, a transportation hub served by subway, bus, and taxi, with both residential and business accommodations. In Annette Meyers's *The Big Killing*, her Wall Street "headhunter," former dancer Leslie Wetzon of Smith & Wetzon, took the IRT Subway south to Wall Street from her Upper West Side apartment. Wetzon hated the subway, which was a garbage bin, but like most New Yorkers she used it for speed and cost. Mystery walkers unfamiliar with the NYC subway system should remember that it is a good idea to travel in pairs; to stay in the middle cars; and, during the day, avoid the time when schools let out.

The very term *Wall Street* is often used in mystery stories with no specific street in mind, much the way the term *the City* appears in London mysteries. A good example is Agatha Christie's *Murder on the Orient Express* about the kidnap/murder of little Daisy Armstrong by a New York gangster. The Anglo-American Armstrongs's wealth came from Colonel Armstrong's mother, who was "the daughter of W. K. Van der Halt, the Wall Street millionaire." The real Lindbergh kidnaping, with its New York connections, has also been written up, by Max Allan Collins in *Stolen Away*.

In many New York mysteries people just "work in Wall Street." In Frances and Richard Lockridge's first mystery, *The Norths Meet Murder*, lawyer Clinton Edwards, a murder suspect, worked there, and in *The Tragedy of X* by Barnaby Ross (aka Ellery Queen), the main offices of brokers DeWitt & Longstreet were also on Wall Street. Isabelle Holland's Episcopal investment banker, Brett Cunningham, too, worked there, at the mythical Chadbourne Guarantee Trust, in *A Death at Saint Anselm's*. In Arthur Maling's *Ripoff*, the investment firm of Price, Potter and Petacque, whose Brock Potter had a way of getting inside Wall Street financial scams, was "on" Wall Street, and in P. M. Carlson's *Murder Unrenovated*, Gordon Banks, tycoon husband of real estate agent Joyce Banks, was "on" Wall Street, too. In Carlson's *Rehearsal for Murder*, the wealthy husband of murdered Broadway star Ramona Ricci was a Wall Street investment banker.

Ironic views of Big Money abound in mysteries. In Amanda Cross's *Poetic Justice*, Professor Kate Fansler (herself a scion of Old New York money) asked colleague Emelia Airhart about her new play. Airhart said it was about parents and college students who changed roles but not opinions, so the colleges got frightfully conservative while Wall Street bankers held constant sit-ins demanding open admission for all seats on the New York Stock Exchange. In *Hyde Park Murder* by FDR's son, Elliott

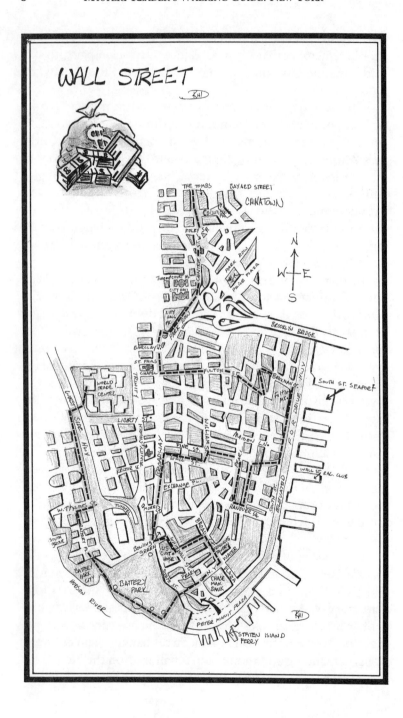

Roosevelt, the plot hinged on an international stock swindle with Nazi connections, uncovered by First Lady Eleanor Roosevelt.

One of the most urbane chroniclers of Wall Street is Emma Lathen, whose John Putnam Thatcher said that "Wall Street is the world's money market. . . . Depending upon your point of view, Wall Street is either awesomely impressive or appalling."

In Annette Meyers's *The Big Killing*, headhunter Leslie Wetzon loved both its historical ambiance and the frenetic bustle, but felt that today's Wall Street was a strange mix of stolid, concrete buildings stained with soot; streets that were dark, narrow caverns; and giant towers of marble and glass. She suggested that the dark old buildings had kept many secrets and invoked a sense of mystery, while the (new) bright lights nearer the river were almost an invitation for the SEC to take a look.

From the World Trade Center subway station you come up in 1 World Trade Center. The World Trade Center has six buildings, including the Vista Hotel, and everything is decorated with large chunks of contemporary sculpture by artists like Miro, Calder, and Picasso. The complex sits in a five-acre semicircular plaza, connected by a ground level concourse with shops, restaurants, and bars. The famous twin towers are each 110 stories high. In the most recent King Kong movie, the poor lovelorn gorilla tried to climb one before he was killed by aerial bomb attacks. (See also Walk 6.) Windows on the World and the observation deck are both on the 107th floor of 2 World Trade Center, but you can also find various restaurants which range from inexpensive to very expensive throughout the complex.

In *The Big Killing*, Annette Meyers's Wetzon met a client, Howie Minton, at a lobby bar to discuss his perennial wish to relocate. In John Grisham's *The Pelican Brief*, Washington reporter Gray Grantham flew from National to La Guardia Airport, took a cab to the Vista Hotel, went to the bar, had a drink or two, then after an hour caught a cab to Fifth Avenue and 52nd Street. He was acting under orders from the Tulane student who knew something about the murders of two Supreme Court justices.

In P. M. Carlson's *Rehearsal for Murder*, Steve Bradford, who had Walter Mitty-like dreams of kidnapping his daughter, Muffin, and using the ransom to go to South America with his girlfriend, worked for his rich father-in-law at Busby Investments, in the World Trade Center.

Global Security, a private security agency in J. C. S. Smith's *Nightcap*, was about a five-minute walk from the Interdine Tower on Washington Street, just east of the West Side Highway. It was a classy skyscraper with the very exclusive Pinnacle Room restaurant on its sixty-eighth floor. It was through Global Security, run by a high school classmate, that ex-NYPD transit cop, Quentin Jacoby, was hired as a special security guard, only to have his new boss, restaurateur Johnny Lombardo, murdered. Jacoby had gone out at lunchtime to look at the "competition"—which was the World Trade Center—and gawk at the crowds.

Ed McBain's non-87th Precinct mystery, *Downtown*, which *is* about New York, began on Christmas Eve. In the book, orange-grower and ex-Vietnam vet Michael J. (for Jellicoe) Barnes had one bizarre adventure after another, all over Lower Manhattan. In *Downtown*, McBain is a little off on some of his New York locales. But McBain had Barnes file a complaint at the First Precinct—which really is just north of the World Trade Center, at 16 Ericsson Place, a tiny street between Hudson and Lower Broadway.

Take Exit 1 on the lobby level and go left out of the southern tower (2 World Trade Center) to Liberty Street. Cross Liberty Street and turn right to take the pedestrian bridge across the West Side Highway to the World Financial Center. This new development is part of Battery Park City, which was built on landfill from the excavation for the World Trade Center. You enter by the Oppenheimer Building (1 World Financial Center). In Meyers's *The Big Killing*, Wetzon meets former client Laura Lee Day there, at her office, and then the two head for a silk undies sale at Century Twenty-One, three blocks east, at the corner of Liberty and Trinity Streets.

Come out of the Oppenheimer Building and walk south down the West Side Highway to West Thames Street. (Unless NYC has completed the South Gardens landscaping, you cannot walk all the way along the Hudson River Esplanade.) Across West Side Highway is the little whitewashed St. Nicholas Greek Orthodox Church with its cross-topped bell gable.

At West Thames Street go right one block to Battery Place and follow it to Battery Park. There is no street sign there and at some point your way may be blocked; if so, return to West Thames Street and continue south on West Side Highway to Battery Park.

In Barnaby Ross's (aka Ellery Queen's) *The Tragedy of X*, deaf actor Drury Lane visited the Uruguayan Consulate (now at 747 Third Avenue) on Battery Place. Drury Lane got vital information there about the Wall Street brokers, murdered Harry Longstreet and John De Witt, who had once been partners in a Uruguayan mining company.

In Ed McBain's *Downtown*, orange-grower Barnes and his newly found Chinese girlfriend, Connie Kee, went to a disco called Oz at 3:00 A.M. on Boxing Day (December 26). They were hunting for a mafia member known as "Mama." Oz was across the West Side Highway between Morris and Edgar Streets, near the entrance to the Battery Tunnel. Once there they found about 100 people dressed like Oz characters standing outside on the yellow brick sidewalk. Inside, the place was Emerald City green. When they found "Mama," Barnes and Connie chased "Mama" up Greenwich Street to Liberty Street, where they all got jammed into a black Cadillac and taken for a ride.

As you walk down the West Side Highway you can also see the Downtown Athletic Club, home of the Heisman Trophy. You then come to a parking lot for the ferry to Liberty and Ellis Islands, and an old fire station in a big white building with a green roof, with fireboats moored by its side. Keep going until you can cross Battery Place to reach Battery Park. You are now at the southern tip of Manhattan, with a wide and wonderful view of both city and harbor.

To your left is the Netherlands Memorial Monument, and the wide walk in front of you leads to Castle Clinton National Monument, or what's left of a circular sandstone fort built to protect the city during the War of 1812. Originally it was joined to the mainland by a causeway and had a twin on Governors Island called Castle Columbus.

General Lafayette landed at Castle Clinton in 1824 to begin a triumphant tour of his adopted country. And the Swedish nightingale, Jenny Lind, had a very successful concert staged here by famous showman P. T. Barnum, in 1850. From 1855 to 1892, Castle Clinton was the immigrant landing depot. Later it became the city aquarium. With only part of its walls still remaining, the former fort is now a memorial to De Witt Clinton, mayor of New York City and Governor of New York State, who was the founder of Tammany Hall. De Witt Clinton also was instrumental in the building of the Erie Canal, which linked Lake Erie (and the Middle West) with the Atlantic Ocean, and made New York America's number one port.

Castle Clinton is now a National Park System's visitors' center (with restrooms), where you can buy tickets for the ferry to Liberty Island and Ellis Island, both recently refurbished. About 100 million Americans trace their ancestry to Ellis Island immigrants, but one distinguished visitor was allowed to "bypass the quarantine place" by getting a special clearance from the U.S. ambassador in London. This was Lord Peter Wimsey, en route to New York to save his brother the Duke's neck in Dorothy L. Sayers's *Clouds of Witness*. Both islands are clearly visible from the mainland and if you don't want to visit them, you can just stand and stare out to sea.

After visiting Castle Clinton, cut to your left across Battery Park, past the statue of fifteenth-century explorer Verrazano and other monuments. At the end of Battery Park you will reach the Port Authority building, the South Ferry subway station, and the Staten Island Ferry.

One of New York's most famous 1920s swingers, poet Edna St. Vincent Millay, captured the 1920s Greenwich Village spirit in her poem about spending the night going back and forth on the ferry. In *Having a Wonderful Crime*, Craig Rice's hilarious romp through Manhattan, young widower Dennis Morrison, Jake Justus, and lawyer J. J. Malone all spent time riding back and forth, getting stabbed and shoved into the harbor, or visiting the murder victim's father, homey Dr. Puckett, on Staten

Island. When Jake Justus took the ferry, however, he did not look at the Statue of Liberty because he wanted to see it first with his missing wife, Helene.

During the March on Wall Street in Emma Lathen's *Death Shall Overcome*, the Stock Exchange's "Three Wise Men" found it difficult to find a quiet place to meet and write a press release, so they spent a blustery November day on the pitching deck of the Staten Island Ferry.

At the eastern edge of Battery Park there is a bus stop on State Street. In Haughton Murphy's *Murder for Lunch*, Wall Street lawyer George Bannard always takes the Express Bus from his home on the Upper East Side to Battery Park. His firm, Chase and Ward, had offices in a new skyscraper with a view of the harbor and East River.

If you don't want to go to Staten Island by ferry or by the Verrazano-Narrows Bridge, cross State Street to Peter Minuit Plaza (a tiny green spot with a few trees between roaring traffic). There is a flagpole memorial to New York's first Jewish settlers, who came in 1654, thanks to some pirates.

At Peter Minuit Plaza you have walked about one mile and may want to stop for refreshment. There is a McDonald's at the corner of Moore and Water Streets, opposite 1 New York Plaza (Chase Manhattan Bank). (McDonald's is America's answer to pit stops, but beware, not all Manhattan's McDonald's keep their public facilities open.) And there are usually street vendors (with pushcarts) selling hot dogs, pretzels, and more exotic ethnic foods during the week. You might also walk a little farther to dine at historic Fraunces Tavern, or you may want to just get a drink and wait to eat until the second leg of the walk, which ends at the South Street Seaport (Fulton Street).

Turn right to cross Whitehall, then walk along Water Street for one block past 1 New York Plaza, the skyscraper home of the Chase Manhattan Bank. The law offices of Haughton Murphy's Chase and Ward are at fictional 1 Metropolitan Plaza. In *Murder for Lunch*, partner Graham Donovan, poisoned by water from his desk carafe, died next door in the Hexagon Club. Donovan (who like many mystery characters had very negative views about New York cabbies) had taken a carefully selected cab from his Upper East Side condo to the corner of Broad and Water Streets. This meant that Chase and Ward was either in 1 New York Plaza or possibly 4 New York Plaza (Manufacturers Hanover Trust).

Walk past the Chase Manhattan Bank and cross Broad Street. Turn left to cross Water Street, which was the original riverside site where the Dutch settlers lived. On Broad Street between Water Street and Pearl Street is the brick, Federal-style Fraunces Tavern, where you might stop for lunch in the wood-paneled dining room with its fireplace and comfortable leather arm chairs. A house specialty is Baked Chicken Washington. Afternoons they serve customary free snacks with drinks.

The original Fraunces Tavern was put up in 1719 but rebuilt in 1927. It belonged to the Delanceys, who remained loyal to king and crown, making it ironic that George Washington said farewell to his Revolutionary troops here in 1783. Upstairs there is a replica of the original tavern room where city business was conducted, while the top floor is a Colonial museum. The museum is open Sundays when the restaurant is closed.

In Meyers's *The Big Killing*, headhunter Wetzon took broker Barry Stark to Fraunces Tavern the first time they met to talk about getting Stark a new job. While they were there, broker Mildred Gleason, the ex-wife of broker Jake Donohue, for whom Stark was currently working, came by their table and yelled at Stark. In Cross's *The Question of Max*, Kate Fansler was dragged to lunch at Fraunces Tavern by her infuriated older brother, who refused to accept the idea that his son, Leo, intended to go to Swarthmore College instead of Harvard.

Leave Fraunces Tavern and turn right to cross Bridge Street. Walk up Broad Street to Stone Street (paved with cobblestones in 1658). Between Bridge Street and Pearl Street, in 1625, there was a small thatched building there that housed the offices of the Dutch West India Company. Go left (west) on Stone to Whitehall and turn up Whitehall to the U.S. Customs House, a 1907 Beaux-Arts building with colonnades that was built on the site of Fort Amsterdam. The Customs Office has since moved to the World Trade Center, but, in the old days, city officials made good money there skimming the top off import taxes on goods.

Cross Battery Place to Bowling Green, where Dutch Peter Minuit paid the wrong Indians twenty-four dollars (or sixty guilders) for the island of Manhattan. This was the site of the original Dutch marketplace. The British made it into a park with a statue of George III, which the Americans melted down for bullets in the Revolutionary War—but they left the iron fence, after tearing off its crowns. Many NYC parades begin here, taking Lower Broadway north. Ticker tape was first used in a parade here for New York native son Teddy Roosevelt; today, however, New Yorkers use shredded computer printouts. As you walk by, take a look at the Bowling Green subway station, one of the cleanest and best in the city. It will give you a feel for the new stations' ambiance if you don't plan to ride the subway. In Emma Lathen's *Death Shall Overcome*, after the March on Wall Street turned into a love-in (and shoot-out) at the New York Stock Exchange, the marchers came back here to picnic.

Walk around Bowling Green to the left. At the far corner, State Street becomes (Lower) Broadway. One Broadway, the home of the famous United States Line, reminds you that New York has been a great port for centuries. Go right to walk up Broadway. In Emma Lathen's *Banking on Death*, John Putnam Thatcher's old Harvard classmate, lawyer Tom Robichaux, had his offices at 4 Broadway, near Bowling Green and Beaver Street. Robichaux's partner was the saintly Quaker, Francis Devane (Robichaux had so many marriages that Thatcher often gets his wives mixed up). Twenty-five Broadway was the headquarters of the Cunard Line, home of the great Queen ocean liners, and across the street at 26 Broadway was the original Standard Oil Building, decorated with oil lamps. When the parade was held for Teddy Roosevelt, the Rockefellers refused to fly a flag from the building because Roosevelt had "trustbusted" the Rockefellers' Standard Oil Company to bits.

Cross Morris Street and walk to Exchange Street. Cross Exchange to look inside 61 Broadway. In *The Big Killing*, Annette Meyers's Leslie Wetzon visits the brokerage offices of Mildred Gleason at 61 Broadway, another wonderful old Art Deco building, with a beautifully restored lobby whose main doors are inlaid with geometric designs in brass on bronze. While there, Wetzon was startled to see murdered Barry Stark's girlfriend, Buffie, get off the elevator. Upstairs, Wetzon saw that the Gleason & Company offices said "old money, you can depend on us," with their dark wood, English antiques, and oriental rugs.

Go up Broadway to Rector Street, where Emma Lathen's Carruthers, one of the New York Stock Exchange's so-called "Three Wise Men," had his cramped law offices. In *Death Shall Overcome*, the Three Wise Men left Carruthers's office when told there was a "race riot" in front of a brokerage house. But it turned out to be just a few dispirited people and a lot of media. As Thatcher hurried to the "race riot" he saw Trinity's gallant spire, dwarfed by the surrounding colossi.

Cross Rector Street to Trinity Church with its green church-yard/cemetery and familiar spire, which has become a modern-day symbol of Wall Street on TV. In Jack Finney's *Time and Again*—a time/travel mystery that took place in NYC in the 1880s and the 1970s, government spy Simon Marley first viewed NYC from the top of Trinity Church, the highest point in the city in 1880. Later, in the 1970s, he brought Julia, whom he had met in Central Park, back to Trinity to prove she was still in NYC.

First built in 1698, the church burned in 1776 when the British torched the city. The second church, built soon after, collapsed from snow on its roof. The third church, built in 1846 in the Gothic Revival style, is the one we know today. Its ceme-tery, though, is much older and contains such notables as Rob-ert Fulton, who sent steamships up the Hudson River, and Al-exander Hamilton, who was killed by his political rival, Aaron Burr, in a duel in Weehawken, New Jersey. The Episcopal Church had forbidden duels but since Hamilton had written a pamphlet against the practice and deloped (fired into the air) he was allowed burial here.

Lathen's Thatcher would also appreciate the fact that Queen Anne's original land grant gave Trinity huge real estate holdings in Manhattan. Columbia University began here as King's College, but now, like Trinity School, where Neal Carey, the street kid raised to be a P.I. went in Winslow's *A Cool Breeze on the Underground*, it is located on the Upper West Side. (See Walk 10.)

After looking at the church, turn right to cross Broadway to Wall Street. The entire block from Wall Street to Exchange Place, Broadway to New Street, was formerly owned by the Irving Trust Company, which is the best candidate for Emma Lathen's Sloan Guarantee Trust. Its old building, 1 Wall Street, was known as the most expensive piece of real estate in the world. Built in 1932, it is famous for its brilliant Art Deco mosaics in the lobby. The Irving Trust's new building was completed in 1964, the year that John Putnam Thatcher complained about Sloan's remodeling in *Banking on Death*. Thatcher's Trust Department, including his very efficient young secretary, Rose Theresa Corsa; Charlie Trinkham, shirt-chasing and casual; Everett Gabler, a fussy old lady; genial research head Walter Bowman; and young Kenneth Nichols, was located on the sixth floor. Another well-known Sloan official was President Brad Withers, the unpredictable WASP figurehead.

In *Death Shall Overcome*, CASH, the civil rights group led by Richard Simpson, author and media manipulator, had a kneel-in at the Sloan. But CASH was outgeneraled by Thatcher, who got the Sloan Employees Chorus sheet music and loud speakers and joined them to sing "The Battle Hymn of the Republic." In *By Hook or Crook*, a mystery about the rug-dealing Parajians, their long lost aunt Veron dropped dead in the Sloan lobby, en route to prove her identity to fussy Everett Gabler.

On another occasion, in Lathen's *Ashes to Ashes*, there was a bomb threat at the Sloan, and the NYPD made everyone clear out. (Thatcher noted that the law department brought all their files with them.) After the NYPD search, the IRS had to help Sloan officials look for a bomb inside every single deposit box. Go inside the Irving Trust Building to admire Thatcher's handsome lobby, then walk to your right down Wall Street.

Wall Street's first financier was probably Frederick Philipse, who bought several barrels of Indian wampum (shells), the colony's legal tender. He created an artificial shortage so anyone who wanted to settle debts or keep in business had to buy from him at his rates.

At 11 Wall Street, on the south side of the street, you come to the colonnaded New York Stock Exchange Building, a 1923 Greek temple to money. The Stock Exchange itself was established in 1792. In Jeffrey Archer's *Not a Penny More, Not a Penny Less*, the American millionaire, Henryk Metelski, defrauds four British investors, who then set out to get even. Metelski got his start as a messenger boy for the New York Stock Exchange. But by 18, acting on a tip about a Standard Oil pipeline, he had begun to make his pile.

After the murder of a stockbroker in Lathen's *Death Shall Overcome*, the Exchange's Board, made up of twenty-nine representatives of the members, three representatives of the public, and the president of the Exchange, wanted someone else to "hold the baby." They therefore appointed the Three Wise Men "to handle things." The wise men they picked were Thatcher (a banker), Hugh Waymark (a broker), and Stanton Carruthers (a lawyer). CASH even sang a song about them to the tune of "The Battle Hymn of the Republic."

Stop to look down on the Floor of the Stock Exchange yourself, from the Visitors' Gallery (entrance on Broad Street). Try to imagine the day of the March on Wall Street when the NYPD tried to arrest the murderer on the Floor. It not only caused pandemonium, but worse there was *no business done for 3 hours and 28 minutes*. One customer, in Minnesota, decided the Bomb must have been dropped on New York.

Across Wall Street, at the north-east corner of Broad Street, is the 1840s Greek Revival-style Federal Hall, built on the spot where Washington took the oath of office as president of the new United States. Its rotunda and the Washington Museum are open to the public. Nearby, at 21 Wall Street, is where S. S. Van Dine put the brokerage firm of Benson and Benson in *The Benson Murder Case*. As amateur sleuth Philo Vance figured out, the Benson's office secretary, who was also the daughter of Alvin Benson's housekeeper, knew a lot about who was "cooking the firm's books."

Cross Broad Street to 23 Wall Street, the offices of J. P. Morgan, "the American banker." Murder has been done there, for in 1920, anarchists tossed a bomb at Morgan's building, killing 33 people and injuring 400 more. You can still see the bomb marks in the wall. In Max Allan Collins's *Stolen Away*, Chicago cop Nate Heller suggested to Lindbergh, after his son was kidnapped, that it was risky to agree to the kidnappers' demands until all the money ($50,000) was ready. Lindy's excuse was that he was a little strapped for cash. In response, Heller asked if Lindbergh's father-in-law, Ambassador Dwight Morrow, "wasn't a partner at J. P. Morgan's?" To which Lindbergh replied that he couldn't accept the ransom money from his wife's family, although they had offered it.

Continue down Wall Street to William Street. In Rex Stout's *Too Many Women*, Archie Goodwin was sent to work at Naylor-Kerr, Inc. at 914 William Street, "down where a thirty-story building is a shanty," to solve the murder of an employee called Waldo Wilmot Moore. The firm employed 500 young women and Wolfe assumed Archie could wine and dine them all to get the necessary clues. Archie was called a "personnel expert" and did very well, not only solving the case (with Wolfe's help) but also staying on good terms with most of the female employees.

Turn left one block to Pine Street. When Lathen's Three Wise Men hurried down Pine to the "race riot," the Sloan's Thatcher decided that the Chase Manhattan Bank building would have to take its chances, especially since he noticed that passersby were still calmly going in and out of the small Roman Catholic Church at the northeast corner of Pine Street.

Turn right to cross William Street and walk along Pine Street. Somewhere on Pine Street Schuyler and Schuyler, the small brokerage firm run by scheming Old Nick Schuyler, scion of a well-known New York family, held a party to introduce new (black) partner Ed Parry, whom Schuyler wanted to take a seat on the Stock Exchange.

Take Pine Street one block east to Pearl Street. In Rex Stout's first Nero Wolfe mystery, *Fer-de-Lance*, grain broker E. D. Kimball, one of the golf foursome present when the university president was murdered with a poisoned dart, had his grain offices on Pearl Street.

Turn right on Pearl Street and walk to the tiny park called

Hanover Square. Delmonico's, a New York landmark restaurant in an 1891 building, faces the Square at 56 Beaver Street. As a restaurant, Delmonico's has been in existence since 1838.

Hanover Square was named for the family of the Royal Georges. And like its London namesake, it was once the center of a residential neighborhood. (See *Mystery Reader's Walking Guide: London*, Mayfair Walk.) Homeowners at the New York Hanover Square have included Captain William Kidd. New Yorkers thought of Kidd as a solid citizen who belonged to Trinity Church, but the British hanged him as a pirate in 1701. Hanover Square was also home to the first New York newspaper, John Peter Zenger's *The New York Daily Gazette*, founded in 1725. Zenger won the first colonial case for freedom of the press, and his paper may have been in Rex Stout's mind when he made *The Gazette* Nero Wolfe's favorite source of information. The Wolfe Pack, however, believes the main model for Stout's *Gazette* was the *Herald-Tribune*.

In Meyers's *The Big Killing*, Jacob (Jake) Donahue & Company, a small and shady brokerage house where murder victim Barry Stark worked, was located at Hanover Square. Its offices were drab and almost unfurnished, but they look out on Hanover Square, with its benches and pigeons—and where drugs were bought and sold. At Hanover Square, every day was "market day," when vendors sold Italian, Chinese, Mexican, Indian, Greek, or Spanish food, or good old American hot dogs.

At the bottom of the tiny park is 1 Hanover Square, or India House, an elegant Italian palazzo/brownstone built in the 1850s to be the Hanover Bank. In addition to a private men's club, India House also houses Harry's Bar, a well-known Wall Street hangout. In *Murder for Lunch* by Haughton Murphy (aka James Duffy, a retired Wall Street lawyer), it was called "Harry's Hangover Bar." Chase and Ward associate Keith Merritt took retired partner Reuben Frost there to talk about the murder of another partner. When they arrived they found it jammed with drinking stockbrokers and a few women dressed for success. (This bar might be the Wall Street bar where Barnes's Christmas adventures began with a pickup, in Ed McBain's *Downtown*.)

Turn left at the bottom of Hanover Square to walk east to Water Street, New York's original shoreline. Everything beyond it is built on landfill. Turn left to walk along Water Street, going past Old Slip (where ships once docked) and the site of the former NYPD First Precinct, then Governeur's Lane, and cross Wall Street to Pine Street. In Haughton Murphy's *Murder for Lunch*, the offices of a P.I. named Russ Doyle were at 24 Water Street. (Doyle was hired by Chase and Ward to investigate partner Graham Donovan's murder.)

Take Pine Street two blocks east to South Street (which is partially underneath the elevated FDR Drive). At one of the piers beyond Marginal Street is the Wall Street Racquet Club. In Murphy's *Murder for Lunch*, Reuben Frost, who disliked his stuffy colleagues, told Executive Partner Bannard that not all the interesting people in this town are to be found at the Racquet Club bar.

Walk up South Street past Maiden Lane, then cross Fletcher Street to Burling Slip. In Rex Stout's *The Golden Spiders*, the elevated FDR Highway was just being built, and the run-over body of rich widow Laura Fromm was found there. At Burling Slip you are at the beginning of the South Seaport Museum complex, a project begun in the mid-1960s to preserve what was left of the original East River Port of NYC. You are standing by the Schermerhorn Row, a group of 1811 brick warehouses built on landfill by Peter Schermerhorn (his family were Dutch Founding Fathers, and a daughter of nouveau riche John Jacob Astor was tickled pink to marry into the tribe). At various times the Row was used for stores, taverns, rooming houses, and dives. They still give you a good idea of how the East River waterfront looked when it was New York's main port.

On the second floor of the Row there is a famous old seafood restaurant, called Sweet's (founded in 1842), which has been preserved. Turn left to the Museum Visitors Center for maps and tourist information. Then walk across the paved pedestrian mall, which is really Fulton Street, to the Fulton Market Building, which has several places to eat both upstairs and downstairs, and outside, in good weather. Behind the Fulton

Market Building is a row of buildings called The Shops on Front Street, a group of galleries and shops in restored waterfront buildings.

Across South Street to your right (under the FDR Drive) you can find Pier 16, where a number of historic ships are moored permanently, and where you can also sign up to take the Seaport Line's ninety-minute NYC cruise.

At Pier 17, just east of the Seaport, there is a pavilion modeled after the recreation piers once popular at seaside resorts, like Brighton. (See also *Mystery Reader's Walking Guide: England*, Brighton Walk.)

The Fulton Fish Market (open at dawn) is just north of Pier 16, on South Street. It is a reconstruction of the 1882 structure that once sold household produce and meat brought from Long Island farms via the Fulton Street Ferry. To your left up Fulton Street is the Titanic Memorial Lighthouse, which originally overlooked the harbor from Seaman's Church Institute on Water Street. It was put up in memory of the 1500 who died (many of them New Yorkers) when the White Star Line's *Titanic* struck an iceberg in the Atlantic.

Among the leading NYC families who got their start in trade, the Vanderbilts began to get rich when Old Cornelius Vanderbilt's ships outran the British blockade during the War of 1812. Vanderbilt went on to control steamboats, then railroads, and ended up being worth about $200 million at a time when the average yearly salary was about $200.

In Jack Early's *Donato and Daughter*, there was a terrifying chase through the South Street Seaport area. The murder suspect had escaped a police cordon at Grand Central Station, forcing NYPD Lieutenant Dina Donato's task force to chase him here, where they had to watch out for tourists. The task force met at the Fulton Street Market Restaurant, luckily nearly empty, then Dina and her father, Sergeant Donato, raced down the cobblestoned street, past the Fulton Market, to check out the piers. At Pier 16 Dina saw the murderer on the schooner *Peking*. She went aboard and ended up as his hostage.

After exploring the South Street Seaport area, look north

to the Brooklyn Bridge, which rises up about three blocks away. In William Marshall's *New York Detective*, about the 1883 opening of the Brooklyn Bridge, NYPD Detective Tillman and Police Officer Muldoon rode the Houston Street–Fulton Ferry horsecar through the Bowery to the harbor. They were on the trail of the murderer of a stagehand at a big Wild West Show. When they arrived at the dirty wharves, the new Brooklyn Bridge filled the sky above them. The final scene was played out on the bridge itself when President Arthur opened it and Detective Tillman thwarted a plot to take over the country in the name of the "Good Old Days." The true story of the Brooklyn Bridge can be found in David McCullough's *The Great Bridge*. Once the world's longest suspension bridge, it was designed and built by a father and son, John and Washington Roebling. John died of an injury to his foot, while Washington got the bends from supervising the underwater work and supervised the remainder of the work from his apartment at the Brooklyn end of the span.

In Stanley Ellin's short story, "The Nine to Five Man," the hero, a professional arsonist, left his office at Columbus Circle to go to Water Street near Montgomery (just north of the Brooklyn Bridge). His job that day was to set a fire for a customer who wanted to collect the insurance on his old warehouse. In Ed McBain's *Downtown*, in another old warehouse near the Fulton Market, Barnes and his Chinese girlfriend, Connie Kee, found five floors of stolen goods of every description, and ended up in a shoot-out in the middle of a room full of furs.

In *One Coffee With*, Margaret Maron placed her invented Vanderlyn College somewhere near the Brooklyn Bridge, along the East River. One of the city colleges, Vanderlyn's campus was two blocks wide and eight blocks long, with 40,000 commuting students. (Its real-life prototype is Brooklyn College on Bedford Ave. south of Prospect Park.)

Unlike Edward Mackin's Lyndon Johnson College in *The Nominative Case*, which was hastily built in the 1970s, Vanderlyn College had Victorian buildings and tree-graced grounds with a fountain in the middle, enclosed by tall, ivy-covered brick walls with wrought-iron gates. But, typical of municipal institutions, its Art Department in Van Hoeen Hall was jammed and had to make do with army surplus furniture.

Return to the walk at Beekman Street and the Fulton Market unless you want to make a detour and walk to the Brooklyn Bridge. In Rex Stout's *The Golden Spiders*, the body of Mathew Birch, an Immigration and Naturalization officer, was found at the South Street Pier off Beekman Street, one block north of Fulton. It was never a good area, as NYPD Sergeant Norah Mulcahaney found out when she parked there in *The Children's Zoo*: At twilight she returned to her car only to find it covered with filth and a mugger waiting for her with a hunk of pipe.

Turn left at the northern edge of Fulton Market to take Beekman Street back to Pearl Street. At 257 Pearl Street there used to be a machinery setup called Edison's Volcano, which was the Electric Illuminating Company's first generating station. William Marshall's Detective Tillman went there hunting the murderer in *New York Detective*.

At Pearl Street, turn left to walk back one block to Fulton Street, then turn right to walk about seven blocks back to Broadway, passing William Street. After William Street you cross Nassau Street. In the 1830s there were nine newspaper offices on Nassau Street, from Wall Street to Beekman Street, including the ones poets Walt Whitman and Edgar Allan Poe worked for. Somewhat later, "newspaper row" was extended north to Park Row.

At Fulton and Broadway you come to the 1766 St. Paul's Chapel of Trinity Church parish. It is NYC's only remaining pre–Revolutionary building and was modeled on London's St. Martin-in-the-Fields, another church no longer in the hinterlands. Walk in and you can see President George Washington's pew and admire the chapel's elegant Georgian interior.

In Isabelle Holland's *A Lover Scorned*, the murdered Reverend Sarah Buchanan (before she was murdered) was assigned to the parish of a chapel with a large cemetery. St. Paul's is the only Episcopal "chapel" of its kind in Manhattan, and it does have a big cemetery in which the Reverend Claire Aldington could have been sick to her stomach after being poisoned at lunch. But

St. Paul's Chapel is not in the right area to have a congregation of Hispanic gang members.

After admiring St. Paul's Chapel, walk past it to Vesey Street, where the Transportation Building, at 225 Broadway, occupies the site of the original Astor House Hotel (1836–1913). Then go one more block up Broadway to Barclay Street, where you will come to the Woolworth Building. Built in 1913 with terra cotta gothic trim, it is known as the "Cathedral of Commerce." Most appropriately, Frank Woolworth paid for the entire building in cash, and there is a statue of him inside the ornate lobby, clutching a nickel. His building was also the world's tallest until the Art Deco Chrysler Building was put up in 1930.

Cross Broadway to your right, to City Hall Park. New York's City Hall, built in 1802–11, is a small but elegant stone palace that combines Federal and French Renaissance styles. Capped with a dome, it has a lovely central hall and sweeping staircase. Although now faced entirely in limestone, it was once faced with marble on its south side and economical brick on the north. In Craig Rice's *Having a Wonderful Crime*, however, Chicago lawyer J. J. Malone noted that Chicago's City Hall is far bigger (and better). City Hall's rotunda is mostly used for fancy official occasions. On the second floor of New York's City Hall are the New York City Council Chambers, as well as a small museum.

In Elliott Roosevelt's *Hyde Park Murder*, young Bob Hannah, after he broke into the apartment of his murdered father's partner, was caught by a bad NYPD cop, who was working for the mob. Bob was rescued by the mayor's Special Unit (dealing with crooked cops) and taken to City Hall, where an angry Mayor La Guardia awaited him. Eleanor Roosevelt had asked La Guardia to look into the elder Hannah's death, but as La Guardia told Bob Hannah, "How can I do that if you [Hannah] stick your nib in and get yourself beaten up?" Later Mrs. Roosevelt herself came to City Hall to meet with Mayor La Guardia. Also in this mystery, the villain, who had Nazi ties, worked on SEC head Joe Kennedy's staff; was that a subtle Roosevelt joke?

La Guardia's election in 1933 signaled the end of Tammany

Hall control of NYC politics. But earlier in S. S. Van Dine's *The Benson Murder Case*, his amateur sleuth, Philo Vance (of whom poet Ogden Nash wrote "Philo Vance/Needs a kick in the pance") told D.A. John F. X. Markham that Bronx alderman Moriarty was "Tammany," meaning "corrupt." (See also Walk 4.) In Haughton Murphy's *Murder for Lunch*, Chase and Ward's murdered law partner, Graham Donovan, although a nominal Roman Catholic, is known to have been married at City Hall. As a result, his partners are not sure what to do about burying him.

To your right, along the eastern edge of City Hall Park is Park Row, also called Printing House Square. At one time this was a theater district, with plays starring Edwin Booth (whose half-brother murdered President Abraham Lincoln), Edmund Kean, and the Kembles. Then it became the new center of the city's newspaper industry (near City Hall and the slums—good for political and human interest stories). Before World War I there were twelve daily papers published there, including Greeley's *Tribune*, Pulitzer's *World*, Dana's *Sun*, Hearst's *American*, and Ochs's *Times*. In Jack Finney's time/travel mystery, *Time and Again*, his twentieth-century hero is present at the historic *World* building fire in January 1882.

Cross City Hall Park from City Hall to the former NYC Courthouse, on the northern edge of the park. City Hall Park has always been New York's commons or public green. It was once even used to pasture cows—until the City built its courthouse in the center of the park, like any other American town. In the park there is a statue of Revolutionary War spy Nathan Hale, who may have been hanged there, and one of Horace Greeley, the Civil War abolitionist editor of the *Tribune*, the country's first nationally distributed paper. Greeley was also the one who wrote "Go West Young Man" journalism, promoting Western settlement.

The former NYC Courthouse is known as the Boss Tweed Courthouse because of Boss Tweed, a famous Tammany official, and his "Ring" of corrupt Democrats, who made off with $10 million of the $14 million earmarked to construct the building. Tweed started as a lowly alderman and died in debtors's prison, but he did well in between.

Walk around the Courthouse to Chambers Street. To your right, Park Row becomes Centre Street. "Centre Street" is the generic name for the central office of the New York Police Department and the criminal justice system, both courts and prison. "Centre Street" means the same thing in a New York mystery that "Scotland Yard" means in an English one, the sleuth, cop, or murderer involved is going to "Headquarters."

The actual area stretches from Chambers Street all the way north to Broome Street, where the original NYPD headquarters were located, at 242 Broome, now an elegant co-op. Its western boundary is Broadway and its eastern side usually is considered to be Columbus Park, which is on the western edge of Little Italy's Mulberry Street and Chinatown's Mott Street. Although the buildings have changed considerably since the early detective stories by S. S. Van Dine and Ellery Queen, the ambiance is still the same.

Walk up Centre Street. On your right you come first to the Municipal Building, a 1914 Beaux-Arts structure by McKim, Mead and White, where you can get a marriage license. Chambers Street once ran through its central arch and is still open to pedestrian traffic. But it is simpler to walk past the Municipal Building and turn right at neo-Georgian St. Andrew's Church, and double back to Police Plaza at the point where Park Row, St. Andrew's Plaza, Chambers Street, and The Avenue of the Finest meet. This complex of buildings, however, does not include the Morgue.) (See Walk 4.)

One Police Plaza, directly ahead of you, is a modern 1970s red-brick building that is currently NYPD Headquarters. You can walk inside the lobby, where, on the wall to your right, is a high, old wooden police precinct desk, and memorials for police killed in the line of duty. You may go through the airport surveillance arch if you have business there, of if there is a police auction being held. In any case, you have to leave cameras outside, the way you do at London's Old Bailey. (See *Mystery Reader's Walking Guide: London*, Inns of Court Walk.) If a tour is forming for school children, or some other group, like senior citizens, you may be allowed to join it, but there are no regularly scheduled tours for the general public.

While exploring, keep in mind that you need to check a mystery's publication date to know which building is meant when it refers to either "Centre Street" or "the Tombs." For example, in the Lockridges' 1940s *The Norths Meet Murder*, Detective Lieutenant William (Bill) Weigland reported to Centre Street to be grilled by his boss on the murder of a lawyer named Brent. (See also Walk 3.) In Mary Roberts Rinehart's 1950s *The Swimming Pool*, about the formerly rich Maynard family, brother Phil commuted to Manhattan from their estate. When a woman's body was found in the Maynards's swimming pool, the Maynards acquired a tenant—or guard—named Bill O'Brien who lived in their cottage. Phil later saw O'Brien going into Centre Street, which suggested he might be an ex-cop.

In the 1960s *Death Shall Overcome*, Emma Lathen's Three Wise Men met at Centre Street the day of the March on Wall Street to tell the police who the murderer was. In Margaret Maron's 1980s *Past Imperfect*, NYPD Captain McKinnon, Lieutenant Sigrid Harald, and Officer "Tillie," her sidekick, all met at Centre Street after homicide staffer Lotty Fischer was shoved in front of a Lexington Avenue subway on her way home from work.

After taking a good look around, return via St. Andrew's Plaza to Centre Street, then turn right to walk up Centre Street to Foley Square. Foley Square, named for a Tammany Hall politician, was once the dismal and dirty Collect Pond. After it was filled in during the late eighteenth century, it was still smelly and boggy and became known as Five Points, the worst crime area in town, averaging fifteen murders a night. British author Charles Dickens, who had "made the name" of London's loathsome Seven Dials slum, insisted on seeing Five Points when in NYC. (See *Mystery Reader's Walking Guide: London*, Soho Walk.) And when New Yorker Al Capone was arrested on tax evasion, he is said to have remarked that he "shoulda never left Five Points."

As you work your way north you will pass many public buildings. One is the U.S. Courthouse (where you can step inside—but not stay unless you are called for jury duty or as a witness). Then cross Pearl Street to the N.Y. County Courthouse, located at Hamill Place. In Barnaby Ross's (aka Ellery

Queen's) *Tragedy of X*, the D.A. and the Police Commissioner both had offices in the 1926 Neo-Classical style, hexagon-shaped building. Drury Lane, the deaf actor who lived up the Hudson River, visited them there. Asked to solve the murder of Wall Street financier Longstreet, Lane told the D.A. and police commissioner not to act like the bad theatrical producers who publicized John Barrymore playing Hamlet instead of the play.

In Hal Masur's *Tall, Dark and Deadly*, lawyer Scott Jordan was obliged to pay a call at the New York County Courthouse on Philip Lohman, former Wall Street lawyer, Washington lobbyist, and Tammany pol, now the D.A., who was hoping to be elected governor. Jordan was accused of manufacturing evidence in a divorce case, then blamed for the murder of a party to the suit.

Keep walking up Centre Street across Worth Street to Leonard Street. To your right is the Criminal Court Building, known as "the Tombs," in memory of another building (long gone) with Egyptian columns that stood across the street in what is now a park. The current building is a kind of Babylonian/Art Deco ziggurat, designed by Rockefeller Center's architect and erected in 1939. (Again, as is the case with London's Scotland Yard [*Mystery Reader's Walking Guide: London*, Westminster Walk], the date of the mystery story will help you determine which building the author is talking about.)

In S. S. Van Dine's *The Benson Murder Case*, Philo Vance uses the Franklin Street entrance (now a dead end just north of you) to enter an ancient building with discolored marble pillars and old-fashioned iron scrollwork. The D.A.'s office was on the fourth floor. It has high ceilings, golden oak wood, dingy walls, a low chandelier, and four narrow windows overlooking the gray tower of the Tombs. It also had a dingy brown carpet, a waiting room, comfortable chairs, and a long oak table. D.A. Markham's desk was set so that his back was to the windows. The final scene was played out here: The murderer went for the D.A., knocking down several detectives before Philo Vance disarmed him with a judo trick. In *The Canary Murder Case*, Philo Vance looked out the D.A.'s window and saw the Bridge of Sighs, which connected the office building with "the Tombs."

This building was also the place in *The Roman Hat Mystery* where Ellery Queen gave a detailed description of the Centre Street office of Inspector Richard Queen. It was homey, small, and cozy, but son Ellery still called it "the Star Chamber." Both Queens went to the D.A.'s office to talk with the very rich Francis Ives Pope, whose daughter was engaged to an actor in the gangster melodrama at the Roman Theater. In *The Greek Coffin Mystery*, the Queens met Wall Street financier James J. Knox there. Knox was mixed up with the theft of a Leonardo Da Vinci painting from London's Victoria and Albert Museum. (See *Mystery Reader's Walking Guide: London*, Brompton Walk.) In *The Chinese Orange Mystery*, a council of war is held in Inspector Queen's office after the police stakeout in Grand Central Station had failed.

Rex Stout's Inspector Cramer had his office here in *Fer-de-Lance*. Big and blustery, Cramer tended to get mad at Archie Goodwin for sticking his nose into police matters (for Nero Wolfe) and mad at Wolfe for making him go to West 35th Street. Cramer had been in NYPD for thirty years. In *The Red Band*, Stout said he was an old friend of Lily Rowan's father who had Tammany Hall connections. Cramer's sidekick was Homicide Detective Sergeant Purley Stebbins. Archie also ended up at "Centre Street," on occasion.

At the Tombs you have walked over three miles from the World Trade Center, and one mile from South Street Seaport. After enjoying the police/criminal ambiance, you can end your walk here.

If you are hungry, walk three more blocks north to Canal Street, and go east two blocks to Mulberry Street, the southern edge of the Little Italy district. This latter area is still popular with Mafioso types in mysteries like Mary Higgins Clark's *While My Pretty One Sleeps*. Or you can walk right around the Tombs to Bayard Street and head east for Chinatown.

Chinatown's center is usually said to be about a block beyond Bayard, at the intersection of Mott and Pell Streets. Some of the oldest buildings in New York are just south of Chinatown around Chatham Square, which is bisected by the Bowery. On the square's south side is the first cemetery of the Portuguese Jews's Shearith Israel Congregation.

The boundaries of Chinatown are somewhat flexible, as noted in Carole Berry's *The Year of the Monkey*. When her "temp" worker, Bonnie Indermill, took a job with Creative Financial Ventures, in an office in a newish building just south of Chinatown, near City Hall, she noted that the address was not truly "Wall Street" as advertised, but it was handy to Chinese restaurants. Since Bonnie's co-worker was Chinese, she spent considerable time there.

In almost every New York mystery, the characters eat or take out Chinese food. Many go all the way down to Chinatown. Chinese immigrants began arriving in New York about 1870 from San Francisco. Today there are over 150,000 Chinese residents in NYC, making it the largest Chinese community outside China. But in spite of the red Chinese arches and pagoda telephone booths, the area is not quaint, just poor, and most mystery adventures reflect that.

In Elliott Roosevelt's *Hyde Park Murder*, young Bob Hannah and the nightwatchman from his dead father's office met in a sleazy bar called the Gum Loo. After the watchman told Hannah his dad was pushed out his office window, he, too, was murdered. In Ed McBain's *Downtown*, his hero, Michael Barnes, teamed up with a gorgeous Chinese girl, Connie Kee, who worked as a chauffeur for the China Doll Executive Limousine Service. After a series of incredible adventures, they ended up at her apartment, above a restaurant called Shi Kai, just off the corner of Mott and Pell. Look for a restaurant there or suit yourself, there are shops and restaurants all over.

2

LOWER EAST SIDE/ EAST VILLAGE WALK

BACKGROUND

Geographically, the Lower East Side and East Village are connected. Together they occupy Manhattan from the East River west to Broadway, and north from Canal Street to 14th Street. The East Village begins north of Houston and is sometimes considered an extension of Greenwich Village as both "neighborhoods" share certain characteristics. Both are populated with a mix of ethnic inhabitants, who range from Hispanics, Asians, Eastern Europeans (NYC's old Irish-Italian neighborhood lies directly west, across the Bowery), to ex-NYU students, artists, poets, and punk rockers, to trendy yuppies. Unlike the rest of the city, the area has no skyscrapers, but many nineteenth-century tenements with street-level stores and restaurants and fire escapes up the front. There are no grand architectural buildings, except for churches, so a walk here is a trip back in time. The best day to go is a Sunday when the very sidewalks are bursting with goods and people.

The Lower East Side is famous in song and story because it has attracted generations of hopeful artists, writers, musicians, and actors. Millions of people, many of whom never even visited the area, also have a sentimental attachment to the Lower

East Side, either because their ancestors once lived there, or because some of America's best-known entertainers have shared their memories of growing up there with audiences. Its colorful counterculture continued into the 1950s with the Beats, the 1960s with the drug-using flower children, the 1970s with the punks, and the 1980s with art galleries moving here from other parts of the city. Today the Lower East Side is still dirty, crime-ridden and—comparatively—cheap, characteristics that appear regularly in the mystery scenes set here.

Until the Revolutionary War, the area was occupied by the estates of great landowners like the Rutgers and Delanceys. The Tory Delanceys eventually lost their land, however, leaving only their name, on streets like Delancey and Orchard Street (which ran through their garden). Peter Stuyvesant's bouwerie (or farm) occupied the future East Village, where he and his descendants are buried at St. Mark's Church.

As the city moved north, the Lower East Side became the "port of entry," a crowded place where "native-born" writers like Henry James and Henry Adams felt overwhelmed by its "huddled masses." (This is the theme of William Marshall's historical mystery, *New York Detective*, with its "man on a white horse" presidential candidate, who dressed like Buffalo Bill and thought like "Know Nothing" Samuel Morse.)

As the Dutch and the English abandoned the Lower East Side they were replaced by the Germans, Irish, Italians, Jews, Chinese, and Hispanics. By 1880 half of all New York City lived above the stores and restaurants of the tenements of the Lower East Side. Educated or not, immigrants either sold goods from pushcarts, worked in the area's restaurants, made cigars, or sewed in the garment trade's "sweat shops." The neighborhood, especially the Bowery, also became famous for its "low life": not just poverty but gambling, gangs, violence, and drugs. Those who could, escaped, and even muckraking immigrant journalist Jacob Riis, author of *How the Other Half Lives,* did not stay there but left as soon as he could.

During the late-nineteenth and early-twentieth centuries, Eastern European immigrants passed through Ellis Island and settled here, giving the neighborhood an unmistakable Jewish flavor. (The Jewish population of metropolitan New York is still larger than that of Israel.) Their descendants still own many of the local businesses, which is why most neighborhood stores and shops shut down on Saturday, for the Jewish sabbath. Jewish families who have moved up and out still cling to their Lower East Side roots. As mystery writer Jerome Charyn said in *Metropolis*, Ellis Island was the place *modern* New York came from. Charyn, himself, had a grandfather who spoke no English and peddled apples for a living on the Lower East Side. (See Walk 1.)

The Lower East Side was also a major literary mecca. The *Jewish Daily Forward*, the largest Yiddish daily in the world, was published south of Delancey, and writers like Sholem Asch, Sholom Aleichem, and Nobel Laureate Isaac Bashevis Singer wrote for it. Other well known Jewish writers, who got their start on the Lower East Side, included Michael Gold, Henry Roth, and Singer's granddaughter, Bel Kaufman, who wrote *Up the Down Staircase*, a story about teaching in the New York Public Schools (and a much more amusing account than the one in *The Blackboard Jungle* by Evan Hunter, aka 87th-Precinct mystery writer Ed McBain).

Non-Jewish writers, like Walt Whitman and Stephen Crane, Lincoln Steffins, John Dos Passos, e.e. cummings, Van Wyck Brooks, and E.B. White, also came here to absorb the atmosphere. In the 1950s, the East village became home to the Beats: William Burroughs, Allen Ginsberg, Frank O'Hara, Jack Kerouac, and Norman Mailer. They lived here because it was cheap, but drank in Greenwich Village. (See Walk 3.) Next came the 1960s counterculturalists with their poetry, street theater, communes, and runaways. Then in the 1970s came the punk rockers with their spike hairdos, who made Alphabet City—Avenues A, B, C, and D—the center of the city's drug trade.

The most recent immigrants to the area are the Hispanics and Chinese, who now run most of the local restaurants and shops. They can be seen on the crowded streets along with little old Jewish ladies, camera-carrying tourists, the homeless curled up in doorways, and NYU students in jeans and earrings, who view with alarm the appearance of stores like Burger King or the Gap.

LENGTH OF WALK: About 2 miles

See map on page 36 for the boundaries of this walk and page 291 for a list of books and detectives mentioned.

PLACES OF INTEREST

This is the NYC home of bargain-hunter shopping, especially along Orchard Street. Remember, Sunday is the day to go.

Strand Book Store, 828 Broadway at 12th Street. Millions of second-hand books on eight miles of shelves. *But* mysteries are lumped with novels! Mon.–Sat., 9:30 A.M.–9:30 P.M.; Sun., 11:00 A.M.–9:00 P.M. Call 473-1452.

New York City Marble Cemetery, Second Avenue at 2nd Street. Started in 1831, it is NYC's oldest nonsectarian cemetery, with burial limited to founding families already there. (No one has been buried there since 1917.)

Grace Episcopal Church (and School), 802 Broadway, at 10th Street. 1846 Gothic Revival bldg. by James Renwick. Open daily, 8:00 A.M.–6:00 P.M.; Sun., for services. Call 254-2000.

CBGB's, 315 Bleecker (and the Bowery). Home of punk rock.

Tompkins Square, Avenues A–B, 7th Street to 10th Street.

Forbidden Planet, 821 Broadway. Ultimate Science Fiction store. Comics. Call 473-1576.

St. Mark's-in-the-Bowery (Bouwerie) Episcopal Church, Second Avenue and 10th Street. 1799 replacement for Peter Stuyvesant chapel. Artist forum, Theater Genesis. Call 674-6377.

Old Merchant's House (1832), 29 E. 4th Street. Victorian house with family furnishings and memorabilia intact. Open Sundays, 1:00–4:00 P.M., or special appointment. Call 473-9008.

Cooper Union, Cooper Square. First free coed university in
   country. Founded in 1859 by Peter Cooper, self-made glue
   manufacturer.

Stuyvesant Street, diagonal street between Second and Third
   Avenues at 10th Street. Early nineteenth-century houses. See
   21 Stuyvesant House (1803–4), country estate of a
   Stuyvesant.

Astor Place, diagonal street between Cooper Square and
   Wanamaker Place, at north end of Lafayette Street (once
   Place) and Colonnade Row. Once the classiest address in
   town: houses of Astors, Vanderbilts, and Delanos, and Astor
   Library bldg.

Streit's Matzoth Company, 150 Rivington (Allen Street). Last
   kosher bakery in Manhattan.

Schapiro's House of Kosher & Sacramental Wine, 126 Rivington
   Street. Last kosher wine firm in Manhattan. Free tours
   Sunday, 10:00 A.M.–6:00 P.M.

PLACES TO EAT

(Many places do not accept credit cards. Some are not on the
walk but found nearby. There are also many others, not listed
here, of every ethnic variety.)

Second Avenue Deli, 156 Second Avenue. Has Jewish Theater
   exhibit in Molly Picon Room.

Gem's Spa, Second Avenue and St. Mark's Place. Best place
   around for kosher egg creams. A neighborhood variety store.

McSorley's Old Ale House, 15 E. 7th Street. Est. 1854. Pleasant
   but dingy (formerly men-only) bar taken over by NYU and
   Cooper Union students (women allowed in 1970s). Also a
   cop hang out. Serves only ale, porter, or Guinness.

Odessa, 7th Street and Avenue A. Typical diner-style restaurant
   overlooking Tompkins Square. Eastern European menu:
   potato pancakes with sour cream, apple sauce, etc.

Katz's Delicatessen, 205 Houston Street. Kosher menu.

Ratner's Dairy Bakery, 138 Delancey Street. Kosher menu.

– LOWER EAST SIDE/EAST VILLAGE WALK –

Begin your walk at Delancey Street, a wide thoroughfare originating at the Williamsburg Bridge, and Essex Street, near the Delancey St./Essex St. subway station. In William F. Love's *The Chartreuse Clue*, he used its name to describe the home turf of his "Delancey Street Irregulars." Love also borrowed part of their name from Sherlock Holmes's "Baker Street Irregulars," a group of London street urchins who brought Holmes useful information. In Love's mystery, the Delancey Street Irregulars were a group of Jewish and Catholic boyhood friends of P.I. Davy Goldman, the ex-cop who lived with and worked for crippled Roman Catholic Bishop Francis Regan. Like their London namesakes, the Delancey Street Irregulars provided a useful network for Goldman to help the bishop solve crimes. Although the group had grown up and long since left the Lower East Side, they still met to play golf and maintained a floating crap game, like Damon Runyon's mobsters in *Guys and Dolls*.

In Jeffrey Archer's *Not a Penny More, Not a Penny Less*, American millionaire Harvey Metcalfe began life as Henryk Metelski. Metelski was born on the Lower East Side. When his father died, the future Metcalfe took to the streets, where he got his first break as a Wall Street messenger. Eventually Metelski/Metcalfe achieved the ultimate ambition of New York's self-made men: his daughter married an English lord. In Marissa Piesman's *Personal Effects*, Bronx-raised lawyer Nina Fischman's Bronx family was two generations removed from the Lower East Side.

South of Delancey there used to be Jewish theaters, cafes, restaurants, and music halls. Some of the famous Jewish restaurants still there are Katz's Delicatessen, at 205 E. Houston, and Ratner's Dairy, at 138 Delancey Street, which began as a bakery.

Cross Essex Street to walk west along Delancey Street to Orchard Street. You will pass the Essex Street Market, a two-block indoor food market that caters to a mixed Chinese, Jewish, and Hispanic clientele. Orchard Street is a "Jewish" bazaar, lined with shops for everything, where the goods spill over onto the

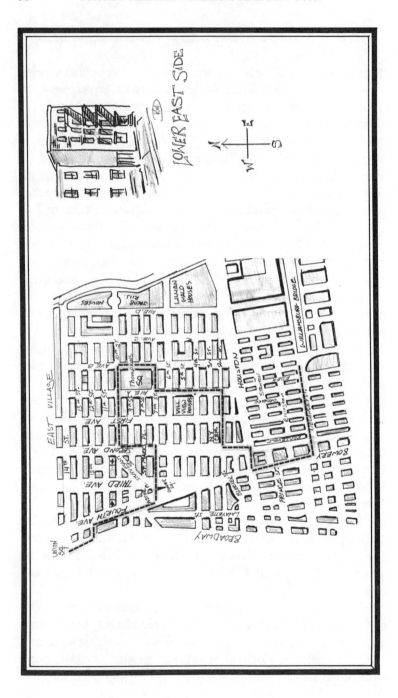

sidewalks. Bargaining is expected, but there are watchers perched on stepladders guarding against thieves.

Walk the eight blocks west to the Bowery, observing the dingy but lively ambiance of old streetlights, buildings, and iron curbs. In *Downtown*, Ed McBain's Michael Barnes's Chinese girlfriend, Connie, got a friend named Louis Klein to open up his Delancey Army & Navy store on Christmas. With Connie's money, Barnes bought a pair of Levi jeans, a blue wool sweater (marked way down), and a pair of woolen socks. When Klein asked how Barnes hurt his arm and Connie told him Barnes had been shot, Klein said he was not surprised and threw in an extra pair of socks.

Forsyth and Chrystie Streets are divided by a tattered Sara Delano Roosevelt Parkway. Chrystie Street (and the Bowery) used to be the chief hooker locale. Unbelievably, up ahead you can see the Empire State Building and the golden gleam of the Metropolitan Life Building at Union Square. (See Walk 4.)

Turn right at the Bowery to head north. Once an Indian trail that became the Stuyvesants' route to the harbor, the Bowery (Dutch *bouwerie* means farm) starts at St. Mark's Place, cuts across Houston to Canal, and dead-ends at Park Row and Catherine Street. Although east-west streets change names here, Broadway, not the Bowery, is the official dividing line.

The Bowery was once NYC's major theater district, but it has since become equally famous for its derelicts and flophouses. Songwriter Stephen Foster died destitute there in 1864, and novelist Stephen Crane set his first novel, *Maggie: A Girl of the Streets*, there in 1893. Still later, a cantor's son, Irving Berlin, got his start singing in its restaurants. Now all the theaters have moved elsewhere and the stores that remain sell lamps and used kitchen equipment, among the flophouses, like the Prince Hotel, and plenty of bums. In Lillian O'Donnell's chilling mystery, *The Children's Zoo*, a group of Upper East Side schoolboys, taken to the Bowery on a "field trip," return there to amuse themselves by beating up on the local street people.

Cross Rivington Street where two blocks to your right is Streit's Matzoh Factory, housed in an old building trimmed with terra cotta. It is the last matzo bakery in Manhattan, just as

Schapiro's House of Kosher & Sacramental Wines a little farther along Rivington is the only kosher winery left. At one time my rock musician cum cabby son, Alec, shared a converted loft on Rivington with some actor friends from NYU and their cat, Pigboy. To reach their apartment over a store you had to climb a narrow staircase. The kitchen was one wall and the bedrooms were the size of a bed, but they had a wide picture window that looked out on Streit's.

Although Amanda Cross left its Lower East Side location vague, Alec's place resembled the loft apartment of Kate Fansler's nephew, Leo, in "Murder without a Text," one of the mystery stories in Sara Paretsky's collection, *A Woman's Eye*. As Dean Cynthia Sterling discovered, and I can testify to, cabdrivers are not always eager to take you there.

In Dorothy Uhnak's *The Bait*, the Orthodox parents of David and Murray Rogoff ran a fish shop in a tenement on Rivington and lived above it. Members of the NYPD Special D.A. Investigations Squad observed "monster" Murray working there before they used Detective Christie Opara as "bait" to catch him.

Walk up to Stanton Street. Across the Bowery, to your left, Stanton becomes Prince Street, where, between Mott and Mulberry, you would find old St. Patrick's Cathedral, built in 1809. Now known as "Little Italy," the area is still considered "Mafia territory" in a number of mysteries, such as Mary Higgins Clark's *While My Pretty One Sleeps*. In real life it was at Umberto's Clam House, on Hester Street, that reputed Mafia capo Joey Gallo was shot dead in 1972.

Turn right at Houston Street (pronounced "How-ston"), another wide roadway that runs from the public housing units on the East River to the Hudson. Cross Houston and go right one block to Second Avenue. Second Avenue once was the Yiddish theater's Broadway.

Walk up Second Avenue to Second Street. You pass by New York's first community garden, founded by the Green Guerrillas in the 1970s. Like the garden far uptown in Richard Barth's mystery *A Ragged Plot*, it too is fenced in.

Turn right on Second Street to walk to First Avenue. To

your left, across the Bowery, Second Street will become Bleecker Street, and at 65 Bleecker Street is the 1898 Bayard-Condict Building, the only Louis Sullivan building in New York. At Bleecker and the Bowery there is a theater mentioned in the Horatio Alger stories, while the CBGB's building, at 315 Bleecker, is the birthplace of American punk rock.

On Second Street you go right past the New York City Marble Cemetery, started in 1831. The tree-filled cemetery grounds are above the sidewalk, surrounded by a tall iron fence. There is no open gate, but you can see ancient mausoleums and gravestones. Members of New York's first families were buried there: Scribners, Varicks, Beekmans, Van Zandts, Hoyts, and even a branch of Roosevelts. Burial is restricted to descendants of the original vault owners, but no one has applied since 1917. There is a rumor in the neighborhood that there is an underground passage from the Liz Mar Lounge on First Avenue into one of the vaults, which was used by gangsters to hide stiffs. The action in Ellery Queen's *The Greek Coffin Mystery* took place in a Midtown block with such an exclusive cemetery. Since half of "Ellery Queen" went to NYU, Manny Lee may have known this cemetery, but similar rules apply at other old Manhattan cemeteries, like Trinity Cemetery, at Broadway and 154th Street, restricting burial to original family members. (See Walk 11.)

Cross First Avenue and walk to Avenue A. You are now in Alphabet City (Avenue A to Avenue D, where ten years ago it was not considered safe for NYU students or tourists to go). Turn left to cross Avenue A and walk up to 4th Street. On your left is modern subsidized housing called Village View Houses, but most of the apartment buildings are old-fashioned brick tenements, with fire escapes running down their fronts. This area has lots of ground floor shops—and many drug busts.

My son Alec's current apartment is in a five-story walk-up above a motorcycle shop. Half the building is unoccupied. To reach the apartment, you must climb up a steep, narrow, dirty staircase, where every door is barred and bolted. From his window you see trees of heaven growing out of the windows and roof. Clearly it is very like the building that housed Len Vandering's apartment in Velda Johnson's *The Face in the Shadows*.

Vandering, the artist brother of wealthy businessman Howard Vandering, was suspected of giving his niece drugs. When he took actress Ellen Stacey to his place, it also had terribly steep, worn stairs, and a heavily padlocked door. But unlike Alec's old plumbing and utilitarian white walls, Vandering's apartment had paneled walls, lowered ceiling fixtures, recessed lights, carpeting, modern furniture, and some of his life-sized sculpture and portraits of the neighbors, done in a stiff Grant-Woods style. A professional artist, Vandering's work was "hung" at MOMA (the Museum of Modern Art) when he was only 25.

In Jack Early's *Donato and Daughter*, Sister Honoria, a nun, was found murdered, having had her ring finger cut off. She had worked at HAFH (Home Away From Home), a place for runaways and drug users on St. Mark's Place. Sister Honoria lived in a dark and smelly tenement walk-up with padlocked doors, but inside her apartment was bright and clean, if austere. NYPD Lieutenant Dina Donato found out quickly that the other tenants were the flotsam and jetsam of down-and-out society, but none were likely to be serial nun killers.

Richard Nusser's *Walking After Midnight* is dedicated to "Sherlock Holmes, Philip Marlowe, Jules Maigret and all their children" (who still walk the mean streets). In the mystery, reporter Max Darenow tried to find out who had fed his photographer girlfriend a fatal overdose and then dumped her body on Staten Island. (See Walk 1.) The trail led him to the Kooks, a Hispanic punk rock group, who lived in the only inhabited building on a block near Avenue A. The Kooks lived on the first floor, and one of the three was always home to guard their electronic equipment. Darenow found them with a drug dealer, and it turned out that his girlfriend had died there.

Take Avenue A north to 7th Street and the southwest corner of Tompkins Park. In Orania Papazoglou's (aka Jane Haddam's) *Wicked, Loving Murder*, one of the nephews of *Writing Enterprises* publisher Alida Brookfield had a "cheap" apartment on Avenue A, furnished from the Salvation Army, because Aunt Alida only paid him $15,000 a year. (To make ends meet, he was also robbing the business.) Beat poet Allen Ginsberg lived at 206 East 7th Street, where his literary friends, like Jack Kerouac, visited him. Kerouac, himself, spent a lot of time at 501 E. 11th Street, in a tenement whose courtyard he and his buddies called "Paradise Alley."

Tompkins Square is a sixteen-acre park that was originally a farmers market. In 1874 it was the site of the first U.S. Labor demonstration, when the carpenters union clashed with club-wielding police, and Samuel Gompers, later the first president of the AFL, was injured. In the 1970s Tompkins Square was the scene of violent clashes between anarchists and the NYPD. In the 1980s it filled up with the homeless. NYC is currently trying to take the park back by closing it, except for a separate children's playground on the north side.

Walk around Tompkins Square looking for a likely building for Art Department secretary Sandy Keppler's apartment in Margaret Maron's *One Coffee With*. According to Maron, the building dated from 1900 and once had only one apartment to a floor. The houses along East 10th Street, just past the local branch of the New York Public Library, seem the best choices. Keppler, who had fetched the poisoned staff coffee, had a single room efficiency with a bay window and old woodwork. In Maron's *Baby Doll Games*, a single mother, whose apartment was also near Tompkins Square, was murdered in front of her daughters on a hot night.

In John Lutz's *Shadowtown*, the smelly apartment of ex-leading man Marv Egan was near Tompkins Square, in a seedy old apartment hotel with twisted iron railings and graffiti. When he checked it out, NYPD Detective "Ox" Oxman saw a bag lady in men's overshoes and overcoat lurking nearby. Not far from here, Beat poet Frank O'Hara lived in a tenement at 441 E. 9th Street, where he was visited by friends like Ginsberg and LeRoi Jones. O'Hara later moved to Broadway across from Grace Church.

Turn left at the northwest corner of the park and walk along East 10th Street back to First Avenue. In Rex Stout's *The Golden Spiders*, Nero Wolfe's Saul Panzer is living in a cheap First Avenue hotel disguised as an illegal alien/DP (displaced person) named Leopold Heim.

Stay on 10th Street to Second Avenue. In Elliott Roosevelt's *Hyde Park Murder*, young Bob Hannah went to a Second Avenue locksmith to find out what kind of box he had found the key to when he burgled his murdered father's Wall Street office. A block to your left, at 156 Second Avenue, is the Second Avenue Deli, famous for its pastrami. It also has a Molly Picon museum with Jewish theater memorabilia.

Cross 10th Street to Stuyvesant Street, which runs diagonally from 11th Street to Cooper Square, where it turns into Astor Place. This is the St. Mark's Historic District. At the corner where 10th Street, Stuyvesant Street, and Second Avenue meet, cross to the church of St. Mark's-in-the-Bowery. The church, built on the site of a chapel on Peter Stuyvesant's farm, is late-Georgian (1799) style, with a steeple and a cast-iron porch (added later), and a small graveyard, where seven generations of Stuyvesants were buried. Peter Stuyvesant's tablet is on the church wall and there is a statue of him to your right as you face the church. In 1878, millionaire merchant A. T. Stewart's body was stolen from here and held for $20,000 ransom, but the Fishes, Schermerhorns, Livingstons, and Stuyvesants rested undisturbed.

St. Mark's is also known for its ministry to the disadvantaged: homeless, drug users, runaways. In Jack Early's *Donato and Daughter*, NYPD Lieutenant Dina Donato's taskforce had to interview a number of the runaways, seeking clues about the nun's killer. St. Mark's also sponsors the Off Broadway Theater Genesis, begun in 1965. The flowering trees in the churchyard were planted in 1975 by the Poetry Project, in memory of W. H. Auden, Paul Blackburn, and Frank O'Hara. A parishioner, Auden lived two blocks south, on St. Mark's Place.

To your right, past St. Mark's on Stuyvesant Street, there is a row of elegant old houses. The Stuyvesant-Fish House, number 21, was built circa 1803; later, its garden was used as the site of other houses. This house is a possible location for Elizabeth Daly's famous old Vauregard mansion in *Murders in Volume 2*, which stood on Traders Row—a mythical spot—and was the oldest house in the city. Uncle Imbrie Vauregard planned to leave it to the city as a museum. Uncle Imbrie was also convinced there had been a "wrinkle in time," allowing a young lady governess, who had disappeared from the garden in the nineteenth century, to reappear in the twentieth. The other Vauregards begged book expert Henry Gamadge to investigate this apparition from the fourth dimension, who had come back, carrying a volume of Bryon's poems. As a result of Gamadge's investigation, Uncle Imbrie was murdered, and Gamadge married a Vauregard greatniece, Clara.

This Daly mystery is also a version of the story about old Commodore Cornelius Vanderbilt, who made his pile in ships and ferries, and steamboats. In his old age Vanderbilt (who actually lived nearby, at 10 Washington Place) was taken in by a pair of sisters who claimed to be mystics and who did get a considerable amount of his fortune when he died. (See Walk 3.)

Although it was built too soon, the history of the Stuyvesant-Fish house makes it one of several that could be substituted for Margaret Maron's fictitious Breul House in *Corpus Christmas*. In the same mystery, Daniel and Gigi DeLucca were renovating an old redbrick row house in the East Village when they found a footlocker in the fourth-floor attic. Opening it, they discovered four dead babies, whose deaths NYPD Lieutenant Sigrid Harald had to investigate.

Turn left from St. Mark's Square to walk down Second Avenue (east of Stuyvesant Street) to St. Mark's Place, one block south. In *Donato and Daughter*, Sergeant Donato remarked that the Main Street in the East Village was St. Mark's Place. In the early 1970s, the streets had been crowded with flower children and the smell of pot was everywhere; later rock clubs and punkers with mohawk haircuts were added to the mix. Two blocks to your left is Gem's Spa, the neighborhood sundries shop famous for its egg creams, where Lieutenant Dina Donato made a phone call.

At 6 St. Mark's Place there used to be the St. Mark's Baths, located on the site of a home of James Fenimore Cooper, who wrote the Leatherstocking Tales—tales filled with plenty of murder, rape, and scalping. Cooper had married a Delancey, and, when her money ran out, he began to write as a spokesman for the American Indian—long before that was politically correct.

W. H. Auden lived at 77 St. Mark's Place for twenty years. Amanda Cross's Professor Kate Fansler adored Auden's poetry and quoted him constantly in *Poetic Justice*. Auden also wrote "Murder in the Guilty Vicarage," in which he insisted mystery stories do not take place in the real world, but are mythical versions of the Garden of Eden story and the Search for the Holy Grail.

Turn right on 7th Street to walk to Cooper Square. There you will see a statue of Peter Cooper by Augustus Saint-Gaudens, a former Cooper Union student, with a base designed by Stanford White, who spent his boyhood in this neighborhood. White, part of NYC's most famous architectural firm of McKim, Mead, and White, was the architect shot by his mistress's husband at the old Madison Square Garden.

Cooper was a self-made man who invented a better glue, invested in Manhattan real estate and iron ore, went into steel rail making, and was partner with Cyrus Field in developing the trans-Atlantic cable. In the middle of the square is the Cooper Union, a big redbrick Italianate building, with a modern annex across the park. Cooper founded the college in 1859 because all his life he had been ashamed that he could neither read nor spell. It was coed, open to all races and creeds, and tuition-free. It was also where Abraham Lincoln delivered the speech that got him nominated for president. And it may be the oldest building in the United States framed with steel beams.

If you didn't detour to Gem's Spa, now is the time to try out McSorley's Old Ale House, at 15 E. 7th Street. McSorley's is an old, atmospheric, somewhat dingy dive, often taken over by Cooper Union and NYU students during the academic year.

Cross Cooper Square and turn right (north) to find Astor Place, another diagonal street going to your left. Astor Place was once New York's Vauxhall Gardens (copied from London's), which were replaced by the popular Astor Place Opera House, where, in 1834, there was a riot over Shakespearean actor William Macready. Astor Place is named for the first John Jacob Astor, who arrived from Germany, in 1789, with $25 and died, in 1848, with about $85 million. Astor had made his fortune in fur trading and Manhattan real estate. He also built the Astor Library here, which now houses the New York Shakespeare Festival.

The offices of the Modern Language Association (MLA) are on Astor Place. And in Cross's *No Word from Winifred*, Kate Fansler went to the MLA to find out about any special sessions on English writer Charlotte Stanton (a cross between Dorothy L. Sayers and Mary Renault) held at MLA conventions. The mystery also involved an MLA love triangle, a husband and wife, both English professors, and Winifred Ashby, who turns out to be the illegitimate daughter of another English scholar, very like Sayers' friend, Muriel St. Clare Byrne. (Byrne edited *The Lisle Letters*, a record of a Tudor family related to Henry VIII.)

To see another house appropriate both for Elizabeth Daly's Vauregard mansion *and* Margaret Maron's Breul Mansion in *Corpus Christmas* (although still too early!), visit the Old Merchant's House, at 29 4th Street. Now a museum, it was lived in—untouched—until the last Tredwell died in 1933.

Walk left down Astor Place, and turn left again on Lafayette Street. Along Lafayette Street is Colonnade Row, a derelict group of elegant houses where the Astors, Vanderbilts, and Delanos once lived. Visit the old Merchant's House if possible (it's open on Sundays), and speculate about its endowment and funding, speculation which proved lethal in Maron's *Corpus Christmas*.

Return to Astor Place and walk back toward Fourth Avenue, going left to Wanamaker Place, which was the beginning of the nineteenth-century famous shopping street: the Ladies Mile. But remember that in John Lutz's chilling *Shadowtown* a wino named Ernest Dickerson was attacked in an alley off Cooper Square by a vampire, fangs and all. Dickerson was then interviewed by newspaper reporters, but soon after disappeared, to be found murdered.

Continue up Fourth Avenue to 10th Street, where, on your right, at the corner with Broadway, is a large, handsome Gothic Revival church with a tall spire called Grace Episcopal Church, set at the bend at Fourth Avenue at the corner of 10th Street. Grace Church is big enough to be a "small cathedral," with its adjoining rectory and school. It was designed by James Renwick, Jr., who won the competition to design the church in 1846, and went on to design St. Patrick's Cathedral, uptown on Fifth Avenue, and many other churches as well.

Grace Church could have been the model for Isabelle Holland's St. Anselm Episcopal Church, in *A Death at St. Anselm's*. But according to Holland herself, St. Anselm's is really based on St. Thomas Episcopal Church on Fifth Avenue. (See Walk 6.) Grace Church, however, fits nicely into the role of the Episcopal Church of St. Jude the Martyr, located (made-up) at 142 Winston Street, near Lower Fifth Avenue, in Byfield and Tedeschi's *Solemn High Murder*.

Coming from Kennedy Airport, his cabby made the Reverend Simon Bede, an emissary of the Archbishop of Canterbury, stop at a Second Avenue and 17th Street drugstore to get cash. It was there that Bede bought a paperback called *Black Mass*. Bede's taxi then turned on Winston, crossing Seventh Avenue to come into a block of beautiful redbrick Federal-style homes. There the Reverend Simon saw a "looming Gothic Revival face back from the street with a half-moon sweep of drive and trees in front and a decorative iron fence connecting smaller houses of later date on either side and gates between them leading to cloisters."

St. Jude's had a gigantic pulpit, outsized Stations of the Cross, and a Lady Chapel, where the rector was bashed with a candelabrum on Good Friday, while hearing confessions. By canon law the parish could not hold his funeral until Holy Saturday, when the bishop of New York officiated. By then Bede had solved the murder.

After admiring Grace Church, turn right to walk up Fourth Avenue past 9th Street and Wanamaker's Place to 10th Street. Go left one block to Broadway. Turn right and walk to 12th Street on Broadway.

Across 12th Street on the corner, at 828 Broadway, is the famous Strand Bookstore, with floors and floors of secondhand—i.e., used—books for sale. In Dana Clarins's *The Woman Who Knew Too Much*, the mystery began here when actress Celia Blandings bought a bundle of mysteries just sold there by Charlie Cunningham, aka Mr. Mystery. Inside a mystery by Michael Warriner, Celia found directions for "Murdering the Director." In fact, however, the Strand does not separate mysteries from other novels for sale.

Across Broadway, at 821, is the Forbidden Planet, the ultimate science fiction/comic book store. Celia Blandings left the Strand, crossed Broadway, passing the Forbidden Planet, and looked at the masks in the windows. Celia also saw actress Vanessa Redgrave and her son come out with some comic books.

When you reach the Forbidden Planet you have walked about two miles. Turn left to go one block north on Broadway to 14th Street (and Union Square) to end this walk. There are plenty of inexpensive places around Union Square to get something to eat, including a McDonald's and street vendors. There are also buses, taxis, and a subway station nearby.

3

GREENWICH VILLAGE WALK

BACKGROUND

Greenwich Village, affectionately known to natives as "the Village," is the "heart" of the New York mystery scene. Mysterious events have happened here ever since Edgar Allan Poe, who lived for a time on West 3rd Street (south of Washington Square) helped run a rooming house on Carmine Street. While living in the Village, Poe wrote both "The Fall of the House of Usher" and "The Purloined Letter," the latter a classic mystery imitated by his admirers, from G. K. Chesterton to John Dickson Carr.

Poe's most recent biographer, Kenneth Silverman, says that Poe picked the ideal time to invade the literary world: 1825–50, the golden age of periodicals. As a brilliant writer of dark melodrama (the Stephen King of his day?), Poe worked at being a celebrity and succeeded, except that he made little money and died broke at 40.

The Village itself began as an Algonquin Indian settlement. Then it became a Dutch tobacco plantation, with landed estates owned by Delanceys, Warrens, and Van Cortlandts. Finally it became a small town, named by the English for Greenwich, a London suburb. (The term *village* is redundant—*wich* means the same thing.)

Like its English namesake, the Village had a pleasant climate, making it a good place to escape smallpox and yellow fever epidemics. It was also originally hilly, but its streets were flattened in the nineteenth century. Its inhabitants, though, insisted on keeping the confusing street names and nongrid numbering system.

Its reputation as a cheap haven for writers and artists began in the mid-nineteenth century. While he lived there, Poe had published his famous hoax article about Mr. Monck Mason's Flying Machine that crossed the Atlantic in three days. (His coup was not matched until Orson Welles's radio broadcast of "War of the Worlds.") At the same time, Greenwich Village played host to other, more successful artists, like painters John LaFarge and Winslow Homer, and established writers like Mark Twain and Henry James, who was born there and lived in the elegant ambiance of Edith Wharton's Washington Square.

As the Village grew, its single-family houses were cut up into "French flats" (so labeled because bedrooms and living rooms were next to each other, a free and easy style of living frowned on in Clarence Day's *Life with Father*). Others were torn down to build tenements, as the Village became a port of entry for black and Italian immigrants. Later still, the Village became New York's version of Paris's Latin Quarter combined with London's Bloomsbury.

This transformation began well before World War I, when heiress Mable Dodge, a so-called bohemian beloved of gossip columnists, lived on the corner of Ninth Street, in a brownstone apartment. She painted her walls white (everyone still does) and held lavish parties, with guests like muckraker Lincoln Steffens, young Walter Lippmann, birth control advocate Margaret Sanger, union organizer Emma Goldman, John (Jack) Reed (who celebrated the Russian Revolution), and moody, sexy D. H. Lawrence.

As the Village's literary population grew (Eugene O'Neill, Theodore Dreiser, and Willa Cather were some of its inhabitants), so did the number of publications produced there. Villagers published the *Masses*, *The Dial* and the *Partisan Review*. After the Great War, the Village became widely known as the tolerant scene of free love and free verse and the home of Gertrude Stein's "Lost Generation" when they "repatriated." There were writers like Edna St. Vincent Millay, Marianne Moore, Sinclair Lewis, e. e. cummings, John Dos Passos, Thomas Wolfe, Sherwood Anderson, the Van Dorens, and critics like Edmund Wilson and Malcolm Cowley. Ever since then it has been a hothouse for the avant-garde in art, clothes, and ideas: in the 1930s, Communism; in the 1950s, Beatniks; in the 1960s, anti-war; and in the 1970s and 1980s, gay rights, women's lib, and punk rock.

At intervals, the Village became too expensive and the artists moved out. This happened most recently in the affluent 1980s, when Wall Streeters, doctors, actors, and lawyers began to buy whole houses (for a million or so), establishing a yuppy middle class there. In *The Medical Center Murders,* Otto Penzler (with Lisa Drake) wrote that there were no "quirky little apartments in the Village with darling little fireplaces and cheery little kitchens with roommates as adorable as Cabbage Patch Kids."

In Mickey Friedman's "The Fabulous Nick," in *Christmas Stalkings,* Santa Claus himself (disguised as Nick Santos, a chimney repairman) visited a Village family made up of a Wall Street broker, a wife who sold real estate, and one kid, Jason, who blamed Santa Claus for his dad being in jail. As editor Charlotte Macleod explained in her notes on the story, the McGuires lived in an Italianate brownstone with a fanlight and leaded glass panels that is a replica of the one where Mickey Friedman herself lives with her husband, a museum director.

Despite waves of gentrification, the Village continues to evoke its old bohemian mystique. Beatle John Lennon said he should have been born in Greenwich Village, though he lived and died uptown at the Dakota. (See Walk 10.) Tourists, too, are attracted to its older buildings and wandering streets, which make the Village seem quaint and European. But most of the bohemian-looking types on the streets are tourists, avidly watching you. Dorothy Salisbury Davis's Julie Hayes, in *Lullaby of Murder,* took guests to the Village for ice cream because it was in "its Sunday night lull," when the tourists gave it back to the natives.

In mystery stories, too, Greenwich Village is *the* place of choice to live or visit. In them its inhabitants are still young—

often advertising or publishing types, or hopeful actors, writers, painters, dancers, and musicians. And, although this is *not* the true Nero Wolfe neighborhood, it is a place where his fans can feel comfortable pursuing Wolfe's adventures.

Note: This walk includes part of SoHo (South of Houston) and the northern boundary of TriBeCa, the triangle below Canal Street. A thriving commercial center in 1840s, with manufacturing, industry, and retail stores, like the original Lord & Taylor, TriBeCa and SoHo now house galleries, rehearsal halls, boutiques, restaurants, and lofts. Recently, TriBeCa residents crusaded to keep their district's few stone streets. But cobblestones of granite, weighing twelve pounds, add up to very expensive paving compared to asphalt.

LENGTH OF WALK: 3.5 miles

This walk is divided into three parts.

See map on page 53 for the boundaries of this walk and page 295 for a list of books and detectives mentioned.

PLACES OF INTEREST

New York University, Washington Square. Founded in 1831 as a nonsectarian alternative to Columbia University by NYC business and professional people. It now occupies most of Washington Square South.

Washington Square Park. Originally a marsh drained by Minetta Brook, then a farm, a potter's field, and parade ground. In 1827 its elegant houses were built and the park laid out. Washington Arch built to mark the centennial of the first president's 1789 inauguration.

SoHo Cast-Iron Historic District, Houston to Canal Streets, Mulberry Street to Sixth Avenue. Fashionable in the 1840s, boomtown in 1960–70s, world center of contemporary art. Visit Saturdays (not Mondays).

Provincetown Playhouse, 133 MacDougal Street. Oldest Off Broadway theater company, begun by playwright Eugene O'Neill. Call 477-5048 for tickets, times.

Sullivan Street Theater, 181 S. Sullivan Street. Where *The Fantasticks* has played for 40 years, the longest run of any New York musical. Call 674-3838 for tickets, times.

Forbes Building and Museum, 62 Fifth Avenue. Museum famous for Faberge eggs, toy boats, toy soldiers, and paintings. Call 206-5548. Free.

New School for Social Research, 66 Fifth Avenue. Founded in 1919 for adult education. Professors included Hannah Arendt. (Combined with Parsons School of Design, 65 Fifth Avenue.)

PLACES TO EAT

(Many places do not take reservations, and you may find long lines.)

Steve's Ice Cream, Sixth Avenue, between 10th and 11th Streets.

John's Pizzeria, 278 Bleecker Street.

Le Petit Cafe, 156 Spring Street.

A. Zito & Sons Bakery, 259 Bleecker Street.

The Gotham Bar and Grill, 12 E. 12th Street. Expensive.

Chumley's, 86 Bedford Street (no sign). Ex-speakeasy. Inexpensive beer and burgers.

Bradley's on University Place, 70 University Place. Famous for live jazz. Cover charge.

The Coach House, 110 Waverly Place. Call 777-0303. Reservations needed. Expensive. Open daily, except Mon.

White Horse Tavern, 567 Hudson Street.

—— GREENWICH VILLAGE WALK ——

Begin your walk at the Canal Street Post Office, on the south side of Canal Street and Church Street. This post office is in a fairly modern building on the corner. In P. M. Carlson's *Rehearsal for Murder,* after Maggie O'Connor had collected the teddy bear stuffed with Muffin's ransom money, she and actor husband Nick mailed the money from here to Sister Alfonsius in Brooklyn.

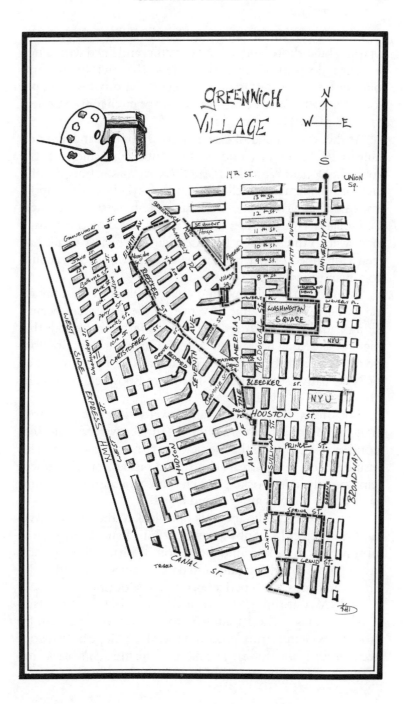

Canal Street, the dividing line between SoHo and TriBeCa, is a wide, busy thoroughfare, full of traffic, and lined with dingy or boarded-up buildings. Many have the metal steps and columns typical of the famous nineteenth century cast-iron period. Originally Canal Street was a drainage ditch for the Collect Pond near City Hall. (See Walk 1.)

At the western end of Canal Street is the Holland Tunnel, built in 1927, the first underwater tunnel for vehicles in the world. In Donald Westlake's *Good Behavior*, master burglar John Archibald Dortmunder fell through the skylight of the impoverished TriBeCa convent of St. Filumena on Vestry Street (near the Holland Tunnel). The burglar was received by the nuns as an answer to their prayers because their Sister Mary Grace had been kidnapped by her rich father and they needed a second-story man to rescue her.

Turn left on Canal Street and walk one block to West Broadway, where Sixth Avenue (Avenue of the Americas) begins. Along Canal Street there are many shops with cheap goods that might be the Ming Bazaar where P. M. Carlson's Steve Bradford hid the rich teddy bear. (A teddy bear is a New York toy named for NYC native son President Theodore Roosevelt because he refused to shoot a bear cub.)

Look for a "hole-in-the-wall" jewelry store like the one in Margaret Maron's *Death of a Butterfly*. In the mystery, Julie Redmond sarcastically said that her jeweler father-in-law treated his business like a grocer treats cheese and pickles, carrying uncut gems casually in his pocket. But en route to a business appointment Redmond was mugged and killed.

Cross Sixth Avenue and walk one block to the Seventh Avenue Canal Street IRT Subway on St. John's Lane. Go down the subway steps to look around the station. With its echoing spaces and columns to hide behind, and dark passages going off in different directions, it's a perfect place for a shooting.

In P. M. Carlson's *Rehearsal for Murder*, the O'Connor family usually caught the 1 train here to transfer to the 2 train for Brooklyn's Grand Army Plaza and their Park Slope brownstone (see *Murder Unrenovated*). The niece of the musical's black choreographer, Daphne, was shot by a masked gunman.

Leave the subway station and turn right (north) to cross Canal Street, then turn right again to cross Sixth Avenue (it's one of those wide open, multiple street corners). Walk one block up Sixth Avenue to Grand Street, then go four blocks east to Greene Street, and turn left on Greene. Looking around you can tell you are in the heart of the Cast-Iron Historic District. On Greene Street alone there are still fifty cast-iron buildings dating from 1869–95. Pre-skyscrapers, they anticipated modern steel-frame buildings, but in their decoration imitated traditional masonry, using ornate columns and patterned facades. Most are four to six stories high, with an iron step up to the store's double front doors.

Walk up Greene Street, crossing Broome Street, to Spring Street. Keep an eye out for a likely looking loft building over a coffee shop. In Carlson's *Rehearsal for Murder*, Guarnen's Coffee Shop was below the studio loft where Ramona Ricci's musical about Queen Victoria was being rehearsed. It had dark booths and ashtrays saying "Mike's Place," and was run by a plump ex-actress who once played Hedda Gabler.

Turn left on Spring Street and pick any handy scaffolded building if you want to try Maggie's gymnast's trick of climbing up to look at the iron ornamentation. (You don't have to do it with a baby in a backpack.) Also in Carlson's *Rehearsal for Murder* there was a (fictional) restaurant called L'Etoile on Spring Street. Star Ramona Ricci was shot nearby by a "masked" kid and then found there by the O'Connors.

You have now walked over one mile. There are a lot of restaurants along here. If you want to stop, try Le Petit Cafe, 156 Spring Street, with its pleasant indoor/outdoor French ambiance, or try any one of the many others in the area.

For the next part of the walk, go four blocks west along Spring Street to Sullivan Street and turn right to walk up Sullivan Street. This area is quite gentrified; it even has a copy place and a Rizzoli's Bookstore, with still more art and antique shops, galleries, and restaurants. The Off-Broadway Sullivan Street Theater, famous for *The Fantasticks*, the longest playing musical in New York history, is at 181 Sullivan. In Carlson's *Audition for Murder*, Nick O'Connor had a good part in *The Fantasticks*, which he gave up to play in *Hamlet* at an upstate college.

In Rex Stout's *Fer-de-Lance*, Archie Goodwin went to murdered Carlo Maffei's rooming house on Sullivan Street near Spring Street. Sullivan Street was littered with rubbish and filled with wild Italian kids, and Archie hated to park Wolfe's car there. But inside Archie found the vital clue to the murder in a *New York Times* clipping. He also met a young girl named Anna Fiore, who supplied more clues.

Fifty years later, in the mid-1980s, in Jack Early's *Donato and Daughter*, Sergeant Donato, walking through SoHo to meet his estranged wife, thought that these "mean streets"—the western edge of Little Italy—had changed drastically in the last ten years. They had gone from factories and luncheonettes to glamorous lofts, galleries, boutiques, and restaurants. Now only successful artists could afford to live here, and most were occupied by business people with money.

Turn left on Prince Street and walk one block to MacDougal Street. Just before MacDougal Street, on the north side of Prince Street, you will see a small redbrick Greek Revival house with a marker. It was built on land once owned by Aaron Burr, whose Greenwich real estate was bought by John Jacob Astor when Burr had to flee the country. Burr had shot and killed Alexander Hamilton in a duel across the Hudson, near Weehawken, New Jersey, ending both their careers. New York University drop-out, Marylyn Coomes, the girlfriend of young NYPD officer Clarence Duhammell, who worked on the kidnaping of poodle Lisa, had an apartment on MacDougal Street, in Patricia Highsmith's *A Dog's Ransom*.

Cross MacDougal Street to Sixth Avenue at Father Fagin Park. There is a McDonald's and a fenced ball court at the park's eastern corner. Turn right to walk up Sixth Avenue to Houston Street.

At Houston you have walked about 1.5 miles and come to the Village proper. If you want to take a rest, or make a pit stop, use the McDonald's on the corner, or try any of the small restaurants in the vicinity.

Like Wall Street, Greenwich Village or the Village is often mentioned in mysteries without the author giving a specific location. Carolyn G. Hart's Annie Laurance, who ran the bookstore called Death on Demand on Broward's Island, had tried her luck on Broadway. Annie had lived in a tiny Greenwich Village apartment (really a closet) and had seventeen tryouts and no call backs.

In Dashiell Hammett's *The Thin Man,* Nick and Nora Charles went to the Village to visit Professor Halsey Edge and his wife, Leda, who lived in an old three-story house. Edge, an archeologist, collected battleaxes and had excellent liquor.

In Ellery Queen's *The Roman Hat Mystery,* murdered shyster lawyer Monte Field had met his current "fiancée" at a Greenwich Village masked ball. (Real masked balls were a pre-war Village tradition as fundraisers for the *Masses,* something the NYU half of Ellery Queen might well have remembered.)

In Byfield and Tedeschi's *Solemn High Murder,* the Reverend Simon Bede, an emissary of the Archbishop of Canterbury, felt that Midtown Manhattan might eat him alive, but he enjoyed the Village because it was such a bazaar.

Mystery characters often live "in the Village." In Britisher Jonathan Gash's *The Great California Game,* antiques expert Lovejoy, having come via Hong Kong, was an illegal alien. He got a job in a sleazy Midtown restaurant and met a regular customer called Rose Hawkins, who lived in the Village. In P. M. Carlson's *Rehearsal for Murder,* a friend of murdered star Ramona Ricci had loaned a Village apartment to Ricci's director, while the male lead also had a dingy fourth-floor Village walk-up, with the obligatory white walls and modern furniture.

In Margaret Maron's *Death of a Butterfly,* NYPD homicide Lieutenant Sigrid Harald parked her car at Father Fagin Park and walked north looking for the Princess Lane loft of Karl Redmond's girlfriend, Bryna. Lieutenant Harald mused that the Village was now third-generation Bohemia, not quite as raffish as in its heyday, nor as free-wheeling as the East Village during the Sixties. But she savored its "yeasty warren of streets, unexpected alleyways, and old two-to-five story brick buildings."

Follow Lieutenant Harald up Sixth Avenue, across Bleecker Street, and turn right on Minetta Street. Follow Minetta Street until it curves back to the left to Minetta (aka Princess) Lane.

Look for a two-story loft/shop building with a green door, where Bryna Leighton might have lived with Karl Redmond. Leighton's loft was furnished in castoffs painted white. To Harald's surprise, she was there when Leighton's baby started to be born, so she stayed until the Chinese midwife appeared.

Take Minetta Lane right to go back to Sixth Avenue, which puts you at Father Demo Square. On the far side of Sixth Avenue you can see the twin movie houses, Waverly I and Waverly II. In Trella Crespi's *The Trouble with a Small Raise*, art buyer Simona Griffo's alibi for the murder of her ad agency's creative director was that she was seeing the funny movie at the Waverly.

Cross Sixth Avenue toward the movie theaters and go left a short distance to Bleecker Street, at the corner of Carmine Street. Look left (or walk) down Carmine Street to the site of the rooming house at 13 1/2 Carmine Street, where Edgar Allan Poe lived. This is also the street where Richard Barth's smalltime mafioso, Donghia, lived above his bakery in *The Condo Kill*. Donghia's flat had little china figurines on every surface and religious paintings—and his daughters had Bergdorf Goodman charge accounts. Margaret Binton went there seeking Donghia's aid and comfort and got it.

If you walked down Carmine Street to Seventh Avenue, you would find St. Luke's Place. It is a tree-shaded street by Walker Park, named for NYC's Mayor Jimmy Walker, who resigned under a cloud in 1932. In Elliott Roosevelt's *Hyde Park Murder*, Jimmy Walker tried to buy off the First Lady herself.

St. Luke's Place has a row of Italianate brownstone houses built for Hudson River merchants in the 1850s. In Ed McBain's *Downtown*, Vietnam vet Michael Barnes and his new Chinese girlfriend, Connie Kee, drove there in her limo to visit Marilyn Monroe look-alike Jessica Wales, a movie star who was the girlfriend of movie producer Arthur Crandall. Her third-floor apartment was nicely decorated for Christmas, but Crandall turned up with a gun.

After exploring Carmine Street as much as you like, return to Bleecker Street and walk up it past Leroy Street to Cornelia Street. Across the street is Our Lady of Pompeii, while on your right at the corner of Bleecker is the famous A. Zito & Sons Italian bakery. The bakery is reputedly popular with Frank Sinatra, who has known a few hoods in his day. It is also (probably) the model for Donghia's Bakery in *The Condo Kill.*

Keep walking up Bleecker Street on the right-hand side of the street, and cross Jones Street. To your left, at the junction with Seventh Avenue, it is called Commerce Street. Cross Barrow Street and keep walking north to Grove Street. According to the Wolfe Pack, Grove Street is really Rex Stout's "Arbor Street," the scene of a number of Nero Wolfe adventures involving his sidekick, Archie Goodwin.

To your left on the north side of the street at 10–12 Grove Street, there is a group of the most authentic Greek Revival houses in the country. Beyond them is Grove Court, an enclave of six brick-fronted buildings built as working men's houses in the days when Grove Court was called Mixed Ale Alley. Turn left and walk down Grove Street. The houses are very suitable for some that appear in Wolfe mysteries.

In Stout's *Too Many Clients*, Julia McGree, who was "Don Juan" Thomas Yeager's secretary (and one of his bimbos), lived on Grove. When she appeared at Yeager's secret Upper West Side love nest, Wolfe had Fred Durkin stationed there, and Durkin tied her up in a yellow coverlet to keep her for Archie Goodwin. (See Walk 10.)

In Stout's short story "Died Like a Dog," 29 Arbor Street, a two-mile hike south from West 35th Street, had an assortment of old brick houses. Archie Goodwin walked there to return a client's raincoat. When he saw NYPD Sergeant Stebbins outside the building, however, he headed back uptown. But when Archie stopped for the light on Ninth Avenue, a dog who was following him saved his wind-blown hat, so he took the dog home with him in a cab to Wolfe's brownstone. The Wolfe Pack also thinks that 63 Arbor Street, in Stout's *The Doorbell Rang,* was the place where Archie used the key of murder victim Morris Althaus to go up two flights of wooden stairs to Althaus's apartment.

In Frances and Richard Lockridge's *The Norths Meet Murder*, the Fullers lived on Grove Street. The murdered man, who was found in the Norths' building, by their cat, Pete, had made a pass at Mrs. Fuller, a gorgeous redhead. As a result, NYPD Lieutenant William (Bill) Weigand went to Grove Street to interview both Fullers. Two blocks west, at the end of Grove Street, you would come to St. Luke's-in-the-Field's, once St. Luke's Chapel, belonging to Trinity Parish.

After exploring Grove Street, continue walking up (north) Bleecker Street to Christopher Street. In Mary Higgins Clark's *Loves Music, Loves to Dance*, Darcy Scott went to her murdered friend Erin Kelley's apartment at 101 Christopher. While there, she ran into the obnoxious superintendent, Gus Boxer, who let her into the apartment. Darcy had helped Erin paint the walls white, put Indian rugs on the floor, and hang framed museum posters on the walls. Erin's workbench, where she made jewelry, was by the windows, but there was no sign of her.

Look left down Christopher, where, four short blocks west, is a tiny north/south street with old warehouses called Weehawken Street. (Weehawken Street is just before West Street.) It was once the Weehawken Market, where New Jersey farmers sold their produce. Number 6 is a strange old building dating to the eighteenth century.

In Margaret Maron's *Baby Doll Games*, NYPD Lieutenant Sigrid Harald lived at 42 1/2 Weehawken, a brick building originally used as a sweatshop. She shared its garden apartment with Roman Tamegra, a friend of her mother's, who knew the owners. In Maron's *Baby Doll Games*, one stormy night Harald and artist Oscar Nauman finally became lovers there, after Nauman sent Tamegra to the movies.

Cross Christopher Street and stay on Bleecker to 10th Street. Bleecker is more commercial than the side streets, where there are many brownstone or brick row houses to admire. The Wolfe Pack thinks that Rex Stout's "Eden Street" was about 10th Street. In *Too Many Clients*, Archie Goodwin found the apartment of another of Yeager's girlfriends, Mrs. Austin Hough, at 64 Eden Street. Dinah Hough's husband was an assistant professor of English literature at New York University. Hough had tried to hire Wolfe, and since he (Hough) quoted both poet Robert Browning and playwright John Webster's *The Duchess of Malfi*, Wolfe had concluded he must be an English teacher. (P. D. James is also fascinated by the bloody vengeance of Webster and quoted him in the title of *Cover Her Face*.)

Cross 10th Street to continue up Bleecker Street to Charles Street. Along Charles Street there are still more handsome, ivy-covered row houses, and trees, and lots of people out with dogs and babies. But, except for Archie Goodwin, who sprang a dog on Nero Wolfe, cats are more popular in Village mysteries.

In Isabelle Holland's *The Flight of the Archangel*, freelance journalist Kit Maitland lived on Charles Street. Kit had a child-hood crush on her half-brother, Joris Maitland, who had myste-riously disappeared. As a result, she married her look-alike cousin, Simon, an alcoholic, whom she left, and moved to the fourth floor of an old brownstone with her alley cat, Topaz.

Kit's brownstone was one of eight on the block that stretched to Perry Street. And when the police came after her, she got in through Perry Street by cutting through clairvoyant Letty Dalrymple's apartment of cats.

In Carol Brennan's *Headhunt*, at 66 Charles Street (near West 4th Street) there is a small antique firehouse, where di-vorced NYPD Homicide Lieutenant Ike (Isaac) O'Hanlon lived. It had a brick facade with decorative cement work and a vestibule done in deep red and white. Upstairs Ike had a big room with a fireplace at either end, white walls, and a window looking out on Charles Street. Ike was the childhood sweetheart of PR person Liz Wareham, who was handling the murder of King Carter. There is no firehouse on Charles Street, but there is one on West 10th Street, off Seventh Avenue.

Keep going north on Bleecker to Perry Street. There are more handsome houses, so pick a brick one for Charlie Cun-ningham in Clarins's *The Woman Who Knew Too Much*. Return-ing home in agony after breaking into Celia Blandings's apart-ment, where his ear lobe was bitten off by her bird, Ed the Mean, Charlie found a dead man. In Rex Stout's *Plot It Yourself*, a story about publishing, Amy Wyn, who now lived on Arbor Street, told Nero Wolfe that she used to live on Perry Street.

Go one more block to West 11th Street. Across Bleecker on the corner is the Biography Bookshop, while on your right is an odd-looking shop called Bird Jungle, where you can buy a parrot or other winged friend, hopefully without the manners of Celia's Ed the Mean.

Between Perry and West 11th Street are the Bleecker Gardens, where the literary Van Doren brothers demolished fences to create an open space with trees and shrubs. In Byfield and Tedeschi's *Solemn High Murder*, St. Jude's parishioner Ivy Wheeler lived in Bleecker Gardens, where she had an odd lavabo planter that was a clue to the murder of St. Jude's rector.

To your left at Hudson and 11th Street is the famous White Horse Tavern, which was the Village hangout of (mystery) writer Norman Mailer and poet Dylan Thomas. Thomas died nearby at St. Vincent's Hospital after a drinking bout. An old bar with a pleasant ambiance, you may substitute it for Edward Mackin's (aka Ralph McInerny's) "The Guillotine" bar in the Village, where Lyndon Johnson College professors met to drink and make up phony poetry to submit under the name of other professors in *The Nominative Case*.

In Craig Rice's *Having a Wonderful Crime*, Chicago lawyer J. J. Malone went with the Justuses to the Village soiree of poetess Wildavine Williams. Wildavine wore orange pajamas and big loop earrings and invited her neighbors, a tall, thin poet and a white-haired painter in tennis shoes, who ate most of the spaghetti. After Malone got the information he needed about the murder, he left to find a steak and a saloon. But after an hour's wandering, Malone found himself at the intersection of West 4th and West 11th Streets. Then at the corner where Waverly Place crossed Waverly Place, he grabbed the first cab he saw. Asked where he wanted to go, he shouted "Chicago!"

Cross West 11th Street and take Bleecker one more block to Bank Street, where, at Abingdon Square, Hudson Street becomes Eighth Avenue. Look left across Hudson for a likely looking Hudson factory converted to lofts to be the "pad away from home" of zany movie director Bernie Barnes, in Steve Allen's *Murder in Manhattan*. After pursuing the murderer there, Steve was rescued from the burning building, not because he ripped off his Clark Kent suit and became Superman, but because he dialed 911.

Holland's Kit Maitland, in *The Flight of the Archangel*, had found a bedraggled alley cat on Hudson and took him to the vet, then adopted him, calling him Topaz. It was also near Hudson that Archie Goodwin found the stray dog whom Wolfe adopted in "Died Like a Dog."

One block north of Bank Street to your left (west) across Abingdon Square is Bethune Street. In Lawrence Block's *The Sins of the Fathers*, ex-NYPD cop Matt Scudder was hired by the father of a murdered Village hooker to find out what had really happened to her. The dead girl had been sharing her apartment at 194 Bethune with a boy named Richard Vanderpoel. The day of the murder, Vanderpoel was found running down Bethune with blood all over his hands. Jailed for her murder, two days later he hanged himself in prison. Scudder went to Bethune to talk to the superintendent, a sculptor named Elizabeth Antonnelli, who gave Scudder a clue: Wendy and Richard had lived together as if they were brother and sister, not lovers.

Two blocks north up Hudson Street is Jane Street. The serial killer in Early's *Donato and Daughter* rented an apartment on Jane Street, then killed his new landlord in an argument. Still farther north on Hudson at Gansevoort Street is the historic Gansevoort Market, a collection of old brick buildings housing the city's wholesale meat market. If you took Gansevoort Street left to the West Side docks and the Hudson River, you would see the Gansevoort Street Piers (53/52) where novelist Herman Melville worked as an outside customs inspector. (Melville's mother was a Gansevoort.) Melville's last novel, *Billy Budd*, the story of the "judicial" murder of an innocent young sailor, was found in his papers after his death.

At Abingdon Square you have walked about one and one-half miles, and should be on the lookout for a good stopping place. Two blocks south down Hudson Street, in *Donato and Daughter*, Lieutenant Dina Donato and her mother met at a Hunan Pan (a Chinese chain) that was decorated in traditional Chinese black and red. Or if you keep walking until you reach Greenwich Avenue, there are a lot of other places to try.

Cross Abingdon Square to a tiny park where West 12th Street meets Eighth Avenue. In Margaret Maron's *Baby Doll Games*, there was a three story brick building on Lower Eighth

Avenue that housed an improvisational dance theater called 8th-AV-8 where a star dancer known as "Emmy" was murdered onstage during a children's Halloween matinee.

Turn right on 12th Street. At 302 W. 12th Street you will find one of the two Foul Play Bookstores. It is a tiny storefront lined from floor to ceiling with paperback mysteries. It's a very friendly place, although there's no place to sit down. In P. M. Carlson's *Audition for Murder*, Lisette and Nick O'Connor had an apartment at West Eighth Avenue and 11th Street, near the Foul Play Bookstore. After Nick found Lisette drunk (or stoned) at Franklin's bar, on Eighth Avenue in the 40s, they walked home to sober her up.

After stopping to buy a book, turn right to walk along West 12th Street. Look for an old brick building for Rex Stout's Gambit Club, the chess club where chess expert Paul Jerin died of poisoning while playing twelve chess games simultaneously, in *Gambit*.

Cross West Fourth Street and go one more block east to Greenwich Avenue. Like Bleecker Street, Greenwich Avenue is a big shopping/eating street. Turn right and walk down Greenwich Avenue to Bank Street, then turn left to West 11th Street, where you come to St. Vincent's Square (at Bank Street and Mulroy Square). The buildings of St. Vincent's Hospital (whose official address is 11th Street and Seventh Avenue) are all over here.

St. Vincent's Hospital was founded by Sisters of Charity in 1849. Bohemian poet and trendsetter Edna St. Vincent Millay was actually named for the hospital where her drunken uncle's life was saved. Millay typified the "new woman," with her short hair and skirts, independent spirit, and greed for life. Raised in Maine, Millay went to Vassar, graduating in 1917, when she also published her most famous poem, "Renascence." In *Murder at Teatime*, Stefanie Matteson's "senior citizen" actress Charlotte Graham went to Maine when she was replaced in the cast of *The Trouble with Murder*. Looking at the seaside view, Graham was reminded of Millay's poem "All I could see from where I stood/Was three long mountains and a wood." But murder had followed Charlotte to Maine.

In Clarins's *The Woman Who Knew Too Much*, when Celia's

bird, Ed the Mean, bit off Charlie Cunningham's ear lobe, Cunningham (aka Mr. Mystery) headed home to Perry Street, stopping to vomit in a trashcan near St. Vincent's.

In Richard Lockridge's *Murder for Art's Sake*, nervous NYPD Lieutenant Nathan Shapiro walked past St. Vincent's Hospital on his way to meet the Widow Jones at murdered Shack Jones's studio. In Byfield and Tedeschi's *Solemn High Murder*, church secretary Ivy Wheeler was taken from St. Jude the Martyr's rectory to St. Vincent's Hospital after she was hit on the head.

In Mary Higgins Clark's *While My Pretty One Sleeps*, undercover NYPD cop Carmen Machado, aka Tony Vitale, who was shot as a stoolie, managed to tell the NYPD that the "hit" on Neeve Kearny was not ordered by mobster Nicky Sepetti. In Ed McBain's *Downtown*, Michael Barnes ended up here with stab wounds after his wild Christmas holiday on the town.

Turn right and stay on Greenwich Avenue as you walk past St. Vincent's Hospital. On your right you should pass first Mulroy Square and, a block later, McCarthy Square. (Both of them are formed by the Seventh Avenue diagonal.) Keep walking to 10th Street. At 10th Street turn left to walk about a half a block to the tiny cul-de-sac called Patchin Place.

Patchin Place has an open iron gate that leads into a tiny cobblestoned mews, with a group of delightful mid-nineteenth century houses. At one time Theodore Dreiser lived here, as did poet e. e. cummings, and recluse novelist Djuna Barnes, whose editor was poet T. S. Eliot, who also visited and liked NYC. A ginger cat, whom Eliot would have spoken with, was sitting on the doorstep of No. 4, where cummings lived.

After you take a look, decide if this is a good time to try Steve's homemade ice cream. His famous ice cream shop is one block to your left, on Sixth Avenue between 10th and 11th Streets. In Crespi's *The Trouble with a Small Raise*, on the night of her boss's murder, Simona Griffo went to a movie at the Waverly, then pigged out on her favorite ice cream, which was Cookeo with Reese's Pieces, at Steve's. Later, when NYPD Detective Sid Greenhouse took Simona to get ice cream at Steve's, the line was around the block.

This is not a good area to park a fancy car at night, as Lillian O'Donnell's Fulton Fish Market merchant, Karl Wespo, discovered. In O'Donnell's *The Children's Zoo*, a group of young blacks, loitering near an all-night hamburger joint at Sixth near 10th Street, attacked and badly damaged his car while chanting "trick or treat."

Walk back from Patchin Place to the corner of Greenwich Avenue and West 10th Street. Across 10th Street is a little red firehouse but, unlike the one lived in by NYPD Lieutenant Ike O'Hanlon in Carol Brennan's *Headhunt*, it's still in use.

In the Lockridges' Mr. and Mrs. North mysteries, "Greenwich Place" was either Greenwich Avenue or Waverly Place—or Village Square. Whichever street it was, the Norths lived in this part of the Village. In *The Norths Meet Murder*, the couple lived at 5 Greenwich Place with their black cat, Pete, in a brownstone that had steps leading up to the double front door, which opened into a vestibule, where you rang to get in, and an inner hallway where the mailboxes were located. Around the basement apartment where their landlady, Mrs. Buano, lived there was an iron railing. The Norths had the second or parlor floor, which boasted high ceilings and deep bay windows. Their cat, Pete, liked to get out on the roof and go up the fireplaces, which was how he found the murder victim, naked in the tub in the empty third-floor apartment (shades of Dorothy L. Sayers' *Whose Body?*). If you see a black cat in the neighborhood, he may be one of Pete's descendents, for Pete was the only real character in the book.

Continue one block south to Village Square, where 10th Street, Christopher Street, Sixth Avenue, and 8th Street meet. The Lockridges commented that Eighth Street (which begins here) was the main street of Greenwich Village. That is less true today, but both Balducci's, the Village's gourmet grocery store, and the Jefferson Market, located in the old Courthouse building on the south-west corner of the square, are here. In *The Trouble with a Small Raise*, Crespi's Simona Griffo called Balducci's the Village's "ne plus ultra grocer," one of the best-stocked specialty stores in the city. According to Griffo, the Jefferson Market was a tamer version. Others disagree. Decide for yourself after sampling both. Griffo lived nearby on 9th Street in a tiny studio decorated with huge photographs of her beloved Italy.

Turn right at Christopher Street to walk about one-half block west to tiny Gay Street, named for the family who lived there in the eighteenth century. On its east side there is a row of Greek Revival houses, and, on the west, a row of Federal houses. The basement apartment of Ruth McKenney, whose play *My Sister Eileen* became the musical *Wonderful Town* was at No. 14. Her sister Eileen was also the wife of writer Nathanael West, who wrote *Miss Lonelyhearts*, and befriended mystery writer Dashiell Hammett.

In Richard Lockridge's *Murder for Art's Sake*, model Rachel Farmer lived in a Gay Street building that was once a house. Its tenants included Farmer and Max (Maxwell) Briskie, a feather-weight boxer who was also a painter, and married to Dottie— Dorothy—Goodbody, a musical comedy composer. Goodbody had been playing around with murdered artist Shack Jones, who had done a nude of her.

At the end of Gay Street you come out on Waverly Place, which begins at Bank Street. As Craig Rice's confused J. J. Malone discovered, Waverly Place first runs north/south, then east/west. It now goes past Washington Square (where it is called Washington Square North), then reappears and continues to Broadway.

Turn left on Waverly Place to walk toward Washington Square. In Emma Lathen's *Banking on Death*, Schneider heir Martin Henderson lived in a basement apartment in a brownstone on Waverly Place. But urbane Sloan Vice-President Thatcher pointed out to young trust officer Ken Nicholas that it was an expensively decorated apartment, with the original wood painted a stark white like the walls, and a rear wall replaced with glass overlooking a pocket-sized garden.

In Don Winslow's *A Cool Breeze on the Underground*, the Upper West Side slum kid, Neal Carey, who was raised by P. I. Joe Graham, was sent to Trinity (prep) School. But mentor Graham made Carey spend his spring vacation learning how to get lost. Carey first tried hiding out in a classmate's third-floor Waverly Place apartment, but Graham easily found him there.

If you are hungry you might stop to eat at the Coach House at 110 Waverly Place, between Sixth Avenue and Washington Square. This restaurant's excellence is attested to by the fact that Emma Lathen's banker John Putnam Thatcher dined there.

Then cross Sixth Avenue and walk left on Waverly Place one block to Washington Square. Washington Square (Park) is the famous "center" of Greenwich Village—and NYU. It is the largest public space south of 14th Street. Once a marsh where the Minetta Brook rose, it was used as a potter's field (or cemetery for indigents, criminals, and unclaimed bodies) and a site for public hangings, like London's Tyburn Hill. (See *Mystery Reader's Walking Guide: London*, Regent's Park Walk.)

On July 1, 1826, when the country celebrated its fiftieth birthday, the area became Washington Square and began to be used as a parade ground. By 1828 it had become a classy public park. Then New York University built its first building, copied from Cambridge University's King's College Chapel, on the east side of the square in the mid-1830s. King's College Chapel was very important in P. D. James's *An Unsuitable Job for a Woman*. (See *Mystery Reader's Walking Guide: England*, Cambridge Walk.)

At the same time, fashionable mansions were being built around the park, where social and literary lights, such as Henry James and Edith Wharton, later lived. Neither of them wrote whodunits, but James is famous for his ghost story *The Turn of the Screw*. James was born at 21 Washington Square. But when he returned from Europe in 1904, he found NYU had torn down his birthplace, and was furious at having half his history "amputated." (James had always dreamed of a tablet to mark his birthplace and, despite the changes, there is a marker for James on NYU's Brown Building one-half block away).

The original Washington Square Arch, built to celebrate the 100th anniversary of George Washington's inauguration, was made of wood, and only later replaced with stone. The arch has 110 steps inside; it was rumored during World War II that a spy had lived secretly inside the arch for several months.

In the north-west corner, Washington Square has a children's playground. (In modern Manhattan if a park is open it usually has segregated child and dog areas.) In Rex Stout's *The Mother Hunt*, Sally Corbet wheeled the baby left on Lucy Valdon's doorstep to Washington Square twice a day. In Steve Allen's *Murder in Manhattan*, one movie scene was shot in Washington Square's playground, with Steve (as a character) and the director's wife, Mimi, sitting on the swings.

In the Lockridges' *The Norths Meet Murder*, Pam North could hear children playing in Washington Square. In Trella Crespi's *The Trouble with a Small Raise*, NYPD Detective Sid Greenhouse and Simona Griffo ate their Steve's ice cream in Washington Square, watching the junkies ply their trade. Greenhouse said the square was the only place in the village to sit down without ordering something.

In Margaret Maron's *Past Imperfect*, NYPD Lieutenant Sigrid Harald went through the square in a snow storm, when it looked like a Currier and Ives print. In Emma Lathen's *Banking on Death*, banker Thatcher had his cabbie drop him at the south side of Washington Square so he could walk through the park on his way to visit Martin Henderson. The snow was crisp and clean and there were many strollers and playground kids. Thatcher went by a large snowman with improbable, but unmistakable, female characteristics. Another older gentleman said with a sniff that he preferred the original kind, but Thatcher tolerantly decided it was the work of some New York University students with fevered imaginations.

In Lathen's *Death Shall Overcome*, the March on Wall Street assembled here. Like the real March on Washington, organizers ran about telling the troops where the Red Cross stations would be. This march went from Washington Square down Broadway, to Foley Square, through City Hall Park, and down Wall Street to the New York Stock Exchange. (See Walk 1.)

New York University now occupies the entire area east and south of the square. It consolidated all its classes here in 1974 when it sold its campus at the far north end of Manhattan. Its current architectural style is shown in Bobst Library, built in what NYU students call "federal prison style." Made of the traditional Washington Square redstone, it is an undecorated skyscraper with glass walls, through which you can see floor after floor of steel stairs. Each stair turn is just right for a guard to stand with a gun.

New York University was the alma mater of one half of Ellery Queen, Manfred—or Manny—Lee. In Rex Stout's *Too Many Clients*, Archie Goodwin came to Washington Square searching for NYU English professor Austin Hough, the husband of Dinah, one of Yeager's love nesters. Archie commented that in a large university a lot of people know where an assistant prof ought to be, or might be, but no one knows where he is. Archie managed to avoid being trampled in corridors, but he was asked for autographs by coeds who thought he was Sir Lawrence Olivier or Nelson Rockefeller.

Walk through the square to Washington Square South, which is also West 4th Street. To your right, at Sixth Avenue, is the Provincetown Playhouse, at 133 MacDougal Street (which becomes Washington Park West). Founded by a Village group that included Eugene O'Neill and Edna St. Vincent Millay, the Playhouse changed American theater. (According to Ellery Queen, in *The Roman Hat Mystery*, theater became strictly for highbrows, while everyone else went to the movies.)

A few blocks farther west is the subway station where the Norths' mailman was shoved under a train on his way home, in the Lockridges's *The Norths Meet Murder*. (Subway shoving is a very popular New York murder method because the subway stations are often poorly lit and unpatrolled in spots.)

Cut back across Washington Square to Washington Square East. Old Commodore Cornelius Vanderbilt, who founded the family's fortune on ferries, steamships, and railroads, lived at No. 10 Washington Place. In his old age Vanderbilt became fascinated by a pair of sisters who claimed to be mystics. They took over his establishment and ended up with a lot of money when he died. This scenario is very like Elizabeth Daly's *Murders in Volume 2*, in which Henry Gamadge had to solve the mystery of how a young English governess, missing for almost a century with the family's volume of Byron's poems, could reappear at the Vauregard mansion and capitivate elderly Uncle Imbrie. (See also Walk 2.)

Walk up Washington Square East to the corner of Washington Square North and University Place, where Washington Square North becomes Waverly Place again. Three blocks to the right is Broadway. In John Lutz's *Shadowtown*, there was a movie house called "The Last Reel," at Broadway and 8th Street, where NYPD Detective "Ox" Oxman picked up the trail of one of the actors in the soap *Shadowtown*. Escaping, the actor Phil Malloy raced down Broadway to Houston, cut back to Bleecker, and ended up dead in a vacant brick building with a second-hand bookshop on the ground floor. Oxman then discovered that Malloy was the soap opera's drug courier.

Cross Washington Square North and turn left to walk back toward Fifth Avenue, passing by the remainder of a row of twenty-eight Greek Revival houses built circa 1831. Number 1 was the home of Edith Wharton, whose neighbors were William Dean Howells and Henry James's grandmother. John Dos Passos wrote *Manhattan Transfer* while living on this block, all of which is now owned by NYU.

Turn right (north) to walk up Fifth Avenue toward the Empire State Building. Fifth Avenue, which begins here, was cut through north to 23rd Street in 1837, then up to Madison Square by 1847. (See Walk 6.)

On Fifth Avenue you pass by Washington Mews, a private alley where the original buildings were stables. Ed McBain's Michael Barnes and Connie Kee drove there Christmas morning to find the S. Gruber of the Gruber Financial Group. Gruber had financed the movie *Winter's Chill*. To Barnes, the Mews looked like a cobblestone lane in Wales. (Was he thinking of *A Child's Christmas in Wales* by Dylan Thomas?) The little houses had freshly painted doors with shiny brass knockers and wreaths, and Christmas trees in the windows. Gruber's place had a black door and the doorbell played "Mary Had a Little Lamb."

Continue up Fifth Avenue to 10th Street. At the corner is the Episcopal Church of the Ascension, an old brownstone building that might be a stand-in for one of the churches in Isabelle Holland's *A Lover Scorned*, "an old red brick edifice that had seen better times." This church was the site of the wedding of President John Tyler and a NYC belle in 1844. It has stained glass windows and an altar mural by John la Farge.

Down 10th Street there are a number of elegant houses including one Mark Train lived in. In Clarins's *The Woman Who Knew Too Much*, Celia Blandings lived near 10th Street and Fifth Avenue, in a building listed in the historic register. Blandings' apartment had one huge room (with the standard white walls) that she shared with her grandfather's pool table (he ran a pool hall in Chicago's Loop) and her hyacinth macaw, Ed the Mean, who could splinter a billiard cue (and bit off Charlie Cunningham's ear lobe when he broke in). Blandings, a would be writer, also had shelves of mysteries and videocasettes of classic mystery movies.

In *A Severed Wasp*, Madeleine L'Engle's retired pianist, Katherine Vigneras, came back to NYC to live in a brownstone she owned on 10th Street between Fifth and Sixth Avenues. She rented out the garden apartment and the upper floor to a dancer and a doctor, respectively, both of whom became embroiled with her in a mystery at the Cathedral of St. John the Divine. (See Walk 11.)

Walk one more block north to 11th Street. In Rex Stout's *The Mother Hunt*, widow Lucy Valdon, who lived at 11th Street off Fifth Avenue, found a baby, supposedly fathered by her dead husband, left on her doorstep. Lucy hired Nero Wolfe to find the baby's mother.

To your left, near Sixth Avenue, was the Second Cemetery of the Shearith Israel Jewish congregation, which came to NYC in 1654. This cemetery opened in 1805 and was used until 1830. (See Walks 1, 4.) Just this side of the cemetery is 18 W. 11th Street, where a new building has replaced the brownstone blown up in 1970 when some SDS Weathermen were making bombs. Three of the bomb manufacturers were killed in the explosion and two other college girls went into hiding for years.

In Arthur Maling's *Ripoff*, about investment chicanery in a Chicago–based company, stock analyst Brockton Potter, of Price, Potter and Petaque, lived in a house near the corner of 11th and Fifth, near the (First) Presbyterian Church. The church, another landmark building, has a tower copied from the Magdalen College Chapel, which appeared in Dorothy L. Sayers's *Gaudy Night*. While coming home from Wall Street with his young Hispanic associate, Jaime Ortega, to meet an art dealer, they were shot at. Jaime, who pushed Potter to safety, was killed.

Keep walking up Fifth Avenue to 12th Street. Heading home after buying a pile of second-hand mysteries at The Strand Bookstore, Clarins's Celia Blandings passed the Forbes Building (No. 62), on the northwest corner of Fifth Avenue. The Forbes Building houses both the business magazine and the founder's museum with his Fabergé Egg Collection. (A friend of mine, Barbara Marshall Frye, has an egg in the collection.)

Across Fifth Avenue, in an old Italianate brownstone mansion, is the Salmagundi Club. You can look at its ornate interior on afternoons from 1:00–5:00 P.M. Named for the satiric periodical that Washington Irving and his friends published, it is the oldest arts club in the country. It is also the only survivor—in this location—of the row of millionaires' mansions once there. It may have been the model for S. S. Van Dine's Knickerbocker Club, except that that club was more political in nature. (See also Walk 4.)

In Anna Green's classic *The Leavenworth Case*, the law offices of Velley, Carr and Raymond were on lower Fifth Avenue. The morning Leavenworth was found shot in his library, young Mr. Raymond was fetched by Mr. Leavenworth's private secretary, Trueman Harwell. Then the two men caught the Fifth Avenue stagecoach to go uptown to the Leavenworth brownstone.

Not far away, at Fifth Avenue and 22nd Street, was the Hoffman House, a luxury hotel which had the most elegant bar in New York, decorated with 25,000 nymphs. This was the hotel where the Englishman Henry Clavering, who was secretly married to one of the Leavenworth sisters, stayed while he tried to claim his bride. NYPD detective, Ebenezer Gryce, insisted that the lawyer, Raymond Everett, go there and strike up an acquaintance with Clavering.

Across Fifth Avenue from Forbes, at 65 Fifth Avenue, is the Parsons School of Design, established in 1896. Parsons was the first school in the world to tie art and industry together. It is now combined with another unique New York institution, the New School for Social Research, located at 66 Fifth Avenue, which was founded after World War I and later became famous for its refuge professors, like Hannah Arendt.

Turn to your right to walk along 12th Street, to University Place, which runs parallel to Fifth Avenue between Washington Square and 14th Street. You are now reaching the end of this walk and may want to stop and eat. There are several good restaurants in this area for you to try, but making a reservation ahead is a good idea.

On the south side, at 12 E. 12th Street, is the expensive Gotham Bar and Grill, with its discreet gray awning. In *The Woman Who Knew Too Much*, Celia Blandings met her agent, Joel Goldman, there for a drink to discuss her theater audition. When Celia complained that Joel was "doing his Clifton Webb" imitation, Goldman admitted his mother was frightened by *Laura* while she was pregnant. At the Gotham Celia and Joel saw Charlie Cunningham have a roaring fight with his mistress, Zoe Bassinetti, the wife of the think tank director.

Continue east to University Place. Just south of 11th Street at 70 University is Bradley's on University Place. Bradley's is a popular jazz club which is as close to being a concert hall as a bar can come. In *The Woman Who Knew Too Much*, Celia Blandings arranged to meet Charlie Cunningham there to return his copy of a mystery story by Michael Warriner that she had bought at the Strand. While they were at Bradley's the place was crawling with CIA, FBI, and Pallisades secret agents.

You might also try the new Cedar Street Tavern, at 82 University Place. Originally located in a six-story loft at 24 University Place, it was a hangout for abstract painters who left paintings as payment. Then it became a drinking spot of the Beats, including writers Jack Kerouac and Allen Ginsberg.

Or just look about for a lunch counter, like the one where Archie Goodwin stopped to have a corned beef sandwich, glass of milk, and a piece of cherry pie when hunting for English professor Austin Hough in Rex Stout's *Too Many Clients*. Or walk up University Place to 14th Street and Union Square, where you can find any number of places to eat and end this walk.

4

LOWER MIDTOWN WALK

Chelsea, Union and Madison Squares,
and Gramercy Park

BACKGROUND

This walk will explore some of New York's most attractive residential areas that have many nineteenth-century treasures. You can choose to walk only one square at a time, or you can walk from one to another. The pleasant ambiance of brownstones and cast-iron buildings, mixed with early skyscrapers, continues until the end of the walk, at the city morgue.

This part of Manhattan from 14th Street north to 23rd Street was originally large farms and country estates. But better transportation in the early nineteenth century made it convenient for people who worked downtown, and the area was developed into a series of private urban parks, like London's West End. (See *Mystery Reader's Walking Guide: London*, Brompton, Belgravia/Pimlico Walk.)

The neighborhood of Chelsea north of Greenwich Village took its name from the estate of Clement Clarke Moore. Moore's maternal grandfather, Captain Thomas Clarke, bought the land from 14th Street to 27th Street, Seventh Avenue to the Hudson River, naming it after London's Chelsea Hospital. In 1835 Clement Clarke Moore, whose father had been bishop of New York, gave a block to the Episcopal Church to build General Theological Seminary. He then developed the rest of the land with great care as the city and its grid system moved north.

Moore was a noted Hebrew scholar, but he is best remembered for his poem "A Visit from St. Nicholas," aka "Twas the Night Before Christmas." He wrote it in 1822 to amuse his daughters, but for years refused to admit his authorship. In that poem, however, Moore's clever combination of Dutch and English traditions created an all-American character–and a merchandizing symbol known worldwide–*Santa Claus*. Ever since, New York City has been closely associated with the jolly old elf.

Moore's mansion, at Eighth Avenue and West 23rd Street, was demolished in the 1850s when the bluffs were leveled along the Hudson River. (Life in this part of Manhattan was described in Gene Schermerhorn's *Letters to Phil, Memories of a New York Boyhood*.) One of the 1991 Christmas windows at Lord & Taylor featured the Moore mansion.

In the nineteenth century the territory east of the Moore estate along Sixth Avenue from 14th to 42nd Streets became known as the Tenderloin, a neighborhood of shops, brothels, and gambling, famous for its graft. Both Stephen Crane and O. Henry wrote about its residents. In the 1880s the famous artists' hotel, the Chelsea, was built. The hotel attracted several writers and the area acquired a literary ambiance. But by the 1980s Chelsea became better known as a swingers' habitat, filled with nightclubs and experimental theater.

Union Square, which runs from 14th to 17th Streets between Park Avenue South and Broadway, was once the site of the Delano and Roosevelt estates. The Roosevelt family came to America in 1649, and native son Theodore Roosevelt was born at 28 East 20th Street, in a house which was later rebuilt and is now open as a museum. By 1847 Union Square had become an affluent residential neighborhood and several grand hotels were built there. One was Eno's Hotel where the young Prince of Wales (Bertie) stayed in 1860; another was the elegant Hoffman House at 22nd Street and Fifth Avenue, with its famous bar decorated with 25,000 nymphs.

After the Civil War, Union Square became the hub of the elegant shopping district along Broadway known as the Ladies

Mile. The Mile began at Eighth Avenue and went north to 23rd Street, spilling over to Fifth and Sixth Avenues. Among the stores once located there were Lord & Taylor, Bonwit Teller, B. Altman, and Best & Co., as well as Tiffany & Co. and Brentano's. There were also a number of exclusive men's clubs, such as the Union, the Manhattan, and the Athenaeum, long since gone or moved uptown.

Union Square was also the scene of many protests. There was a big demonstration/riot against President Lincoln and the draft in 1860. And by the early twentieth century, Union Square had become a place like London's Hyde Park Corner and Chicago's Bughouse Square, where political soap-box orators spoke their minds. Then it became the haunt of criminals, oddballs, and drug addicts, until the 1980s, when both the square and the old shopping district began to undergo renewal.

Today, Union Square is somewhat of a mixed bag. It has been cleaned up and its shrubs cut back, and holds a large farmers' market on Wednesday, Fridays, and Saturdays. Around the square are expensive restaurants, landmarks like the neo-classical headquarters of Tammany Hall, and expensive high rises, like Zeckendorf Towers. Publishing and advertising companies, as well as printers, art and photography studios, and suppliers are returning, but there are still bums and homeless people about.

Madison Square (Park) is directly north of Union Square, where Broadway crosses Fifth Avenue. It was the site of the 1890 Madison Square Garden (there have been three since), designed by Stanford White. White was the third partner in the Beaux Arts architecture firm of McKim, Mead and White. A notorious playboy, who maintained his own love nest, complete with a red velvet swing, he was shot and killed at the Garden while watching a revue starring his former mistress, Evelyn Nesbit. His murderer was Nesbit's rich and jealous husband, Harry R. Thaw. This real-life crime story has been the basis for several mysteries and movies.

When Fifth Avenue was cut north from Union Square, a corner of Madison Square was chopped off to give "The Avenue" more room. But Madison Square still is famous for its marvelous view of "old" New York skyscrapers on its eastern

side, along Madison Avenue, including the 1902 Flatiron
Building near its southwest corner.

East of Union and Madison Squares lies the most charming
square of all, the only private park left in the city: Gramercy
Park, still serene and quiet, with brownstones on almost all
sides. In the late afternoon, neighborly dog walkers circle outside the locked park as children play within. Real-life VIPs, like
former *New York Daily News* publisher James Hoge, still live
here, the way the young and the rich did in Edith Wharton's
day. At the southwestern corner, at Nos. 15 and 16, are the National Arts Club and the Players, a club begun by actor Edwin
Booth in 1888. The NYC Chapter of Mystery Writers of America holds its monthly meetings there, while the Wolfe Pack has
used the Gramercy Park Hotel on the northeast corner to host
its Nero Wolfe Black Orchid Weekends.

Other famous authors lived nearby: from Washington Irving, who visited his nephew at Irving Place; to O. Henry, who
drank at Pete's Tavern; to Nathanael West, who was the night
manager at the Kenmore Hall Hotel and let his friend Dashiell
Hammett stay there when he was broke. North on East 26th
Street at 68 Lexington Avenue is the Armory, where the famous
1913 Armory show of Post Impressionists was held. To the east
is the Police Academy Museum, and, on the East River, famous
Bellevue Hospital and the NYC Morgue.

LENGTH OF WALK: About 3 miles

See map on page 81 for boundaries of this walk and page 300
for a list of books and detectives mentioned.

PLACES OF INTEREST

Chelsea Historic District, 20th to 22nd Streets, Eighth to Tenth
    Avenues. Cushman Row (1840): 406–418 W. 20th Street;
    Italianate houses (1855): 446–450 W. 20th Street; General
    Theological Seminary (1836): Ninth Avenue at W. 20th Street.

Gramercy Park Historic District, area just east of Park Avenue
    South, between 20th and 21st Streets. Park developed in 1831.

See National Arts Club, No. 15, and the Players, No. 16, as well as Nos. 3 and 4.

Flatiron Building, 175 Fifth Avenue, at Broadway and 22nd Street.

Tammany Hall, Park Avenue and East 17th Street, on Union Square.

The Chelsea Hotel, 222 W. 23rd Street, between 7th and 8th Avenues.

Theodore Roosevelt's Birthplace (replica), 28 E. 20th Street. Museum is open Wed.–Sun., 9:00 A.M.–5:00 P.M. Admission fee.

Kenmore Hall Hotel, 145 East 23rd Street.

NYPD Police Academy Museum, 235 East 20th Street. Open Mon.–Fri., 9:00 A.M. 2:30 P.M. Admission free.

PLACES TO EAT

(Not many are named in mysteries, but there is every variety: from diners for Stout's Archie Goodwin to famous bars to expensive restaurants to choose from.)

Empire Diner, 210 Tenth Avenue, at the corner of West 22nd Street. Twenty-four hour Art Deco establishment that serves the late crowd from Chelsea's discos. Inexpensive.

Sam Chinita's, Ninth Avenue and 20th Street. Diner specializing in Spanish/Chinese cuisine, including Cuban pot roast and stir-fry chicken. Inexpensive.

Pete's Tavern, 66 Irving Place/129 E. 18th Street. Dates from 1874. Put on map by O. Henry. Open daily, including Sunday brunch. Inexpensive. Call 473-7676.

Union Square Cafe, 21 E. 16th Street. Publishing lunch crowd. Noisy, high-ceilinged rooms. Expensive. Call 243-4020.

——— LOWER MIDTOWN WALK ———

Begin your walk at Madison Square at the southwest corner where Broadway meets Fifth Avenue near the 7th Avenue (BMT) subway stop. You will see a tiny plot of ground with a gigantic pair of crutches in front of the world-famous and much photographed triangular Flatiron Building. Designed by D. M. Burnham and built in 1902, the Flatiron Building occupies the entire triangle of 22 and 23 Streets at Fifth Avenue where it crosses Broadway. Among its most famous photographers were Alfred Stieglitz (lover/husband of bare bones and clouds artist Georgia O'Keeffe) and Edward Steichen (brother-in-law of poet and folk singer Carl Sandburg).

In S. S. Van Dine's *The Canary Murder Case*, a street cleaner named Potts found the murdered "Canary's" jewelry in a D.S.C. can near the Flatiron Building. The Flatiron Building was also directly across Madison Square Park from Philo Vance's and D.A. John F. X. Markham's favorite place to meet, the Stuyvesant Club.

Visiting the Flatiron Building puts you in the vicinity of several mystery publishers. One of the best known mystery publishers, St. Martin's Press, has its offices in the Flatiron Building, and calls its monthly mystery newsletter *Murder at the Flatiron Building*. In Rex Stout's 1950s mystery about the publishing business, *Murder by the Book*, Archie Goodwin had to interview nearly all the big publishing firms. The Wolfe Pack is inclined to think the publishing house called Scholl and Hannah, where the murdered editor, Joan Wellman, worked, was really Viking (now a division of Penguin Books, which once had its NYC offices nearby at 40 W. 23rd Street.) In Mary Higgins Clark's *Loves Music, Loves to Dance*, Darcy Scott, daughter of a famous American acting couple, also had her office there. Called Darcy's Corner, Budget Interior Designs, Darcy helped people decorate their homes and offices on a shoestring.

The second Madison Square Garden (on the site of the converted railroad station called the Hippodrome, run by P. T. Barnum) was designed by Stanford White in 1890. Built in the Spanish Renaissance style of yellow brick and white terra cotta, with arcaded sidewalks, this building included a theater, roof garden, and a tower with a nude statue of the goddess Diana. In 1906, Stanford White was shot dead in the Roof Garden Theater by Evelyn Nesbit's jealous husband as he watched her perform in a revue. (She had been White's mistress and posed in his famous red velvet swing.)

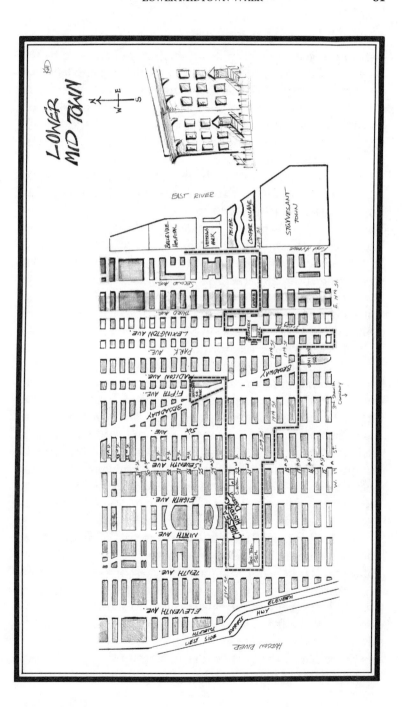

White's Madison Square Garden stood at the park's northeast corner, but it was torn down in 1925 and replaced by the New York Life Insurance Company, with its bright gilded pyramid tower. Another Madison Square Garden, at 50th Street and 9th Avenue, was also torn down. The present Madison Square Garden, built in 1968, is located above the "new" Pennsylvania Railroad Station, on 7th Avenue between 31st and 33rd Streets. (See Walk 5.)

It is important to look at the publication date when checking out Madison Square Garden in mysteries. For example, in Emma Lathen's 1964 *Death Shall Overcome*, John Putnam Thatcher, the urbane vice-president of the Sloan Guarantee Trust, said he remembered "the long count" at Madison Square Garden in the fight between Dempsey and Tunney. He was talking about an earlier Madison Square Garden located at 50th Street, not the present one perched on top of the Pennsylvania Railroad Station. In the same mystery, Thatcher attended a huge CASH rally at Madison Square Garden in support of a N.Y. Stock Exchange seat for Ed Parry.

In Richard Lockridge's *Murder for Art's Sake*, the luxurious apartment of murdered painter Shackleton Jones was in an old house at Fifth Avenue and Broadway. Shack's apartment was carpeted in pale green and his paintings, full of jagged shapes and flagrant colors, hung on the walls. His style made it comparatively easy for the artist wife of NYPD Captain Bill Weigland to recognize Shack's paintings for sale in department stores. In the Lockridges' *The Norths Meet Murder*, the office of Louis Berex, the inventor, whose business affairs were handled by murdered lawyer Brent, was at Broadway and Fifth Avenue.

Madison Square Park is filled with statues of many famous leaders, including Presidents Washington and Arthur, General Lafayette, Gandhi, and Admiral Dewey, among others, but has been cleared of shrubbery and underbrush for safety's sake. At the southwest edge of the square there is a statue of Lincoln's Secretary of the Interior, William Henry Seward, who bought Alaska from the Russians.

Look across the park at the beautiful view of early skyscrapers along Madison Avenue, among them the New York

Life Insurance Building and the Metropolitan Life Building and Tower. The Jerome mansion, where Winston Churchill's mother lived, was located next to the New York Life Insurance Building. Her father was a crony of August Belmont who loved fast horses and racing.

Walk to Madison Avenue, cross it, and turn left to walk toward 26th Street. You will pass by the 1900 Palladian palace (with its famous murals), which houses the Appellate division of the New York State Supreme Court. At the northern end of the park there is a statue of Admiral David Farragut by sculptor Augustus Saint-Gaudens, with a base designed by the murdered Stanford White.

Beyond the limits of this walk, but within reach if you want to extend it, are several other NYC "sights." About halfway between Union and Madison Squares at 28 E. 20th Street there is a museum replica of the 1858 birthplace of Theodore Roosevelt. Roosevelt not only was mayor of NYC and governor of New York, but was elected vice-president, becoming president when President McKinley was shot. Roosevelt had fought the Democratic political machine known as Tammany Hall.

Also south of Madison Square near Fifth Avenue and 22nd Street there was the "Doge's Palace," which first housed the Academy of Art. It was built by Samuel F. B. Morse, the painter and inventor. He invented Morse code and was an NYU professor who belonged to the "Know Nothing" party, which demanded that only native-born Americans hold office, and wanted immigrants to wait twenty-five years before they could become citizens. His membership in the Know Nothings makes Morse a good model for William Marshall's Professor Quarterknight in *New York Detective*. Quarterknight was a "Buffalo Bill" on a white horse who planned a coup when the Brooklyn Bridge was opened in 1888. (See Walk 1.)

At East 27th Street one block north of Madison Square at 120 Madison Avenue is the American Academy of Dramatic Arts. It is in a building originally designed to be the Colony Club. (See Walk 8.) In Velda Johnson's *The Face in the Shadows*, actress Ellen Stacey was a student at the "Academy of Dramatic Arts," where she had met her husband, Richard. Tragically, both he and her daughter Beth were killed in a plane crash, just as Ellen got her first big break in an Off Broadway show.

In the early twentieth century, West 28th Street was known as "Tin Pan Alley," where music publishers sold songs to singers and musical producers. Still farther north and east, between Madison and Fifth Avenues, at 1 E. 29th Street, is the 1848 Gothic Church of the Transfiguration, better known as the Little Church around the Corner. It won the nickname when it held a funeral for a "mere" actor. Ever since it has had a tradition of being NYC's actors' church, and has a John La Farge stained glass window showing Edwin Booth as Hamlet. For murder fans, Booth's great claim to fame, however, is that he was the half-brother of President Lincoln's assassin, John Wilkes Booth, another actor.

At Fifth Avenue and West 28th Street is the Gothic Marble Collegiate Reformed Church, built in 1854. For many years, Dr. Norman Vincent Peale was pastor there, and, if he had not been long gone, Dr. Peale might have been the model for Haughton Murphy's incurably contemporary and nondenominational cleric in *Murder for Lunch*, a minister who Reuben Frost said would bury anyone.

Turn left to walk along 26th Street on the northern side of Madison Square. Several of the remaining brick buildings around the park could have been men's clubs, but S. S. Van Dine's Stuyvesant Club had to be opposite the Flatiron Building. The Stuyvesant was Philo Vance's favorite club, one whose members were mostly businessmen and not very bright ones (which gave Vance lots of room to shine?). Not only was D.A. Markham a member, but most of Vance's suspects were, too, allowing him to hold several confrontations there. Van Dine described the Stuyvesant as a glorified hotel with an extensive political, legal, and financial membership. Members ate in the Palm Room, a dining room with a high rotunda. At that time, most NYC politicians would have been Tammany men, but Philo Vance invariably only referred to dumb or venial "pols" as members of Tammany, never his friend, D.A. Markham.

Continue east along 26th Street. At the northeast corner of Madison Square past its children's and dogs' play areas at the former site of White's Madison Square Garden, there is a memorial to Major General Worth, a hero of the mid-nineteenth century's Mexican War. Go past it and walk back down the west side of the square to West 23rd Street and the Flatiron Building, passing by a McDonald's.

Cross Fifth Avenue and walk along 23rd Street to Sixth Avenue, where you are in the old Tenderloin district, famous for its graft and crime. Cross Sixth Avenue and keep going to Seventh Avenue. When 23rd Street became a major el stop, it destroyed the residential nature of the area. As you walk along, you are surrounded by cast-iron buildings, many of which are being rehabbed.

You are now in Chelsea. In Margaret Maron's *Past Imperfect*, NYPD Lieutenant Sigrid Harald's mother, the famous photographer Anne Harald, lived in a spacious Chelsea brownstone's basement, which she decorated with her own photos, blown up. Mother and daughter celebrated their combined birthdays there and found out that their Southern mother and grandmother, respectively, was giving them both "the works" at an Elizabeth Arden-style salon called "Imagine You."

On the south side of West 23rd Street, in the middle of the block between Seventh and Eighth Avenues, you come to Hotel Chelsea, a redbrick building with New Orleans style ironwork balconies and a huge neon sign. It opened in 1884 as one of NYC's first cooperative apartments. It was converted to a hotel in 1905 and is famous as a place where many artists and writers stayed. On the front of the hotel, on either side of the awning, on a series of brass plaques, are the names of many of the hotel's famous guests: Mark Twain, Virgil Thompson, O. Henry, Edgar Lee Masters, James T. Farrell, Dylan Thomas, Thomas Wolfe, actress Sarah Bernhardt, singer Janis Joplin, painter Jackson Pollack, and playwright Arthur Miller. Arthur C. Clarke wrote *2001: A Space Odyssey* here, and William Burroughs, *Naked Lunch*. Also engraved there is Brendan Behan's tribute, in which, sounding like Dr. Johnson's remark about London, he exclaimed, "To America, the man who hates you hates the human race."

The hotel is rather shabby, but go inside to admire the grand staircase, carved fireplace, and the lobby art gallery. Its rooms are far from fancy, and comparatively cheap. Writer Thomas Wolfe wrote and lived here the last year of his life, drinking in the hotel bar. Poet Dylan Thomas was taken from here to St. Vincent's Hospital to die. And rock star Sid Vicious probably murdered his girlfriend, Nancy, here in 1978. In Margaret Maron's *Death in Blue Folders*, murdered lawyer Clayton Gladwell's personal sidekick and investigator, the elderly law clerk Dan Embry, lived here—and was found murdered here.

Walk west on West 23rd Street toward the Hudson River. At Tenth Avenue look about for a likely Chelsea duplex for Carolyn Sue Hoopes. In Joyce Christmas's Lady Margaret Priam mystery, *Suddenly in Her Sorbet*, Texas oil heiress and former princess Carolyn Sue Hoopes, now married to a banker, explained that the apartment was not quite her life-style. But she kept it because "you never know when some big ol' bank is going to hanker to build a skyscraper right in your backyard barbeque. . . ."

Hoopes's son Prince Paul Castrocani lived there while apprenticing at a bank. One night he attended a society benefit with Lady Margaret when their hostess Helene Harpennis (aka Brooke Astor?) was poisoned. Mama promptly arrived in NYC to collect all the gossip and set Paul up with a NYPD detective as a roommate, both to protect him and to give him some extra spending money. (Prince Paul did not pay Mama rent, but his allowance and bank salary were inadequate for his social needs.)

Turn left on Tenth Avenue and go one block south to 22nd Street. You pass the Empire Diner, a Chelsea "landmark" with Art Deco decor, which is open twenty-four hours a day. You are also now in the Historic Chelsea District, which runs from 22nd Street to 20th Streets between Eighth and Tenth Avenues. It is lined with lovely mid-nineteenth-century brick and brownstone houses (now cut up into apartments), many of which are owned by General Theological Seminary.

These brownstone houses are exactly the kind in which Rex Stout's Nero Wolfe lived and the Wolfe Pack suspects that West 35th Street may really have been West 22nd Street. "Brownstone," which has come to mean a style of house, was actually a chocolate-colored stone that NYC writer Edith Wharton hated because it was so gloomy (but practical in the dirty city).

Built for single families, brownstones characteristically have "English" basements surrounded with iron fencing, high Dutch stoops, and three or four stories. In Chelsea there are still big old trees (mostly sycamore or plane) along the parkways.

Go one more block south on Tenth Avenue to 21st Street. You have now reached the gothic campus of General Theological Seminary, which occupies the entire block between Ninth and Tenth Avenues, from 21st to 20th Streets. It is the oldest theological school in the country, and was built on land donated by Clement Clarke Moore, whose father was a bishop and whose materal grandfather, Captain Thomas Clarke, had named his estate for Chelsea Hospital in London. Clement Clarke Moore was a Hebrew scholar who taught at General, but he achieved his lasting fame by writing the poem "A Visit from St. Nicholas," which gave rise to the all-American Santa Claus.

The Episcopal seminary is surrounded by a high iron fence with a locked gate, so you can only look through at the Romanesque redbrick and limestone buildings. In the middle of the block where the main gates are located is a large chapel. A multistory library is on the northwest corner. In Isabelle Holland's mystery, *A Lover Scorned*, the Reverend Claire Aldington of St. Anselm's parish went to General Theological Seminary searching for clues to the serial murders of Episcopal women priests like herself.

Across the street from the seminary is a whole row of beautiful Greek Revival houses. Some are known collectively as Cushman Row, and date from the 1840s. Others are Italianate rowhouses dating from 1855. Both have handsome molded cornices and ironwork, very much like the brownstones of Brooklyn's Park Slope. Since the O'Connors had lived in Chelsea, these houses were probably the reason P. M. Carlson's Maggie and Nick O'Connor had a yen for an affordable brownstone in *Murder Unrenovated*.

You will note that the street numbers (in the 400s) do not match up with those in Holland's *A Lover Scorned*, where the murdered Reverend Ida Blake lived at 116 W. 20th Street in a third-floor apartment in a row of Greek Revival houses facing the campus. The Reverend Claire Aldington met NYPD Lieutenant O'Neill there to look for clues concerning Blake's murder. They also invited medium Letty Dalrymple, first seen in *Flight of the Archangel*, to come get a "sense" of the scene of the crime.

Walk left along West 20th Street to Ninth Avenue. You will pass St. Peter's Episcopal Church, another old redbrick Gothic-style church currently being renovated. It holds services in both Spanish and English and houses the off-Broadway Atlantic Theater. Like many other Episcopal churches, it might be a model for Holland's St. Timothy's in *A Lover Scorned*.

You have now walked about one mile and may want to stop for a snack. You can go back to the Empire Diner, at 22nd Street and Tenth Avenue. Or you can cross Ninth Avenue to try Sam Chinita's, an ordinary diner on the southeast corner. It features a strange New York specialty: Spanish/Chinese cuisine, which means you can order dishes with red beans and rice, Cuban pot roast, and Chinese stir-fried broccoli, but it does not have Archie Goodwin's kind of sandwiches and pieces of pie. You might also try Pete McManus's bar, two blocks down 20th Street, at the corner of Seventh Avenue, which has tables outside, London style, in warm weather. McManus's has been used to shoot TV shows such as *Miami Vice*.

As you walk along, you can tell that you are getting back into an area with lots of old warehouses and cast-iron department store buildings built in pre-skyscraper days. Many of these old buildings are now filled with advertising firms, photographic shops, and art suppliers, as well as lofts for rent.

In Dana Clarins's *The Woman Who Knew Too Much*, actress Celia Blandings had a tryout for a Broadway production in a Chelsea rehearsal hall. In the play, a mystery thriller called *Misconceptions*, Celia played a sister of the lead who thought she was pregnant, got murdered, but returned in the second act. The play was actually put on at the Martin Beck Theater. (See Walk 5.)

Cross Seventh Avenue and go one block south to walk along 19th Street to Sixth Avenue. Across Sixth Avenue is the Episcopal Church of the Holy Communion, an 1846 church begun by the Sisterhood of St. Luke's, who built St. Luke's Hospital in St. Luke's Square. (See Walk 3.) Now deconsecrated, it houses a trendy disco cum theater called Limelight. In Annette Meyers's *The Big Killing*, headhunter Leslie Wetzon went to a nightclub called Caravasarie in an abandoned church. It was run by a friend of Wetzon's murdered client Barry Stark.

If you walked down Sixth Avenue all the way to West 11th Street, you would come upon another one of the tiny, crowded Shearith cemeteries belonging to the Spanish and Portuguese Synagogue. This one opened in 1829 and was used until 1852. It is the third cemetery of NYC's first Jewish congregation, established in 1654. (Their first cemetery is in Chinatown, the second in the Village.) The cemetery, set in the middle of the block and surrounded by tall buildings, is locked, with the usual high iron fence around it, making it seem like a place out of time.

In Jerome Charyn's *Paradise Man*, Saxe and Son, morticians to the mob, buried bumper Sidney Holden's old family friend Mrs. Howard (who was not Jewish) in a Sephardic cemetery with only her initials on the marker because it was quiet there; no questions would be asked, and there was less of a chance of having her dug up.

If you don't make this detour (having no sinister interest in checking out more old cemeteries), cross Sixth Avenue and turn right and walk south to 17th Street. Walk east along 17th Street to Fifth Avenue. Cross Fifth Avenue and go one more block back to Broadway and the northwest corner of Union Square, where pop artist Andy Warhol had his studio. In *Murder Unrenovated*, P. M. Carlson located a bar called Palomino's just north of Union Square, on 18th Street. Actor Nick O'Connor went there on a tip he got from his friend Franklin. O'Connor was hunting a young man implicated in the Park Slope brownstone murder.

At Union Square you have walked about one and one-half miles. If you want to end the walk you can easily get a cab, or a bus, or take the subway at the southwest corner of the square. (The subway station is decorated in shiny Art Nouveau style. This is a major stop, but during 1991, a drugged or drunken engineer caused a major subway crash here.)

By 1850 Union Square (originally Place) had become a genteel residential park, with major stores like Tiffany & Co. and
Lord & Taylor, and restaurants like Delmonico's located nearby
on Ladies Mile. It was briefly New York's main theater district,
and—after an Irish draft riot, caused by the fact that richer men
could buy their way out—Union troops were shipped out from
here during the Civil War.

Then, along with its lower-priced department stores and
second-hand bookstores, the square gradually became the center of NYC's radical movement and a forum for soapbox speakers. May Day parades traditionally end here. The *Daily Commu-
nist* was published nearby, on 13th Street, as is the still-powerful
Village Voice. Isabelle Holland's freelancer, Kit Maitland, did
work for *The Public Eye*, a 1960s activist paper that had survived,
in *The Flight of the Archangel*.

Many artists and writers lived in the 14th Street lofts facing
the square. And, until recently, Klein's discount house was on
the square's eastern side, emphasizing the fact that Union
Square was seen as the "working peoples' " square.

After being "demonstration turf," as well as dirty and full
of drugs, the park was closed and cleaned up. Today Union
Square is somewhat chic again, with a fresh fruits, vegetables,
and eggs market held three times a week. In Marissa Piesman's
Unorthodox Practices, Nina Fischman went to Union Square's
greenmarket on her way home from housing court to buy
some eggplants. There are a number of cafes and restaurants
where authors and editors often lunch, such as the Union
Square Cafe, at 21 E. 16th Street. Klein's and the bookstores
have gone, replaced by the huge, upscale high-rise Zeckendorf
Towers.

All of this was yet to come in Emma Lathen's 1964 *Death
Shall Overcome*, where Union Square was one of the preliminary
rally points for the March on Wall Street. In the 1980s, in Trella
Crespi's *The Trouble with a Small Raise*, Simona Griffo worked at
HH&H Advertising near Union Square, where her murdered
boss, Creative Director Fred Critelli, had an office looking south
toward the World Trade Towers. Simona also supervised "ad
shoots" at Scriba's studio, just off Union Square in a classic

warehouse loft: one enormous room, bleached wooden floors, bare white walls, and 12-foot-high ceilings.

If you plan to keep walking, there is a McDonald's if you need to make a pit stop. Then walk across Union Square along 17th Street to see Tammany Hall. It is on the northeast corner in a stately neo-classical building built in 1928. Tammany Hall was the headquarters of NYC's famous Democratic Machine, which began as a protest group organized by De Witt Clinton and others, including Aaron Burr, in 1776. In the late-nineteenth century, however, Tammany became corrupt, most notably under the infamous Boss Tweed. (In S. S. Van Dine's Philo Vance stories, small-time pols and suspects were routinely said to have Tammany Hall connections.) Its well-organized machine was not defeated until after Fiorello La Guardia became mayor, in 1933.

La Guardia's campaign song was "Who's Afraid of the Big Bad Wolf." It was sung by thousands as they watched the election returns in Times Square for the first time. As mayor, La Guardia not only read the comics to NYC children over the radio during a newspaper strike, but in Elliott Roosevelt's *Hyde Park Murder*, he also gave Eleanor Roosevelt a hand with a Wall Street murder case.

Turn right to walk down Park Avenue along the eastern side of Union Square. At 14th Street turn left. The famous Consolidated Edison building, with its chiming clock, has been hidden by the Zeckendorf Towers, but it was clearly heard striking the hour in Gypsy Rose Lee's *The G-String Murders*, when she was a stripper in a burlesque theater nearby.

Across 14th Street you can see the boarded up, green cast-iron building with gold trim that once housed Luchow's, NYC's most famous German beer garden. In Gypsy Rose Lee's autobiographical mystery, *The G-String Murders*, Gypsy herself was a featured stripper in H. I. Moss's burlesque show at the "Old Opera Theater." After a cast member was strangled with her own G-string, the rest of the large cast and chorus, including Gypsy's boy friend, Biff, decided to "shoot the wad" and eat at Luchow's. They never figured out why Luchow's would never serve them again. It might have been because a stripper called

Dolly walked off with half the silverware in her purse, or because Biff tried to take the hall tree with him. Even more likely, it was because paying the bill "was an ordeal," as the waiters tried to collect an installment from each of the cast.

Luchow's was still there in *Death Shall Overcome* when Lathen's John Putnam Thatcher had dinner there with Bradford Withers, his WASPishly unpredictable boss at the Sloan. They went there to enjoy Luchow's dark-paneled ambiance and good food after the unsettling murder of a stockbroker at a Wall Street cocktail party. Luchow's was also popular with writers like Theodore Dreiser and H. L. Mencken, Lewis Mumford and George Jean Nathan. Now all you can see of Luchow's is the facade.

Next to Luchow's are two other New York landmarks: the Palladium and Julian's Billiard Hall. The Palladium at 126 East 14th Street is no burlesque house, but it is about the right location for Gypsy Rose Lee's Old Opera, and it does still operate as a disco. It has a huge mural by Hank Pressing and Jeff Green over the door, with Greek Goddess Pallas Athena pulling back a curtain to show a rock concert.

Cross 14th Street if you want to take a closer look, otherwise walk one block left along the north side of 14th Street to Irving Place. Turn left to walk up Irving Place to 17th Street. The house on the southwest corner there has a marker indicating it was the home of Washington Irving, the first successful native-born American author. In fact it was not, although Irving Place was named for him. In town Irving stayed with his nephew John at 46 E. 21st Street, several blocks north.

As a young journalist (a trade followed by many New York writers from Poe on) Washington Irving had pulled off quite a spoof with his mock-pompous Diedrich Knickerbocker's *History of New-York*. As the author proclaimed in the lengthy introduction, this volume was meant to preserve and protect the fame and reputation of our Dutch ancestors in the style of Gibbon and Herodotus. It certainly preserved all the gossip about the early settlers, from Peter Minuit's good twenty-four-dollar buy to Peter Stuyvesant's peg leg.

The pseudo-Irving brownstone with its bay window (and an elegant restaurant in the basement) is one of many in a very handsome block that stretches all the way back to Tammany Hall. Writer/editor William Dean Howells (*The Rise of Silas Lapham, The Atlantic Monthly*) also lived on East 17th Street, as did short story writer O. Henry, who had no love for New York, the city he labeled "Baghdad on the subway."

O. Henry, whose real name was William Sydney Porter, was a Southerner, and kissing kin to Katherine Ann Porter. He came to NYC to work as a newspaper man, and wrote surprise-ending short stories like the sentimental "Gift of the Magi" and the amusing "Ransom of Red Chief." Many of his stories featured this part of NYC (and the Tenderloin), and included some Damon Runyon-type hoods long before Prohibition.

Admire the brownstone row, then walk one block up Irving Place to 18th Street. Across the street at 66 Irving Place is Pete's Place (once Healy's Cafe), dating from 1864. It is a reminder of Old New York, with its carved-wood bar and beveled glass. On the walls are memorabilia to remind patrons that O. Henry drank and wrote there, but he behaved less genially than his British counterpart, the journalist and mystery writer G. K. Chesterton, who liked to write and drink and chuckle in such Fleet Street pubs as El Vino or the Cheshire Cheese. (See *Mystery Reader's Walking Guide: London*, Inns of Court/Fleet Street Walk.)

Stop off for a drink or continue to walk up Irving Place past 19th Street, known as the Block Beautiful for its remodeled houses and mews. At 20th Street you are at Gramercy Park, the only private residential park left in the city, with a locked garden to which only the owners whose houses surround the square have keys.

In 1882, in Jack Finney's sci-fi mystery, *Time and Again*, his time traveler cum government operative, Simon Morley, rented a room at No. 19 Gramercy Park. Looking out the window, Morley saw houses on all four sides of the square, with mounting blocks and hitching posts at each house. Later, on the run from the police, Morley ducked into Gramercy Park as the lamplighters were working their way down Lexington Avenue, but did not dare go back to No. 19 because he feared there might be a trap.

During the murders at the Old Opera Theater in *The G-String Murders*, narrator Gypsy Rose Lee and her boyfriend, Biff, walked from the theater to Gramercy Park, where the surroundings changed abruptly. There were large apartments with doormen, and when Gypsy said she was going to live in one of them when she got rich, Biff kidded that he would be one of the doormen, after which both chose the uniform they liked best. The park itself looked green and cool and they stared through the bars at the children playing there, all starched and combed with governesses watching them. Gypsy told Biff that she had been in show biz for years at their age. Biff looked at the benches and said that he thought there could be a few outside the railings, for outsiders to sit on. "It's things like that start revolutions," he suggested.

Today on the south and west sides there are still row houses, both Greek Revival and Victorian, while on the north and east sides there are taller buildings in 1920s pseudo-gothic. At the southwest corner is an old Friends Meeting House, now a Jewish synagogue. Just past the Quaker Meeting House is the place where a major gas pipe exploded, killing two workers and a woman in an apartment nearby.

This is the neighborhood that most of the Wolfe Pack feel is closest to the "true" ambiance of Nero Wolfe's West 35th Street brownstone, so choose one you like. Oddly enough, a recent literary guidebook stated that this neighborhood does not serve any important literary function today! That, despite the fact that groups like NYC's Chapter of MWA (Mystery Writers of America) hold their monthly meetings at the Arts Club and the Wolfe Pack holds its annual Black Orchid banquet at the Gramercy Park Hotel!

The park has also appeared in many other mysteries. In Haughton Murphy's (aka James Duffy's) *Murder Saves Face*, retired Wall Street lawyer Reuben Frost and his former ballerina wife, Cynthia, attended an annual New Year's Eve party here with other older couples who were still married to one another. Because the guests had already made their marks, Frost noted that this usually made for a very pleasant, elegant, nonthreatening party, although he was seated by a very dramatic young black opera star.

Margaret Maron was thinking of Gramercy Park when she described the superb, kept-as-is Breul house, which was a privately endowed museum running short on funds. True NYC entrepreneurs, the Breuls made their money in barges on the Erie Canal and blockade-running during the Civil War. Third-generation, Harvard-educated Erich Breul developed a taste for paintings, which he collected in Europe—along with a charming Swiss wife. His father built them a gem of a Victorian mansion at 7 Sussex Square (Gramercy Park), where the junior Breul used the ballroom for his art gallery (like the Fricks). (See Walk 8.) When Erich, their only son, was killed in Paris, his father left the mansion to be a museum.

In *Corpus Christmas*, when an art historian was found dead at the Breul mansion, one of the suspects NYPD Lieutenant Sigrid Harald had to check out was docent Mrs. Beardsley, a jealously protective resident of the square. Another suspect was Rick Evans, the photographer grandson of Jacob Munson, who handled artist Oscar Nauman's work in his Fifth Avenue art gallery.

Maron's descriptions allow you to experience the proper Victorian ambiance in marvelous detail. According to Maron, her real-life models for the Breul home were Theodore Roosevelt's birthplace at 28 E. 20th Street and the National Arts Club at 15 Gramercy Park South. (Certain parts of the mystery also use details from the Frick and the Old Merchant's House.) (See Walks 2 and 8.)

Turn left to walk around the park. Number 15 Gramercy Park South was built in 1845 and remodeled in 1874 for New York Governor Samuel J. Tilden, who lost the most controversial presidential election in U.S. history to Republican Rutherford B. Hayes in 1876. In 1898 it became the National Arts Club. To get inside visit either its Artists Exhibition Gallery (which probably gave Maron her idea of having major artist Oscar Nauman hold a retrospective at the Breul) or Heritage Theater.

Next door at No. 16 is the Players, another brownstone remodeled into a more Italianate style by architect Stanford White. It houses a famous theatrical club, founded by actor Edwin Booth in 1888 to give the profession better social stature. (Booth's statue is in the center of the park, but there is no mention here of his half-brother, Lincoln assassin [and actor] John Wilkes Booth.)

On the front facade of the Players there are plates listing its famous members. In Jane Dentinger's *Murder on Cue*, actress Jocelyn O'Roarke was at a Players' Ladies Dinner in the long, oak-paneled dining room, when she made a drunken crack about leading lady Harriet Weldon, causing her best friend to spill wine on her blouse. Later, when Josh was understudying Weldon in a play, Weldon was murdered, and Jocelyn went to the Players to have a drink in the Grill with Frederick Revere, a famous old actor and friend, who gave her the lowdown on Weldon's past. Arriving, Jocelyn deliberately got out of the cab a few blocks away to savor the early twilight effect on the old and gracious houses surrounding the square.

Walk on around Gramercy Park to your left. On the west side look at Nos. 3 and 4, a pair of "New Orleans" style row houses with cast-iron porticos and porches. The offices of Writing Enterprises, who published *Writing Magazine* and read manuscripts for a fee, were only a block away on Park Avenue between 20th and 21st Streets in Orania Papazoglou's *Wicked, Loving Murder*. Its seedy-looking offices were on the twentieth floor of an overly ornate pre–World War I building whose elevators seldom worked. Patience McKenna—six-feet tall with long blond hair—had been recruited by her college roommate, now the president of Romance Writers of America, to edit the issue on romance writing because the organization suspected Writing Enterprises would be insulting to authors of the genre. Alida Brookfield, the owner/publisher, who was in the writing trade purely for money, retaliated by putting McKenna in a closet office, where McKenna found the body of one of Brookfield's nephews.

In Margaret Maron's *Death in Blue Folders*, the apartment of murdered lawyer Clayton Gladwell was on 21st Street between Park and Lexington Avenues. Gladwell had the entire third floor of a lovely eighteenth-century townhouse, furnished in comfortable eclectic, leaning toward French Provincial. NYPD Lieutenant Sigrid Harald noted that his books ran to spy thrillers by John le Carré, Somerset Maugham, Eric Ambler, even golden oldie storywriter E. Philips Oppenheim, the forerunner of Ian Fleming. Sigrid and her assistant, "Tilly the Toiler," found $46,000 in cash, plus a Swiss bank account number in Gladwell's old butternut kneehole desk, suggesting a lot of unreported income.

Turn right on 21st Street to walk to Lexington Avenue. The Gramercy Park Hotel is at 2 Lexington Avenue. In December 1991, as in other years, the Wolfe Pack celebrated its Black Orchid Weekend here. It was also the last home of humorist S. J. Perelman, brother-in-law of Nathanael West and college friend of Dashiell Hammett, who wrote the trend-setting *The Thin Man*.

In Rex Stout's *The Golden Spiders*, 315 Gramercy Park (a fictional number) was an old, yellow brick building, with a uniformed doorman, a spacious lobby (with fine old rugs), an elevator, and the home of lawyer Dennis Horan. Rich widow Laura Fromm came to dine there the night she was (later) bashed on the head and then run over by a car. Archie Goodwin went there after her death to talk to Mrs. Horan, an ash blond in black. They talked in a high-ceilinged room, done up in yellow, violet, green, and maroon.

In Carole Berry's *The Year of the Monkey*, Bonnie Indermill, still seeking a career, got a job at a shady operation called Creative Financial Ventures, located on the edge of Chinatown. The night of the office Christmas Party, Bonnie and her current lover, Derek Thorensen, shared a cab with Ashley Gartner, CFV's CEO. They dropped him off at his apartment in Gramercy Park, but the next morning, at Thorensen's elegant pad in the Village, they were informed by NYPD Homicide that Gartner had been found murdered. Later Bonnie, playing amateur sleuth, went back there to talk to the handyman, Hector Rodriquez. She found him repainting the apartment—a relic from a more genteel time.

Pause to look up Lexington Avenue for one of many gorgeous views of the Art Deco Chrysler Building. Then turn left on Lexington Avenue and walk north to the Kenmore Hall Hotel at 145 E. 23rd Street. Stephen Crane lived at the Art Students League (two doors away at 143 E. 25th Street) while he wrote *Maggie: A Girl of the Streets*, a story set in the Bowery.

Kenmore Hall Hotel was the place where Nathanael West, who wrote the grim novel about an advice-to-the-lovelorn columnist, *Miss Lonelyhearts*, was once the night clerk. West used to treat his friends to a swim in the hotel pool, and he let Dashiell Hammett stay there, under a false name, when he couldn't pay the rent, so that he could finish *The Maltese Falcon*.

The apartment of one-armed P.I. Graham was north of 23rd Street between Second and Third Avenues in Don Winslow's *A Cool Breeze on the Underground*. Graham had adopted Neal Carey, an Upper West Side pickpocket, and taught Carey everything he knew.

Turn right at 23rd Street to walk to Third Avenue. Turn right and walk south on Third Avenue to 20th Street. Go left to 235 E. 20th Street, where, in the middle of the block, you will find a cement block building with a NYPD sentry on duty. This is the Police Academy Museum. It is only open to the public Monday through Friday, from 9:00 A.M. to 2:30 P.M., but it is worth an effort because it houses one of the largest collections of police memorabilia open to the public. (Scotland Yard's Black Museum is only accessible to other cops.)

The modern cinderblock building goes through to 21st Street, where it becomes the HQ of the NYPD's 13th Precinct, one of many where detective story characters have gone to "interact" with Homicide. In William Love's *The Chartreuse Clue*, ex-cop P.I. Davy Goldman, who lives on the West Side with crippled Roman Catholic Bishop Regan, had some dealings with the NYPD's Homicide Department on 20th Street. In the Lockridges' *The Norths Meet Murder*, the NYPD precinct station on 20th Street was mentioned both as the Police Academy Museum and as the office of NYPD Lieutenant William (Bill) Weigland. Stout's Archie Goodwin occasionally came here, too, as well as to Centre Street headquarters. (See Walk 1.)

You have now walked over three miles. If you are tired, hop a cab or walk back to the Park Avenue South (IRT) subway station on 23rd Street.

If you want to take a look at two more places that are very popular with mystery writers, turn right on 20th Street to walk to First Avenue. On First Avenue, head north to 27th Street.

On the way you will pass a huge hospital complex, which extends along the East River from 23rd to 34th Streets. It contains the NYU Medical Center, Bellevue Hospital, and Veterans Hospital. It is really too far south, however, to be the medical center where Lisa Drake worked in *The Medical Center Murders*.

Bellevue Hospital, located at East 27th Street and the East River, began in 1736 as a place where anyone who needed care could get it. Not only is it the place where "crazy" people go, but its emergency room is famous because all NYC accident victims and emergencies are routinely taken there.

In Isabelle Holland's *A Lover Scorned*, the mentally disturbed street woman Althea, a former history professor who felt she must stay on guard to protect Arthurian England from the barbarians, had to be taken there. Althea had a cat called Dalrymple, named for the medium Letty Dalrymple, and, while Althea was hospitalized, the Reverend Claire Aldington had to take in the cat. Claire's son Jamie had a large dog called Motley, but the animals got along.

In P. M. Carlson's *Rehearsal for Murder*, musical comedy star Ramona Ricci was taken to Bellevue after she was attacked and died in the hospital several days later. Maggie and Nick O'Connor came to see her at the hospital, and met her childhood friend, Sister Alphonsius, to whom Ramona used to send money to help other slum girls. When they got the ransom money for Muffin, the O'Connors sent it to Sister Alphonsius.

The City Morgue—technically the Office of the Medical Examiner—is in a separate turquoise brick building at 520 First Avenue. It was built in 1959 when Bellevue Hospital became too crowded to handle bodies. Only the lobby is open to the general public, Monday through Friday, 9:00 A.M to 5:00 P.M. According to the Office of the Chief Medical Examiner (coroner, to you) this is the *only* Manhattan morgue, no matter what you may read in some mysteries. So you may assume that this is the place where mysterious characters came to view/identify dead bodies.

In Craig Rice's hysterical put-down of NYC, *Having a Wonderful Crime*, the bereaved young husband Dennis Morrison, Helene and Jake Justus, a number of suspects, and Chicago lawyer John J. Malone all came here to look at the bride's decapitated body. It took Malone, however, to figure out that the body belonged to the bride and the head to somebody else.

In Richard Lockridge's *Murder for Art's Sake*, NYPD Detective Tony Cook came here to view the body of murdered artist Shackleton Jones, who signed his paintings as "Shack." Cook noticed that Shack had been a big rugged man with strong square hands.

In "Firecrackers," written by Wolfe Pack member Charles E. Burns and published in the Wolfe Pack's *Gazette*, Archie Goodwin came here the night old Rusterman himself was murdered. Much later in the corpus when Rusterman's protégé and heir Marko Vulcic was murdered, Nero Wolfe actually walked here to put two gold coins on Marko's eyes, Montegnegrin style.

Stockbroker Brock Potter of Price, Potter and Petacque came here to try to identify a little old lady who had been hit by a subway train in Arthur Maling's *Lucky Devil*. As Brock told the NYPD, he had never seen her before, but she had his name on a piece of paper.

In *Loves Music, Loves to Dance*, Mary Higgins Clark's Darcy Scott came here to identify her best friend Erin Kelley's body, after Erin was murdered on a date set up through a personal ad. In Richard Nusser's *Walking After Midnight*, down-and-out reporter Max Darenow went to the morgue to talk with an assistant medical examiner about his dead girlfriend Denise's autopsy. The doctor had style, wearing white clogs, brown tweed slacks with fancy suspenders, and a Grateful Dead T-shirt. He told Darenow that Denise had ingested a large quantity of heroin and possibly scopolamine (a knockout drug). Darenow, realizing that Denise's death had to be murder, remembered the Latin inscription over the door of the Medical Examiner's Office. Translated, it said, "Let laughter cease, let conversation flee: this is where death delights in helping the living."

The Morgue is the end of the walk. At First Avenue you can get a cab, catch a bus, or turn left on 28th Street and walk three blocks to the Lexington Avenue subway.

5

MIDTOWN WEST WALK

BACKGROUND

This walk covers the two trades for which New York City is known worldwide: theater and fashion. Broadway's Theater District—the Great White Way—and the Garment District intersect at about Seventh Avenue and Times Square, where you can still hear people talking like characters in a Damon Runyon story. Both Herald Square and Times Square were originally newspaper centers that became popular meeting places. Seedy as it is, Times Square is still New York's answer to London's Piccadilly Circus, where crowds gather to watch election results or see the New Year in, while Herald Square continued to be the city's best known shopping center, starring Macy's and Gimbel's, until Gimbel's closed in 1989.

Historically, the neighborhood just west of the theater district, from West 59th to West 34th Streets, Eighth Avenue to the Hudson River, was called Hell's Kitchen. Known for gang warfare and immigrant tenements, it was the setting for Leonard Bernstein's 1950s *West Side Story*. Gentrification has since set in and the area is now called Clinton, but it is still a tough neighborhood. The businesses that have moved into the new highrises are fortress-like and security-mad, like the Wall Street law firm Ward and Chase, in Haughton Murphy's mystery *Murder Saves Face*.

The Great White Way started around Times Square in the early 1900s, as new theaters began to appear on Broadway. One of the area's most important mythmakers was Damon Runyon, a star Hearst reporter, playwright, and short story teller. Runyon preferred associating with Broadway's mobsters, gamblers, touts, and sports stars to the upper crust, and in his writing immortalized them with his famous streetwise style.

Many of the area's landmark theaters, like the Belasco (1907), the Lyceum (1903), and the Shubert (1913), still have their elaborate columns and marquees. Oscar Hammerstein I, who built four theaters, was known as the "creator" of Times Square, whose best season was 1927–28, when there were 71 theaters in operation, with 257 separate productions. The 1930s Depression, movies, and television, however, have changed Broadway into a half-darkened group of "legitimate" theaters mixed with sleaze and pornhouses.

The Garment District, or "Seventh Avenue," extends from Sixth to Ninth Avenues, from 41st Street to 25th Street. The fashion and clothing industry had moved north from the sweatshops of the Lower East Side around the time of the first World War. But even today much of its business is done in small shops not open to the general public. Its famous congested street traffic, where pedestrians (and cars) must avoid delivery trucks, wheeled clothing racks, and pushcarts, makes "Seventh Avenue" a popular daytime chase scene in mysteries, second only to Fifth Avenue and Central Park.

Just as Broadway has given way to Off Broadway and Off Off Broadway theaters, so has shopping in New York gone north and east, up Fifth, Madison, and Park Avenues in the East 60s and 70s. But in classic mystery fiction you find that NYC's "old" Midtown still exists because Herald Square's department stores made excellent scenes of the crime, while Times Square retained its tawdry image as the haunt of hookers, junkies and gangsters with murder on their minds.

Most important to mystery fans, it was south of Clinton and west of the Theater and Garment Districts that Rex Stout's portly Nero Wolfe lived with his "All American" sidekick, Archie Goodwin. Mystery fans and authorities agree that Rex Stout is America's answer to England's Agatha Christie. His mysterious pair are also typical New Yorkers because Wolfe was an immigrant Montenegrin and Archie a Midwesterner come to try his luck in the Big Apple. As a result, Wolfe and Goodwin have become mythic NYC personages, in a class with Knickerbocker's peg-legged Peter Stuyvesant and Clement Moore's Santa Claus. This is also true of Wolfe's celebrated brownstone on West 35th Street. As does Sir Arthur Conan Doyle's Sherlock Holmes, Nero Wolfe has his own organization, the Wolfe Pack, presided over by the Werowance. It is the Wolfe Pack's considered opinion that the West 35th Street location of Nero Wolfe's brownstone was a mysterious deception. As those of you energetic enough to walk over there will find, there are not and never were any of the right kind of brownstones there. Moreover, according to Archie Goodwin's misnumbering, its location would be in the middle of the Hudson River, or under the Jacob Javits Convention Center.

LENGTH OF WALK: About 2 miles

The walk covers one mile from the Mysterious Bookshop to Times Square and another mile to Herald Square. See map on page 107 for the boundaries of this walk and page 304 for a list of books and detectives mentioned.

PLACES OF INTEREST

The Mysterious Bookshop, 129 W. 56th Street. Open Mon.–Sat., 11:00 A.M.–7:00 P.M. Call 765-0900.

Times Square, 42nd Street and Broadway at Seventh Avenue.

Broadway Theater District (aka the Great White Way), 42nd Street to 53rd Street, between Sixth and Eighth Avenues. Special tours available.

TKTS (Times Square Ticket Center), West 47th Street between Seventh Avenue and Broadway. Place to buy cheap theater tickets shortly before curtain time.

Herald Square, West 34th Street and Broadway at Sixth Avenue. Home of New York *Herald*, later *Herald-Tribune*.

General Post Office, 33rd to 34th Street, Eighth to Ninth Avenues. 1913 McKim, Mead and White building. Letters to Santa displayed here. Tours available. Call 330-2767.

Madison Square Garden (1968), 31st to 33rd Streets between Seventh and Eighth Avenues. Sports, events, and offices. For tickets or info., call 563-8000.

Pennsylvania Railroad Station (1963), under Madison Square Garden. Major rail center for city/suburbs. Place to wait, check bags, use restrooms, get snacks.

R. H. Macy and Company (1902), Herald Square, 34th Street and Broadway. World's largest department store. Open Mon., Thurs., Fri., 10:00 A.M.–8:30 P.M.; Tues., Wed., Sat., 10:00 A.M.–7:00 P.M.; Sun., 11:00 A.M.–6:00 P.M. Foreign interpreters available.

Carnegie Hall, West 57th Street at Seventh Avenue. Concerts, recitals, etc. Special tours available. Call 247-7800.

Jacob Javits Convention Center, West 39th–34th Streets on Eleventh Avenue. Twenty-two-acre exhibition hall. Call 216-2000.

Circle Line Cruises, Pier 83, Hudson River and 43rd Street. Three-hour cruises around Manhattan. Open daily mid-March–Nov. Harbor lights night cruises June–Aug. Call 563-3200.

Intrepid Sea-Air-Space Museum, Pier 86, Hudson River and 46th Street. Moored World War II aircraft carrier turned museum. Naval and space travel exhibits. Open daily in summer, Wed.–Sun., 10:00 A.M.–5:00 P.M. Admission fee. Call 245-2533.

NYC Passenger Ship Terminal, 48th–59th Streets on Twelfth Avenue. Passenger/tourist lounges. Parking. Call 765-7437.

Weehawken Ferry, entrance just north of Lincoln Tunnel. Major ferry to and from New Jersey. Pre-dates Lincoln Tunnel.

Lincoln Tunnel, West 39th Street, near the Hudson River. Opened
  in 1937, added to since. Approaches take up much of the
  roadway between 40th and 37th Streets, making it hard to
  check out Nero Wolfe sites on Ninth Avenue at 35th Street.

Manhattan Plaza, West 42nd–43rd Streets, Ninth to Tenth
  Avenues. Housing for performing artists who pay one-fourth of
  their yearly income in rent.

Theater Row, 42nd Street between Ninth and Tenth Avenues.
  Several Off Broadway theaters and restaurants.

POSSIBLE SIDE TRIPS

New York Harbor, including the *New York City Passenger Ship
  Terminal*, 48th to 55th Streets at Twelfth Avenue (Piers
  88–92). *Intrepid Sea-Air-Space Museum*, 46th Street and
  Hudson River (Pier 86).

Nero Wolfe Walk, 42nd Street west to Hudson River and *Circle
  Line* (Pier 83), south to 40th Street. Includes *Weehawken Ferry*,
  Jacob Javits Convention Center. Goes east to Eleventh Avenue,
  south to 35th Street, east to Ninth Avenue.

Places to Eat

(In the Broadway Theater district there are many places to eat;
in the Garment District there are small delis and coffee shops.
Nearer the Hudson River, however, places to eat are few and far
between, except for an occasional motel or McDonald's.)

Carnegie Deli, 854 Seventh Avenue. Crowded, shared long tables.
  Take out menu. Inexpensive (cash only). Open daily,
  6:30–3:45 A.M. Call 757-2245.

Lindy's (contemporary location) Seventh Avenue and 33rd Street,
  off lobby of the New York Penta Hotel (a Ramada Inn).
  Cheesecake celebrity hangout, once upon a time.

Macy's Department Store, West 34th Street between Sixth and
  Seventh Avenues. There are a number of places to choose from,
  including the Cellar Café and Café L'Etoile.

Russian Tea Room, 150 W. 57th Street, slightly to the left of

Carnegie Hall. Old Russian menu. Expensive. Open 11:30
A.M.–midnight. Sun. brunch. Call 265-0947.

Sardi's, 234 W. 44th Street. Famous for Opening Night parties.
Place to see and be seen. Open 11:30 A.M.–midnight. Sun.
brunch. Expensive. Call 221-8440.

Nathan's Kosher Deli, southwest side of Times Square at 42nd
Street. Located inside Kentucky Fried Chicken franchise.

Cafe New York, New York Hilton, 1335 Sixth Avenue, on
concourse level. American. Inexpensive. Open daily, 6:00
A.M.–midnight. Call 586-7000.

Beefsteak Charlie's, Madison Square Garden. Good burger chain.

———— MIDTOWN WEST WALK ————

Begin your walk at The Mysterious Bookshop, at 129 W. 56th
Street between Sixth and Seventh Avenues, whose proprietor
is Otto Penzler of The Mysterious Press. This bookstore—
sandwiched in between much taller and more modern
buildings—has a lovely old New York ambiance. This brownstone would serve Rex Stout's Nero Wolfe well, except that it
has one more floor than his, no orchids, and more than seven
steps to the stoop. Its basement has a big display window full
of mysteries and The Mysterious Press and *The Armchair Detective* (TAD) have their offices on its upper floors. The bookstore
specializes in used and out-of-print mysteries but sells new
books, too. (See Walks 3, 7, and 10 for other mystery bookstores.)

In Dana Clarins's *The Woman Who Knew Too Much*, actress
Celia Blandings and P.I. Greco visited Otto Penzler. The book
gave a wonderful description of the bookshop, including its circular iron staircase (shades of New Yorker Mary Roberts Rinehart's *The Circular Staircase* and English Dorothy L. Sayers's
Murder Must Advertise). Penzler refused to tell them who mystery writer Michael Warriner was, but slyly left them alone with
his Rolodex.

This brownstone also makes a suitable substitute for George

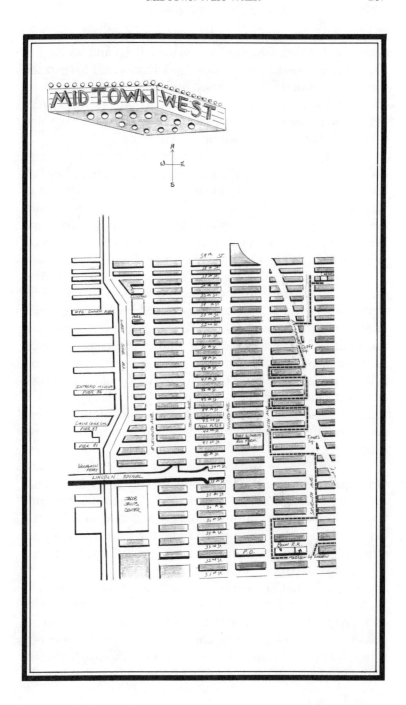

C. Chesbro's brownstone on West 56th Street, where the Frederickson brothers—Mongo and Garth—lived and worked in *The Second Horseman Out of Eden*. Frederickson & Frederickson was on the ground floor, and each brother had an apartment on an upper floor. Mongo lived on the fourth floor and had a patio. When the brothers brought twin spacey Apocalypse conspirators there, the twins jumped off the patio roof.

The Mysterious Bookshop is across the street from the stage door of City Center, 131 W. 55th Street, where the Joffrey Ballet, Alvin Ailey's Dance Company, and the Dance Theater of Harlem all perform. Haughton Murphy's *Murder Takes a Partner* was about a dance company like the Joffrey. Chase and Ward's retired partner Reuben Frost's wife Cynthia had been a prima ballerina so he knew the ballet world well.

After browsing, turn right up 56th Street to Seventh Avenue. Turn right again to walk one block north to West 57th Street, where you will see caramel-colored brick Carnegie Hall at 881 Seventh Avenue. The nation's premier concert hall, it was built in 1891 and named for Andrew Carnegie, the steel magnate who spent his golden years being a public benefactor. It is still the ultimate place to perform. (In the old joke, a passerby asks a musician, "How do I get to Carnegie Hall?" and is told, "Practice.") The main hall was refurbished in 1986, but people still bicker over whether the sound was improved or ruined.

In Clarins's *The Woman Who Knew Too Much*, Celia and Greco passed Carnegie Hall en route to The Mysterious Bookshop. In Amanda Cross's *A Trap for Fools*, Kate Fansler had gone there to hear an Arlo Guthrie concert with her nephew Leo and her niece Leighton. This proved to be the perfect alibi for her after the murder of an unpleasant fellow professor at her university. (See Walk 10.)

Next door to Carnegie Hall is the Russian Tea Room at 151 W. 57th Street. It is a famous "Russian emigré" restaurant with dark green walls and pink lamps, and where tea is served in glasses. It is known for its lunchtime clientele of show biz personages who do business there. In Orania Papazoglou's (aka Jane Haddan's) *Wicked, Loving Murder*, Marty Lahler, the wimpy accountant at Writing Enterprises, insisted on taking amateur sleuth Patience McKenna to the Russian Tea Room for a very uncomfortable lunch: McKenna did learn that the magazine's publisher, Alida Brookfield, paid her nephews virtually nothing.

Cross Seventh Avenue at 57th Street and walk south one block to the Carnegie Deli, a narrow storefront restaurant with plain benches and long wooden tables. The Carnegie serves traditional deli food, such as corned beef and Reuben sandwiches (all gigantic), and is very popular with natives and tourists alike. In Crabbe Evers's (aka Bill Brashler's) *Murderer's Row*, retired Chicago sports columnist Duffy House went to the Carnegie Deli after he consulted with the Baseball Commissioner about the murder of the New York Yankees' obnoxious owner. House did not have to stand in line. You may.

Continue walking down Seventh Avenue to 54th Street. Here you are in the middle of "Convention Town NYC." There are not only many small hotels along the cross streets but two of the biggest in the city, which house enormous conventions like the Modern Language Association (or MLA). The New York Hilton occupies the entire block between 54th and 53rd Streets from Seventh to Sixth Avenues, and the Sheraton New York is directly across 53rd Street from the Hilton at Seventh Avenue.

To your right at 54th Street and Broadway, there are several older buildings that could be John Lutz's twenty-story office building, which had a marble lobby full of small shops in *Shadowtown*. Agent Manny Brokton had his office there. While chasing suspects, NYPD Detetive E. L. "Ox" Oxman not only saw the TV soap opera producer Harry Overbeck coming out of the elevator there, but he also saw a fleeing vampire. Later, going up to Brokton's office, "Ox" found Brokton murdered.

Somewhere along West 54th Street was CAN, the television network headquarters, where on Tuesday, May 20 (1973), at 3:17 P.M., Peter J. Odell opened the liquor drawer of his boss and died instantly from a bomb explosion in Rex Stout's *Please Pass the Guilt*. Archie Goodwin and the rest of Nero Wolfe's operatives spent a considerable amount of time there afterward interviewing staff, but the vital clue turned out to be in Inspector Cramer's own NYPD homicide department.

Still farther west on Tenth Avenue there are warehouses and garages, like Nunn's Garage in Rex Stout's *The Golden Spiders*, where Wolfe's operative Fred Durkin was taken for a ride by Lips Egan, and later rescued by Archie Goodwin.

Walk south one block to 53rd Street on Seventh Avenue. You are at the Sheraton Hotel. In recent years the annual Edgar Allan Poe Awards Dinners have been held here, and the invitations always specify "Dress to kill." In 1991, the affair honored the birth of the detective story with Edgar Allan Poe's "Murders in the Rue Morgue," published in 1841. This annual party of the Mystery Writers of America is commonly known as the "Edgars Awards," and winning an Edgar—like winning a Hollywood Oscar—is the pinnacle of a crime-writing career. (A double-whammy is also winning the British Gold Dagger, given by their CWA, or Crime Writers Association.)

Edgar Awards are given in twelve categories, from first novel to drama to short story. Each year an important writer in the genre is also given the title of Grand Master (or Mistress). Many New Yorkers have won Edgars and been honored as Grand Masters, among them Ed McBain, Ellery Queen, Dorothy Salisbury Davis, Dorothy B. Hughes, and Rex Stout.

Take a moment to investigate the enormous lobbies of these two hotels. They are the most likely sites for mysterious conventions (with murders). Conventions held in a hotel represent one variety of the classic "locked room" mystery: like theater and department store locales, they limit the possible suspects.

I first saw Professor Carolyn Heilbrun (aka Amanda Cross) at the 1978 MLA (Modern Language Association) convention at the Sheraton. She was in a Special Session on Virginia Woolf and I was there to give a paper on Dorothy L. Sayers. (I was also reading *The Question of Max*, through which I learned she, too, was fascinated by Sayers and her college friends.) So, despite Kate Fansler's lack of experience of MLA convention life, her creator not only knows all about it, but also, as Professor Heilbrun, has been president of the organization.

For those of you who have never attended the MLA—or any other academic convention—Cross's *No Word from Winifred* contains a marvelous tongue-in-cheek description of an MLA convention as an academic slave market. In it Fansler was trying to get a clue to the whereabouts of a missing English heiress, which involved her in a triangular love affair among MLA members, as well as with another professor who tried sexual harassment to get a card to Fansler's university library. (See Walk 10.) This mystery even included a timid biographer from the Dakotas (New Yorkese for the boonies) with a name (Alina) like mine, right after I published my Sayers biography, *Maker and Craftsman* (which is being reissued this year).

In Elizabeth Peters's *Not for Love*, librarian Jacqueline Kirby went to a NYC Romance Writers Convention out of boredom and got involved in the murder of a nosy reporter. Peters beautifully described the fetid, hothouse "pink" atmosphere of "professional" romance writers. Kirby also came to the inevitable conviction that even she could "do better than that," and started writing her own romances, which became best sellers like Peters's own.

NYC also plays host to trade conventions like the ABA (American Booksellers Association). Isaac Asimov's *Murder at the ABA* was written about their 1975 convention. While attending the convention Asimov wrote a mystery about it, in which the protagonist was a writer named Darius Just, and the murder victim another egotistical writer named Giles Devore, who had to autograph books with a special kind of pen. Asimov also put himself in the mystery and included cameo appearances by other real authors. (His mystery requires a hotel locale, although the current ABA conventions are held at the Jacob Javits Convention Center.)

The Sheraton was also the hotel in *Second Horseman Out of Eden* where George Chesbro's Mongo Frederickson went to hide out from the NYPD and some crooks after an unhealthy dip in the Hudson River.

The New York Hilton has also had mystery characters staying there, like the Arab prince in Margaret Maron's *Death of a Butterfly*. Karl Redmond's father was on his way to show the prince some uncut gems when he was mugged, robbed, and left to die.

(If you want to do the side trip of New York's Harbor on the Hudson River, you can either walk due west along 52nd Street to Eleventh Avenue and De Witt Clinton Park, or you can take a cab there. See Side Trips.)

Continue the walk by crossing Seventh Avenue at 52nd Street. Walk west on 52nd Street one block to Broadway. Cross Broadway and turn left to walk south, following Broadway, which bends slightly to the east as it heads south to merge with Seventh Avenue at Duffy Square at 47th Street. From now on this walk will zigzag on and off Broadway, so you can check out the theaters mentioned in mysteries. But be warned: many mystery writers either make up a theater or give a real one a new name, while some just use the generic term "Broadway theater" and don't give a cross street at all.

Walk down Broadway to 50th Street. Across Broadway to your left is the Winter Garden Theater. In S. S. Van Dine's *The Canary Murder Case*, a revue called *The Scandals* was at the Winter Garden. A friend of murdered musical star Margaret Odell, "the Canary," had a part in it and Philo Vance went to see the revue to time her alibi, which turned out to be phony. During the 1991–92 season, poet T. S. Eliot's *Cats* was playing there. A star of that show is the mysterious Macavity, a feline impersonation of Sir Arthur Conan Doyle's sinister Moriarity. Eliot was a Sherlock Holmes buff who also quoted Holmes in his play *Murder in the Cathedral*.

Keep going south to 49th Street, looking about for a seedy substitute for Ellery Queen's Hotel Benedict in *The Greek Coffin Mystery*. That was the cheap hotel where ex-con Grimshaw went when he was released from Sing Sing Prison. Grimshaw was visited by five different suspects during one evening, then murdered.

In Dashiell Hammett's *The Thin Man*, ex-P.I. Nick Charles went to a speakeasy on West 49th Street called the Pigiron Club. It was run by ex-con Studsy Burke, whom Charles had helped to put away. Later another mobster from there went to the Charles's hotel and "accidentally" shot Nick. (The last real speakeasy in New York is not far away; it is the 21 Club, at 52nd Street between Fifth and Sixth Avenues. See Walk 6.) In Mary Roberts Rinehart's saga *The Lamp in the Window*, the story of a NYC publishing family (like the Rineharts), the publisher's niece married an NYC bootlegger who was killed in a NYPD ambush.

Jack Dempsey Corner is located at 49th Street and Seventh Avenue. Seventh Avenue here begins to merge with Broadway, separated from Broadway by smaller and smaller islands until it becomes a wide open space, surrounded by huge neon billboards. Cross West 49th Street on Broadway and keep going to West 48th Street.

Cross West 48th Street and turn right to walk past the Longacre Theater on the south side of the street. Its age, handsome terra cotta facade, and two stage doors on either side of the main marquee, make it one of the best substitutes for the new (1920s) Roman Theater in Ellery Queen's first mystery, *The Roman Hat Mystery*. This was the first collaboration of two cousins, Frederic Dannay and Manfred Lee, who used different "locked room" milieus for their early mysteries. (The Roman Theater is supposed to be two blocks south, at West 47th Street, but Queen often chose a site a block or two from a real-life prototype for his fictional sites.)

The Roman Theater was showing *Gunfire*, a gangster play with a romantic (Runyonesque) view of tommy guns, crooks, and gangs. Ellery Queen said it was popular because there was no new Eugene O'Neill play for the intelligentsia, and the lowbrows had gone to the movies. After the murder of shyster lawyer Monte Field the NYPD kept the entire audience, staff, and cast there to question and search them, but no clues were found. Neither was Field's top hat. Later NYPD Inspector Richard Queen and his book-collecting son Ellery sat in the murder victim's row during a full-scale re-enactment at the scene of the crime.

Walk along West 48th Street to Eighth Avenue. To your right, until 1968, was the third Madison Square Garden. Emma Lathen's John Putnam Thatcher recalled in *Death Shall Overcome* that he had seen the "long count" there in the famous Dempsey vs. Tunney prize fight. Thatcher was taking a taxi to the Garden to attend CASH's enormous rally in support of Ed Parry, who was trying to become the first black member of the New York Stock Exchange.

Walk one block south to 47th Street, then go back along 47th Street to Broadway. Among the theaters you pass are the Lunt-Fontanne, the Brooks Atkinson, the Barrymore, and the Biltmore. One of them could easily be Hugh Pentecost's "Quartermayne Theater" in *The Substitute Victim*, where a terrorist bomb killed forty-two people just before curtain time. The Quartermayne was an old theater, just off Broadway in the West 40s, recently bought and restored by millionaire Duke Maxwell, who was one of those blown to bits. So was Elissa Hargrove, a famous film star making her Broadway debut. Hargrove was also famous for her support of unpopular causes (a kind of Vanessa Redgrave mixed with Jane Fonda).

One of these theaters (on West 47th Street) must be the Ambassador Theater in Jane Dentinger's *Murder on Cue*. Actress Jocelyn O'Roarke was understudying a great—but unpopular—lady of the theater, Harriet Weldon, in a play called *Term of Trial* there. Jocelyn got to go on when Weldon was found murdered in her dressing room. The murder also led to the meeting of NYPD Detective-Sergeant Philip Gerrard and Josh, who later teamed up to solve the case. (In many contemporary mysteries, the female sleuth becomes enamored of the NYPD detective.)

At 47th Street and Broadway you are at Duffy Square, named for the fighting chaplain of the 69th regiment in World War I. There is also a statute of "Give My Regards to Broadway" song-and-dance man George M. Cohan. And on an island between Broadway and Seventh Avenue is TKTS (Times Square Ticket Center), where you can buy cheap theater tickets shortly before curtain time.

In George Chesbro's *Bone*, a horrifying mystery about NYC's homeless, Bone and his social worker Anne Winchell met near Times Square. They bought hot dogs from a street vendor, then walked over the TKTS island in the middle of Broadway and sat on a bench to discuss his case. (Bone had been accused of killing several dozen homeless and cutting off their heads.)

Look across Broadway/Seventh Avenue to spot the Palace
Theater (now called the Embassy). In S. S. Van Dine's *The Benson Murder Case*, the "Piccadilly Theater" was just around the
corner from the brownstone mansion of murdered Wall Street
broker Alvin Benson. That was the mystery that introduced
Philo Vance, a gentleman sleuth and aesthete, whom Julian Symons called an (American) "aristocrat," but Ogden Nash
wanted to give a "kick in the pance." Van Dine based his mysteries on real-life cases, this one on the murder of a New York
bridge expert. Suspect Colonel Ostrander had been at the Midnight Follies at the Piccadilly with a Tammany Hall alderman
from the Bronx, but had gone into the theater's alley at the cru-
cial time (of the murder).

Walk south to West 46th Street. Across Broadway to your
left there were some old brownstones which might have been
Alvah Benson's elegant mansion, but they are being torn down.
On the north side of the street at 119 W. 45th Street, there was
once a small hotel called the Normandie. That was the name of
the first-class hotel where Dashiell Hammett's Nick and Nora
Charles stayed. Today, however, it is hard to imagine this transi-
tional area populated with classy hotels.

Go down Broadway to West 45th Street, and turn right to
walk west to Eighth Avenue. On the way you will pass the tow-
ering Marriott Marquis Hotel and the Marquis Theater (inside
on the mezzanine floor). The hotel has all the typical contemporary details: transparent elevators, long escalators that take
you to a second floor (where there are restrooms), a hanging garden atrium, and a revolving restaurant on the rooftop. During
the 1991–92 season a short-lived musical called *Nora and Nick*,
based on Hammett's *The Thin Man*, opened—and closed—here
almost simultaneously. Since the musical's locale, the
Charleses, and Asta, had all been moved to California from
NYC, what did the authors expect? If you don't want to read
the book, rent the William Powell/Myrna Loy movie. It has
marvelous 1930s clothes and hairdos, but very few outside locations.

Across Eighth Avenue, on the south side of 45th Street,
you can see the Martin Beck Theater. In Clarins's *The Woman*

Who Knew Too Much, Celia Blandings got a part in a play here called *Misconceptions*. Her role was a pregnant ghost who came back.

Across the street from the Martin Beck Theater there are several good substitutes for John Lutz's small residential Penmont Hotel in *Shadowtown*. It was in the Penmont that the landlord found the body of TV soap opera actor Burt Lassiter, a member of the group using a vampire costume to scare the soap's leading lady.

Go left one block to West 44th Street, then cross the street and head back to Broadway. You will go past the St. James Theater, where a memorial service was to be held for murdered theater critic Jason Saylin in Jane Dentinger's *First Hit of the Season*. Saylin was a college friend of NYPD Detective Philip Gerrard, with whom actress cum amateur sleuth Jocelyn O'Roarke was in love. Next door is the Helen Hayes Theater, named for a real grande dame of the stage.

Across 44th Street is the Majestic Theater. In Rex Stout's *Too Many Clients*, one of the many visitors to the love nest of murdered Thomas Yeager was actress Meg Duncan, star of *Back Door to Heaven*. She had no alibi for Yeager's murder, but she could prove she had been at a benefit at the Majestic Theater when Maria Perez, the daughter of Yeager's landlord, was later murdered.

Next door to the Majestic on the north side of 44th Street is the Shubert Theater with its famous gathering place, once a kind of open-air casting parlor, called Shubert Alley. The three Shubert brothers created a theater empire which had a virtual monopoly on the try-out circuits and bookings nationwide. Even in the 1980s the Shubert Organization still controlled half of Broadway's remaining theaters.

Patrick Quentin's Dagonet Theater, "west of Broadway at 44th Street," was somewhere near here. In *Puzzle for Players*, producer Peter Duluth, back in business after a breakdown, went past the Shubert, the Broadhurst, and the St. James to reach the Dagonet. Duluth was putting on a problem play called *Troubled Waters* in a theater that was still "haunted" by a 1902 murder. Duluth's girlfriend had a part, and his principal backer was his psychiatrist. But a bit actor died onstage during a rehearsal, and the production ran into real hot water.

Walk back east along 44th Street, admiring the Art Deco mosaics on the Shubert, until you reach one of the famous spots to see and be seen in town, Sardi's, at 234 W. 44th Street. With its red canopy and big green neon sign, it is easily recognizable. Traditionally actors, producers, and playwrights came here on opening nights to wait for the reviews to come out.

In Hammett's *The Thin Man*, Nick and Nora Charles went to the opening night of a play called *Honeymoon*, then to a party at a place like Sardi's. In Dorothy Salisbury Davis's *Lullaby of Murder*, Julie Hayes, who worked for the *New York Daily*'s gossip columnist, was taken there by her husband. Older, and rather insufferable, Jeff Hayes was a *New York Times* foreign correspondent who was far too sophisticated to enjoy Sardi's, but Julie did.

In Steve Allen's *Murder in Manhattan*, Steve was told to follow a set of "treasure hunt" clues that began at Sardi's. Allen commented that even the walls at Sardi's were crowded with famous caricatures of all the Broadway personalities who had been there over the years. Avoiding the people he knew who wanted to buy him a drink, Steve hung around until 10:05 P.M., when he gave the mysterious claim check to the coatcheck girl and got a second note telling him to go to the Four Seasons. (See Walk 7.)

Walk to Broadway, passing by the rear of the new *New York Times* Building, which goes through to 43rd Street. On the southwest corner of 43rd Street is a famous Broadway kosher deli called Nathan's. It has been swallowed up by a Kentucky Fried Chicken franchise, but it still has Nathan's sign and you can get the famous hot dogs there. Looking back up Broadway from here you can see the huge neon Camel (cigarette) sign, which originally featured Wrigley's Gold Fish. Across Seventh Avenue at 123 West 43rd Street is the 1921 Town Hall, the only concert hall in the vicinity.

Turn right to walk south to 42nd Street and Times Square, where the Great White Way begins (or ends). Broadway's most famous "historian" was short and dapper Damon Runyon, a Middle Westerner who came to New York before World War I.

As a Hearst reporter, Runyon acted out the "wise guy" journalist and Broadway was his beat, whether he hung out at the Astor Bar or the original Lindy's, when he was not covering sports or crime. His biographer Jimmy Breslin writes that Runyon created the whole idea of the "Roaring Twenties" with its bootleggers, gangsters, gamblers, and hit men, giving it class. It is startling to remember that the movie that made Shirley Temple a star was *Little Miss Marker*, his story about betting.

Runyon co-authored a Broadway play called *A Slight Case of Murder*, which was made into a movie starring Edward G. Robinson. In addition to writing, Runyon co-sponsored Joe Louis's first big fight—at Yankee Stadium—and was the star reporter at the Lindbergh kidnapping trial. (That real life mystery was retold by Max Allan Collins in *Stolen Away*.) When Runyon died of cancer in 1946, his ashes were scattered over NYC from a plane flown by Eddie Rickenbacker, with Mike Todd and Damon Runyon, Jr. along for the ride.

Times Square was once known as the crossroads of the world. It is still the place all tourists want to see, like London's Piccadilly Circus. As early as 1891, Times Square was lit up with electric advertising signs (which were later replaced by neon). They are the "bright lights" that all aspiring actors, dancers, writers, and artists yearn for. But on a lecture trip to America, British mystery writer G. K. Chesterton commented, "What a glorious garden of wonder this would be, to any one who was lucky enough to be unable to read."

During the twentieth century, the more Times Square has changed, the more it has stayed the same. Despite periodic cleanups and rebuilding, the area is still considered NYC's "home" of sin, where one can buy porn, comic books, newspapers, sex, and dope, as well as attend movie theaters; a street with hookers and pawn shops. The "new" Times Square is still dirty and unkempt, with bundled up homeless sleeping in doorways, lots of dark theaters, and pickpockets and junkies about.

In Michael Wolk's *The Beast on Broadway*, Minnesotan John Sugarman had only been in NYC fifteen minutes when he had his pocket picked in Times Square. Luckily, a Mediterranean-looking hawker for a girlie show tripped the thief and gave Sugarman his wallet back. That led to Sugarman visiting the Apple & Eve Go-Go Lounge, where one thing led to another—like murder. In Wolk's *The Big Picture*, literary agent Max Popper had an office only a knife's throw from Times Square, where he witnessed a murder. Kidnapped by the killer, who shoved him into Times Square with a gun in his back, Popper got away by enticing a strong-armed hooker to grab him, then escaped from her clutches by dashing into a dirty bookshop with pulsating red lights.

Times Square is an important junction for NYC's transportation system. In Byfield and Tedeschi's *Solemn High Murder*, British Reverend Simon Bede, after a superb lunch at Grand Central Station's Oyster Bar with Jeremy Baxter, the Executive Director of the Episcopal Church Center, followed the arrows to the shuttle to Times Square to get the subway south to 14th Street.

In Margaret Maron's *Past Imperfect*, NYPD Lieutenant Sigrid Harald went to Times Square looking for Jerry the Canary, a homeless bird-caller, who had witnessed a murder. Times Square was a blaze of Saturday night's light and color, with flashing marquees up and down Broadway and along 42nd Street.

In Haughton Murphy's *Murder for Lunch*, after the funeral of his murdered Chase and Ward partner, suspect Roger Singer went to Times Square to drown his sorrows in a movie. Singer was an ex-CIA operative, whose wife had been having an affair with the murdered man. Singer went into Loews to see the comedy hit of the year, then took a taxi home, packed a bag, and left for Paris from JFK airport.

In John Lutz's *Shadowtown*, the soap opera's set designer admitted buying the magazine *Babes Fit to Be Tied* at a Times Square porno shop. In Velda Johnson's *The Face in the Shadows*, Ellen Stacey, the actress who found the rich school girl Cecily Vandering stoned at the Cloisters, had a part in a coffee commercial being shot in an old movie theater near 42nd Street and Broadway. In the commercial, Ellen had to race down the balcony steps. When the railing came off, she was nearly killed.

Times Square got its name from *The New York Times*.

Founded in 1851, the paper unmasked Boss Tweed in the 1870s, but was not highly visible or successful until bought by Adolph Ochs in 1896. His heirs, the Sulzbergers, still run the paper, whose motto is "all the news that's fit to print." One Times Square, the newspaper's first building, put up in 1904, still stands on the triangle formed by Broadway, Seventh Avenue, and 42nd Street. In 1960, *The Times* sold the old building and moved all its offices to 43rd Street just west of Broadway.

In NYC mystery stories, the existence of *The New York Times* is a "given." In Rex Stout's first mystery, *Fer-de-Lance*, Nero Wolfe sent Archie Goodwin to Times Square to get 20 copies of the Monday *Times* so he could figure out what the clipping in Carlo Maeffi's room meant. At *The Times* a cop Archie knew let him leave his car parked outside while he went in, even though the theater and movie mob were coming out. In *The Golden Spiders*, Archie saw Wolfe's operator, Saul Panzer, at *The Times* office. Panzer was boning up on how to pretend to be a DP (displaced person), who would need help from the organization called ASSIDIP.

In Ellery Queen's *The Greek Coffin Mystery*, millionaire Knox was told to leave a ransom of $30,000 for his missing da Vinci painting at *The Times* checkroom before 10:00 P.M. in a package addressed to Mr. Leonard D. Vincey. Knox was now cooperating with the NYPD, so Lieutenant Richard Queen set up a police watch in the basement of *The Times* to catch the ransom collector.

Turn west to walk along 42nd Street, crossing Seventh Avenue, and continue to Eighth Avenue. The original Lindy's, the home of the world-famous Lindy's cheesecake, was on the south side of 42nd Street near Eighth Avenue. As you go along, look for a Midtown joint like the greasy spoon/bar Manfredi's, where Jonathan Gash's Lovejoy, a British antiques dealer, found a job when he arrived here illegally from Hong Kong in *The Great California Game*.

Between Eighth and Ninth Avenues you come to the Port Authority Bus Terminal, which goes from 42nd to 40th Streets. The Port Authority replaced individual company terminals, like the Third Avenue Railways Line in Ellery Queen's (aka Barnaby

Ross's) *The Tragedy of X*. When the guests at the engagement party of model Cherry Browne and Wall Street broker Harley Longstreet could not get taxis, they took the crosstown streetcar to the Weehawken Ferry, located just south of 42nd Street. But when Longstreet was murdered on the car near Ninth Avenue, the NYPD took car and passengers to the barn. Then NYPD Commissioner of Police and the D.A. asked the help of amateur sleuth Drury Lane, a deaf former actor who lived in a castle on the Hudson River. The Weehawken Ferry was the only way to get to Weehawken, New Jersey, before the Lincoln Tunnel was completed. It is an important part of the plot in Queen's *The Tragedy of X* because most of the murder victims lived in New Jersey. (See Possible Side Trips at end of walk.)

In Dana Clarins's *The Woman Who Knew Too Much*, Charlie Cunningham had written an exposé on the government's spy network. He let his editor at Pegasus Press, Jeff Lefferts, take the manuscript out of a Port Authority lock box. Lefferts decided it would make his name in publishing but his boss at Pegasus Press, a retired admiral, buried the book below the Pentagon for security's sake.

Along 42nd and 43rd Streets between Ninth and Tenth Avenues is a redbrick complex called Manhattan Plaza. Part of the gentrifying of the West Side, it was designed as luxury apartments. When the project failed it became federally subsidized housing for performing artists. Around the same time some warehouses along 42nd Street were converted into a group of Off Broadway theaters.

In Jane Dentinger's *First Hit of the Season*, actress Jocelyn O'Roarke belonged to a health club inside Manhattan Plaza. Josh met her friend Irene Ingersoll for lunch at the complex's Gardenia Club, after Irene's lead role in *Hedda Gabler* was savaged by reigning critic Jason Saylin. Unfortunately, Saylin was there, too, so Irene dumped a plate of fettucine on him.

Walk east to Eighth Avenue past the Port Authority. Then walk along 40th Street to Seventh Avenue. You are now entering the Garment District, often called Fashion Avenue, or just "Seventh Avenue." The district is roughly bounded by Sixth to Eighth Avenues from 41st to 34th Streets. Its heaviest traffic is down Seventh Avenue and on the cross streets.

Before you push through the crowded streets, filled with garment carts, trucks, messengers, and confusion, look west toward Broadway. Over on 39th Street and Broadway is the former site of the Metropolitan Opera House. (See Walk 10.) In Ellery Queen's *The Greek Coffin Mystery*, two suspects, Mrs. Vreeland and Dr. Wardis, the latter an undercover agent of London's Victoria and Albert Museum, shared an alibi for the second murder because they went to the opera there together.

In S. S. Van Dine's *The Canary Murder Case*, Philo Vance had tickets for the matinee performance of Giordana's *Madame Sans-Gene*, which he hated to miss while sleuthing. Then in Edgar Box's (aka Gore Vidal's) *Death in the Fifth Position*, the grand St. Petersburg Ballet Company performed at the Metropolitan Opera House. Young Peter Cutler Sargent III was hired by the company to handle PR because they were putting on a new ballet called *Eclipse*, by a "Red" named Jeb Wilbur. That publicity was nothing to what they got when ballerina Ella Sutton was killed when her cable was cut and she fell, holding the fifth position to the bitter end.

Walk down Seventh Avenue. In Lisa Bennett's *Seventh Avenue Murder*, Seventh Avenue was described as one of the least stylish thoroughfares in the city, an architectural hodgepodge of delapidated sweatshops and soulless new high-rises, with their tinted glass already grimy. Art Director Peg Goodenough—a large, handsome girl, who was the daughter of world-famous abstract painter Theo Goodenough—came to Seventh Avenue to see client Beryl Merriweather, who had invented a line of loose, comfortable leisure clothes. Merriweather's office was in the Zabin Building, whose lobby, like the building itself, had seen better days. The elevator was covered with graffiti and wheezed all the way up to the 11th floor, where Peg found Beryl murdered.

In *While My Pretty One Sleeps*, Mary Higgins Clark's boutique owner Neeve Kearny came to Seventh Avenue every Monday afternoon to shop. She loved the bizarre bedlam of crowded sidewalks, delivery trucks double-parked on the narrow streets, agile delivery boys manipulating racks of clothes through the traffic, and the sense of everyone rushing. Neeve visited several well-known designer shops, but always ended up at the shop of her father's childhood friend Anthony della Salva near West 36th Street. During the last chase when mob hit man Denny Adler was after Neeve, she ended up there, too. In Richard Barth's *A Ragged Plot*, senior citizen Margaret Binton chased one young suspect through this district on foot to catch and question him about the murder of their city garden's planner, her Puerto Rican friend Luis.

Walk south down Seventh Avenue, keeping an eye out for hit men. Due west on 37th Street you would find (if it existed) the residence of William Love's crippled Roman Catholic Bishop Regan and his "Archie Goodwin," former Lower East Sider and ex-NYPD cop Davy Goldman. Goldman worked with the bishop solving strange cases, like *The Chartreuse Clue*. They lived in a brownstone run by housekeeper Sister Ernestine, with a chapel upstairs where the bishop spent hours praying (instead of breeding orchids).

When you reach West 35th Street, remember that due west on Eleventh Avenue, at the Jacob Javits Convention Center (or in the Hudson River) was the legendary brownstone of Rex Stout's massive Nero Wolfe. (If you want to look at the scene of the crime, consult Possible Side Trips at the end of the walk.) Or take a right to get to Eighth Avenue. On Eighth Avenue go left (south) to 33rd Street to see the General Post Office building. Designed in the grand manner by McKim, Mead and White to echo their equally famous Pennsylvania Railroad Station (the old one), which used to be across the street, the colonnaded, neo-classical Post Office Building takes up an entire block. On its classic facade is inscribed the memorable quotation from Herodotus: "Neither rain nor heat nor gloom of night stays these couriers from the swift completion of their appointed rounds." (Those were the good old days, but you might apply the message to the NYPD instead.)

Cross 33rd Street and walk up the massive flight of steps to go inside the post office's main entrance. The marble lobby has a magnificent (internal) staircase, too. Operation Santa Claus began here fifty years ago when the post office began the custom of making children's letters to Santa available to potential Santa

Clauses. Today these letters are laid out in a small, handsomely decorated anteroom off the main marble lobby. In George Chesbro's *The Second Horseman Out of Eden* the Frederickson brothers always read the letters to Santa. One year Garth Frederickson found one from a little girl living in a religious commune, where a Reverend Jones was sexually abusing her. The brothers instantly set out to locate—and rescue—her, using soil samples from her letter which turned out to be from a rain forest.

Just west of here near 33rd Street and Ninth Avenue, the storyteller Zulu, in Chesbro's *Bone*, found Bone, the mute homeless man who carried a human femur as a weapon. The NYPD believed Bone had murdered some of his fellow homeless. Later Bone and Zulu went on a hunt for the real murderer, who, as they discovered, had a cavern "cathedral" filled with grisly heads below the city streets. You may prefer to limit your underground excursions to Penn Station. NYC really is honeycombed with many tunnels and water systems that date back to Aaron Burr.

Come out of the post office and recross Eighth Avenue (aka Joe Louis Plaza) to the new, subterranean Pennsylvania Railroad Station. (The latest Madison Square Garden complex was built above it in 1968.) In P. M. Carlson's *Rehearsal for Murder*, Maggie and Nick O'Connor changed (subway) trains at Penn Station to take the A train (aka the 8th Avenue Express). They had baby Sarah with them in the backpack. Later they took a train to Long Island from Penn Station, trying to solve the mystery of Muffin's kidnaping.

Either walk through the Madison Square Garden lobby or duck underground and cut through the Pennsylvania Railroad Station, where you can check bags for the day. There are some benches for travelers, restrooms, and fast food places, like Wendy's.

On the upper, Madison Square Garden level, at the Seventh Avenue entrance, you can find a Beefsteak Charlie's restaurant (one of a chain), a good burger place. In Mary Higgins Clark's *Loves Music, Loves to Dance*, NYPD Detective Vince D'Ambrosio met his fifteen-year-old son Hank there to eat hamburgers "with everything," before they took in a Rangers hockey game at the Garden. D'Ambrosio, however, left before the game was over to go to the morgue after word came that the body of the missing Erin Kelley had been found. All kinds of events take place at Madison Square Garden. In Pete Hamill's *The Deadly Piece*, his reporter Sam Briscoe took his girlfriend, Marta Torres, a gorgeous Hispanic "Nuyorican" who was also a Columbia Law School graduate, to hear a sold-out Salsa concert. But the Mafia chose that concert to make a hit. Briscoe's cousin Ike was involved in the hit and later murdered.

Walk out of Madison Square Garden on Seventh Avenue and cross to the New York Penta Hotel (now a Ramada Inn). Built in the 1920s, the hotel was a famous home of the Big Bands, and its phone number, Pennsylvania 6-5000, the subject—and title—of a Glenn Miller song. Today it is a huge convention hotel, with many kinds of tourist groups. It is also suitable for murderous affairs. On the Seventh Avenue side of the hotel is a Lindy's, still serving the famous cheesecake. An L-shaped restaurant with dark wainscotting and white walls, and etched glass over the long bar, it would not be too easy to hide in the back because there are no booths, just open tables. But in *Headhunt*, that's where Carol Brennan's PR person Liz Wareham found one of the partners of a fancy firm of headhunters she represented. He had always pretended to be a Lower East Side Jewish boy who made good; now he admitted he was really the son of a minor Italian mafioso.

After checking out Lindy's, walk around the Penta Hotel to your right. Walk east on 33rd Street. One block east you will come to Herald Square, where it crosses Broadway at Sixth Avenue. Herald Square was named for the NYC newspaper begun by the Bennett family in 1835. The son of the founder was raised in Paris and turned the paper into a scandal sheet full of racy gossip and human interest tales. One of his coups was to send H. M. Stanley to look for David Livingston in "darkest Africa." Eventually the competition between the Hearst and Pulitzer papers forced *The Herald* to merge with *The Tribune*, creating *The Herald-Tribune*, which lives on as the Paris-based *International Herald Tribune*.

Across Broadway at the southern end of Herald Square is a statute of *Tribune* editor Horace Greeley, who told young Americans to "Go West, young man." At Broadway and Sixth Avenue is a white building with psychedelic neon lights called A & S Plaza. This was once the home of Macy's archrival, Gimbel's. It now houses a vertical mall with floor after floor of brand-name boutiques. On the seventh floor you can get all kinds of food, from pizza to Chinese, and there are plenty of tables to sit at. There are also restrooms open to the general public.

Turn left to walk up Broadway. One block north is R. H. Macy & Co. department store, which takes up the entire block from Broadway to Seventh Avenue, 34th Street to 33rd Street. The world's largest store, it has big clocks on the front of the building and comfortably traditional, but upscale feeling inside. Founded in 1858 by a Quaker boy from Nantucket Island, on the theory of low fixed prices, cash payments, and heavy advertising, Macy's sells almost as many things as London's famed Harrod's, living up to its motto: "If you haven't seen Macy's, you haven't seen New York." There are several places to eat, restrooms, and, of course, many things to buy. Macy's still sponsors the huge televised Thanksgiving Day Parade, made famous also by the movie *Miracle on 34th Street*, which starred the young Natalie Wood, who was to die mysteriously on her yacht many years later. (Interestingly, her husband, Robert Wagner, was playing a "Nick Charles" type in TV's *Hart to Hart* at the time.)

In Margaret Maron's *Death in Blue Folders*, NYPD Lieutenant Sigrid Harald, one of the world's worst dressers, went to Macy's to look for a gown for a MOMA benefit. Ellery Queen's French's department store was located on Fifth Avenue, but there are almost no stores left there that are both family-owned and full-scale department stores. (See also Walk 6.) Macy's, therefore, is a prime suspect for the department store in *The French Powder Mystery*, where the wife of the store owner was found murdered in a display window. The crime turned out to be linked to a drug ring being run out of the store's book department. This Queen story was like Phyllis Whitney's first, *The Red*

Carnelian, based on Marshall Field's department store in Chicago.

Since Macy's sells paintings, although it does not have an art gallery, it could also have been the model for Richard Lockridge's Bryant and Washburn department store. NYPD Captain Bill Weigand's artist wife, Dorian, used to be a staff artist there in *Murder for Art's Sake*. She tried to investigate a crooked art dealer selling her client's paintings to department store galleries behind his back.

Explore Macy's as long as you like, especially checking out the departments that sell paintings and books, located on the eighth floor. Then have something to eat.

You have now reached the end of the walk and walked about two miles.

POSSIBLE SIDE TRIPS

Clinton/New York Harbor. Begin at De Witt Clinton Park, on Eleventh Avenue and 52nd Street. NYC's Passenger Ship Terminal is directly west, on the Hudson River at Piers 92, 90, and 88. Go south along the Hudson River to Pier 86, home of the *Intrepid* Sea-Air-Space Museum. Continue past Pier 83, the Circle Line Pier, to 42nd Street.

In Haughton Murphy's *Murder Saves Face*, Reuben Frost's Wall Street law firm of Chase and Ward moved uptown (from Wall Street) to "Clinton Place." Its new building was known as "Fort Bliss" and had heavy security, but associate Julianna Merriman was still found murdered in the library. Merriman lived nearby, in an apartment with her boyfriend, Marshall Genakis, who ran a trendy restaurant called Marshall's.

In Dorothy Salisbury Davis's *A Gentle Murderer*, the church where the young murderer came to confession was St. Timothy's, located in the midst of Hell's Kitchen. Father Murphy, having heard the whispered confession, traced the murderer across NYC and beyond because he could not break the seal of the confessional and go to the NYPD.

In Marilyn Wallace's short story "The Cutting Edge," a

self-portrait by a young artist called Rico who was having his first show was slashed at the opening by a jealous NYU film student. The student thought Rico was a rival for his girl. This opening took place at Porterfield's, a (fictional) new art gallery on West 51st Street run by an old friend of Rico's mother, who was able to stop the carnage in the "nick of time" so it was not a bloody "slice of life."

As you walk along the Hudson you will see many piers, which run along the Hudson down to Manhattan's southern tip. But in spite of Clinton's gentrification, this is not a safe area to walk without company. In Mary Higgins Clark's *Loves Music, Loves to Dance*, the body of Erin Kelley was found by a homeless wino, Petey Potters, near the West 56th Street pier, west of Greenwich Village.

Ocean liners are a popular venue for mystery stories, and you may want to visit the NYC Passenger Lounge at the piers. In Charlotte Armstrong's *The Unsuspected*, Mathilda Frazier, the ward of a radio personality called Grandy, turned up in port unexpectedly after her ship was sunk, only to find out she had a handsome husband whom she did not remember marrying. There was a gala shoving-off in Marion Babson's *Murder Sails at Midnight*. It was the first sailing of the Italian liner the *Beatrice Cenci* (aka the *Andrea Doria?*). On board were four wealthy women, one of whom was the intended victim of another passenger who had been hired to eliminate her en route. The murderer was given ample opportunity to do the job as the ship ran into heavy weather and was delayed. In Amanda Cross's *In the Last Analysis*, Kate Fansler, having solved the mystery of her student's murder, decided to take a trip abroad. She sailed out of New York harbor, but as the ship rounded Manhattan to the East River on its way to the open sea, Assistant D.A. Reed Amhearst appeared, unwilling to let her out of his sight.

As you walk south you will go past Pier 92, the NYC Convention Pier, and Pier 86, where the *Intrepid* aircraft carrier, which has been converted to a floating museum, is moored. In Clark's *While My Pretty One Sleeps*, Neeve Kearny has been taken there for a Labor Day charity party by a date she decided was too possessive, so she dumped him.

At Pier 83 you can take the Circle Line around Manhattan, or go to Pier 81 and take the Dayline cruise. In Margaret Maron's *Death in Blue Folders*, artist Oscar Nauman, head of Vanderlyn College's Art Department, took NYPD Lieutenant Sigrid Harald to a MOMA charity do on a cruise ship from here.

One Sunday in Jonathan Gash's *The Great California Game*, British antiques dealer Lovejoy, in NYC as an illegal alien, spent part of his day off on the Circle Line's three-hour cruise around NYC.

Nero Wolfe Walk. Begin this walk at the Weehawken Ferry just before the Lincoln Tunnel at 39th Street. Past the ferry are the entrances to the Lincoln Tunnel and the Jacob Javits Convention Center, which make walking there a bit difficult, despite Archie Goodwin's habit of taking a morning stroll "about the piers and back." If you want to explore the Javits Center (perhaps to attend a murderous ABA convention, courtesy of Isaac Asimov), it's safest to take a cab.

Along Tenth and Eleventh Avenues are plenty of garages where Wolfe could have stored his two cars, but there are no handsome brownstones on West 35th Street and Eleventh Avenue—and there never were. At 367 W. 35th Street, the first block east of the Hudson River with any houses, there is a five-story brownstone apartment building, with a fire escape on the front, a stoop, and a basement, but no greenhouses on top. Next door at 337 W. 35th Street is the NYPD Midtown Precinct South, a modern, green cinder block affair that claims to be the busiest precinct in the world. You can go inside and look at the official complaints desk in the lobby.

However elusive in real life, Nero Wolfe's brownstone is as famous as Sherlock Holmes's 221B Baker Street, or Lord Peter Wimsey's 110A Piccadilly, London. It is on the north side of West 35th Street, and has three stories, with greenhouses on the top and a basement with iron railings where the chef, Fritz, lives. It has a Dutch stoop with seven steps leading up to the double front door with one-way glass, and, inside, an elevator. There is a front parlor on one side of the hall with the dining room on the other. Behind these front rooms Wolfe has a big office with a cherry desk, bookcases, and souvenirs of cases. There are also two big red leather chairs reserved for suspects, and a picture of a waterfall—with a peephole. Archie's desk is at right angles to Wolfe's under the windows. In the kitchen is a small table where Archie eats breakfast and reads his newspaper, while Wolfe sleeps in the back, on the second floor, in his yellow pajamas. And on top of the brownstone, in the temperature-controlled greenhouses, are 10,000 orchids, overseen by Theodore Horstmann, Wolfe's plant expert. In Margery Allingham's *The China Governess*, Albert Campion said he would prefer pottery figures of Maigret, Poirot or Nero Wolfe with an orchid to statues of murderers.

In *Method Three for Murder*, Mira Holt parked a cab with a dead body in front of Wolfe's brownstone. Most of his cases begin and end there, simply because Wolfe will not go out. Clients, suspects, and the NYPD all come here for both consultation and confrontation. In "Died Like a Dog," Archie Goodwin adopted a dog found at the scene of the crime and brought it home to annoy Wolfe. But Wolfe protected the dog's rights when the NYPD wanted to impound it, and later he and Archie officially adopted it.

Down the block to your left, at the corner of West 35th and Ninth Avenue, are more Lincoln Tunnel entrances (and a lot of heavy traffic), making it a very hard place these days for a boy to wipe off windshields—and many do. In *The Golden Spiders*, 35th Street and Ninth Avenue is the corner where young Pete Drossos was working the wipe game, and was run over and killed. From this point you can go back to 33rd Street to pick up the main walk at the General Post Office, or end your walk here.

6

THE AVENUES WALK

Fifth, Madison, and Park

BACKGROUND

This walk gives you a chance to pursue mystery "on *the* Avenue," as it is called in the Judy Garland movie *Easter Parade*. The two major activities on and around Fifth Avenue are shopping and dining, and, as a result, NYC-based detective stories have more chases in and out of stores along Fifth Avenue than anywhere else on Manhattan. *The* Avenue, from 34th Street to Central Park (59th Street), also extends its shadow east, to include Madison and Park Avenues, with their public relations, advertising, and publishing offices, and many famous hotels.

Historically, Fifth Avenue began north of Washington Square in the Village. (See Walk 3.) It was first residential, then became mercantile and business-oriented as the stately mansions moved relentlessly north to "Millionaires Row" across from Central Park. (See Walk 8.) Later, the Avenue became home to fabulous restaurants, department stores, hotels, and the ultimate NYC skyscraper—the Empire State Building—making the story of Fifth Avenue a capsule history of Manhattan.

The area from 34th Street north was developed after 1827 when John Jacob Astor, a German immigrant who started in furs and clipper ships, and his son William bought farms on Fifth Avenue from 32nd to 36th Streets. In 1890, William

Waldorf Astor opened the Waldorf Hotel next door to his aunt, famous as *the* Mrs. Astor (whom he loathed). Born Caroline Webster Schermerhorn, with impeccable Dutch antecedents, Aunt Caroline ran society, then passed into American folklore.

In *The American Scene*, Henry James wrote about the Waldorf's famous maitre d' Oscar, who learned his trade at Delmonico's and Hoffman House. The Waldorf hotel (like its successors) was famous for its charity balls and the fact that women could come there alone and smoke in public.

Farther north at 40th Street, NYC's answer to London's Great Exhibition was held in 1853 in a cleaned up Bryant Park, located behind the Croton Reservoir. By 1893, the reservoir was gone and the handsome marble New York Public Library with its famous sitting lions was being built, helped by Astor money.

While Columbia University, which owned the land from 47th to 51st Streets, decided not to build there, members of high society and celebrities, like Tammany Hall's Boss Tweed, built brownstones and houses of worship north of the library on Fifth Avenue. The first Jewish Temple Emanu-El was located at 43rd Street; the second St. Patrick's Roman Catholic Cathedral was consecrated in 1879, at 50th and 51st Streets; and fashionable St. Thomas's Episcopal Church was completed in 1911, just a few blocks north, at 53rd Street. Two famous restaurants occupied the corner of 44th Street: Delmonico's and Louis Sherry's, where murdered architect Stanford White created a "Versailles look," and a Horseback Dinner was held in 1903.

Nouveau riche railroad millionaire Jay Gould built a mansion at the corner of 47th Street, where his daughter Helen lived until 1934. The Astors built new Italianate houses with marble staircases and conservatories nearby. The Rockefellers also built homes at W. 54th Street, where their neighbors included William Waldorf Astor and his hotel, The Netherland, and the Marble Row, a group of townhouses, one of which was owned by Edith Wharton's very fat aunt, Mary Jones. Until World War I, Fifth Avenue from 34th Street to Central Park was known as the village with the most money in the world. Today along this stretch of Fifth Avenue only the Morton F. Plant mansion (aka Cartier's) is left.

After World War I when Saks relocated here, building itself an Italian palazzo, Fifth Avenue from 34th to 59th Streets became home to the world's most famous department stores. Then in 1931 the Empire State Building, easily the world's most famous skyscraper and for a long time the tallest, opened on the site of the original Waldorf-Astoria Hotel at 34th Street. Finally, during the 1930s, Rockefeller Center was built. An outstanding Art Deco complex, it is Fifth Avenue's "village square."

This walk includes parts of Madison Avenue, the advertising capital of the world and home to publishers, agents (including mine), and bookstores, and Park Avenue, with its luxury hotels. To the west it includes some special attractions, such as the Algonquin Hotel, which is Number One with mystery writers, though their rich characters usually stay at the Plaza or the Waldorf-Astoria.

LENGTH OF WALK: 3 miles

The walk covers 1.5 miles to 59th and 1.5 miles back to site of B. Altman's.

See map on page 139 for the boundaries of this walk and page 310 for a list of books and detectives mentioned.

PLACES OF INTEREST

Empire State Building, Fifth Avenue at 34th Street. Open daily, 9:30 A.M.–midnight. A perfect place to get the whole NYC picture. Built in 1931, it has 73 elevators and 1,860 stairs to the 102nd floor, where the concessions stand and observation deck are located. In 1945, an airplane crashed into it, killing fourteen people. It was also the scene of the crime in the classic 1930s *King Kong*, where the poor, unloved gorilla climbed to the top of the building for the woman he loved but fell to his death, murdered by buzzing little airplanes.

St. Patrick's Roman Catholic Cathedral, Fifth Avenue and 50th Street. Parish House, 14 E. 51st Street. Open daily. Victorian

Gothic building consecrated in 1879. Three-hundred thirty feet high, seats 2,400.

St. Thomas's Episcopal Church, 1 W. 53rd Street. St. Thomas Choir School, 202 W. 58th Street. 1914 French Gothic church, famous for deep-blue stained glass windows and tall carved-marble reredos over high altar.

Algonquin Hotel, 59 W. 44th Street. An elegant landmark with a cozy English ambiance in its lobby. Since 1902, home away from home to many of NYC's literary and theatrical lights. Dashiell Hammett drank here, and the Algonquin Round Table members, including Dorothy Parker and Robert Benchley, ate and broadcast from the hotel's Oak Room, later the Rose Room. Call 840-6800.

New York Public Library, Fifth Avenue and 42nd Street. Built in 1911. One of the world's most famous research libraries. Its fiction collection includes many mysteries, with a strong emphasis on detective stories with a NYC setting. It also has a collection of obituaries, death notices, and guides to burial places, all housed in a magnificent Beaux-Arts palace, with a wide outside staircase flanked by the two seated lions Mayor Fiorello La Guardia named Patience and Fortitude. Free. Tours Mon.–Wed., 11:00 A.M.–2:00 P.M. Public restrooms in basement and park. Gift shop. Call 930-0501.

Rockefeller Center, 47th to 52nd Streets, Fifth to Sixth Avenues. Art Deco "city within a city" made up of nineteen buildings on twenty-two acres. Over 1,000 firms and thirty-four restaurants of all kinds and prices. Home to Radio City Music Hall, GE (RCA) Building, Time-Life Building, and Rockefeller Plaza, which includes the Channel Gardens and sunken ice skating rink. J. D. Rockefeller, Jr. had agreed to buy the land from Columbia University for the Metropolitan Opera. When the Met backed out, he developed it himself. Now owned by the Japanese, but still quintessence of twentieth-century NYC and USA.

Grand Central Railroad Station, 42nd Street to 45th Street and Park Avenue, including Vanderbilt and DePew Places. (Pan Am Building and Helipad above it to the north.) Beaux-Arts terminal built in 1871 by railroad millionaire Commodore

Cornelius Vanderbilt. Preserved as landmark in 1970s, but "terminated" as NYC's main railroad station in the 1980s. Grand Concourse home of the famous clock and vaulted ceiling with signs of the Zodiac. Seating almost all gone. Somewhat cheerier on lower levels, where the Oyster Bar, shops, fast food places, and suburban and subway trains are located. Tours meet at the clock Wednesdays at noon.

Museum of Modern Art (MOMA), 11 W. 54th Street. Art from 1880 to present. Founded in 1929 with help of Mrs. Rockefeller and son Nelson. Special exhibits and film showings. Sculpture Garden backing up to University Club, but overshadowed by high-rise built over the museum. Two restaurants. Open 11:00 A.M.–6:00 P.M., Thurs., 11:00 A.M.–9:00 P.M. Closed Wed. Admission fee. Phone 708-9480.

The Pierpont Morgan Library, 29 E. 36th Street. Part of the home of millionaire financier J. P. Morgan. Built to house his collections. Son J. P., Jr. enlarged it and opened it to public in 1924. In 1988, trustees bought 1852 brownstone next door. Special exhibits. Open daily, except Mon. Admission fee. Call 685-0610.

The Waldorf-Astoria Hotel and Waldorf Towers, 301 Park Avenue at 50th Street. Named after the German village the Astors came from and the original Waldorf Hotel (on Fifth Avenue and 34th Street), it was connected to the original Astoria Hotel by a passage called Peacock Alley (named for its well-dressed clientele). Twin-towered Art Deco masterpiece, with a three-level ballroom for charity functions, many restaurants, two lobbies, and private suites occupied by presidents and the ex-royal Windsors. For fine dining, try either Peacock Alley or the Cocktail Terrace. Luxury class. Phone 355-3000.

St. Regis–Sheraton Hotel, Fifth Avenue at 55th Street. Lovely Beaux-Arts building, recently renovated. Attractive lounge where you can sit, take tea, or have a drink. Luxury class. Call 872-6140.

The Peninsula New York Hotel, 700 Fifth Avenue. Formerly the Beaux-Arts Gotham Hotel. Twin of St. Regis. Recently

redone with Art Nouveau decor. Bar/lounge, the Gotham,
off lobby. Luxury class. Call 247-2200.

Lord & Taylor, Fifth Avenue between 38th and 39th Streets.
Started in Lower Manhattan in 1826. In World War I
building. Noted for women's accessories, children's clothes,
furniture, and linens—all from American designers.

Saks Fifth Avenue, Fifth Avenue between 49th and 50th Streets.
Landmark 1920 Italian Palazzo. Opened 1924 by Saks and
Gimbel. Famous for designer clothes, good taste, and
excellent service. No furniture and no restaurants. Open
daily. Call 940-4200.

Morton F. Plant Mansion (aka Cartier's), Fifth Avenue and
52nd Street. Only remaining mansion from turn of the
century. Landmark status. Worth a look inside even if you
are not buying jewelry.

Villard Houses, 451–55 Madison Avenue. Landmark group of
Italianate brownstone mansions designed for railroad tycoon
Henry Villard in 1884 by McKim, Mead and White. Once
housed Random House, now part of Helmsley Palace Hotel.

St. Bartholomew's Episcopal Church, Park Avenue and 51st
Street. 1919 Byzantine style structure. In 1981 its parish
tried to sell front lawn—the last piece of open land on Park
Avenue—and air rights to a developer to build a high-rise
office tower, but failed to get approval from Landmark
Commission.

PLACES TO EAT

(This walk has so many places to eat in the stores and hotels
that this list includes only places mentioned in mystery stories.)

New York Public Library. Outdoor vendors on either side of the
front staircase.

The "21" Club, 21 W. 52nd St. Only remaining (former)
speakeasy in landmark brownstone. Lunch, dinner,
afternoon tea, cocktails. Closed Sun. Formal dress.
Reservations needed. Call 582-7200.

Waldorf-Astoria Hotel, Park to Lexington Avenues between
49th and 50th Streets. Cocktail Terrace in lobby, serving
afternoon tea, cocktails. Open daily, 2:30 P.M.–2:00 A.M.
Peacock Alley. French. Open daily, including Sunday
brunch. Reservations needed. Call 355-3000.

Harry's New York Bar, Helmsley Palace, 455 Madison Avenue.
Lunch, sandwiches, and cocktails daily, 11:00 A.M.–2:00
P.M. Formal dress. Expensive. Call 888-7000.

Hotel Peninsula New York, 700 Fifth Avenue. Gotham Lounge
and Bar. Cocktails. Formal dress. Reservations needed. Very
expensive. Call 247-2200.

Algonquin Hotel, 59 W. 44th Street. Oak Bar (Blue Bar)/Lounge.
Open daily, noon–1 A.M. Formal dress. Afternoon tea,
cocktails. Oak Room. Supper club/entertainment. Lunch,
dinner. Reservations needed. Expensive. Rose Room. Breakfast,
lunch, supper, and Sunday brunch. Open daily, 7:00–12:30
A.M. Reservations needed. Expensive. Call 840-6800.

The Oyster Bar, Grand Central Station, Vanderbilt Avenue at
42nd Street. Lower level. Opened in 1913. Seafood
specialties. Clam chowder cheap, makes marvelous lunch.
Table or counter service available. Call 490-6650.

Museum of Modern Art (MOMA), 11 W. 53rd Street. Cafeteria.
Indoor/outdoor seating. Good food at moderate prices.

The Rainbow Room, 30 Rockefeller Plaza (at 48th Street). 1930s
ambiance. Celebrated nightspot and view. Open Tues.–Sun.
Reservations needed. Call 632-5000.

--------- **THE AVENUES WALK:** ---------
FIFTH, MADISON, AND PARK

Begin your walk at Fifth Avenue and 34th Street, one block east
of Herald Square, where Sixth Avenue and Broadway intersect.
As you walk up "The" avenue remember that in mystery stories
the general ambiance is wealth and privilege. In Carolyn G.
Hart's *Death on Demand*, for example, mystery bookstore
owner Annie Laurance recalled that wealthy and handsome
Max Darling had lived in a Fifth Avenue penthouse, a Long Is-

land country house, a Scottish castle, and a Connecticut mansion.

At the same time, suspects and murderers chase one another through the stores of Fifth Avenue more than anywhere else in Manhattan. Since many mystery characters are at one time either the hunter or hunted, hiding from the NYPD or murderers, *and* shoppers, this walk combines their adventures into one fun-thrilled hike, with time out for shopping and eating. If you find a body in Bloomingdale's, however, it is your civic duty to report it, instead of behaving like a Gothic romance heroine and grabbing a cab back to your hotel.

The Empire State Building is at 34th Street and Fifth Avenue. It is the best-known building in Manhattan, possibly in the world, and you must take the time to visit its Observation Deck and survey NYC. It opened in 1931, and shortly afterward had a starring role in the movie that featured the poor gorilla, King Kong, who died climbing the skyscraper for the woman he loved.

The Empire State Building gives NYC its glittering, indestructible image. Not only the home of real-life heroes, like Charles Lindbergh, NYC has been home to mobsters, like the "Godfather" John Gotti; and classic comic heroes, like Superman and Dick Tracy.

In Rex Stout's *Too Many Clients*, the corporate offices of murdered love nester Thomas Yeager's Continental Plastic Products were located in the Empire State Building. Benedict Aiken, president of Continental Plastics, hired Wolfe to solve the Yeager murder (and protect the company from scandal). In Frances and Richard Lockridge's *The Norths Meet Murder*, the sleek, new, impersonal apartment building of murder victim and lawyer Clyde Brent was near the Empire State Building. More recently, in *The Great California Game*, Jonathan Gash's antiques expert, Lovejoy, who entered America illegally from Hong Kong, stayed at a sleazy Midtown hotel nearby.

After touring the Empire State Building, go three blocks up Fifth Avenue to 37th Street. (NYC was built on hills, so it is *up*.) There are no mansions in this part of Fifth Avenue, but this is the block where the Leavenworth mansion once stood in Anna

Green's epoch-making 1878 mystery, *The Leavenworth Case*. A satisfactory substitute is the Morton F. Plant Mansion (aka Cartier's) farther north, at Fifth Avenue and 52nd Street.

In Green's mystery, the Leavenworth mansion had a raised basement with windows and an area gate, a hallway with antique flooring, carved woodwork and bronze ornaments, and a large parlor with wide windows looking out, where the NYC Coroner and his grand jury (hastily taken off nearby streets) met over the body of Mr. Leavenworth. He had been shot in his second-floor library adjoining his bedroom. His nieces Mary and Eleanore lived on the third floor in rooms with gorgeous carpets and azure walls. The secretary Mr. Harwell lived in front (noisier), the maids in the attic, and the butler in the basement. In the back was a carriage house with a driveway.

Continue walking up Fifth Avenue to 38th Street and cross the street to Lord & Taylor with its green-and-white awnings. It is known for its calm, conservative atmosphere and all-American merchandise. It also has several restaurants, including the Soup Bar, a NYC institution—as are its Christmas display windows. In 1991 Lord & Taylor's windows featured historic Manhattan buildings, like the Chelsea home of Santa Claus creator Clement Clarke Moore.

Although Lord & Taylor does not sell books, it does have furniture and a penthouse. It is therefore a possible substitute for French's Department Store in Ellery Queen's *French Powder Mystery*, in which books and drugs resulted in murder. French's display windows were a Christmas tradition (like Lord & Taylor's), and there was a penthouse on the sixth floor. A board meeting was going on there at noon when a model opened a new show window display and found the body of Mrs. French, the owner's wife. (This scene of the crime is very similar to the one in Phyllis Whitney's *The Red Carnelian*, or *Red Is for Murder*, written about Chicago's Marshall Field's, where Whitney once worked.) An important clue was the books found in the French penthouse apartment. They should have been the Frenchs' favorites, the novels of Graustark, Jack London, Sherlock Holmes, and Richard Harding Davis, but were not.

Lord & Taylor may be an even better choice for Richard

Lockridge's Bryant & Washburn in *Murder for Art's Sake*, where the wife of NYPD Captain Bill Weigand, Dorian, was a staff artist. Dorian Weigand went back to talk to buyer Ursula Fields about the new practice of selling paintings in furniture departments. Later, when she also investigated the seventh-floor furniture department, she found a missing Shack (Shackleton Jones) cityscape for sale—much too cheap.

Besides being home to Lord & Taylor, 39th Street is also the location of the apartment hotel where the Kirk family lived in Ellery Queen's *The Chinese Orange Mystery*, but none of the hotels south of 42nd Street are quite right.

Walk up Fifth Avenue to 40th Street to the imposing New York Public Library, guarded by the two lions Patience (downtown) and Fortitude (uptown) who were given those names by Mayor Fiorello La Guardia. La Guardia appeared as himself in Elliott Roosevelt's *Hyde Park Murder*, in which First Lady Eleanor Roosevelt helped a young couple, whose parents disapproved of their romance.

The library, with its wide outdoor staircase used by New Yorkers to sit and eat or people-watch in good weather, was built in 1911, after the old reservoir was torn down and the potters' field in Bryant Park was emptied. Inside and out the library is one of NYC's finest examples of the Beaux-Arts style, especially its elegant white marble lobby, known as Astor Hall. Upstairs in Room 315, the spacious, wainscotted Reading Room, with long tables and tall windows, is a refuge for scholars, students, and people who want to get out of the rain, like the famous circular Reading Room in London's British Museum. (See *Mystery Reader's Walking Guide: London*, Bloomsbury Walk.) There is a gift shop on the main floor, and public restrooms are in the basement. There are no restaurants, but there are vendors outside.

During Edgars Week each spring (when the annual awards are given), the MWA (Mystery Writers of America) and the John Jay College of Law jointly hold a symposium workshop and reception here. Sessions include panels with members of the John Jay faculty, the NYPD, and mystery writers. There is a charge, but any interested mystery fan can attend. (For more information, call MWA at 888-8171.)

The New York Public Library is no longer a circulating library, but it has many special collections, including one of NYC detective stories and the Berg Collection, which contains the papers of T. S. Eliot, Virginia Woolf, and their contemporaries. Amanda Cross's English professor, Kate Fansler, must have come here—one way or another—since Amanda Cross is actually Columbia Professor Carolyn G. Heilbrun. Dr. Heilbrun is a noted authority not only on mystery writer Dorothy L. Sayers and her Somerville College circle, whom she uses as models in her detective stories, but also on Virginia Woolf.

NYC mystery characters automatically come here for information. In Margaret Maron's *Death in Blue Folders*, millionaire Justin Trent told the NYPD he had walked to the NYPL to see if it had a biography of the artist Mabuse, whose works were on exhibit at the Pierpont Morgan Library. In Emma Lathen's *Banking on Death*, Sloan Guarantee Trust Vice-President John Putnam Thatcher needed the Buffalo, New York newspapers. Young trust officer Ken Nichols jokingly told the Sloan office boy to steal them from the public library. When he did, Thatcher's properly brought up secretary, Miss Corsa, was horrified, but Thatcher was amused. After reading them he told Miss Corsa to get them returned without anyone being caught!

In Frances and Richard Lockridge's *Murder Comes First*, Pam North's Aunt Lucinda (Lucy), under suspicion of murder, sneaked out of her hotel to go to the library. There she found out the name of the Long Island town where her murdered friend Grace Logan had a cottage. She then took the train from the Grand Central Station all by herself to Westchester County, where she met the murderer.

In George Chesbro's *The Second Horseman Out of Eden*, Garth Frederickson went to the NYPL to get information on suppliers of the organization Nuvironment to help him locate the site of their Armageddon biosphere. In Zev Chaffets's *Inherit the Mob*, journalist William Gordon (aka Velvel Grossman) was taken to the library at age seven, by his mother, and shown how to take out books, which made him into a reader. His successful writing career, however, turned out to have been orchestrated by his Uncle Max, co-capo of the Organization (Mob, Mafia).

In Mary Roberts Rinehart's *The Swimming Pool*, mystery writer Lois Maynard lived with her lawyer brother Phil at The Birches. When their sister Judith dumped her rich husband and came to The Birches, bringing murder with her, Lois went to the city to read the old newspapers about her father's suicide at the NYPL.

In Elizabeth Daly's *The Book of the Crime*, book detective Henry Gamadge visited the library on business regularly. He had ordered some books and was about to look at them when he was approached—on purpose—by Gary Austen, the crippled husband of young Rena Seton, who had run away from home. Austen wanted to hire Gamadge as a private investigator to find Rena. Rena, however, was actually hiding at the Gamadges', pretending to be their baby nurse. In *The Book of the Lion*, Gamadge also went to the library to check in the catalog department for any works by Isabel Wakes. He found none by her, but several by her late husband, Jeremy Wakes, another Lost Generation member of an old New York family.

After visiting the library, turn right on 40th Street to walk behind the library toward Sixth Avenue (west), to look at Bryant Park. Named for poet and abolitionist NYC editor William Cullen Bryant, the park was the site of America's first World's Fair and the Crystal Palace Exhibition of 1853. The park has just reopened and has public restrooms, complete with an NYPD guard. It has nice benches, old trees, and ground myrtle, as well as a large grassy lawn with "Keep Off" signs.

In William A. DeAndrea's *The Lunatic Fringe*, in which Teddy Roosevelt is NYC police commissioner, Roosevelt and NYPD Officer Dennis Patrick Xavier Muldoon capture and destroy an anarchist called Baxter, who was planning to blow up a group of VIPs assembled in NYC for a wedding. Their confrontation took place on the walls of the Croton Reservoir, which filled the land now occupied by the library and the park.

It was in Bryant Park on a windy Sunday morning, in Mary Higgins Clark's *While My Pretty One Sleeps*, that mob hit man Denny Adler met mobster Big Charlie, whom he had known at Attica Prison. They drove up the Henry Hudson Parkway to the George Washington Bridge and crossed the Hudson River to the lookout point at Exit 3, where Big Charlie told Adler to "waste" Neeve Kearny, the daughter of former NYPD Police Commissioner Myles Kearny.

At the west end of the park, walk up Sixth Avenue to the statue of William Cullen Bryant at 42nd Street. (From here you have a grand view [east] of the Chrysler Building, for one year the tallest building in the world, with its scalloped Art Deco top, which is equally lovely lit up at night.)

Between Fifth and Sixth Avenues at 33 W. 42nd Street, there is the old Aeolian Building, an architectural gem built in 1925, now the City University Graduate Center. You can take time out to walk through its elegant bluestoned arcade, where there is an art gallery, or go upstairs to eat at the buffeteria, open to anyone who pays a minimum charge. In S. S. Van Dine's *Benson Murder Case*, Philo Vance went to a concert at Aeolian Hall to hear a string quartet from San Francisco.

Walk one more block north to 43rd Street and look right again. Just down the block is another NYC landmark, *The New Yorker* magazine, which has its offices at 25 W. 43rd Street. Begun in 1925, the magazine's list of contributors reads like a course on twentieth-century literature: J. D. Salinger, John Hersey, I. B. Singer, John Cheever, Saul Bellow, Philip Roth, E. B. White, John Updike, Anne Sexton, Dorothy Parker, Robert Benchley, James Thurber, S. J. Perelman, and many more.

James Thurber wrote the hilarious short story "The Macbeth Murder Mystery" for *The New Yorker*. In it a woman read Shakespeare's *Macbeth* as if it were a detective story. Truman Capote held a party at the Plaza Hotel to celebrate the publication of his famous true life crime story, *In Cold Blood*, which first ran in *The New Yorker*. Capote also wrote *Breakfast at Tiffany's*, which we will pass shortly. In *Murder in Manhattan*, Steve Allen had a cameo role as an aging Southern writer called Toots Gable, which was loosely based on Capote, according to the zany director Bernie Barnes.

Original publisher Harold Ross had insisted that *The New Yorker* would not write for "the Old Lady from Dubuque," a snide remark often quoted and mixed up with another about "little old ladies in tennis shoes." As a Midwesterner who did these walks in sneakers, I find this comment amusing since so many "native" New Yorkers are really Middle Western immigrants, just like Rex Stout and his Archie Goodwin.

Walk up Sixth Avenue to 44th Street. You are now at the site of the famous Biltmore Hotel, with its big lobby clock where everybody used to meet. In Mary Higgins Clark's *A Stranger Is Watching*, Room 932 was rented by psychopath "Foxy," a serial killer. He had murdered the wife of Steve Peterson, the editor of *Events Magazine* (aka *Time*) and now planned to kidnap Peterson's son for ransom and make off with it after blowing up NYC.

Cross 44th Street and turn right to walk back towards Fifth Avenue. Down this rather narrow, London-looking side street at 59 W. 44th Street is the Algonquin Hotel. If you don't want to stop in now for tea, or a drink, or lunch, either come back or go in long enough to appreciate its cozy, paneled lobby with comfortable chairs, sofas, and small tables (and the current hotel cat stalking about). Although it is pleasantly preserved, not ossified, the Algonquin could be the American version of the hotel in Agatha Christie's *At Bertram's Hotel*. It harks back to the days when *Thin Man* author Dashiell Hammett used to frequent the tiny Blue Bar, located just inside the street door. Marketing manager Christina Zeniou told me the bar was moved to the Oak Bar because there had only been enough room for Hammett himself to drink there!

The hotel was the site of the famous Algonquin Round Table lunches. Originally held informally in the Oak Room, they were moved to the Rose Room when they "went on the air," doing radio broadcasts. The Round Table itself was back in the Oak Room when I took my family there for a birthday lunch, and maitre d' Danny Reggio kindly let us sit there. I remarked how *small the table was* (five of us filled it completely) and he chuckled and told us that people used to come and sit three deep to be included in the show.

The Algonquin Round Table first became famous when Franklin P. Adams (FPA), a *Herald-Tribune* columnist, wrote about it. The most famous member, still remembered today, is probably Dorothy Parker, a tiny witty woman who was the *New Yorker's* book reviewer, aka "Constant Reader." Her crack about *Winnie the Pooh*, that "tonstand weader fwode up," was a typical, if intemperate, Parker remark about the most famous work of mystery writer A. A. Milne (who also wrote *The Red House Mystery*, a spoof of the genre).

In Emma Lathen's *Banking on Death*, Ken Nichols, the Sloan's trust officer for the Schneider family, fell for daughter Jane Schneider. She came to NYC to shop—and see him. They met in the Algonquin lounge, where Jane was charmed by its substitution of comfortable chairs and couches and convenient tables for the usual bar and booth arrangement. But Ken's boss, John Thatcher, was there, too, and joined them, much to Ken's dismay.

In Dana Clarins's *The Woman Who Knew Too Much*, the gorgeous, but temperamental, Zoe Bassinetti, the wife of the crippled Director, had picked up Charlie Cunningham (Mr. Mystery or MM) at an Algonquin publisher's party for an ex-Mafia moll. Two years later, woozy but hanging in there, Charlie was still in thrall to her bossiness, sexiness, and ambition.

In *Murder Unrenovated* by P. M. Carlson, Julia Northrup, a retired fifth-grade teacher who lived in the basement apartment of a Brooklyn brownstone Nick and Maggie O'Connor wanted to buy, quoted the Algonquin Group a lot. Later, in Carlson's *Rehearsal for Murder*, Julia, now the O'Connors' tenant, offered to babysit their baby Sarah one Sunday afternoon—taking her to the Algonquin, so she (Northrup) could pretend to be Dorothy Parker.

In *Murder Comes First* by Frances and Richard Lockridge, Pam and Jerry North had a long lunch at the Algonquin before meeting Pam's three aunts' train from Cleveland. In Edgar Box's (aka Gore Vidal's) *Death in the Fifth Position*, the new PR man for the Grand Street Petersburg Ballet, Peter Cutler Sargeant III, joined the principal male ballet dancer for a night on the town that began at the Algonquin and ended in Harlem. (See Walk 11.)

The Algonquin is not just popular with bankers, writers, and actors. In Crabbe Evers's *Murder at Wrigley Field*, retired

Chicago sports writer Duffy House came to NYC to talk with Baseball Commissioner Granville Canyon Chambliss about the shooting of star Cub pitcher Dean (Dream) Weaver. Chambliss had agreed that House could stay at the Algonquin on an expense account while he played P.I. for the baseball industry.

In Jerome Charyn's *Paradise Man*, dapper "bumper" (aka hit man or waster) Sidney Holden went to the Algonquin to waylay a British furrier who owed Holden's patron a bundle. (Holden disdainfully characterized the Algonquin as practically a British hotel.) Once there he met NYC's D.A. Abruzzi, the D.A.'s writer son Rex, and Rex's wife Fay. Holden had rescued Fay from a Mafia kidnaping so they wanted to thank him. As they sat, people kept coming to the table to give their regards to the D.A. and his daughter-in-law, making Holden wonder if the Algonquin was the D.A.'s Manhattan office.

Come out of the Algonquin Hotel lobby and turn left to walk east along West 44th Street. Across the street is the American Bar Association, while on your side, at 217 W. 44th Street, is the venerable Harvard Club, built by NYC's McKim, Mead and White. Here it helps to be or know a member if you wish to explore. When I bravely walked in to ask if ordinary people could look around, the answer was a quick "no." But I took a peek at the portraits of benefactors, hung on Harvard crimson walls, which contrasted with the colonial white paneling.

In Lathen's *Banking on Death*, the Sloan's John Putnam Thatcher and his much married Harvard classmate, broker Tom Robichaux, always met there the day before Christmas to avoid office Christmas parties. Robichaux talked about a Buffalo felt company with a new process, which gave Thatcher a clue to the whereabouts of the missing Schneider heir.

The two also lunched there the day after the near miss on Ed Parry at a Stock Exchange cocktail party in *Death Shall Overcome*. But when they heard on the television that black author Richard Simpson's group, CASH, planned to manipulate stock and "march on Wall Street," they left quickly for their respective offices.

In Amanda Cross's *No Word from Winifred*, Kate Fansler lunched at the Harvard Club with Toby Van Dine, a law partner of her brother, to talk about the papers of English author Charlotte Stanton. In the lobby, Kate sank into a huge leather chair, noting that the chair was clearly meant to intimidate any women allowed inside. She also commented unfavorably on the head of a dead (presumably male) elephant nailed to the wall of the lounge.

In Zev Chaffets's *Inherit the Mob*, William (Velvel) Gordon, a prize-winning journalist whose Mafia Uncle Max had left him the "business," refused to meet another mob representative at the Harvard Club because he would have had to wear a tie.

Keep walking east along 44th Street. In plush Edwardian days, Louis Sherry's famous restaurant stood on the southwest corner of Fifth Avenue at 44th Street. In S. S. Van Dine's *The Benson Murder Case*, D.A. Markham's gentleman friend, Philo Vance, came there for tea after viewing some tapestries about to be auctioned. Across Fifth Avenue, on the northeastern side, was Delmonico's, an equally resplendent establishment that followed society north from the Wall Street area and has moved back there again. (See Walk 1.) Between 44th and 45th Streets, on the west side of Fifth Avenue, there used to be one of the popular Schrafft's chain where ladies (and lawyers, etc.) lunched. Cross's Kate Fansler met school chums at Schrafft's once upon a time.

Turn left on Fifth Avenue to walk north to 46th Street. As you cross 46th Street, look to your left and see if you can pick out a building that might have been the Chatham Arms Apartment. In S. S. Van Dine's *The Benson Murder Case*, it had a simple, dignified facade, and a lobby with a switchboard, reception room, and elevator. Major Anthony Benson, brother of murdered Wall Street broker Alvin Benson, had an apartment on the third floor. Amateur sleuth Philo Vance and his friend D.A. Markham searched the apartment and found the pistol that shot Benson, and a box of jewels belonging to Miss St. Clair, an operatic hopeful.

Keep walking up Fifth Avenue, heading towards 47th Street. This area, from 44th Street to 47th Street, is known as the Diamond Center. It has many retail and wholesale jewelers and you can walk through the arcades and watch gems changing hands. Forty-Seventh Street from Sixth to Seventh Avenues is called Diamond and Jewelers Way on the street signs. At the corner of 47th Street, across Fifth Avenue, you can see the old F. A. French Building being restored. The name may have given Ellery Queen ideas, although the location is wrong for the department store in *The French Powder Mystery*. The current offices of the Mystery Writers of America are at 17 E. 47th Street, to your right.

Cross 47th Street and keep going north to 48th Street. Look left for any remaining brownstone mansions. In S. S. Van Dine's *The Benson Murder Case*, the brownstone scene of the crime where Alvin Benson was murdered was on 48th Street near Sixth Avenue. The brownstone had an elegant carved facade, the typical iron railing, shallow basement areaway, and a front door about six feet above street level. There were two heavily grilled front windows, one in the parlor, the other in the library, where Benson was shot from behind. Around midnight, a NYPD cop walking his beat saw a Cadillac filled with fishing gear parked in front of the house. The Cadillac turned out to belong to a playboy with a rich wife called Pfyfe. (The kind of house Benson had still exists in the Murray Hill district near the Morgan Library.)

On 48th Street across Fifth Avenue is the 1913 black-and-gold book emporium where I once saw a copy of my first book, a biography of Dorothy L. Sayers, on sale. Then the retail outlet of Charles Scribner and Sons, it is now a Brentano's. Forty-eighth Street is also the beginning of fabulous Art Deco Rockefeller Center, which stretches to 52nd Street from Fifth to Sixth Avenues.

Built in the 1930s by John D. Rockefeller, Jr., Rockefeller Center is a city within a city, alive by day and lit up by night, serving as Midtown Manhattan's village square. Its seventy-story limestone GE (formerly RCA) Building, with its observation deck and the Rainbow Room, is the centerpiece. The Metropolitan Opera had arranged for Rockefeller to rent the land from Columbia University and develop it for them, but when they backed out, he developed the land for himself.

Walk up Fifth Avenue to the main promenade entrance to

Rockefeller Plaza where you can see the statue of Atlas holding up the world. Inside the plaza are the Channel Gardens, planted year round; at Christmas they feature a huge Christmas tree and gigantic wire angels. A statue of Prometheus stands at the far end of the plaza, and there is a sunken area with restaurants in summer and a rink in winter, surrounded by the flags of foreign nations. The entire Center, ringed by tall office buildings, is always thronged with tourists with cameras.

In Donald Westlake's *Good Behavior*, master burglar John Dortmunder had "dropped in" on St. Filumena's Convent in TriBeCa and been persuaded he must help them rescue Sister Mary Grace. Kidnaped by her tycoon father, Sister Mary Grace was locked up on the upper floor of a Midtown skyscraper that—like many Rockefeller Center buildings—housed a bank. As a result, Dortmunder sat for hours in the ground-floor garden of the Avalon State Bank building near a waterfall and a wall of glass, watching a maintenance door and drinking cup after cup of cappuccino.

In Clarins's *The Woman Who Knew Too Much*, fleeing Charlie Cunningham saw the tourists gaping at Rockefeller Center's Atlas. In Ellery Queen's *The Chinese Orange Mystery*, publisher Donald Kirk's secretary, James Osborne, invited Dr. Kirk's nurse to go see a new John Barrymore film at Radio City Music Hall. Instead they wound up spending the evening being questioned about the dead stranger found in the Kirks' hotel suite.

In Hammett's *The Thin Man*, Nick Charles and his rich wife Nora went to a show at Radio City Music Hall, but left after an hour. In Ed Hoch's short story, "A Winter's Game," secretary Sunny York spent the 1952 Christmas season searching for a job. But during the holidays no one was hiring, so she spent Christmas Day at Radio City Music Hall.

In Martin Meyers's *Kiss and Kill*, Patrick Hardy, the food-and-fun-loving P.I., who owned a dog named Sherlock Holmes, was hired to find the killers of a stripteaser with mob connections. The dead stripper's sugar daddy worked at Louis White and Associates at Rockefeller Center (Louis White was reputed to be the Mr. Big of the Organization on the eastern seaboard). Hardy went to the NBC Building, took the escalator to the underground shopping arcade, cut through the mob in the post office, and headed for Suite 1735, Louis White's offices, where he met Mr. Big, who told him to get lost. But Hardy returned on a Wednesday (matinee day, when no native New Yorker should be in midtown) and got into the dead stripper's strongbox, also in a Rockefeller Center bank.

In Haughton Murphy's *Murder Saves Face*, restaurant owner Marshall Genakis, the boyfriend of murdered Chase and Ward law associate Juliana Merriman, banked his restaurant's take at a Rockefeller Center bank each night. In Velda Johnson's *The Face in the Shadows*, actress Ellen Stacey walked along Fifth Avenue to the office of Vandering (aka Rockefeller?) Enterprises. She was meeting Howard Vandering, whose daughter Cecily, Ellen had found drugged at the Cloisters. The Vanderings represented "old" NYC money, and the Vandering Foundation served public causes in the way the real-life Rockefeller Foundation does.

In *Murder in Manhattan*, the cast, including Steve Allen, spent the day filming at Rockefeller Center, which Steve said was "once the proud symbol of American capitalism, now owned by the Japanese." At the end of the day, Steve, carrying his F.A.O. Schwarz baseball bat, walked to the Plaza, where he got a mysterious message to go to Sardi's after ten that night. (See Walk 5.) The movie they were shooting, *Murder in Manhattan*, had its gala premier at Radio City Music Hall a week before Christmas and got rave reviews.

Explore the lower-level shopping arcade or look at the NBC building, where on Saturday night you see crowds arriving to be the audience for TV's *Saturday Night Live*.

The famous (and gigantic) Radio City Musical Hall, considered part of Rockefeller Center, is at Sixth Avenue and 52nd Street, where the Rockettes still prance, although the 6000-seat theater no longer shows first-run movies. (In 1991, an ex-Rockette was stabbed to death walking her dogs on the Upper West Side; see Walk 10.)

The *Time/Life* Building on Sixth Avenue at 50th Street is also considered part of Rockefeller Center. It is also the probable site of *Globe*, where freelance photographer Helen Bullock got assignments in Byfield and Tedeschi's *Solemn High Murder*. It is also likely to be the home of *Events Magazine*, where Steve Peterson was editor, in Mary Higgins Clark's *A Stranger Is Watching*. In the mystery, Peterson's wife had been killed by a crazy serial killer who was now planning to kidnap his young son.

After exploring—and possibly getting something to eat—at Rockefeller Center, cross Fifth Avenue at 49th Street to visit Saks Fifth Avenue. Saks takes up the block between 49th and 50th Streets. Its 1920s Italian-style palazzo was built to fit in with Fifth Avenue's other European-style mansions. Though called Saks, it was founded by a Saks and a Gimbel, so, in a way, there still are a Macy's and a Gimbel's in NYC.

In Allen's *Murder in Manhattan*, activist actress Suzanne Tracy had marched outside Saks in a snowstorm to scream at women wearing furs. Steve himself met the impulsive Italian actress La Volpa in the lingerie department there, giving her ideas about him. In Clarins's *The Woman Who Knew Too Much*, Charlie Cunningham saw his reflection in Saks's plate glass windows. In Jane Dentinger's *First Hit of the Season*, actress Jocelyn O'Roarke argued with her best friend, Ruth Bernstein, about a baby shower gift in the infant's department of Saks. O'Roarke was upset because she had just visited the fiancée of murdered theater critic Jason Saylin. The two women then went across Fifth Avenue to watch the skaters at Rockefeller Center.

In a typical Fifth Avenue chase/shopping spree, in Frances and Richard Lockridge's *Murder Comes First*, after eating lunch with murdered Grace Logan's nephew, Sandford, Pam North walked to Saks. She shopped for stockings and men's handkerchiefs until she realized she was being followed. She grabbed a cab to go home, but told the cabby, who was scared of guns, that she was being followed. When he cravenly protested, Pam returned to Saks. Once there, Pam spent the afternoon trying on clothes and buying them as a disguise. When she left to go home to Greenwich Village, wearing a new dress and hat, she found out she was being followed by the FBI.

Come out of Saks, turn right, and cross 50th Street to St. Patrick's Cathedral (Roman Catholic), which occupies the entire next block from Fifth to Madison Avenues. The Cathedral was designed in 1879 by the great Victorian Gothic architect James Renwick, who also designed Grace Church. Big (state) funerals are held here and tickets for midnight mass at Christmas are very hard to come by. A tall, twin-towered gray Gothic limestone building, it is very restrained inside, without "pink plastic" Madonnas or votive candles. The huge front doors are only opened for important events or VIPs; tourists and worshippers, however, can go in the side doors any time.

Clarins's fugitive, Charlie Cunningham, saw tourists gaping at St. Patrick's Cathedral as he raced along Fifth Avenue. In Clark's *While My Pretty One Sleeps*, boutique owner Neeve Kearny liked to sleep late on Sundays and then go there to Pontifical Mass. The Sunday after mobster Nicky Sepetti was let out of prison, Neeve's father, retired NYPD Police Commissioner Myles Kearny, came with her. When Neeve was ten, her mother Renata was murdered in Central Park and her funeral was held at St. Patrick's, with a NYPD honor guard in attendance.

Cross 51st Street and walk up the block to Cartier's, at 725 Fifth Avenue. The jewelry store is in the only remaining Fifth Avenue mansion, built in 1902 for Morton F. Plant. It is a lovely marble and granite neoclassic palazzo. In Mignon Eberhart's *Danger Money*, young Susan Beach, a secretary (and "temporary" fiancée) of GM (the Great Man), went there with his assistant, Greg Cameron, to buy a ring for his secretary. The clerk assumed it was for them and Cameron played up to him, much to Susan's embarrassment, buying a huge star sapphire.

Take a peek inside, then go back across Fifth Avenue at 52nd Street. Called Swing Street during the Roaring Twenties, it was once lined with speakeasies and jazz clubs. Walk left along 52nd Street. In the middle of the block on the north side of the street, sandwiched in between taller, more modern buildings, is a handsome brownstone undergoing extensive rehabbing. This is the famous "21" Club at 21 W. 52nd Street. A speakeasy during Prohibition, it is the only one left in NYC, and is still a hangout for famous names and familiar faces.

It is a very likely place for Nick and Nora Charles to have gone if they were bored by a Radio City show a block away. It is also a place where Nick Charles might have waited for Nora and Asta, their dog, to finish their Christmas shopping as the mystery opened. It was while waiting that Nick Charles met Dorothy Winant and became involved in her father's disappearance in Hammett's *The Thin Man*. He told Dorothy her father's lawyer had an office in the Tishman Building "around the corner on Fifth Avenue."

Walk west to Sixth Avenue, turn right, and go one block north to 53rd Street. Turn right again and walk back towards Fifth Avenue. On the south side of the street, at 40 W. 53rd you pass the very new American Craft Museum, with displays of quilts and bedspreads, and demonstrations of native crafts, like weaving and potting. In Haughton Murphy's *Murder Saves Face*, the WASP wife of a Chase and Ward partner held her husband Bill Richardson's fiftieth birthday party here. Retired partner Reuben Frost, who attended the party with his wife Cynthia, said they would probably eat off Amish quilts on the floor; in fact, the food was almost cold and the entertainment strictly family amateur night.

Cross 53rd Street (which is closed for a street fair on Sundays) to the Museum of Modern Art (MOMA) at 11 W. 53rd Street. Looming above MOMA is Museum Tower, built on the air rights to the museum. MOMA's sculpture garden, however, backs up to a less contemporary building, the University Club, on 54th Street. Affectionately known as MOMA, the museum was another gift to NYC by the Rockefellers, Abby and her son, Nelson, one-time governor of New York and vice-president of the USA. On a Sunday morning, it's a lovely place. Its lobby has benches and its sculpture garden and restaurants and wonderful modern art are all available to you. But avoid going on Wednesdays, when the museum is closed. This museum is real New York City, not a copy of a European institution, and mystery characters who are real artists are hung there.

In Johnson's *The Face in the Shadows*, it was pointed out that MOMA was the first museum to have film, photography, and architectural departments. It also hung a painting by Vandering's half-brother Len when he was only 25. In Allen's *Murder in Manhattan*, at the end of the mystery MOMA was plan-

ning a retrospective film show of the work of murdered director
Bernard L. Barnes.

In Tony Hillerman's *The Thief of Time*, Navajo Lieutenant
Joe Leaphorn was sent to NYC to check out the auction catalog
at "Nelsons Auction House." It listed a piece of prehistoric
pottery whose theft was tied up with the mysterious disappearance of a woman anthropologist, Dr. Eleanor Friedman-Bernal.
After going to Nelsons, Leaphorn went to MOMA, where years
earlier he and his dead wife Emma had seen Picasso's she-goat in
the sculpture garden. Emma had decided it made a good symbol
of the Navajo people: starved, gaunt, bony, tough, but enduring. This time, Leaphorn had coffee at the MOMA cafe, looking at the Picasso goat. But, feeling very lonesome, he left to
keep his appointment with the crippled "voyeur" collector
who had bought the Anasazi St. John Polychrome pottery
bowl.

In all of Margaret Maron's mysteries about Lieutenant Sigrid Harald there are references to MOMA because Harald became involved with celebrated abstract artist Oscar Nauman.
Nauman was not only head of Vanderlyn College's art department, but hung at MOMA. In *Death in Blue Folders*, Nauman
took her to a MOMA benefit on a cruise ship where she met the
mayor.

Turn left when you leave MOMA to head back to Fifth Avenue. On the southwest corner of Fifth Avenue you will come
to another graceful, but very narrow, limestone French-Gothic
church, St. Thomas's Episcopal Church, built in 1913. St.
Thomas's is considered *the* Society church, with a dollar sign
carved over the archway used for the bride's entrance. You will
pass by the entrance to the parish office, but St. Thomas's Choir
School is not on this block. It's farther west, at 202 W. 58th
Street. It is an English-style choir school run for the boys who
sing in St. Thomas's men's and boys' choir.

The church's front steps are another favorite Manhattan
hangout for tourists and the homeless, as well as a grand place to
see the Easter Parade, as Rex Stout's Archie Goodwin discovered. In George Chesbro's *Bone* the storyteller Zulu, who rescued Bone, used St. Thomas's corner as his pitch. Both tourists

and homeless people like Mary Kellogg sat on the church steps to listen to him. Once Zulu used his tall staff to beat up the members of the vicious Wolfpack gang, who tried to steal his begging bowl.

St. Thomas's is open daily, so it is easy to go inside and look at the imposing carved marble reredos over the high altar and the famous deep-blue stained glass windows. In its lady chapel there are also some tall candlesticks, which would work as the murder weapon in Byfield and Tedeschi's *Solemn High Murder*.

This church was the model for Isabelle Holland's fictional St. Anselm's Church. Its basic ambiance is right: a very wealthy church with a social outreach program, where someone like the Reverend Claire Aldington could have served as both counselor and clergy. The only difficulty is that Holland put St. Anselm's on the Upper East Side. (See Walk 8.)

In one Holland mystery, *A Fatal Advent*, the Reverend Claire, now married to Wall Street lawyer/vestryman Brent Cunningham, was asked to play hostess to the Rector's former professor, the British Alec Maitland, the former Dean of St. Paul's Cathedral, London. Maitland got mixed up with a nasty Choir School conspiracy and was murdered by being pushed down the stairs. (St. Anselm's Choir School was in a building next to the church.) In Holland's *A Lover Scorned*, the murderer was anti all women priests and systematically eliminated them; while in *Flight of the Archangel*, St. Anselm's white elephant of a Hudson River mansion was the scene of the crime.

Investigate as much as you like, then leave St. Thomas's to walk up Fifth Avenue to 54th Street, where the stately University Club sits on the corner. This club makes a good substitute for the various private men's clubs where well-connected mystery characters, like Elizabeth Daly's Henry Gamadge, went for lunch with elderly publishers in mysteries like *The Book of the Lion*.

Across Fifth Avenue is the familiar red door of Elizabeth Arden's beauty salon. In Maron's *Past Imperfect*, NYPD Lieutenant Sigrid Harald and her widowed mom Anne were given "the works" at "Imagine You" as a birthday present. (Harald would not go if they admitted their relationship.) In Trella Crespi's *The*

Trouble with a Small Raise, Art Director Bertrand Monroe took Simona Griffo to lunch with his formidable mother, who came to town every Thursday to be "done" at Elizabeth Arden's and then met her son at the Colony Club. (See Walk 8.) The Arden building is about the right place, too, for the imaginary 1 E. 54th Street, where Liz Wareham worked for a public relations firm called the Gentle Group on the eighteenth floor in Carol Brennan's *Headhunt*.

Cross Fifth Avenue at 54th Street. This block, from Fifth Avenue to Madison Avenue, is the block where Ellery Queen set his *Greek Coffin Mystery*, right on top of Gucci's and the St. Regis Hotel. In the mystery the block had a tradition—a mellowed church and a row of brownstone mansions, which all opened into a common garden and the churchyard/cemetery. The family of blind art dealer Georg Khalkis, who owned a gallery around the corner on Park Avenue, had been parishioners for 200 years and had their own burial vault in the churchyard. (There is no such churchyard in Midtown Manhattan, but there are several elsewhere. See Walks 1, 2, and 11.)

When Khalkis was buried in his family vault, no one could find his new will, so NYPD Inspector Richard Queen (and his son Ellery) were called in. Khalkis's body was then exhumed and another murdered man's body was found buried with him in the coffin. The murders turned out to be related to a Leonardo Da Vinci painting stolen from London's Victoria and Albert Museum. Khalkis's friends, relatives, and employees, including an elusive millionaire, James J. Knox, were all involved in the crime.

Since the St. Regis Hotel and Gucci's occupy this block, the place most like the one Ellery Queen described is the Villard Houses, a block east on Madison Avenue at 51st Street behind St. Patrick's Cathedral, where the walk will take you shortly.

Meanwhile, turn right to walk up Fifth Avenue to 55th Street and the St. Regis Hotel, a beautiful 1904 Beaux-Arts building, which was recently renovated to a high gloss. Inside it is not only luxurious, but comfortable. There are actually places to sit down in the lobby where you can look out at the street, have tea or a drink, or wait for someone. There are also powder rooms in the basement, with attendants who do not sneer at ordinary tourists.

In Emma Lathen's *Death Shall Overcome*, the New York Stock Exchange took a suite there "for the duration" of the activities associated with the March on Wall Street. Their "Three Wise Men," Sloan banker John Putnam Thatcher, lawyer Stanton Carruthers, and broker Hugh Waymark met there with the demonstration leaders for CASH: black novelist Richard Simpson; Dr. Mathew Ford, a well-known social scientist; and Mrs. Mary Crane, who was active in hostilities against the Board of Education and told them with a steely smile, "Oh, I'm really just a wife and mother. . . ."

In Richard Lockridge's *Murder for Art's Sake*, nude model Rachel Farmer went dancing at the St. Regis the night painter Shackleton Jones (Shack) was murdered in his Greenwich Village loft studio. In Mary Higgins Clark's *While My Pretty One Sleeps*, Neeve Kearny went to a party given by *Women's Wear Daily* at the St. Regis and tried to find out where her good client, nosy free-lance writer Ethel Lambston, had disappeared. No one knew, but Neeve got to meet Jack Campbell, the new head at Givvons and Marks, a publishing house.

In Shannon O'Cork's *The Murder of Muriel Lake*, the world-famous Hepplewhite Hotel was located on the site of the St. Regis. It was the site of the annual Writers of Mystery convention (aka Mystery Writers of America?), whose highest award was not the Edgar or CWA's Golden Dagger but the Black Cape. Grand Maven mystery writer Muriel Lake had organized the occasion, but the main event was the murder of Lake herself. A murder in his beloved hotel totally upset the prissy banquet manager Eduardo Vinici, although the murder was solved by novice mystery writer Cecila Burnett, marking her for future fame and fortune. (A nice locked room puzzle featuring "one of us," but MWA in recent years has held its Edgar Awards [convention] at the Sheraton Centre on Seventh Avenue; see Walk 5.)

Across Fifth Avenue at 55th Street is the St. Regis's Beaux-Arts twin, once known as the Gotham Hotel, now the Peninsula. Equally splendid in its redone glory, it is also about the right place for Ellery Queen's hotel in *The Chinese Orange Mystery*, in which the Kirk family lived in a suite of rooms. In the mystery, Donald Kirk walked from the Fifth Avenue hotel to Central Park. He returned to find Ellery Queen in the lobby of the hotel. Kirk had asked Queen to dinner, but when a body dressed backwards was found in his suite, he tried to withdraw the invitation.

Across 55th Street on the west side of Fifth Avenue is the Fifth Avenue Presbyterian Church. It, too, is a handsome Gothic edifice, but it does not have any cemetery for pew holders' families. It did, however, serve as a kind of shelter for the homeless in Chesbro's *Bone*.

Continue up Fifth Avenue to 56th Street to Trump Tower. Donald Trump—bankrupt or not—is the kind of latter-day New York jet setter cum socialite that socially conscious 1930s mystery writers like Hammett disapproved of. Trump Tower is a very glitzy, glittery skyscraper, with dark glass and sixty-eight floors. The six-story atrium lobby is done in salmon-colored marble and shining brass, with escalators and a waterfall (a startling contrast to the St. Regis). The upper floors are princely condominiums (Prince Charles owns one, although he gives no-no lectures about this style of architecture in London).

In Annette Meyers's *The Big Killing*, headhunter Wetzon, wearing her pink Reeboks, left her office and took the scenic route home, up Fifth Avenue to Central Park South. She was followed from 49th Street by a leggy female in a Robin Hood SoHo-style costume. Wetzon eyed Saks's short metallic dresses skeptically, marched into I. Miller's at 57th and Fifth for a sale on Ferragamo shoes, and bought three pairs. Then, crossing 57th Street toward the Plaza Hotel, Wetzon heard a woman with a Bergdorf shopping bag ask her friend if she wanted "to go Trumping."

In Clark's *While My Pretty One Sleeps*, designer Anthony della Salva, Neeve's "Uncle Sal," lived in Trump Parc on Central Park South (aka Trump Tower combined with the Plaza Hotel). Della Salva watched the funeral of mobster Nicky Sepetti, who had died of a heart attack soon after his release from prison, there on TV. Neeve Kearny, leaving the St. Regis, began to walk north toward Central Park but got a cab, which stopped hit man Danny Adler from killing her as she walked home through Central Park. In Trella Crespi's *The Trouble with a Small Raise*, Simona Griffo's ad agency's cosmetics client Jean Janick had an apartment in Trump Tower.

In George Chesbro's *The Second Horseman Out of Eden*, Nuvironment was in a building whose description sounds like Trump Tower: a tall tower of pink marble and steel with a three-story, smoked-glass, tree-filled atrium and shops. Nuvironment was the organization funding the sect called "Apocalypse," which was run by a crazy (Jim Jones-like) minister. Apocalypse had smuggled rain forest soil into the country to build a new Eden that followers would escape to after they set off bombs in all the big cities. (Biosphere II, in Arizona, bears an eerie resemblance to the Apocalypse project, although Biosphere II consists of scientists, not millennialists.)

On the ninth floor in an office looking out toward Central Park was the triplex penthouse and private quarters of weird millionaire Henry Blaisdel (half Howard Hughes, half Donald Trump). Blaisdel turned out to be dead, but, stuffed as a mummy, he was left in a glass case on a throne in his penthouse. Searching for a child molester, Garth Frederickson broke in to the building, but was captured. When brother Mongo came to rescue him he found the model for the Eden project, but was captured before they could escape. The brothers were rescued by the NYPD, who got them safely to JFK Airport. From there British Concorde pilots flew them out—despite one of the worst snowstorms in NYC history—to find Eden.

At the northeast corner of Fifth Avenue and 57th Street is Tiffany & Co., another old New York landmark, known not only for fine jewelry but for stained glass and Tiffany lamps. In Steve Allen's *Murder in Manhattan*, Jayne Meadows persuaded Steve to be "terribly chivalrous" and go inside to buy her some earrings.

On Christmas Eve in Chesbro's *The Second Horseman Out of Eden*, the Frederickson brothers walked along Fifth Avenue, hearing Christmas carols playing and seeing Salvation Army bands (shades of Damon Runyon's *Guys and Dolls*). In Don Winslow's *A*

Cool Breeze on the Underground, apprentice P.I. Neil Carey was taught to shadow by his mentor Graham, who led him along Fifth Avenue where every store window offered a reflection.

You have now walked about a mile and a half, not counting stops to shop, eat, or explore. Now leave Fifth Avenue to go south along Madison and Park Avenues back to 36th Street, which will be another mile and a half walk.

Turn right and walk along 57th Street, past what was once Bonwit Teller, at 4–10 E. 57th Street. In Emma Lathen's *Banking on Death*, Jane Schneider came from Massachusetts to see young Sloan Guarantee Trust officer Ken Nichols. Before she met him at the Algonquin Hotel, she "shopped up a storm" at Bonwit Teller. The store is now another Trump venture, the Galleries Lafayette, which opened at the end of 1991 with a gala benefit for the American Ballet. The ballet was danced in the new AT&T building at Madison between 55th and 56th Streets.

Go down Madison Avenue past the AT&T building to 54th Street. To your left, on the north side of the street, was one of "the" New York restaurants, Le Cygne (now closed), which was where Mary Higgins Clark's heroines, like Darcy Scott, got taken to dine in *Loves Music, Loves to Dance*. On these side streets you can also glimpse older buildings where many publishers, advertisers, and public relations firms have offices.

Across 54th Street between Madison and Park Avenues is a 1920s building with a tiny chimneylike tower, standing between two much taller buildings. This is the Elysée Hotel, still a first-class establishment, with its famous Monkey Bar, where you can eat lunch, or have a drink, or order dinner. In S. S. Van Dine's *The Benson Murder Case*, Philo Vance and his faithful Watson, Van Dine, lunched at the hotel, then went to Knoedler's Art Gallery to see an exhibition of French Pointillists. (See Walk 8.)

Continue along Madison Avenue to 51st Street. Cross 51st Street to the Parish House of St. Patrick's Cathedral. Its vast plant—Parish House, Rectory, Chancery, and parochial school—occupies an entire block. In Clark's *While My Pretty One Sleeps*, a childhood friend of Myles Kearny, Bishop Devin

Stanton, was having a cocktail with the cardinal at St. Patrick's Rectory when the TV news reported a murderer had confessed to ordering a hit on Myles's daughter, Neeve. In Emma Lathen's *Ashes to Ashes*, Monsignor Miles was stuck with the touchy issue of letting a developer buy a parochial school building so that he could tear it down and build a high-rise. At the Rectory the Monsignor was told there was talk of a suit against the Archdiocese (this meant *war*). Because the Sloan Guarantee Trust was making the loan to the developer, John Putnam Thatcher found himself going to meetings at St. Patrick's. During the development row there were two bomb scares that forced personnel to evacuate the Chancery and jammed all Midtown traffic between 42nd Street and Central Park.

Recross Madison Avenue to the famous group of brownstones called the Villard Houses, located between 51st and 50th Streets. An Italian Renaissance-style palazzo, designed in 1884 by McKim, Mead and White for Henry Villard, a newspaper and railroad tycoon, they used to house the publishing firm of Random House. But now they merely form the facade of the gigantic Helmsley hotel that rears up behind them. You can go inside the Madison Avenue courtyard to see some of the old buildings. The lobby has a huge chandelier and two curving staircases with a red marble fireplace. To your left is the Gold Room, which murdered Stanford White designed like the Music Room of a Renaissance palace, where tea is served. The old walnut-paneled Dining Room, now a bar, opens off the Gold Room and leads to a lobby of one of the original houses with a mosaic floor and colonnaded staircase. Beyond it is the Madison Room, with its green-marble pillars and gilt decor.

Since the Villard Houses are only a block west and about two blocks south of the site Ellery Queen gave for the Khalkis's block in *The Greek Coffin Mystery*, it seems obvious where his description of the block came from. In addition, an aerial view over the spires of St. Patrick's Cathedral shows the Villard Houses in such a way that the block looks like the Queen block.

After exploring the Villard Houses walk east along 51st Street to Park Avenue. On the far side of Park Avenue, with its center parkway where Grand Central Railroad lines ran, is the

Byzantine Episcopal St. Bartholomew's Church, built in 1910. For many years the church has had a row with NYC over the fact that it wanted to sell its air rights to a high-rise developer, so the church could have money for its outreach programs. This is similar to the problem Isabelle Holland's St. Anselm's experienced in *A Death at St. Anselm's*. (See also Walk 8.)

Continue walking down Park Avenue, past St. Bartholomew's to 50th Street. The entire block between 50th and 49th Streets, Madison to Park Avenue, is occupied by the most recent (1931) incarnation of the venerable Waldorf-Astoria Hotel. Its past is so famous that a biography of the hotel was published in 1990 to celebrate its 60th birthday (which it shares with the Empire State Building and King Kong).

The Waldorf began farther south, at 34th Street and Fifth Avenue, as the Astor Hotel. It then became the Waldorf-Astoria, in a French château-like building, much like the Plaza. In 1929 that building was torn down to make room for the Empire State Building and the present Art Deco building was put up on Park Avenue.

With two towers, forty-two stories, and 1,850 rooms, it was possible for Golda Meir and Yasir Arafat to stay at the Waldorf at the same time (without seeing each other). It also has both permanent suites and transient rooms for its VIP guests, like the late duke of Windsor. In the main lobby is an eight-sided bronze clock, made in 1893 for the original hotel by the Goldsmith's Company in London, which has since replaced the lost Biltmore clock as a Midtown rendezvous.

The Waldorf's mysterious connections go back to its beginnings. Mystery writer Leslie Charteris (Leslie Charles Bowyer Yin), son of an English woman and a Chinese doctor, was born in Singapore in 1907, went to English schools, studied art in Paris, and entered Cambridge, but quit to be a writer. In 1928 he took the legal name of Charteris from the notorious eighteenth-century Colonel, Francis Charteris, who was a gambler, duelist, and founder of the Hellfire Club.

In Charteris's *The Saint in New York*, he introduced Simon Templar, aka the Saint. Bright, cultured, and very athletic, the Saint was hired by a NYC millionaire William K. Valcross for one million dollars to clean up Manhattan. Millionaire Valcross lived in the (new) Waldorf-Astoria, where he talked to Templar about "the city, his home . . . [which] others see as a place to be looted."

The Saint looked out the Waldorf windows and saw "the wonder island of the West . . . expanded upwards . . . a modern Baghdad . . . whose towers . . . looked like . . . solid gold to hungry eyes . . . where civilization and savagery . . . climbed . . . on each other's shoulders." The Saint cleaned up the city in forty-eight hours, with help from a smart aleck immigrant cabby and a classy call girl.

In Mary Roberts Rinehart's *The Swimming Pool*, the youngest Maynard sister, Lois, who wrote mysteries, had lunch at the Waldorf with her rich ex-brother-in-law, Ridgley Chandler. Lois had come to NYC to get her sister Judith clothes for a sea voyage. Chandler seemed nervous despite two martinis, and would not talk business until his demitasse was in front of him.

In fact and fiction most NYC balls and civic extravaganzas are held at the Waldorf. In Dorothy B. Hughes's 1942 thriller, *The Fallen Sparrow*, which she dedicated "to Eric Ambler, Second Lieutenant in the Royal Artillery, because he has no book this year," Kit McKittrick, who had just returned from the Spanish Civil War, went to a Refugee Benefit at the Waldorf-Astoria the first night he came home.

According to the Wolfe Pack, the Waldorf-Astoria is also the fictional Churchill Hotel, where Archie Goodwin often went dancing with Lily Rowan or came on Nero Wolfe's business. In *Too Many Women*, when Archie was romancing 500 female employees of a Wall Street firm, he took Gwynne Ferris to the Silver Room at the Churchill to check out the food and music.

In *The Golden Spiders*, rich young widow Laura Fromm, who came to see Wolfe after he put an ad in the paper about some Golden Spider earrings, had cocktails there with her lawyer Dennis Horan and later with Angela Wright, Executive Secretary of the Displaced Persons agency, ASSIDIP. In Stout's *Too Many Clients*, Archie Goodwin got a newspaper clipping from Lon Cohen showing the murdered Thomas Yeager at the Waldorf banquet of the National Plastics Association.

In Emma Lathen's *Death Shall Overcome*, the Stock Exchange's "Three Wise Men" drew lots for who went to what function (that might affect the Stock Exchange's image). Sloan Guarantee Trust's John Putnam Thatcher drew the ADA banquet at the Waldorf, where he realized his vision of politically progressive women was outmoded. He observed that these women were smartly dressed and looked like prosperous reactionaries, only a shade more intense.

In Clark's *While My Pretty One Sleeps*, the murdered journalist Ethel Lambston had a framed photo of herself at the Waldorf with the Mayor. Shannon O'Cork's *The Murder of Muriel Lake*, a story about the annual Writers of Mystery Convention (aka MWA), may have taken place at the Waldorf. Her fictional Hepplewhite Hotel was father north at 55th and Fifth Avenue, but, although it catered to the rich and famous, it had a very "family" atmosphere, kept alive by Eduardo Vinici, its banquet manager, who also helped to solve the crime.

In Margaret Maron's *Death in Blue Folders*, the Waldorf-Astoria Hotel was "still one of city's most prestigious hotels." A room was reserved there for the odd sister of the drug addict who had kidnapped millionaire Justin Trent's grandson, Jamie Logan. Murdered lawyer Clayton Gladwell had found the boy in California and the sister was bringing him to NYC—for a suitable reward.

In Zev Chaffets's *Inherit the Mob*, William (Velvel) Gordon, journalist nephew of dead Mobster Max Grossman, held a dinner party in a wood-paneled private dining room at the Waldorf. His guests were the old Jewish mobsters who once worked for Uncle Max and came back from Florida to save him. Even Gordon's dad, who was shot in Grand Central Station, came, with his buxom nurse. At the party, Gordon's former editor admitted that he had taken over as the Mob's media consultant.

Stop to look over the Waldorf-Astoria or get something to eat there. Then go out the Park Avenue entrance and turn right (south). The original Ritz Hotel was located between 47th and 46th Streets on Madison Avenue. (See also Walk 9.) Walk three blocks to 46th Street and the 1963 Pan Am Building, built on top of Grand Central Station and behind the rococo 1929 Helmsley Building.

In Martin Meyers's *Hardy: Hung Up to Die*, his P.I. Hardy had a bum knee, for which his doctor had recommended therapy. Following the doctor's directions to the Pan Am Building, where therapist Natasha Tamarova's dance studio was, Hardy mistakenly went down the escalators to Grand Central Station, which was filled with people coming and going. Eventually, however, he found the right elevator and rode up to the ninth-floor dance studio where he promptly became involved in a murder.

One of NYC's Beaux-Arts icons, Grand Central Station was "saved" as a landmark in the 1970s, a decade after its fellow terminal, the grand (old) Pennsylvania Railroad Station, was torn down. Once a busy intersection for travelers, Grand Central is now a commuter terminal, handy passageway, and subway junction. The huge echoing concourse is virtually empty most of the time, especially since the homeless have been driven away, and the whole place seems to be a ghostly shadow of its former self, despite the great gold clock and vaulted ceiling filled with twinkling stars.

Perhaps detective fans can rescue it from oblivion as they come to admire one of the most frequently mentioned meeting spots/stakeouts in classic NYC mystery stories. But don't be startled if you are almost alone there, except for a gaggle of tourists who assemble at noon on Wednesdays for a weekly tour.

To get inside the station from Park Avenue, bear right to tiny Vanderbilt Avenue. Then turn left and go through the main doors by the taxi stand, where a posted sign announces that the station is closed from 1:30 to 5:30 A.M.

In George Chesbro's *Bone*, a number of homeless hung about the station. Bone himself went there, seeking a clue as to his identity, but he panicked at the feeling of being trapped in the taxi tunnel. Later, after he was attacked by Lobo and his gang, Bone was rescued by the tall, black storyteller, Zulu, who had a living place hidden away on the lower level of the terminal. (There are many levels below Grand Central and mystery characters make good use of them. Be careful how much you explore on your own, though.)

Having gone through the main doors you are on the upper

level of the Grand Concourse, standing above the central ticket office and the huge four-faced clock. To reach the main concourse, where long distance trains used to arrive and depart, go down the stairs to the main level. There are no longer benches or lockers there.

In Elliott Roosevelt's *Hyde Park Murder*, young Bob Hannah took a cab to Grand Central Station with an old friend, Moira, a Wellesley College graduate and a call girl, and his murdered father's senior partner, Arthur Lindemann. They then headed by train for Washington, D.C., seeking help from First Lady Eleanor Roosevelt.

In Dorothy B. Hughes's *The Fallen Sparrow*, Kit McKittrick arrived from the West via Grand Central Station, determined to avenge the murder of his childhood buddy. As the train pulled into the station, a beautiful girl brushed by him, leaving a clue in his coat pocket.

In Elizabeth Daly's *The Book of the Crime*, crippled war hero Gray Austen tried to make a getaway from Grand Central Station but was stopped by the NYPD, who had been alerted to Austen's movements by Henry Gamadge. Gray's wife had gone to the Gamadges for help after he threatened her. They hid her by pretending she was their baby nurse.

In Emma Lathen's *Death Shall Overcome*, Ed Parry, a black candidate for a seat on the NY Stock Exchange, came in from his home in suburban Westchester to be met by a KKK-type group tossing rotten eggs. The NYPD quickly broke up the attack, but it did not help the Stock Exchange's image, which John Putnam Thatcher was trying to preserve.

In Ellery Queen's *The Chinese Orange Mystery*, the Queens, father and son, set a trap to catch whoever picked up a suitcase belonging to the murder victim at Grand Central. Inspector Queen's trained crew: Velie, Johnson, Ritter, Piggot, all hid around the Grand Concourse to capture the person who claimed the ratty old canvas bag. But two and one-half hours later no one had showed up.

In Jack Early's *Donato and Daughter*, a serial murderer kept disguises in a locker at Grand Central Station. When he was on the run he went there. The cops were waiting for him, but he got away and took off, heading for the South Street Seaport. (See Walk 1.)

In Frances and Richard Lockridge's *Murder Comes First*, Pam and Jerry North came here to meet Pam's three aunts, who were stopping off en route from Cleveland for their annual trip to Florida. Their trip was delayed, however, when their old friend Grace Logan was poisoned while they were all having tea together. Later Pam's timid Aunt Lucy, after her investigations at the New York Public Library, lunched at the station's Commodore Grill (long gone) and took the train to Long Island to meet the murderer.

Turn right and walk under an archway to the stairs to the lower level where you can catch subway and suburban trains. Down there go left through the gates where some suburban trains still come and go. Look around and try to decide if it would be possible for someone like "Jerry the Canary" to sleep on the pipes above the trains. It seems neither very safe nor very hidden—and extremely uncomfortable—but he did in Margaret Maron's *Past Imperfect*. It was at Grand Central Station that the NYPD first caught "Jerry the Canary" doing his bird imitations, but they let him go.

Down on the lower level are plenty of locked doors to which a bag lady, station employee, Zulu the storyteller, or a restaurant worker might get a key—and use it with impunity. No one questioned me as I snooped about.

In Clark's *A Stranger Is Watching*, Grand Central Station itself was the scene of the crime/kidnapping. Foxy, a serial killer, kidnapped the son of *Events* editor Steve Peterson. Foxy meant to get a huge ransom for the boy, so he could "start over" and make everyone in the world notice him. Foxy had explored the station and discovered a basement room under the tracks, where he dumped the boy and journalist Sharon Martin. But a retired school teacher named Lally, who came to NYC from Nebraska, had discovered and used the room Foxy had for his den and rescued the victims. Since Lally had joined the crowd of celebrities like Jackie Onassis, who demonstrated to make Grand Central Station a landmark, the authorities put up a sign in her memory in the station.

Go to your right and walk across the lower concourse. In the connecting and sloping passageways toward 42nd Street are fast food shops, shoe repair stands, flower stalls, and the usual flotsam and jetsam you find in any station, as well as a place to check luggage. It is not easy to find the restrooms, however; the place to ask is the Oyster Bar, and it helps to have a native guide.

The remaining jewel in Grand Central's crown is also here on the lower level: the subterranean Oyster Bar, with its red-checked tablecloths and marvelous clam chowder, one of the better and cheaper items on its good but expensive menu. There is also a take-out bar for a faster meal.

In Byfield and Tedeschi's *Solemn High Murder*, the Reverend Simon Bede, official representative of the Archbishop of Canterbury, met Jeremy Baxter, head of the Episcopal Church Executive Council for lunch at the Oyster Bar. When he tasted his oyster stew, Bede told Baxter that there had to be a God.

In Zev Chaffets's *Inherit the Mob*, Al Grossman, the father of prize-winning journalist William (Velvel) Gordon and brother of dead Mobster Uncle Max, went to the Oyster Bar to eat his way through a bucket of steamers, but he got shot outside the restaurant near the escalator.

After looking around for suspects or the police, take the 42nd Street exit and walk out of Grand Central. Then turn right and walk along 42nd Street to Madison Avenue. Cross 42nd Street and walk south on Madison Avenue to 41st Street.

Madison Avenue is known as publishers/advertising row, although many firms are located elsewhere in Manhattan. In Lisa Bennett's *Madison Avenue Murder*, the office of the ad agency where Peg Goodenough became art director (after her boss was murdered) was located somewhere on Madison Avenue. As a result, Peg, the large daughter of world-famous abstract painter Theo Goodenough, became involved with the NYPD's investigating detective, Dan (for Dante) Cursio.

In Clark's *While My Pretty One Sleeps*, the publishing house of Givvons and Marks was at 41st Street and Park Avenue, one block to your left. New publisher Jack Campbell had talked to the soon-to-be-murdered Ethel Lambston about a half-million dollar book deal, an exposé on the garment industry, which led to her murder.

Walk down Madison Avenue to 38th Street and go left towards Park Avenue. You are now in a noticeably hilly neighborhood called Murray Hill. Along the south side of the street are a number of well-cared-for brownstones. Philo Vance's apartment was located inside one on East 38th Street between Park and Madison Avenues, in S. S. Van Dine's *The Benson Murder Case*.

Vance's apartment occupied the two top floors of a beautifully remodeled old mansion. Its spacious rooms with lofty ceilings were filled with rare specimens of oriental and occidental art, ancient and modern, from Michelangelo to Picasso. S. S. Van Dine had been breakfasting there so that Vance could tell him which Cezannes to buy. Vance was in a surah silk dressing gown and slippers, eating strawberries and eggs Benedict. When D.A. Francis Xavier Markham came to get Van Dine's help, the three caught a cab up Madison Avenue to the Benson mansion, where a murder had taken place.

Choose the best brownstone for Vance, then return to Madison Avenue. Walk south on Madison Avenue to 36th Street where you will find the home of banker J. P. Morgan, a lovely Italianate brownstone with a garden, connected to the Beaux-Arts Pierpont Morgan Library, built by his son to house the family's growing collection. The library has a handsome rotunda, and, nearby, is Morgan's private study, the West Room, a rich and elaborately Gothic Victorian chamber, with a gilded ceiling and walls hung with red silk. The brownstone next door has since been added to the property. It has a charming hallway with a museum bookstore.

The Morgan collection contains many wonderful items and sponsors many marvelous exhibitions. In Maron's *Death in Blue Folders*, after hearing from his lawyer that his kidnapped grandson, Jamie, would soon arrive, millionaire Justin Trent walked to the J. Pierpont Morgan Library to see a special exhibit on the artist Mabuse. In E. L. Doctorow's *Ragtime*, a kind of "faction" set in NYC at the beginning of the twentieth century, Henry Ford came to lunch with J. P. Morgan at his home. After lunch the two men went to the West Room and talked about reincarnation and mysticism.

Leave the Morgan Library and walk one more block south on Madison Avenue to 35th Street. Then turn and walk back to Fifth Avenue. At the corner of 35th Street and Fifth Avenue you are at the site of the former B. Altman & Co. department store, which closed in the late 1980s. It may have been the best model for Ellery Queen's French's Department Store in *The French Powder Mystery*, although its founder had no children. Completed in 1906, it was the first of the great department stores built in this exclusive residential area. To make it fit in McKim, Mead and White deliberately made it look like an Italian palazzo. In its day B. Altman, like Lord & Taylor, had fabulous Christmas windows with animated figures, and its departments stocked goods of every kind. Though the building still stands, it is no longer a place you can either shop or snoop. Therefore it is time to end this walk by returning to Fifth Avenue across from the Empire State Building where you began.

7

MIDTOWN EAST WALK

BACKGROUND

The eastern half of Manhattan's Midtown between Lexington Avenue and the East River represents a richer and cleaner side of town, which has come back up in the world, especially since the elevated trains were taken down. Not only is it the home of NYC's 1920s and 1930s Art Deco designer skyscrapers and a showcase for contemporary buildings from Citicorp Centre to the United Nations, but it also combines these architectural wonders with streets lined with lovely old brownstones, small, elegant hotels, and classy restaurants. These make it a most attractive place to walk.

Near the East River, where the UN dominates, is the area still known as Turtle Bay. Its name came either from the turtles that inhabited the shoreline in colonial times or from a Dutch word *Deutal*, or "bent blade." Historically, like Chelsea on the west, the Turtle Bay area was made up of large estates; then in the mid-nineteenth century it became more of a rural suburb, where important editors like Horace Greeley of the influential *New York Tribune*, writer/critic Margaret Fuller, and the peripatetic Edgar Allan Poe came for the healthy sea breezes. Poe wrote bitterly about the inevitable development of this scenic part of Manhattan; he also divided humanity into three classes: men, women, and Margaret Fuller.

By the 1860s streets of brownstones had replaced the farms and mansions as the area developed from west to east with the expansion of the businesses and offices on Fifth, Madison, and Park Avenues. But the building of the Second and Third Street els in the 1880s and the development of waterfront industry caused the area to decay. By the close of the century it was mostly gangland turf, occupied by ethnic immigrants and filled with breweries and slaughterhouses.

In the early part of the twentieth century, artists, actors, and writers discovered the East Side had attractive but inexpensive places to live near their work; by the 1920s the neighborhood was on the way up again. Places like Tudor City, a group of high-rise mock Gothic buildings with lovely views, were built, and Turtle Bay Gardens, twenty brownstones back-to-back on 48th and 49th Streets, was rehabbed. Many of the Algonquin wits and other prospering writers like Padraic Colum, Dorothy Thompson, and John P. Marquand came to live here, as did people in related trades like Scribners' editor Maxwell Perkins, who launched so many writers—including Thomas Wolfe, who often visited here.

Finally, in the early 1950s building the UN headquarters created a massive face-lift for the East River and completed the neighborhood's rebirth. The UN buildings now occupy the riverfront where Turtle Bay had been, on land partly purchased by John D. Rockefeller, Jr., and partly donated by the city. Begun in 1947, they were built on landfill shipped from London buildings destroyed in the Blitz. Its distinguished international architectural board was led by American Wallace K. Harrison, who had designed Rockefeller Center, and included other architects such as France's LeCorbusier.

North of the UN between Second Avenue and the river people like the Beekmans had been careful about the development of their property, and Beekman Place and Sutton Place continued to be residential enclaves of quiet elegance. In the 1950s despite the creation of the raised FDR Highway along the shoreline (it disappears below street level at the UN and again at Sutton Place), the charm of this area was enhanced when the els were torn down. This major development also led to the building of more contemporary towers and open-air plazas along Park and Lexington Avenues to the west, like the Seagram's Building, Lever House, and Citicorp Centre.

LENGTH OF WALK: About 3 miles

It is 1.5 miles from Grand Central Station to Beekman Place and 1.5 miles from Beekman Place to the Plaza Hotel. See map on page 177 for the boundaries of this walk and page 316 for a list of books and detectives mentioned.

PLACES OF INTEREST

Turtle Bay Gardens Historic District, 48th and 49th Streets between Second and Third Avenues.

Beekman Place, 50th to 52nd Streets, First Avenue to the East River.

Sutton Place, 54th to 59th Streets, First Avenue to the East River.

Chrysler Building, 42nd Street and Lexington Avenue. Opened in 1930. Art Deco design by William Vam Alen (tallest building in world until Empire State Building in 1934).

Daily News Building, 220 E. 42nd Street. Opened in 1930. Designed by Howells & Hood. Site of the film *Superman.*

Ford Foundation, 42nd Street and Second Avenue. 1967 building with elaborate multistory atrium.

Episcopal Church Headquarters, 815 Second Avenue. Bookstore and chapel on ground floor.

Tudor City, 40th to 43rd Streets, between Second and First Avenues. 1925–28 apartment complex.

United Nations Plaza, visitors entrance, First Avenue at 47th Street. Open daily, 9:00 A.M. to 5:00 P.M. Guided tours: daily, in twenty languages. On your own visit the General Assembly Building lobby as well as its basement book/gift shop and coffee shop. Free. Tickets for UN sessions available on first-come, first-served basis. Call 963-7539 for information.

Alexander's Department Store, Lexington Avenue between 58th and 59th Streets. Midprice merchandise, largely self-service.

Bloomingdale's, Lexington Avenue, between 59th and 60th Streets. Family store begun in 1872. NYC's most crowded and popular department store with famous sales. Trendsetting styles, expensive and upscale.

The Plaza Hotel, Fifth Avenue and 59th Street. One of NYC's two legendary hotels (the other is the Waldorf-Astoria). 1905 French chateau with national landmark status. Many movies shot here. Kay Thompson's "Eloise" lived here. Now owned by Donald Trump. A must-place to see or eat, but no lobby seating.

PLACES TO EAT

This part of New York has every kind of restaurant. The walk will not mention every restaurant you pass unless it appears in a mystery. It will list some not on the walk but nearby and easily found.

Alexander's Department Store, Lexington between 58th and 59th Streets. Café Alex. Counter serving hamburgers, etc. Inexpensive.

Bloomingdale's, Lexington between 59th and 60th Streets. Call 705-2100. Le Train Bleu (shades of Agatha Christie), Showtime Cafe, Forty Carrots, Espresso and Tasting Bars. Wide variety and price range.

UN Plaza, First Avenue at 47th Street. Call 963-7525. Coffee shop in Public Concourse. Open from 9:30 A.M. to 4:30 P.M. daily. Delegates Dining Room open to visitors on weekdays for lunch (good buffet and view).

P. J. Clarke's, 915 Third Avenue, at 55th Street. NYC institution for beer, hamburgers, chili, etc.

Neary's Pub (Restaurant), 358 E. 57th Street (at First Avenue). Irish bar/restaurant with long bar and a few tables. Lunch or dinner or drinks. Expensive.

Smith & Wollensky, 49th Street and Third Avenue. "The quintessential New York steak house. Bar, sidewalk café. Lunch and dinner, Mon.–Fri. Expensive. Call 753-1530.

Plaza Hotel, Fifth Avenue and 59th Street. Call 759-3000.

   Palm Court serves breakfast, brunch, lunch, afternoon tea à la Ritz Hotel, London. Reservations. Expensive.

Oak Bar offers very English (men's club) ambiance. (Old New
York vibes, caters to famous, rich, and powerful.) Call
759-3000.

Edwardian Room, a high-ceilinged, dark wainscoting, NYC
answer to Simpsons on the Strand. Continental. Open 7:00
A.M.–11 P.M. Sunday brunch. Reservations. Call 759-3000.

Trader Vic's, basement location. Entrance at Central Park
South. Hawaiian decor and bar food. Expensive. Call
759-3000.

——————— MIDTOWN EAST WALK ———————

Begin your walk at Park Avenue at the southeast corner of
Grand Central Station and 42nd Street near the Lexington Avenue subway station. Turn left to walk along the north side of
42nd Street. It is a very wide, major cross street with lots of traffic. Often called NYC's "Main Street," its hotels, restaurants,
and businesses run the gamut from luxury to sleazy. One block
east at Lexington Avenue across 42nd Street on the opposite
(southwestern) corner is the Chanin Building, a famous Art
Deco building, with bands of decorative terra cotta and bronze.

Cross Lexington Avenue to New Yorkers' own favorite skyscraper, the Chrysler Building. Its scalloped tower lit up at night
is visible all over Manhattan. Look inside at its famous African
red marble and inlaid wood lobby, now a Consolidated Edison
exhibit, but once *the* Chrysler automobile show room. Just two
blocks north, near Lexington and 44th Street in S. S. Van
Dine's *The Canary Murder Case*, there was a brownstone that
held the offices and home of murder suspect Dr. Lindquist.

Cross 42nd Street at Lexington Avenue and walk east to
Third Avenue. The last NYC automat, Horn and Hardart, with
coin slots and cheap food under glass, used to be on the southeast corner. As with other long-gone NYC traditions—Schrafft's
and Chock-Full o' Nuts—many a mystery character (and writer)
ate in these inexpensive places. Originally founded in Philadel-
phia before World War I, Horn and Hardart now holds the

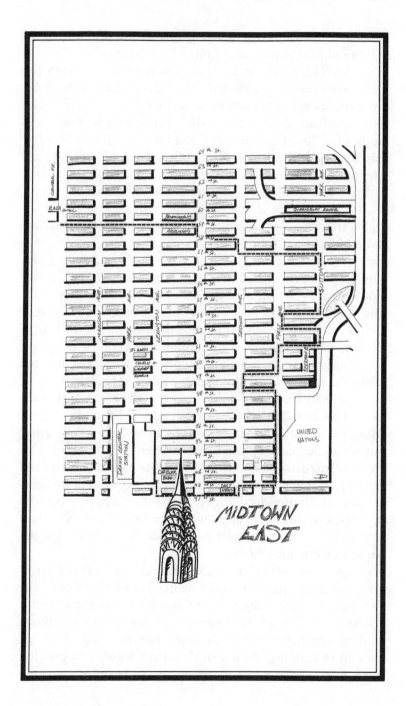

NYC franchise for Burger King, so one way to deal with automat nostalgia is to patronize Burger King instead.

Cross Third Avenue and keep going until you reach the Daily News Building, a modern-looking skyscraper with an Art Deco frieze over the doorway. In its lobby you will see the famous revolving globe of the world. This building is another example of 1930s "Gotham City" architecture, but—although it was designed by Raymond Hood, the same architect who built Chicago's Tribune Tower—it has no Gothic trimmings. Like Tribune Tower, however, it sports a lot of flagpoles.

The tabloid, the *Daily News*, was founded by Captain Joseph Patterson, first cousin of the Chicago *Tribune*'s Colonel Robert McCormick, both of them grandsons of Chicago newspaper owner and editor Joseph Medill, who helped make Abraham Lincoln president. It was McCormick who hired Chester Gould to draw the comic strip *Dick Tracy* in a studio atop Tribune Tower, but Dick Tracy's city is more NYC than Chicago. Gould was succeeded in the strip by mystery writer, Max Allan Collins, who wrote *Stolen Away* about his fictional P.I. Nate Heller and the Lindbergh kidnapping, which was also the basis of Agatha Christie's plot in *Murder on the Orient Express*.

The Daily News Building was used in the movie *Superman*, in which Clark Kent is a bashful reporter. (In Steve Allen's *Murder in Manhattan*, Steve was cast in a cameo role, playing Superman because he looks like Clark Kent. He had always secretly wanted to wear Superman's blue tights and the red cape.) In real life the *Daily News* was recently bought by flamboyant British press lord Robert Maxwell. Maxwell's mysterious death off his own yacht, which he brought to NYC and kept nearby at a private pier on the East River, has made the paper's future uncertain.

Nero Wolfe's fan club, the Wolfe Pack, thinks that *The Gazette*, where reporter Lon Cohen worked in a little office on the twentieth floor, two doors from the publisher, is a stand-in for the late New York *Herald-Tribune* (now only published abroad as the *International Herald Tribune*). But the *Daily News* has enough in common with Stout's *Gazette* for you to give it a once-over.

In Stout's *Too Many Clients*, Archie Goodwin consulted Cohen's file and found out it wasn't Thomas Yeager, the murdered love nest owner, who had hired him to do surveillance. It was the NYU professor and estranged husband of Dinah Hough, one of Yeager's many bimbos. Robert Goldsborough's later "add-on" Wolfe mystery, *Death on Deadline*, was the story of a British press lord (Ian MacLaren) who bought a New York newspaper. MacLaren, an unpleasant cross between Rupert Murdoch and Robert Maxwell, dealt in late-twentieth-century yellow journalism, an NYC tradition since the pre–Civil War days of the Bennett family and the *New York Herald*. As a result, when Goldsborough had Wolfe "ride" to the rescue of a free press, he was reacting more like Rex Stout than Wolfe himself.

In Dana Clarins's *The Woman Who Knew Too Much*, during a pre-Maxwell *New York Daily News* strike, Debbie Macadam, an actress friend of Celia Blandings, read in Liz Smith's syndicated column that she was only thirty-one, which meant she was growing younger. (Liz Smith left the *Daily News* when Maxwell bought the paper.) Later in that mystery, reporter Teddy Birney explained to Celia and P.I. Greco that the dead men they kept finding were CIA and FBI operatives.

In Mary Higgins Clark's *A Stranger Is Watching*, the *News Dispatch* Building was at E. 42nd St. and Second Avenue (on top of the *Daily News*). Sharon Martin was a columnist there who wrote a book opposing capital punishment. As a natural result she appeared on a TV talk show on capital punishment where she met Steve Peterson, a magazine editor whose wife had been murdered by a young man about to hang. In *Lullaby of Murder* by Dorothy Salisbury Davis, Julie Hayes, the young wife of *New York Times* foreign correspondent Jeff Hayes, worked as a legman for *The Daily's* gossip columnist Tony Alexander. *The Daily* was published in a building at this very address with a huge globe in the lobby. Tony Alexander was shot to death in the office on the fifteenth floor, and Julie was a suspect because Alexander had bawled her out about her story on a dance marathon palace near Harlem.

After looking the building over, go to Second Avenue and cross 42nd Street. Down the block on 42nd Street between Sec-

ond Avenue and First Avenue you can see the Ford Foundation
building, with its high atrium visible through its multistoried
glass walls. This famous not-for-profit organization, together
with the equally famous Rockefeller Foundation, are some real-
life models for the Vandering Trust in Velda Johnson's *The Face
in the Shadows*. Each is a family organization set up to distribute
money to worthy causes with family members serving on the
board the way Howard Vandering did.

Walk up Second Avenue to 43rd Street and cross. On the
northwest corner at 815 Second Avenue is a modern-looking
building. This is the national headquarters of the Protestant
Episcopal Church, known to its communicants as "815." You
can walk into the lobby, which has an information desk and pro-
vides access to a bookstore and chapel. In Byfield and Tedeschi's
Solemn High Murder, the widowed Ivy Wheeler worked at
"815" for its executive director, Jeremy Baxter. Ivy had to
work because her husband, Fred Wheeler, a cousin of the murdered rector of St. Jude the Martyr, had run through his share of
the family money. After the rector's murder on Ash Wednesday, the Reverend Simon Bede, a representative of the Archbishop of Canterbury, met with Baxter at "815" to discuss new
candidates for an Anglican Communion job Bede had offered
the dead rector.

Turn right and cross Second Avenue to walk along 43rd
Street to First Avenue. You are now in Turtle Bay, where Theodore Roosevelt lived (see also Walk 4). You go past Tudor City,
a 1920s pseudo-Tudor (beams and stained glass) development
of twelve towers, each facing an internal park. Tudor City
stretches north to 43th Street. South of Tudor City is the area
known as Kip's Bay, named after the Dutch farm that occupied
the area in the 1700s.

At First Avenue go down the steps to the lower level where
you are in Ralph Bunche Park, which in turn leads into United
Nations Plaza, stretching from 42nd to 48th Streets. Dispos-
sessed nationals sometimes choose to demonstrate here or at the
other end of the plaza in Dag Hammarskjöld Plaza, named for
the former UN secretary general who died in a mysterious plane
crash while on a peace mission.

The UN visitors entrance is at the northern end of the complex at 47th Street where there are TV cameras and protesters stationed almost permanently. They hang out near a large modernistic statue of St. George and the Dragon. St. George was one of G. K. Chesterton's heroes, and his role model for detective-knights errant in his famous essay, "In Defense of Detective Stories." In Clarins's *The Woman Who Knew Too Much*, en route to Zoe Bassinetti's Sutton Place apartment Celia and Greco drove north on First Avenue past the UN.

In Lillian O'Donnell's *The Children's Zoo*, suspect Alfonse Lamont, who often escorted the murdered wife of rich businessman Roland Guthrie, worked in a cubbyhole on the twenty-second floor of the UN building. A youthful, romantic-looking scion of a French family that dated back to Louis XVI, Lamont had diplomatic immunity. But he was terrified of what Papa in Paris would say when he learned that NYPD Sergeant Norah Mulcahaney questioned Lamont's alibi in the murder.

Inside the UN the very dramatic murder of a UN representative took place in Alfred Hitchcock's thriller movie, *North by Northwest*, starring Eva Marie Saint and Cary Grant. (This film ends with a chase across Mount Rushmore where NYC native son Theodore Roosevelt is preserved in stone.) Fewer murders and mysteries occur at the UN than do spy stories and thrillers. But it must be only a matter of time before Margaret Truman writes about "Murder at the UN."

One exception that may prove the rule is Barbara Paul's *Liars and Tyrants and People Who Turn Blue*. Shelby Kent had the unenviable talent of knowing when people were telling lies: to her they gave off a red aura. She was recruited by Sir John Dudley, head of the special UN intelligence agency. Sir John was hunting the leader of a secret organization that sold defective weapons to terrorists, making the work of the newly established UN Militia impossible.

Three very reputable UN ambassadors were accused of spearheading these strange attacks, so Shelby found herself in a UN hearing room, listening to the testimony of the accused. She pushed a button to indicate when the ambassadors were lying, but the UN ambassadors, having diplomatic immunity, were able to flee.

Several other mysteries have scenes that take place outside the UN. Technically, this is international territory where diplomats (and their families) can murder at will, so you will see plenty of New York's finest keeping watch, especially if a major VIP like the president or Khadafy is coming to address the General Assembly. You will not see homeless people here, although they reappear nearby at Sutton and Beekman Places.

In 1967 there was a huge Fifth Avenue parade in support of the war in Vietnam. Then Martin Luther King, Jr. led a counter-march from Central Park to the UN Plaza, where he spoke. In P. M. Carlson's *Audition for Murder*, Nick O'Connor and his first wife, Lynette, took time off from the *Hamlet* production they were working on at an upstate college to come join the countermarch with the other students.

In Emma Lathen's 1971 *Ashes to Ashes*, an absentee (aka slum) landlord who planned to build a high-rise on parochial school property lived in a fancy high-rise on UN Plaza. (Probably 866 United Nations Plaza at the north end of the complex.) The Sloan's John Putnam Thatcher found out that the developer had Sloan Guarantee Trust backing, so he became involved. A local community group and parochial school parents, plus a group of allies who included pro-choice demonstrators, arrived at UN Plaza by subway from Queens to picket the developer's apartment.

Their demonstration confused the NYPD because it contained neither Arabs nor Jews, whom police were under orders to keep separated at all costs! Much to the amusement of John Putnam Thatcher, everyone got buddy-buddy—sharing food, blankets, expertise—and closed ranks to protest lousy landlords. Inevitably the media arrived, which led to a CBS TV editorial: "We saw Jews and Arabs joining their Catholic brethren . . . for the common good." Thatcher was annoyed when this simplistic idea was picked up and commented on by everyone: do-gooders, prelates, and pols.

You can see the East River from the UN promenade, which was built on the rubble of war-bombed London and Bristol brought over in ships as ballast. But you will have to imagine the scene that took place when comedian Steve Allen, in *Murder in Manhattan*, went on the white yacht called "Easy Money." It was docked at the end of 37th Street to the south and belonged to a thirty-three-year-old Wall Street whiz kid who had "retired" to a penitentiary. The zany director Bernie Barnes decided to sail out "to sea" so the NYC skyline would be in the background of the film he was working on.

There was an explosion on board and the yacht sunk. Steve Allen, wearing his Superman costume, landed in the East River, where he was rescued by NYPD helicopter and made the front page. The East Side Heliport is at 34th Street and the East River, and the private yacht of press lord Robert Maxwell was anchored near there while he negotiated to buy the *Daily News*.

You can either tour the UN building and/or go there to get something to eat. Or if it's a particularly nice day, join a demonstration and get the demonstrators to share their sandwiches with you.

Then cross First Avenue at 47th Street to Dag Hammarskjöld Plaza. This street was vacated when the plaza was built. Go right along First Avenue to 48th Street and then turn left to walk along 48th Street west to Second Avenue. You will enjoy the ambiance: a well-dressed, international crowd of people hurrying back and forth to the UN against the backdrop of the East Side's brownstone neighborhood.

Turn right on Second Avenue and go north one block to 49th Street. The Turtle Bay Gardens Historic District, which was remodeled in 1920, is located here between Second and Third Avenues. The district has two rows of ten houses, back to back, which share a common garden. They have since been occupied by a wide variety of celebrities, from Mary Martin and Katharine Hepburn (still there), to Judge Learned Hand and Leopold Stokowski. In his famous essay, "Here Is New York," *New Yorker* writer E. B. White described an old willow tree in the common area. Edgar Allan Poe, however, would not consider one scrawny willow worth the stately oaks and elms lost by the relentless expansion of the city.

On the northeast corner of 49th and Second Avenue there

is a well-known steakhouse called Smith & Wollensky's, which may—along with handguns—have helped inspire Annette Meyers's name of Smith & Wetzon for her team of headhunters in *The Big Killing*. Turn to your right and walk back toward the East River, enjoying the brownstones. Many have brass plates that indicate that they house business or embassy offices. Choose a brownstone "off Second Ave. and 49th Street" where Annette Meyers's team can have their small office. It consisted of a one-bedroom apartment on the ground floor that opened into a garden, for which Xenia Smith bought white cast-iron Victorian furniture. An odd couple, Smith was dark and divorced, with a Ph.D. in psychology and a son Mark. Leslie Wetzon, a former dancer, was nicer, more naive, and blond.

In *The Big Killing*, en route to her fateful meeting with Barry Stark at the Four Seasons, Wetzon went past the Gardens, hoping for a glimpse of "Katie" (Hepburn) or "Steve" (Sondheim). She had been a fan of Sondheim's since she had danced in his revival of Leonard Bernstein's *West Side Story*.

Movie star Katharine Hepburn has lived in Turtle Bay Gardens since 1931. In a *New York Times* interview about Hepburn's autobiography, *Me*, the reporter wrote that entering her home was "like entering a Hepburn movie." The maid led the way up a narrow, red-carpeted staircase to a large, but cozy, sitting room hung with Hepburn paintings, where Kate, in khaki slacks, turtleneck, and Reeboks, waited in state. *Me*, however, does not exactly tell the story of a liberated female, 1980s style.

Besides Sondheim, Hepburn's neighbors have included writers such as Dorothy Thompson (she was once married to Sinclair Lewis) and E. B. White; Maxwell Perkins and other editors and publishers; and Ruth Gordon, Garson Kanin, and other actors.

One of these old houses could also double for Evelyn E. Smith's limestone-fronted building on a quiet, expensive street on NYC's quiet, expensive East Side. In Charlotte MacLeod's mystery collection *Christmas Stalkings*, Smith wrote about Miss Susan Melville, a world-class painter and native New Yorker with "old money." Miss Melville was an updated Edith Wharton, with touches of Amanda Cross's Kate Fansler. She had let the Melville Foundation for Anthropological Research (run by her aging lover Dr. Peter Franklin) use the first two floors, but kept a hideout for herself in the basement and all the keys to the building. Miss Melville's own "hands on" community service was murdering undesirable individuals. She now planned to eliminate African Matthew Zimwi, called "Monster of the Year" by *Time*, at a party in his honor at the Foundation. Zimwi was to be the party's Santa Claus. Miss Melville was duly horrified at the Monster of Mazigaziland impersonating one of her culture's most cherished icons. (See Walk 4 for origins of Santa Claus.)

Keep walking east on 49th Street past any number of elegant restaurants and hotels to First Avenue. Turn left to walk north on First Avenue to Beekman Place at 50th Street, which dead-ends in a railing above the park and the FDR Drive and the East River. At 51st Street there is a staircase down to the park where people jog and walk dogs. Turn left to walk to 51st Street.

Beekman Place was named for the Beekman family, who once owned much of the area and whose mansion, Mount Pleasant, stood at the river near 51st Street. It served as British headquarters during part of the Revolutionary War. The Beekmans got it back, but it was torn down in 1874 as the area became more developed.

Among other celebrities who have lived on Beekman Place was John P. Marquand. After winning the Pulitzer Prize in 1937 for *The Late George Apley*, Marquand rented the duplex at 1 Beekman Place. Marquand was a displaced New Englander (a great nephew of the redoubtable Margaret Fuller) who had supported himself writing "Mr. Moto" mysteries about a Japanese sleuth, loosely based on the Charlie Chan stories until his "serious" books sold.

In S. S. Van Dine's *The Greene Murder Case*, Philo Vance was once again called upon by his friend, D.A. John F. X. Markham, to solve a series of family murders that took place in the Greene Mansion. The mansion had stood for three generations at the eastern end of 53rd Street, where its two oriel windows overhung the East River. It had a great iron double gateway and occupied an entire block. It was not built in Federal style, however, but was a Gothic "chateau flamboyant," with gabled spires and chimney clusters, stained glass, and dark woodwork. Since Old Tobias Greene's will had stipulated that the mansion must remain intact for a quarter of a century after his death as a monument to him and his ancestors, his descendants were still living there and murdering one another.

As you stand at Beekman Place overlooking the park, you can see that some of the houses have patios that overlook the river. In Stefanie Matteson's *Murder at the Spa*, her elegant sleuth, raven-haired, 60ish actress Charlotte Graham was a four-time Oscar winner. Graham was also highly intelligent, with a no-nonsense manner. She lived in a brownstone on E. 49th Street with a river terrace. Beginning after her co-star in a Broadway play, *The Trouble*, had been shot onstage, Graham kept busy as an amateur detective. In *Murder at the Spa*, she went to the upstate spa of an old friend, cosmetics queen Paula Langenberg, to discover who was sabotaging the business. In *Murder at Teatime*, Graham took a Maine island vacation only to get mixed up in a murder over development of the island. But, like Katharine Hepburn, Charlotte Graham always returned to her East Side brownstone.

Go left back to First Avenue and turn right. Two blocks away at 163 E. 51st Street and Third Avenue is the NYPD's 7th Precinct. If you have not stepped inside one of the precinct stations, walk over to take a look at the charge desk. In Dorothy B. Hughes's *The Fallen Sparrow*, Kit McKittrick, the quixotic son of a dead NYPD detective, burst into the 17th Precinct to demand that the NYPD help him avenge his childhood friend, NYPD officer Louie Lepetino. The 17th Precinct also is a possible substitute for Ed McBain's "87th Precinct," which he insists is *not* in NYC, but everyone else—including *The Wall Street Journal*—is sure it is.

Keep walking north on First Avenue to 53rd Street. Then go right and head back to Sutton Place (a north–south street that runs from 53rd to 59th Street where it ends under the Queensboro Bridge). Sutton Square is on the river at 58th Steet. This is a very, *very* elegant neighborhood. A Morgan had a house at Number 1 and the secretary general of the UN lives at Number 3. To the north (almost under the looming Queensboro Bridge, completed in 1909) there is a small cobbled street called Riverview Terrace, where five nineteenth-century houses face the East River. Along this stretch the FDR Drive disappears in a tunnel. There are no subway stops along here and only one bus route, but there are lots of taxis.

Beyond the Queensboro Bridge, Sutton Place becomes York Avenue. In Patricia Highsmith's *A Dog's Ransom*, the ransom for the kidnapped poodle Lisa had to be stashed by the railings of the little York Avenue Park. (Lisa had been kidnapped across town in Riverside Park. See Walk 10.)

There is also another large medical complex along the East River from East 60th Street to East 72nd Street, which includes the world-famous Sloan-Kettering Cancer Center; Rockefeller University, on the site of the old Schermerhorn estate, which specializes in medical research; and New York Hospital–Cornell University Medical College, part of which was the first hospital in the city. The presence of this complex just north of the Queensboro Bridge makes it the most likely site for the Blackheath Medical Center in Otto Penzler's unfinished *The Medical Center Murders.* Amateur sleuth and medical records clerk Lisa Drake could see the Pepsi sign and the Triborough Bridge from her office there. Drake uncovered a medical insurance scam that led to murder. It was also the place in Chesbro's *Bone* where the murderer found Dr. Ali Hakim, professor of psychiatry and neurology at NYU Medical Center. Dr. Hakim had taken a great interest in the "case" of the homeless mute known as Bone, which led to Hakim's being beheaded in his office.

Walk through Sutton Place to 57th Street. You will see many apartments with balconies and window boxes. In a cul-de-sac off 56th Street there is a building with a quiet, unassuming doorway and a wrought iron lantern, as well as larger buildings that look more like Lord Peter Wimsey's Bellona Club, with driveways in and out. At 57th Street there is another clublike building with a blue door, showing you why people say the area is like St. James's, London, in spite of the fact that these buildings date from the 1920s and 1930s and sport awnings and doormen. (See *Mystery Reader's Walking Guide: London*, St. James's Walk.)

In *The Woman Who Knew Too Much*, Zoe Bassinetti (the director's wife) lived on Sutton Place in a lavish apartment with window boxes. It was brick with an oak door and a gorgon's head knocker. Zoe's Japanese maid liked the Yankees (P.I. Greco was fortunately wearing a Yankees T-shirt), but when Greco and Celia Blandings met the "Dragon Lady" herself, things got rougher. Later Greco went back alone to stake out the apartment, heard shots, went in, and found Zoe's dog and another operative dead. Greco then got chopped by Zoe's lover, Charlie Cunningham, but was able to escape using the balcony.

Turn left at 57th Street to walk to First Avenue. Just past the corner on the south side of 57th Street you will find Neary's Pub at 358 E. 57th Street. It is in a three-story building with a green awning. It was hospitably open at 11 A.M. on a weekday morning, with Jimmy Neary himself beaming behind his long shining bar. With his friendly Irish accent he seemed amused by the mystery fans who keep coming to see places mentioned in the mysteries of Mary Higgins Clark. (Her photograph is on the celebrity wall across from the bar.) The long, narrow room is wainscoted and rather dark, with gleaming glass, many Irish momentoes, and only a few tables.

In Clark's *While My Pretty One Sleeps*, Jimmy Neary was described as a "twinkly-eyed Irishman with a leprechaun's smile." The Kearnys and publisher Jack Campbell had dinner there after meeting Kitty Conway, who had found reporter Ethel Lambston's body. Clark called Neary's a NYC Irish hangout where politicians and clergy gathered.

In Clark's *Loves Music, Loves to Dance*, Darcy Scott and Nona Roberts of Hudson Cable TV, who recruited Darcy and her murdered friend Erin Kelley to answer personals ads, met at Neary's to have dinner. Jimmy had saved them the left back-corner table, where they were joined by NYPD detective Vince D'Ambrosio, who was working on the case.

Although Neary's is not on Second Avenue in the Upper 80s, it could also be used as a substitute for another "Irish" pub, the Galway Bay Bar and Grill in *Lullaby of Murder*. Dorothy Salisbury Davis's stringer Julie Hayes met Mary Ryan there the night Hayes's boss, columnist Tony Alexander, was murdered in his office. That bar also had a masculine and gaslight atmosphere with dark wood, brass fixtures, and photographs and prints of horses and riders.

If you're hungry or thirsty now, try Neary's. Then leave and walk left toward Second Avenue, passing by NYC P. S. 59, which showed no signs—not even graffiti—of being a "blackboard jungle" like the one described by Evan Hunter, aka 87th Precinct chronicler, Ed McBain. Second Avenue, however, is an urban shopping street, lined with dingy shops and stores and old buildings. Turn right and walk up Second Avenue to 58th Street, then go left to Third Avenue.

There are both a Burger King (the heir of the automat) and a McDonald's on Third Avenue if you need a quick break or have to make a pit stop. If you want something more elegant than fast food and didn't try Neary's menu, walk three blocks left down Third Avenue to 55th Street, where you will find a New York "institution," P. J. Clarke's, at 915 Third Avenue. Known as a "grown-up frat boy's dream" with a bar, plenty of beer, chili, and hamburgers, it, too, has a wood-trimmed, masculine decor.

In Carol Brennan's *Headhunt*, PR person Liz Warender met a fellow worker there before they went to burgle the Upper East Side offices of Liz's murdered client. For this caper both wore dark slacks and black leather jackets. In *Inherit the Mob*, "Velvel" Gordon, the prize-winning reporter who was the nephew of a dead mobster, insisted on going to Clarke's instead of the Harvard Club for a formal meeting with the representative of his dead uncle's partner.

If you are not ready to stop yet, continue walking up Third Avenue to Alexander's Department Store at 58th Street. Alexander's is a medium-priced department store with few clerks and inexpensive merchandise. Its real interest for mystery fans lies in the fact that most of the Wolfe Pack (including the Werowance) think that this is where you *should* find the Rex Stout restaurant called Rusterman's.

Nero Wolfe called Rusterman's the best restaurant in NYC. It had been run since 1926 by Marko Vukcic, a Montenegrin childhood friend and fellow partisan of Nero Wolfe's, and it was the only place in town where Nero Wolfe would go to eat. As usual with Stout's stories, there are location problems for Rusterman's because Archie Goodwin changed its street address from tale to tale. In *Fer-de-Lance*, Rusterman's was at 58th and Lexington Avenue, which would be Alexander's. Later in *In the Best Families*, Rusterman's was on East 54th Street. At that time it was run by Herman Rusterman (aka Emil Wolfgang Rusterman) who immigrated in 1893 and worked on the Lower East Side until he opened Rusterman's in 1904. But at the time when Vukcic was murdered and Wolfe had to go to the morgue to place the traditional coins on the deceased's eyes, Rusterman's had moved north again. Vukcic himself was one of the fifteen master chefs of the world and some fans believe he was Nero's twin brother.

Alexander's itself has a counter-style restaurant that will never take the place of Rusterman's. Explore Alexander's, then cross to 56th Street to Bloomingdale's, one block north between Third Avenue and Lexington. Bloomingdale's is a trendy and upscale store, quite possibly the most popular with native New Yorkers. Since it started as a family store, it might even be a stand-in for Ellery Queen's French's Store. The oldest part of the store was built in 1882. At that time brothers Joseph and Lyman Bloomingdale had been in business only ten years.

Bloomingdale's has women's and men's clothes, furniture, housewares, a bakery and meat counter, expensive restaurants and modest health bars, you name it. The book department, however, has become a Rizzoli's in recent years. Bloomie's famous sales rival Harrod's in London. (See *Mystery Reader's Walking Guide: London*, Brompton Walk.)

In Isabelle Holland's *A Fatal Advent* the Reverend Claire Aldington took a visiting Anglican VIP to Bloomingdale's to experience "an American Christmas." After being sprayed in the face with perfume and hustled to buy candy, the elderly cleric admitted he was absolutely "awe-struck" by the mad commotion. Shortly afterward, he was shoved down the stairs at St. Anselm's Choir School, which finished him off.

After eating or shopping there yourself, leave Bloomingdale's by the 59th Street exit. Turn right and cross Lexington Avenue and keep going west, window-shopping in fancy shops along the way. Across the street on the northwest corner of Park Avenue and 59th Street you will see the world-famous Christie's Auction House at 502 Park Avenue. This is undoubtedly the best substitute for the Midtown "Nelsons's," where Tony Hillerman's Navajo cop Lieutenant Joe Leaphorn went for information about a prehistoric Indian pot listed in their catalog. The pot matched one that had been stolen out of a dig in *The Thief of Time*. (See also Walk 6.)

Cross over to look in Christie's if you have time or keep walking along 59th Street toward the south-east corner of Central Park. Cross first Madison Avenue and then Fifth Avenue to reach the Pulitzer Memorial Fountain just south of the Grand Army Plaza and your destination, the NYC landmark Plaza Hotel.

This French chateau built in the opulent Edwardian era (1907) to serve the well-to-do still does so, while having been "Trumped." It is also one of *the* favorite NYC rendezvous for mystery characters who gather either in the bright, airy Palm Court—which reminds you of the Ritz on Piccadilly in London—or in its very English Oak Bar or the Edwardian Room with its atmosphere so much like Simpson's-in-the-Strand. You can easily imagine Agatha Christie taking tea there, just as Mary Roberts Rinehart undoubtedly did. (See *Mystery Reader's Walking Guide: London*, St. James Walk; Covent Garden Walk.)

The Plaza's mystery mystique goes back to Dashiell Hammett's *The Thin Man*, when Herbert Maccaulay, the lawyer of the missing (and murdered) inventor Clyde Winant, told the NYPD that he had had a phone call telling him to meet Winant at 2 P.M. in the Plaza lobby. When Maccaulay got there at 3 P.M., there was no Winant, and nobody at the Plaza remembered seeing him. The lobby now has no chairs, which makes waiting for an appointment with murder much more tiring.

In Frances and Richard Lockridge's *Murder Comes First*,

Pam and Jerry North met at the Oak Room to celebrate the fact that Pam was not a maiden aunt. (Her three maiden aunts had just arrived by train on their annual pilgrimage from Cleveland to Florida by way of NYC. They were shortly to be accused of murdering a childhood friend with whom they had tea.)

In Mignon Eberhart's *Danger Money*, the innocent and easily bemused heroine Susan Beach, a sort of society girl typist under the wing of the "Great Man" (GM), met the GM's aide-de-camp, Greg Cameron, at the Plaza for lunch. The GM had sent them to NYC from his Secret House to buy a huge engagement ring, for whom no one was sure, since his wife had just been murdered.

In Amanda Cross's *The Theban Mysteries*, Reed Amhearst and his recently acquired wife Professor Kate Fansler met at the Oak Bar for dinner after she had taught the first session of the senior seminar on *Antigone* at her old school. It was clear to Kate that the seniors were out to get her. Reed took one look at her and ordered two martinis. Not being health food nuts, Kate and Reed drank several more martinis and had pâté and a bottle of wine with their steaks.

In Jerome Charyn's *The Education of Patrick Silver*, which pitted NYPD First Deputy Commissioner Isaac Sidel against both the Guzmann clan and a renegade Irish-Jewish cop called Patrick Silver, Silver left the Guzmann's so-called baby, Jeronimo, in the lobby of the Plaza Hotel while he ran an errand. Silver was guarding the baby because the Guzmanns had a feud going with the NYPD and he knew no cop would remove a big middle-aged goof like Jeronimo from the lobby. After taking Jeronimo for a brief assignation with a whore on the third floor, Silver then left the Plaza, leading Jeronimo by the hand.

In John Grisham's *The Pelican Brief*, after the murders of two Supreme Court justices, reporter Gray Grantham of the *Washington Post* met a Tulane University student called Darby at the Plaza to get the inside story on the murders. Following Darby's instructions, Gray had to fly in from Washington, D.C. to La Guardia, take a cab to the Vista Hotel at the World Trade Center, have a drink, then take another cab to the corner of Fifth Avenue and 52nd Street and walk to the Plaza Hotel.

(Shades of Watergate's "Deep Throat" adventures and the cab rides of Cary Grant in Hitchcock's movie *North by Northwest*.) At the Plaza Gray had to go through the lobby to the Central Park South exit and turn west to walk to Sixth Avenue, where he next ducked into the St. Moritz Hotel where Darby had reserved them a room.

The exact location of Hugh Pentecost's fabulous Hotel Beaumont is unknown but the Plaza is one real possibility because of its world-class ambiance and glitz. Run by the legendary manager Pierre Chambrun, the Hotel Beaumont was the place the rich and famous always stayed. In Pentecost's *Beware Young Lovers*, famous glamour queen Sharon Brand acted outrageously in the main dining room, then was found murdered in her room. But Pierre Chambrum managed both the hotel and the crime with his usual urbanity.

In Steve Allen's *Murder in Manhattan*, the entire cast of the movie being shot in NYC was put up at the Plaza. Because the director had decided he must have Steve for a cameo part as his look-alike Clark Kent (Superman), Steve asked for a corner suite with a piano and got it. He also found one corpse in his suite. While staying there, Steve ate in all the Plaza restaurants. He drank at Trader Vic's in the basement by the Central Park South entrance and the Oak Bar, and ate in the Oak Room and Edwardian Room and the Palm Court, meeting with various cast members, his wife Jayne Meadows, and the NYPD, while trying to solve the murders.

In Zev Chaffets's *Inherit the Mob*, Pietro, the younger son of Mafia Don Spadafore, with whom journalist Velvel Gordon's uncle had worked, came to the Palm Court, where he picked up Gordon's bisexual girl friend Jupiter. The new twosome went to his secret hideaway, where they were blown up in Pietro's car.

In Trella Crespi's *The Trouble with a Small Raise*, amateur sleuth/art buyer Simona Griffo, returning through Central Park from a romantic visit to the apartment of NYPD detective Greenhouse, was followed. Simona first considered hiring a horse and buggy to escape, but then decided to go to the Plaza Hotel because nothing could go wrong near the Plaza. But someone gave her a shove in front of a bus on 59th Street.

In *Headhunt* by Carol Brennan, a British P.I. named Anthony Swift was investigating a leaked deal to sell trade secrets known to the King Carter Agency. He had placed a call to PR person Liz Wareham who handled the account, just before he was found strangled with pantyhose in his room at the Plaza.

In Mary Higgins Clark's *Loves Music, Loves to Dance*, Darcy Scott always stayed at the Plaza with her parents, a famous movie couple. En route to an appointment with a shady jewelry salesman who had known her murdered friend Erin, Darcy dropped by the Oak Room where the maître d', Fred, was an old friend. Later a clue to the murderer was found in the guest list for the 21st Century Playwrights' Festival Benefit held at the Plaza, with its glittery guests, who included Helen Hayes and Tony Randall.

In Velda Johnson's *The Face in the Shadows*, in an effort to "reach out" to his daughter Cecily, who was getting drugs from someone, Howard Vandering asked actress Ellen Stacey to meet them at the Palm Court for lunch. They had an elegant lunch while a string band played, but Cecily did not respond to Ellen at all. Treat yourself there, however, to end your walk.

8

UPPER EAST SIDE WALK

BACKGROUND

This is *the* NYC residential neighborhood, where the rich and well-connected live. It has been the home of New York's "old money" since the 1870s when Central Park was opened. Then the very rich like Andrew Carnegie or J. P. Morgan moved there to live in peace and quiet far from the madding crowd and the trade and manufacturing that were creeping up Manhattan. The millionaires first built stately limestone mansions between Fifth Avenue and Park Avenue, then from 1900 to 1920 came elegant brick, limestone, and brownstone townhouses. (In the 1980s, an Upper East Side brownstone cost several million dollars.) Because of the serene uniformity of the buildings, the area from 60th Street to 79th Street, Fifth Avenue to Lexington Avenue, has been made an official historic district, contributing, of course, to the general impression of a neighborhood of wealth and gracious living.

On the maps and in real life, the Upper East Side is the "right side" of the park. On Fifth Avenue by Central Park it has tall apartment buildings with doormen and limousines out front. Madison Avenue is its very upscale shopping street, especially for art and antiques (most places are closed on Sundays), while Park Avenue specializes in hotels, churches, and restaurants. The Upper East Side for years has also been the home of select private clubs like the Colony or the Metropolitan, and private schools like Chapin School, which relocated in the 1920s from 57th Street to 84th and East End and today owns most of its block. It is also home to much of New York's culture along "Museum Mile," which begins at the Metropolitan Museum of Art at 82nd Street and stretches north up Fifth Avenue to Central Park North at 104th Street.

South of 96th Street stretching to 86th Street is the community of Yorkville. Yorkville was once farmland, then a German community, then tenement territory, but recently it has been losing "turf" to new developments. Much of the urban blight that used to exist east of Lexington Avenue has vanished, thanks to the construction of new clusters of trendy high rises along the East River during the 1970s and 1980s.

The walk focuses on the older, more historic district closer to Central Park, whose upper-class ambiance, faithfully reflected in mysteries stories from the 1930s to the 1990s, makes it New York's Belgravia. (See *Mystery Reader's Walking Guide: London*, Belgravia/Pimlico Walk.) Museum-sponsored art and architecture tours abound to tell you about the styles to be found among its handsome, well-maintained private and public buildings.

In mysteries the Upper East Side is definitely home to the "Social Register" (high-society's private phone book), as you will see in stories by Dorothy B. Hughes, Elizabeth Daly, Mignon G. Eberhart, Mary Roberts Rinehart, and Rex Stout. In more recent mysteries by people like Steve Allen or Lawrence Sanders, you also catch a glimpse of the new high-rise territory to the east, which is outside the boundaries of the walk itself.

LENGTH OF WALK: About 2.5 miles

Note: Because it would make the walk too long, "Museum Mile" is treated as a "Side Trip," as are historic Gracie Mansion in Carl Schurz Park and Yorkville, East 86–96th Streets.

See map on page 201 for the boundaries of this walk and page 321 for a list of the books and detectives mentioned.

PLACES OF INTEREST

Knoedler Gallery, 19 E. 70th Street. Established 1846. Still one of the major art galleries in area. Closed Sun.–Mon. Call 794-0557.

Whitney Museum of Modern Art, 75th Street and Madison Avenue. Contemporary and avant garde collections. Open Wed.–Sat., 11:00 A.M.–8:00 P.M.; Sun. and holidays, noon–6:00 P.M. Admission fee. Call 570-3676.

Frick Collection, Fifth Avenue at 70th Street. Built 1914 for Henry Clay Frick, chairman of Carnegie Steel (U.S. Steel). Houses his private collection/belongings. Open Tues.–Sat., 10:00 A.M.–6:00 P.M.; Sun. 1:00 P.M.–6:00 P.M. Admission fee. *No children*. Call 288-0700.

Temple Emanu-El, 1 East 65th Street. Largest Reform synagogue in U.S.A. Pioneer congregation formed in 1845. With congregation Beth-El moved into Byzantine and Romanesque building in 1927. Weekdays ask the guard to let you inside.

POSSIBLE SIDE TRIPS

Museum Mile, Fifth Avenue, 82nd Street to 104th Street. (Most museums are closed on Mondays, many have free admission on Tuesday afternoons. Most of these listed are visited by mystery characters.)

Metropolitan Museum of Art, 1000 Fifth Avenue at 82nd Street. Sunday, Tues.–Thurs., 9:30 A.M.–5:15 P.M. Fri.–Sat., 9:30 A.M.–9:45 P.M. Closed Mon. Admission fee. Call 535-7710.

NYU Institute of Fine Arts, Fifth Avenue and 78th Street. Originally home of James Duke; built in 1912.

Guggenheim Museum, 88–89th Streets. Frank Lloyd Wright building with spiral internal ramp. Modern art. Tues., 11:00 A.M.–8:00 P.M.; Wed.–Sun, 11:00 A.M.–5:00 P.M. Admission fee. Call 360-3500.

National Academy of Design, 1083 Fifth Avenue. Founded by
Samuel F. Morse, the painter and inventor in 1825. It
claims to be the first art gallery in NYC. Morse was also a
Know Nothing politician.

Church of the Heavenly Rest, Fifth Avenue and 90th Street.
Host to Heavenly Jazz Series and York Theater Company.

Cooper-Hewitt Museum, East 91st Street. Originally the home
of Andrew Carnegie. Mansion built in 1901 at cost of $1.5
million. Gorgeous conservatory and gardens. Home of
Smithsonian Institution's National Museum of Design.
Thurs., 10:00 A.M.–9:00 P.M.; Wed.–Sat., 10:00 A.M.–
5:00 P.M.; Sun., noon–5:00 P.M. Closed some holidays.
Admission fee. Call 860-6868.

Museum of the City of New York, 103–104th Street.
Tues.–Sat., 10:00 A.M.–5:00 P.M.; Sun. and holidays,
1:00 P.M.–5:00 P.M. Admission fee. Call 534-1672.

El Museo del Barrio, 104th Street. Latin American art and
performances. Tues.–Fri., 10:30 A.M.–4:30 P.M.;
Sat.–Sun., 11:00 A.M.–4:00 P.M. Admission fee. Call
831-7272.

Yorkville, East 96th Street to East 86th Street, Central Park to East
River.

Gracie Mansion, Carl Schurz Park, 90th Street and East River.
Original Federal-style mansion was the country home of
merchant seaman Archibald Gracie; had other rich owners
until 1924 when taken over by New York City. During La
Guardia's term as mayor made Official Residence (1941). In
the 1980s Mayor Ed Koch opened it to public. Tours on
Wed. Call 570-4751.

Sotheby Parke Bernet, 1334 York Avenue at 72nd Street. The
"other" great auction house (Christie's). Also the
American branch of a British institution. Famous for sale of
Andy Warhol's estate and van Gogh's *Irises* for $53.9
million. Call 606-7000.

PLACES TO EAT

(Most of those mentioned in mysteries are expensive. For less
expensive food your best bet is the museum restaurants.)

Bergdorf Goodman, Fifth Avenue, 58th to 59th Streets. Café Vienna, luncheon or afternoon tea with Viennese goodies. Pasta and Cheese, Italian, with sandwiches and salads. Expensive. Call 753-7300.

Hotel Carlyle, 35 E. 76th Street. Cafe Carlyle, upscale restaurant with murals by Vertes, featuring singer/pianist Bobby Short. Buffet, French. Breakfast, lunch, dinner, and afternoon tea. Expensive. Call 744-1600.

Regency Hotel, 540 Park Avenue at East 61st Street. Home of the "power breakfast," classy Continental brunch, lunch, and dinner. Expensive. Call 759-4100.

Le Cirque, 58 E. 65th Street. In the Mayfair Regency Hotel. Lunch and dinner. Very expensive. Call 794-9292.

Mezzaluna, 1295 Third Avenue between 74th and 75th Streets. Trendy, crowded, gentrified pizza parlor. No credit cards or reservations. Call 535-9600.

Museums
Metropolitan Museum of Art
Museum Cafeteria, Tues.–Sun., 9:30 A.M.–10:30 A.M., 11:00 A.M.–4:30 P.M. Inexpensive.
Museum Restaurant, Tues.–Sun., 11:30 A.M.–3:30 P.M.; Fri.–Sat., 11:30 A.M.–10:00 P.M. Call 570-3964.
Museum Dining Room, Sat.–Sun., public brunch 11:30 A.M.–2:30 P.M. Call 879-5000, ext. 3614.
Whitney Museum of American Art, basement café and sculpture garden. Lunch: salads, sandwiches, plat du jour. Call 570-3641.
Guggenheim, tiny restaurant, good salads, sandwiches, desserts. (If you have an admission ticket to other museums on Museum Mile, you can use restaurant without paying admission fee.)

——————— UPPER EAST SIDE WALK ———————

Begin your walk at Bergdorf Goodman at Fifth Avenue and 59th Street. One of New York's most popular and expensive department stores, the original 1928 store is just south of the Plaza Hotel, while its men's apparel shop is across Fifth Avenue. Bergdorf's is a very elegant store, with a black and gold and crystal ground floor—a class act. It even has a superb home furnishings department that sells antiques. But the store is much too upscale to be "Bryant and Washburn," the department store in Richard Lockridge's *Murder for Art's Sake*, in which an unscrupulous art dealer was selling off her clients' work using department store "art galleries."

In Richard Barth's *The Condo Kill*, the daughters of the minor mafia capo Donghia, who ran a bakery on Carmine Street in the Village, both had Bergdorf Goodman charge accounts. Their father kept them paid up as a sign of his own prestige.

Before you start your walk have lunch here (reservations are a good idea). Try either Café Vienna or Pasta and Cheese. But most mystery characters come here to do "heavy shopping." The prime example was Carol Brennan's PR person Liz Wareham in *Headhunt*. While she was involved in the murder investigation of her client King, Wareham went shopping at Bergdorf Goodman for solace. For Wareham "shopping is the therapy of choice for frustration, anger, self-pity and brain clog." Wareham went through Bergdorf Goodman like a cyclone, hitting every department, and left with a blazer, pants, top, and new Coco cologne, and decided to think (about the cost) tomorrow.

After looking around, leave Bergdorf Goodman at the 58th Street exit and cross Fifth Avenue. Then cross 58th Street to go north to F.A.O. Schwarz, the famous toy store. It is located inside the GM Plaza Concourse between Fifth and Madison Avenues. Go inside and ignore the teddy bears (despite Swiss pretensions, teddy bears have been native to NYC after the first one was made to honor Teddy Roosevelt because he had refused to shoot a bear cub). Instead, you need to hunt for a solid wooden baseball bat. In Steve Allen's *Murder in Manhattan*, Steve suspected he was being followed as he tried to solve a murder, so he went into F.A.O. Schwarz and bought himself a good solid wooden baseball bat to take back to his suite at the Plaza.

Then cross 59th Street to the Sherry-Netherland Hotel at 781 Fifth Avenue. The Sherry-Netherland is on the northeast corner of Fifth Avenue, facing Central Park. It has a delicate facade and a fifteen-story tower, and its display windows are espe-

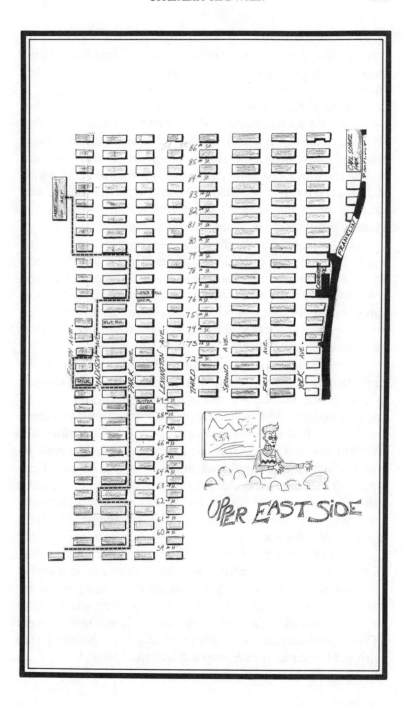

UPPER EAST SIDE

cially lovely, featuring items like Fabergé eggs. Inside, there is no place to sit (or lurk), partly because the building has become largely co-op apartments, partly for fear of the homeless settling in.

Built in 1922, its handsome wood paneling and traditional furnishings make it a fine example of an earlier age. There is an Italian restaurant called Quaglino in the Sherry-Netherland, which serves the hotel guests breakfast and gives room service. After mayhem among the movie cast Steve Allen made his wife Jayne Meadows secretly get a room at the Sherry-Netherland, where she was seen eating alone by the director's wife Mimi, who then went to the Plaza to pursue Steve in *Murder in Manhattan*.

The Sherry-Netherland is only one of several hotels that might have been Rex Stout's "Balfour Hotel," among them, the more famous Pierre Hotel a block north of you at 61st and Fifth Avenue. The Pierre Hotel, built by and named for a Corsican who had run restaurants in Paris, London, and New York, is still a top drawer hotel (and partial co-op), which serves an elegant tea under its Rotunda.

In Rex Stout's *Too Many Clients*, the Balfour Hotel in the East 60s near Madison Avenue was the home of musical comedy star Meg Duncan. She was one of love nester Thomas Yeager's many mistresses. The Balfour doorman knew Archie Goodwin because he had once been a carhop at the Churchill (aka Waldorf-Astoria). The penthouse apartment of theater critic Jason Saylin was at Central Park and 61st Street in Jane Dentinger's *First Hit of the Season*. During a party there attended by both actress Jocelyn O'Roarke and her NYPD lover Philip Gerrard, Saylin was poisoned with some strychnine mixed with his party supply of cocaine.

Around the corner from the Sherry-Netherland at 14 East 60th Street is the Copacabana, which was once a famous nightclub and is now a disco. The Copacabana became known nationwide on radio, where it featured the big name acts that later would go to Las Vegas and other venues. It was one of many NYC nightclubs that were visited by Craig Rice's Helene Justus with her hired escort in *Having a Wonderful Crime*.

After taking a quick look around the Sherry-Netherland come out on 59th Street and turn left to Madison Avenue. Cross Madison Avenue and continue east on 59th Street to Park Avenue. On the northwest corner you will find Christie's Auction House. (See also Walk 7.) At Park Avenue (a double road with a planted parkway in the center) turn left to walk up to 61st Street.

Cross Park Avenue to the northeast corner where you will find the Regency Hotel at 540 Park Avenue. Its lobby has marble walls hung with tapestries, with a great chandelier; its rooms are done in eighteenth-century decor, very chic but cozy. This hotel is the place where the idea of the "power breakfast" was born (its clientele is largely VIP) but you, too, can enjoy afternoon tea in the lounge, eat at the classy Regency 540 Restaurant, or have a drink at its bar.

In Carol Brennan's *Headhunt*, the partners of murdered executive headhunter King Carter went to stay at the Regency while the murder investigation was going on. Carter was murdered just a few blocks away on 64th Street at their office in an old brownstone called the Manse. Liz Wareham, their PR person (who had discovered the body), met the partners at the Regency to decide how to keep the murder from destroying their business. (Murder is very poor PR.)

Turn right as you leave the Regency to walk up Park Avenue. This block on Park Avenue between 61st and 62nd Streets is the location given for Isabelle Holland's St. Anselm's Episcopal Church, which appears in her mystery series about the Reverend Claire Aldington. In fact, just one block north two churches do share the block between Park Avenue and Lexington Avenue: the Third Church of Christ Scientist and the Central Presbyterian Church, both near fictional St. Anselm's. The Christian Science Church has classic New England columns, but the Central Presbyterian Church, which takes up half the block, is a large Gothic edifice.

In Holland's first mystery, *A Death at St. Anselm's*, as well as in its sequels, *The Flight of the Archangel, A Lover Scorned*, and *A Fatal Advent*, the action is centered at her imaginary St. Anselm's Episcopal Church at East 62nd Street. It had a Gothic

stone front and—like St. Thomas's—was once the most fashionable church in the city. St. Anselm's occupied half a block, with
the church itself facing Park Avenue and the parish house on
Lexington. Originally it was surrounded by the townhouses of
wealthy parishioners, which now housed shops and boutiques,
together with delicatessens and coffee shops. This is the scene
today on Lexington Avenue. But looking out of her church office window the Reverend Claire Aldington decided that she
would measure Park Avenue against any comparable scene in
the world as the sun set on trees in the center parkway and as the
lights came on in the great glass skyscrapers to the south.

In *A Lover Scorned*, the church's mission to the homeless
(feeding them and letting some stay overnight) included,
among others, the mentally ill bag lady Althea with her cat
Dalrymple. Althea, who stayed on the street all day, believed
she was guarding Arthur's Britain from a Viking invasion. St.
Anselm's social outreach programs not only included beds and
food for the homeless, but also the counseling service run by the
Reverend Claire Aldington, work with pregnant teenagers, drug
addicts and AA, a hospice, a half-way house, *and* a choir school.

St. Anselm's had once supported a mission, Saint Matthew's Chapel in the West 40s, and it also owned St.
Cuthbert's, a huge Victorian house above the Hudson River
which a California guru wanted to buy for his sect. In short,
Holland's St. Anselm's is a mixture of the two wealthiest and
most socially conscious Episcopal churches in NYC: Trinity,
Wall Street; and St. Thomas, Fifth Avenue, with more than a
touch, too, of Byzantine-style St. Bartholomew's on lower
Park Avenue. St. Bart's is the wealthy Episcopal church that
wanted permission to sell its air rights to fund its welfare programs. (See also Walk 1 and Walk 6.)

In *A Fatal Advent*, St. Anselm's housed its famous Choir
School in a building next door. First the dead body of the elderly
retired dean of St. Paul's Cathedral, London, the Reverend Alec
Maitland, was found dead at the bottom of a steep Victorian
staircase in the school, then a young choirboy's mother was also
found murdered in the school building.

Although Holland agrees that St. Thomas, Fifth Avenue,

was her main model, St. Thomas's choir school is several blocks west of the church in a separate building. Trinity Church, Wall Street also has a school, to which the young street arab Neal Carey was sent by the Friends of the Family who employed his mentor, P.I. Joe Graham in *A Cool Breeze on the Underground*. In addition, both the Cathedral of St. John the Divine and Grace Church in the East Village have church schools attached. (See Walk 2 and Walk 11.)

Like its English models, St. Anselm's Choir School provided a top-notch private education for boy sopranos aged 9–13 in return for their singing in its famous Men and Boys Choir. This is exactly the kind of school that Dorothy L. Sayers's clergyman father headed in Oxford when she was born. (See *Mystery Reader's Walking Guide: England*, Oxford Walk.)

St. Anselm's weekday services schedule matches St. Thomas's, including Daily Morning Prayer. This was the service Wall Street banker and vestryman Brett Cunningham attended. If you want to explore a church building, it is often a good plan to attend a service, then look around or take a tour.

Across 62nd Street on the west side of Park Avenue is the Colony Club with its blue awning. It is one of the most prestigious women's clubs in the world. Its building is pure Georgian architecture, with a granite ground-level facade and brick upper floors. Cross Park Avenue to walk slowly by, unless you know a member who will take you in to look around.

In Isabelle Holland's *A Death at St. Anselm's*, stuffy Wall Street banker Brett Cunningham had his annual luncheon at the Colony Club with a very important client, Mrs. Chadbourne, who happened to be the Reverend Claire's mother-in-law. (Claire's husband Patrick was dead.) Cunningham and Mrs. Chadbourne discussed Claire's stepdaughter Martha and the Chadbourne estate.

In Trella Crespi's *The Trouble with a Small Raise*, HH&H Ad Agency's Art Director Bertrand Monroe took amateur sleuth and art buyer Simona Griffo to lunch there with his formidable mother. Mrs. Monroe came to town every Thursday to be "done" at Elizabeth Arden, and he was expected to lunch with her. Griffo went by the guest waiting room, with its wall that displayed hundreds of names. The doormen took pride in recognizing the over 2,000 women members, putting a peg by the name of each when she was in the club. Simona managed to see four Rockefeller names in a row. The guests' waiting room was done up in baby blue with rose armchairs—sweet and genteel, the ladies' restroom was functional pink and white.

"Mummy" (aka Mrs. Monroe) was tall and majestic, walking with a cane. She had her usual table by a sealed window. The large room was decorated with gilt wall sconces of proud American eagles, pink tablecloths, delicate chairs, many mirrors, and a long buffet table. All the attendants, like the members, seemed to be over sixty. Mummy ordered skim milk for herself and Bernard but let Simona, who was Italian, have a glass of white wine. She sent her son to get her soup so she could grill Simona. When she found out Simona's father had been Italian consul general in Boston, she began to act as if Simona's marriage to Bertrand was a foregone conclusion, provided the children were brought up Episcopalian!

The "other" women's club is the Cosmopolitan Club, north and east of here on 66th Street. In Amanda Cross's *Poetic Justice*, English Professor Kate Fansler met Polly Spencer there to reassure Kate that there was still sedate stability to be found in NYC. Although Polly Spencer had also gone to the Knickerbocker Club's dancing classes and cotillions (a few blocks away on Fifth Avenue at 62nd Street), they met again on campus during the 1960s student uprisings. Polly turned out to have gone to University College as a returning scholar and become a teaching assistant to avoid babysitting her grandchildren.

In *The Question of Max*, Kate Fansler invited art historian Max Reston to lunch at the "Cos Club" to pump him about the papers of Cecily Hutchins, a fictional English contemporary of Dorothy L. Sayers. Fansler knew that Max, who was a terrible snob, loved the club's ambiance, from the comfortable lounge to luncheon at a window table. From there Fansler went to Central Park to watch her nephew Leo play baseball for St. Andrew's, an Upper East Side private school, whose questionable academic standards and values remind you of the scandal over college test scores at Eastern prep schools in Emma Lathen's *Come to Dust*.

Look down 62nd Street toward Central Park. Somewhere just off Park Avenue on 62nd Street where "Park Avenue met Bohemia" (in 1942) was the bachelor girl apartment of Laura Hunt in the mystery *Laura*. Her mentor, fussy bon vivant and columnist, Waldo Lydecker, was a cross between critics Alexander Woollcott and Edmund Wilson. Lydecker snootily told NYPD detective Mark McPherson that when he read that the president (FDR) was a devotee of mystery stories, he voted a straight Republican ticket. In Dana Clarins's *The Woman Who Knew Too Much*, when Celia Blandings accused her agent Joel of going into his "Waldo Lydecker" act, he admitted his mother had been frightened by the movie *Laura* when pregnant with him.

Laura's murder turned 62nd Street into "Coney Island moved to the Platinum Belt," with street vendors and gapers and Central Park lovers strolling by arm in arm. Lydecker was appalled; he wished to be the chief (and only) mourner. The apartment where Laura was shot to death was one of a row of converted Victorian mansions whose high stoops had given way to red-lacquered doors and bright blue and green window boxes. Laura lived on the third floor, where her living room had a black marble fireplace, faded chintz curtains, lots of books, comfortable chairs, and the famous portrait of her that made NYPD detective McPherson fall in love with a dead woman.

Go left along 62nd Street until you reach Madison Avenue, enjoying the expensive atmosphere of quiet restaurants, attractive apartments, hotels, embassies, and old mansions—many of limestone with bay windows, all very well kept. Choose a nice building for Laura's apartment, then pick out a narrow brownstone as the home of the strange Austen family in Elizabeth Daly's *The Book of the Crime*. Wounded vet Gary Austen's second wife, Rena, used to hurry down the steep steps to walk the family's old Boston terrier. She had been observed by her neighbor, young Mr. Ordway and his house-bound grandmother, and when Rena was terrified by her husband's locking her up and ran away, Ordway took her in a cab to Henry Gamadge's house. Gamadge, his wife Clara, and their baby and pets lived in an Upper East Side townhouse located somewhat farther north nearer

Central Park. They hid Rena from her husband by disguising her as their baby's nurse while Gamadge investigated the Austen "ménage."

Go right on Madison Avenue to 63rd Street and walk back along 63rd Street to Park Avenue on the south side of the street. You pass both the Lowell Hotel with its terra cotta facade and the Leonard Hotel. Both have penthouses and the Leonard has a roof garden, too. In Rex Stout's Nero Wolfe stories, the penthouse apartment of Archie Goodwin's "best girl" Lily Rowan was on 63rd Street between Park and Madison Avenues. Archie Goodwin had met Lily in *Some Buried Caesar* (a mystery about a prize bull, which led to Lily calling him "Escamillo"). Lily's old man was an Irish immigrant contractor with Tammany Hall connections who left her loaded. (See Walk 4.)

Lily bought her penthouse when she moved out of the old Ritz Hotel. She furnished it with a Kashan carpet, 19 feet by 34 feet, with a garden design; Impressionist paintings by Renoir, Monet, and Cezanne; and an off-white grand piano. There were glass doors that led to a terrace planted with flowers in the summer and evergreens in the winter. On a similar elegant terrace in Mignon G. Eberhart's *Woman on the Roof*, the wife of politician Marcus Desart had been pushed off the terrace and fell to her death twelve floors below.

In Joyce Christmas's *Simply to Die For*, Lady Margaret Priam had lunch with the wealthy Stafford family who lived in a four-story, redbrick Federal townhouse on East 63rd Street. The Staffords wanted Lady Margaret to run the debut of Camilla Stafford, the debutante daughter whose mother had been found murdered recently.

Across 63rd Street on the north side of the street, there is a nice row of brownstones where the Great Man's assistant Greg Cameron had his apartment in Mignon Eberhart's *The Secret House*. Susan Beach stayed overnight there when she and Greg came to NYC to buy the GM a huge engagement ring. Much to Susan's embarrassment, while she was there, Greg's Aunt Lalie dropped in. (Today's Aunt Lalies would not bat an eye, nor would Susan.)

Turn left on Park Avenue and walk north to 68th Street. In *Headhunt*, Carol Brennan located the Manse at 159 E. 64th Street, to your right between Lexington and Third Avenue. It was one of NYC's few nineteenth-century mansions with a perfect limestone facade. Liz Wareham's murdered client, King Carter, had cleverly bought it at auction and renovated it into a combined office/apartment. Its entrance rotunda had a marble floor and a graceful marble staircase that lead to King's office on the second floor, where Liz found him dead. Wearing black leather jackets and black slacks, Liz and her assistant, Angela Chappell, later tried to burgle the Manse but they were caught in the act by NYPD Lieutenant Ike O'Hanlon, who had dumped Liz after their senior prom.

At 65th Street you will pass the Mayfair Regent Hotel, which contains the famous French restaurant Le Cirque. It caters to the well-heeled, well-connected crowd up to and including the president of the United States. In Mary Higgins Clark's *Loves Music, Loves to Dance*, Darcy Scott's movie-star parents always went there, and Darcy met Michael Nash on a personal-ad date there, while trying to solve her friend Erin's murder.

In *Somewhere in the House*, Elizabeth Daly placed an H. H. Richardson Romanesque mansion somewhere "up" Park Avenue—which could mean all the way to Central Park North. Henry Gamadge walked there to meet members of the old New York Clayborn family. Made of red brick with a tiled roof and separate carriage house, the Clayborn house was solid but decorative, like Richardson's famous Trinity Church in Boston. In fact, the only NYC H. H. Richardson mansion is on Staten Island, where Richardson lived briefly. Unlike the Clayborn mansion, that house never had a corpse in a sealed room waiting twenty years to be discovered. But the Richardson legacy is all over the Upper East Side—and the rest of Manhattan—because three of his best-known pupils made up the firm of McKim, Mead and White, which designed many NYC buildings.

Nearby on East 65th Street senior Wall Street partner Arthur Lindemann had a brownstone in Elliott Roosevelt's *Hyde Park Murder*. Young Bob Hannah, whose father had been pushed from a Wall Street window, was caught hunting clues to his father's murder by a crooked NYPD cop. Hannah was then rescued by a clean cop whom Mayor La Guardia had ordered to keep watch on him because he was a friend of First Lady Eleanor Roosevelt.

In William Love's *The Chartreuse Clue*, ex-NYPD cop Davy Goldman's girlfriend lived at 225 E. 65th Street. Goldman had trouble with the NYPD because while driving to pick her up for a ballgame, he went the long way around from West 37th Street to go past the scene of the crime on the Upper West Side, and then through Central Park.

In Annette Meyers's *The Big Killing*, there is a trendy nightclub called the Caravanserie run in a historic church on 65th Street near First Avenue. It had been bought and turned into a health club by Georgie Travers, a childhood friend of murdered Barry Stark. Wetzon went there seeking clues to the Stark murder. Although this is about the right location, there is no such nightclub here, and Meyers's nightclub is more like Limelight, the Chelsea disco in a former Episcopal church. (See Walk 4.)

The Upper East Side has mostly well-dressed types, who are often walking pairs of matched dogs. But once I saw a tall, grayhaired man walking along in a black, flowing Dracula cape. He seemed perfectly cast for a role in the mysterious hauntings in John Lutz's *Shadowtown*.

The Upper East Side is also home to many private schools, and when school lets out in the afternoon, uniformed students of both sexes and all sizes are collected by nannies, mothers, or school buses. The Brearly School, for example, is at East 83rd Street; the Chapin School occupies two connected buildings at 84th Street and East End. Amanda Cross's fictional Theban School, where Professor Kate Fansler taught the seniors *Antigone*, was in the East 70s near Central Park. These fancy private schools are known in the trade as the "curtseying sisters" for their emphasis on manners.

In *The Face in the Shadows*, Velda Johnson's fictional Mainwaring School was at 68th Street between Madison and Park Avenues. Midway down the block in an old mansion you can see the real Dominican School. Like it, the fictional Mainwaring School was in a tall eighty-year-old brownstone with bulging bay windows, a highly polished brass nameplate, and ilex trees in tubs on either side of the double door. Actress Ellen Stacey had found schoolgirl Cecily Vandering drugged, wearing the Mainwaring School uniform, at the Cloisters. Curious, Ellen later walked by the school and was accosted by old Miss Mainwaring herself, lurking nearby in a navy coat and pillbox hat.

Fictional 340 E. 68th Street was the home of love-nester Thomas Yeager in Rex Stout's *Too Many Clients*. Yeager's wife persuaded Archie Goodwin to take her to view the love nest itself, across Central Park on the West Side. In Stout's *The Golden Spiders*, murdered rich widow Laura Fromm lived at 743 E. 68th Street (really in the East River). Her house was granite, set back a couple of yards from the street, with iron railings higher than Archie's head. To get in, Archie pretended to be the funeral director.

In Lillian O'Donnell's *The Children's Zoo*, the Dowd School, whose principal was called the headmaster, occupied two buildings on 69th Street. Co-ed, it had affluent junior high and high school students, some of whom were appallingly and senselessly violent. But it was extremely difficult for Detective Norah Mulcanhaney to get information about individual students because neither the school nor the parents wished to share it.

Between 68th and 69th Streets, from Park to Lexington Avenues, there is a large, utilitarian-looking building that houses Hunter College. The biggest of the city colleges, it was originally founded in 1870 for working-class women, when women's education had become a national issue. B. J. Rahv, an authority on the detective story, teaches mystery fiction there and wrote an article on the importance of "place" or "setting" in the detective story for the 1989 "Edgars's Award Dinner" program book.

Walk past Hunter College on Park Avenue and go north to 70th Street. Turn left on 70th Street to walk to Madison Avenue. At the northwest corner of Madison Avenue and 70th Street is Knoedler's, an old, very famous art gallery and NYC institution. Since the entire Upper East Side is covered with art galleries, this is a good one to use as a model for those that appear in mysteries.

While Knoedler's has the space to stash away the snooping wife of a NYPD captain, its staff would never do such a thing. In Richard Lockridge's *Murder for Art's Sake*, Dorian Weigand, the artist wife of the Norths' old friend, NYPD Captain William Weigand, was trying to find evidence that gallery owner Myra Dedek had sold her client Shackleton Jones's paintings too cheaply. She had visited department store art galleries, checking up, then she visited Dedek's gallery and was kidnapped.

In Mary Higgins Clark's *Loves Music, Loves to Dance*, Chris Sheridan ran the Sheridan Gallery on 78th Street just east of Madison Avenue. Sheridan's twin sister Nan had been murdered by the serial killer running loose in NYC, and, after Erin Kelley's murder by the killer, her best friend Darcy Scott came to Sheridan's Gallery to look for faces she might recognize from his old family photographs.

Two blocks north of here on 72nd Street you can see an ornate French chateau built in 1898 for NYC Police Commissioner Rhinelander Waldo. Waldo was fictionalized in E. L. Doctorow's *Ragtime*, played by actor Jimmy Cagney, known for playing archcriminals and crooks.

Cross Madison Avenue and walk west to Fifth Avenue and Central Park. When you reach Fifth Avenue, look to your left. At 1 E. 65th Street is the huge Byzantine-Romanesque Jewish Temple Emanu-El, which has the largest Jewish Reform congregation in America. In Marissa Piesman's *Personal Effects*, lawyer Nina Fischman, who was trying to solve the murder of her oldest friend Susan Gold, had answered personal ads and met Irwin Smolkowitz. Irwin was the son of a South African gem dealer. He demanded to know if Nina had ever been to services at Temple Emanu-El on Fifth Avenue. When she admitted she had not, he announced there was not a Jewish woman in the temple. Nina told him he was mixing up cosmetic surgery (on their noses) with Christian blood.

In Velda Johnson's *The Face in the Shadows*, the classy apartment of Janet Vandering (Cecily's mother) was at 68th Street and Fifth Avenue. Decorated with Aubusson carpets and eighteenth-century French antiques, it occupied the entire twelfth floor, as Ellen Stacey discovered when she took Cecily Vandering home after finding her at the Cloisters.

On the northeast corner of 70th Street and Fifth Avenue is one of the most famous private residences left in New York, the Frick mansion, now called the Frick Collection. It is a neoclassical limestone building with grounds surrounded by a high iron fence. Although a bit too far north, it's still a possible model for the East 60s home of Margaret Maron's millionaire Julius Trent in *Death in Blue Folders*. His grandson was kidnapped when Trent took him for a secret ride during naptime. In *A Lover Scorned*, walking back to St. Anselm's after lunch, the Reverend Claire Aldington came out of Central Park near the Frick, which she admired. What she did not know was that the murderer had followed her.

Called NYC's favorite museum, the Frick is worth a visit to see how the other half lived in the early part of the twentieth century. It has a private art gallery with genuine Old Masters, sitting rooms decorated with eighteenth-century French paintings and antiques, and a gorgeous paneled library looking out at Central Park with its pair of Holbein portraits on either side of the mantelpiece. Supposedly Frick, a business associate of Andrew Carnegie, never read any of his leather-bound classics, preferring the daily newspapers, and had to be taught about art. But his home has been compared—favorably—with London's famous Wallace Collection. The Wallace Collection is also housed in a private mansion and was mentioned in Agatha Christie's *The Secret of Chimneys*. (See *Mystery Reader's Walking Guide: London*, Regents Park Walk.)

In Aaron Elkins's *A Glancing Light*, Seattle Art Museum Curator Chris Norgren stated that the finest small art museum in Europe was the Mauritshuis (in the Netherlands) because "there isn't a second-rate piece of work in the place. . . . Every painting, every object, is a jewel. It's like the Wallace Collection in London or the Frick in New York: a limited but superb collection in an elegant old town house."

The Frick might also work as the model for the city house of the once wealthy Maynards in Mary Roberts Rinehart's *The*

Swimming Pool, but it may be too light and large. The Maynard mansion was located in the East 70s near Central Park, but it had dark halls and curtained windows. Children like Lois Maynard, who grew up to write mystery stories for a living, were banished to the fifth-floor nursery or to supervised play in Central Park the way Cross's Kate Fansler's mother had been.

Because it was left "as is" with family possessions, the Frick could also be a substitute for Margaret Maron's Erich Breul House. But it is not on a small park like Gramercy Square in the East 20s and the best choice is still probably the Old Merchants House at 29 4th Street. (See also Walks 2 and 4.)

In Margaret Maron's *Corpus Christmas*, she lovingly describes the Breul House, lavishly built in the Gilded Age by a family who made their money in canal barges and blockade-running, like the Clintons and Vanderbilts, not in coke and steel, like the Fricks. But like Frick, the Breuls were great collectors of paintings and their mansion was also kept as a museum just as the Breuls left it. When its endowment became inadequate, its trustees looked for new sources of revenue, which led to murder. (See also Walk 2.) In Margery Allingham's *The China Governess*, the Kinnet family, who were art dealers, had a set of the famous Staffordshire Murder Cottages that was more complete than the collection held by the Van Hoyer Museum in NYC. This fictional museum sounds as if it might well be the Frick.

Turn right and walk along Fifth Avenue. Across from Central Park you pass row upon row of elegant apartment houses, which have replaced the mansions of Millionaire's Row. In Steve Allen's *Murder in Manhattan*, one movie scene was being shot in a Fifth Avenue penthouse at 71st. Steve walked there at dusk from the Plaza Hotel where the entire cast was staying just in time to see the director come close to scaring the Italian ingenue La Volpa into jumping off the penthouse balcony. (Her acting skills were very poor.)

Many of the buildings have discreet brass signs that indicate they are the offices of doctors, lawyers, orthodontists, and other well-paid professionals. Both the buildings and brass plates make it obvious this is a very appropriate area for the office/

home of Amanda Cross's psychiatrist Emmanuel Bauer in *In the Last Analysis*. Bauer was a former lover of Professor Kate Fansler, who noted that all psychiatrists were confined to the elegant East Side on Park, Fifth, and Madison Avenues, where they could be reached only by taxi, bus, or foot. A true-blue NYC native, Fansler had walked from her West Side apartment near Riverside Drive through Central Park. A murdered patient who turned out to have been a graduate student of Kate's was found dead in Bauer's office.

Turn right at 72nd Street to walk back to Madison Avenue. On the north side of 72nd Street in a landmark building you will see another private school, a co-ed elementary school, the Lycee Francaise de New York. If you want to get the feel of such institutions, at about 3 P.M. on a weekday afternoon, you'll see milling students in blue sweaters or blazers, skirts or pants occupy the entire block, together with their school buses, nannies, pet dogs, and mothers' cars.

Much farther east beyond First Avenue at 72nd Street and York Avenue is the oldest art auction house of them all. Founded in England, Sotheby Parke Bernet Auction House is at 1334 York Avenue. (If you want to see it, take a cab there, then return to complete the walk.) In Margaret Maron's *Death in Blue Folders*, "Satterwaites" was auctioning off the Cinderella glass slippers worn by famous movie star Elena Dorato, a kind of Mary Pickford-Jean Harlow-Greta Garbo mix. Adored in her day, Elena had drowned on an ocean liner trip.

Close by at Third Avenue and 73rd Street, there is a trendy little restaurant called Mezzaluna. It is really a gentrified pizza parlor—very popular and crowded all the time—but it won't take either credit cards or reservations. In Annette Meyers's *The Big Killing*, her Wall Street headhunter Leslie Wetzon went there with her old dancing buddy Carlos to celebrate his new job.

In Elizabeth Daly's *Murder in Volume 2*, most of the old New York Beauregard family lived with their aunt, the famous retired actress Mrs. Morton, on East 74th Street. The exception was Great Uncle Imbrie who lived in the old family mansion near Astor Place. The family included the attractive, animal-loving Clara, with whom book collector/sleuth Henry Gamadge fell in love and later married.

Still farther north and east at 75th Street and Lexington Avenue ballet conductor Miles Sutton was found dead in Edgar Box's (aka Gore Vidal's) *Death in the Fifth Position*. Sutton was married to the prima ballerina Ella Sutton, who had died during a new ballet called *Eclipse* when her supporting cable was cut. Mr. Washburn, the head of the Grand St. Petersburg Ballet where the Suttons had worked, and his young PR man, Peter Cutler Sargeant III, went to the scene of the crime from a reception at the Park Avenue mansion of Lady Edderdale, an important ballet backer. Her living room reminded Peter of the waiting room at Penn Station. Lady Edderdale (née Alma Shellabarger) was a Chicago meatpacking heiress who had married into the aristocracy.

Unless you detoured east to Sotheby's, turn left on Madison Avenue to walk north to 75th Street. Across Madison Avenue is the (main—there are several branches) Whitney Museum of American Art. Built of cement blocks with a skylight like a cyclops's eye, it is both unusual and modern. All its work in its collection is by American artists. It has a basement restaurant with a sculpture garden, as well as a museum store. In Johnson's *The Face in the Shadows*, Len Vandering, Cecily's artist uncle who was suspected of giving her drugs, asked Ellen Stacey to go there to see a nineteenth-century American landscape show.

After taking in the Whitney, keep going up Madison Avenue to 76th Street. The Hotel Carlyle is on the northeast corner. Its Café Carlyle has a famous daily lunch buffet and serves afternoon tea. At dinner there is a classical French cuisine and Bobby Short on the piano. In Mary Higgins Clark's *While My Pretty One Sleeps*, publisher Jack Campbell took Neeve Kearny there, partly to talk about the disappearance of writer Ethel Lambston, whom Neeve "dressed" and Jack was going to publish.

You have now walked two miles and might like to stop for something elegant to eat or drink yourself, perhaps afternoon tea. (Never say "high tea," that is a totally different English meal more like Sunday night supper.)

Whether you stop at the Carlyle or not, cross Madison Avenue and walk east on 76th Street past the hotel to Park Avenue. In Amanda Cross's *A Trap for Fools,* the wealthy retired Mr. Witherspoon, who studied the Middle East for amusement under murdered Professor Canfield Adams, lived on Park Avenue in the 70s. Kate Fansler visited him in a duplex that reminded her of her childhood, when family rooms were on one floor, public areas on another. They talked in his library, and when he realized she did not like sherry, he offered her an exquisite English tea.

The redbrick Lenox Hill Hospital sits on the far corner of Park Avenue at 76th Street. The hospital complex occupies the entire block, and it really is on a hill. (Most people forget that Manhattan is quite hilly, but that's what its Indian name meant.)

The Lenox Hill Hospital is famous not only because one of mystery's "Grand Masters," Dashiell Hammett, died there, but also because it "housed" various mysterious characters. In Emma Lathen's *Banking on Death*, the entire murder sprang from the fact that Hilda Schneider Henderson, daughter of the dynasty's founder, was dying at the hospital. Her death would wind up the family trust being administered by John Putnam Thatcher's Sloan Guarantee Trust.

In Annette Meyers's *Tender Death*, Wetzon's elderly friend Hazel Osborn, a self-described professional volunteer whom headhunter Wetzon had met at the American Folk Art Museum, was brought here for observation. Hazel's rich friend "Peepsie" Cunningham had jumped out of her apartment at 999 Fifth Avenue, across from the Metropolitan Museum of Art. In Shannon O'Cork's *The Murder of Muriel Lake*, which is about a Writers of Mystery Convention (aka MWA?), grande mistress Muriel Lake was murdered. When novice mystery writer Cecilia Burnett figured out who committed the murder she was attacked. She was then taken to Lennox Hill Hospital and given seventeen stitches.

Still farther east at Third Avenue was the Rensselaer Apartment Building, where murder victim Julie Redmond lived in Maron's *The Death of a Butterfly*. In Tony Hillerman's *A Thief of Time*, Navajo Lieutenant Joe Leaphorn visited the crippled, voyeur buyer of the stolen Anasazi St. John Polychrome bowl at First Avenue and 78th Street, in a neighborhood of uniformed doormen and expensive dogs that were being walked by people hired for the jobs. Richard DuMont liked stories of blood with his treasures and sent Leaphorn off with an avid, "Call me with all the details. When you find her body."

Walk three blocks up Park Avenue to 79th Street. This is "fat cat territory," filled with rich doctors, lawyers, and merchant chiefs. Individual buildings described in mysteries may not exist, but there are similar examples all about you. At Third Avenue and East 79th Street in William Love's *The Chartreuse Clue*, there was a high-rise co-op with a marble facade and a big black doorman who was very solicitous of elderly Abe Nathanson. Nathanson was a sort of Bernard Baruch type who was consulted by VIPS of all kinds, very much like "framed" elder statesman John Paul Marcus in Charlotte Armstrong's *Alibi for Murder*. Love's Nathanson was a friend of crippled Bishop Regan, who helped the bishop and Davy Goldman solve a family bank business murder.

Haughton Murphy's retired Wall Street law partner Reuben Frost lived in the East 70s near Lexington Avenue. Frost took taxis back and forth across town to "Fort Bliss," the nickname for the new fortresslike quarters of Chase and Ward. Frost was called back to solve the murder of associate Juliana Merriman in *Murder Saves Face*. (See Walk 5.) Earlier, in *Murder for Lunch*, Chase and Ward's Executive Partner George Bannard lived at 79th Street and Park Avenue and took the Wall Street Express bus to work, unlike his murdered partner Graham Donovan, who lived in a fancy co-op on 82nd Street and preferred to use preselected cabs. (See Walk 1.)

Turn left to walk along 79th Street to Madison Avenue. You will pass an entire block of art galleries, which is why this was a perfect location for Myra Dedek's art gallery in Lockridge's *Murder for Art's Sake*. Feel free to stop and look at them; it is unlikely that you will be shanghaied the way Dorian Weigand was.

At the southeast corner of 79th Street and Fifth Avenue there is a limestone landmark mansion built in the French

"Jacques Coeur" medieval style that houses the Ukrainian Institute of America. Built in 1899 as the home of August van Horn Stuyvesant, it is typical of the mansions that once lined these streets. It, too, would make an excellent home for millionaire Julian Trent in Maron's *Death in Blue Folders*.

Cross Fifth Avenue to Central Park and turn right to walk to 82nd Street and the main entrance to the Metropolitan Museum of Art. As you go, glance at the apartments that line the eastern side of Fifth Avenue and pick one for the Reverend Claire Aldington. In Holland's *A Death at St. Anselm's*, using her dead husband's money, Claire was able to live in an expensive co-op with three bedrooms and a view of the Metropolitan Museum of Art at 28 E. 82nd Street. Of its various holiday decorations, Claire liked the Museum's Christmas exhibit with the Baroque crèche the best. You also should look for a substitute for 999 Fifth Avenue, where Meyers's Leslie Wetzon and her older friend Hazel saw Hazel's college chum "Peepsie" Cunningham fall to her death.

The Met is a place you must investigate, now or another time. Mystery characters seem to go to the Metropolitan Museum of Art far more than any other museum except for the Natural History Museum across Central Park. (See Walk 10.) The Metropolitan Museum of Art is one of the largest in the New World and one of a half-dozen great museums anywhere. No other museum rivals the scope of its collections, which range from Egyptian mummies and Greek chariots to Chinese, Islamic, and Indian pottery, European Old Masters, French Impressionists, and Modern and Post-Modern paintings. It also holds frequent and impressive special exhibitions.

In Aaron Elkins's *A Glancing Light*, Chris Norgren, curator of Renaissance and Baroque Art at the Seattle Art Museum, who was sent to Italy to ship paintings for a special exhibition, commented that most world-famous art museums are "provincial." He meant that places like the Uffizi, the Prado, and the Rijksmuseum are primarily showcases for their native sons. He added that it takes a museum without much cultural pedigree of its own (like the Metropolitan), or with a long history of big spending (like London's National Gallery), or with the help of the world's most preeminent looter, Napoleon (like the Louvre), to be truly eclectic.

Its grand staircase outside on Fifth Avenue is used as a park bench by pedestrians of all kinds, but to your left as you face the museum there is also a student/handicapped entrance you can use. Inside on the ground floor there is a museum shop, a place to buy tickets for the museum, and restrooms.

This walk ends here. Many visitors settle for a look at one or two galleries at a time and this may be a good idea if you have already completed a three-mile walk. If you want to go inside now, pick your own poison, as the saying goes. This also a good place to get something to eat or drink.

In Piesman's *Personal Effects*, when Nina Fischman, tracking her friend Susan's murderer, met her mother Ida there for a council of war, Nina gave them five bucks for two admission fees. Her mother, a retired school teacher who had become a full-time museum groupie, was outraged, because she never paid more than twenty-five cents to get into any museum.

Since her mother had seen all the current exhibits, they went to have tea in the museum restaurant where Nina remembered a fountain in the expensive section, now reserved for sleek society matrons and impeccably groomed gay men. In Jane Dentinger's *First Hit of the Season*, actress Jocelyn O'Roarke met her friend Irene's lover Marc here for a secret confab about the murder of critic Jason Saylin. Heads swiveled as handsome Marc followed Josh to their table, and their lunch was interrupted by Irene's arrival. When Irene got nasty, Josh shoved her into the fountain, then left, only to be picked up outside by the NYPD for questioning about the murder.

In Dorothy B. Hughes's *The Fallen Sparrow*, Kit McKittrick's widowed mother had married Geoffrey Wilhite. The Wilhites had endowed a wing at the Met, where Kit hoped to display the fabled jeweled Babylon Goblets. Kit had rescued them during the Spanish Civil War when "the other side" tried to get them for Adolph Hitler's personal collection. (Hitler—and Göring—tried hard to outloot Napoleon. The remnants of their efforts are still reappearing in Europe, as they did in Aaron Elkins's *Fellowship of Fear*, which also starred curator Chris Norgren.)

In Carol Brennan's *Headhunt*, Liz Wareham found out that her murdered (and childless) client King Carter had done the proper NYC thing and left the bulk of his estate to the Metropolitan and Harvard University. In Lisa Bennett's *Madison Avenue Murder*, Peg Goodenough, daughter of world-famous abstract painter Theo Goodenough, was working at a Madison Avenue ad agency where someone was murdered. As a result, Peg met NYPD detective Dante Cursio (Dan). Later, on a date, they walked through an exhibit of Degas paintings. Dan had an M.F.A. from Columbia University but he had decided that teaching art was not as good as being a cop.

In Maron's *One Coffee With*, Vanderlyn instructor David Wade, the lover/fiancé of the Art Department's secretary Sandy Keppler, was supposed to be at the Met seeing an exhibit when someone poisoned the coffee of art professor Riley Quinn. In Mary Higgins Clark's *While My Pretty One Sleeps*, NYC Police Commissioner Myles Kearny's Italian-born wife Renata was found murdered near the Egyptian wing soon after Kearny had "put away" mobster Nicky Sepetti.

If you want to quit now, and it's not rush hour, you can take a leisurely Fifth Avenue bus trip downtown. This bus stops at the museum door. Or you can make one or more of the following side trips. You probably will want to take a cab to your destination.

POSSIBLE SIDE TRIPS

Museum Mile. In Maron's *Corpus Christmas*, NYPD cops Matt Eberstadt and Bernie Peters went to the Guggenheim Museum to check out the recent movements of murdered Dr. Shambley. A museum shop clerk with a punk haircut remembered that Shambley had bought two identical Fernand Léger posters. She remembered being surprised because Dr. Shambley's period was late-nineteenth-century American art.

In Joyce Christmas's *A Fete Worse Than Death*, Lady Margaret Priam met social climber Emma Ross at a black-tie opening in a "large white art museum opposite Central Park, with swirling ramps and white walls." This sounds just like the Guggenheim.

So does the Gary, in Emma Lathen's *Come to Dust*. Sloan Guarantee Trust vice president John Putnam Thatcher was taken there by his boss, George Lancer, to see an opening. Thatcher considered the Gary an eccentric exercise in spiraling ramps. They saw an exhibit of European gouaches, hung by an Old Brunsie, that is, a graduate of Ivy League Brunswick College, where all male Lancers always went.

Yorkville. It would be about the right area for an Anglican retreat house called the House of the Savior in an old house on 94th Street in Holland's *A Fatal Advent*, where the Reverend Claire Aldington took an abused wife who was her client. It was run by an Anglican nun, Mother Mary Margaret, who was very like Madeleine L'Engle's Mother Catherine of Siena in *The Severed Wasp*.

By contrast, in John Lutz's *Shadowtown*, the very classy apartment of soap opera star Lana Spence was at 96th and Lexington. This was the place where NYPD Detective "Ox" Oxman chased and almost caught one of the vampires playing hide-and-seek with Lana. In Clark's *While My Pretty One Sleeps*, Neeve Kearny's boutique Neeve's Place was at 84th and Madison.

To the south and east along FDR Highway and the East River there are many contemporary high rises. In Lawrence Sanders's *The First Deadly Sin*, his protagonist Daniel Blank, who stalked the Upper East Side armed with an ice ax, lived in a bare apartment house of glass and enameled steel that occupied an entire city block on East 83rd Street. It was built in a U shape with a blacktopped driveway and a stainless steel portico with green outdoor carpeting. Inside, the lobby had chairs and sofas of black chrome and plastic, abstract paintings, and a heavy bronze sculpture called *Birth*. Blank, who was the ultimate fitness freak, lived in an exceptionally large apartment where one long wall was covered with mirrors.

In Steve Allen's *Murder in Manhattan*, the movie's producer Nashville Stuart lived in a brand-new skyscraper on the

East River, which rose in a dramatic series of terraces and curves like an Aztec temple. Seeking clues, Steve visited Stuart there after Stuart's bastard son Trip had been murdered.

Gracie Mansion. In Richard Barth's *The Condo Kill*, senior citizen Margaret Binton organized her senior-citizen-center friends to stop a shady Upper West Side developer who was trying to empty a building on 93rd Street. When one of the remaining tenants, Angelo Varonetti, was murdered, it turned out he had managed to shoot the developer's hit man. Afraid of being caught, the developer killed his hit man and dumped his body in the East River. It was found near Gracie Mansion with Angelo Varonetti's old bullet in his leg and a new one at the base of his skull. In Haughton Murphy's *Murder for Lunch*, retired Wall Street lawyer Reuben Frost's wife Cynthia told him she was going to Gracie Mansion for another "dreary ceremony," involving another effort to bring culture into the schools.

9

CENTRAL PARK WALK

BACKGROUND

Central Park is the great wide open space where New Yorkers romp and recruit their energies for the week ahead. It is also regularly the scene of the crime, where more mystery characters go to play or be preyed on than any other place in Manhattan, with the possible exceptions of Greenwich Village and Fifth Avenue.

The idea of conserving centrally located open land for recreational use came from editor-poet William Cullen Bryant, who started a campaign for such a spot in The *New York Post* in 1850. Surprisingly, the New York legislature did agree that NYC needed a version of London's Kensington Gardens/Hyde Park. But future Tammany Hall Boss Tweed, then a city alderman, managed to convince them to build the park in very unpromising terrain—the rocky and swampy territory between 59th and 110th Streets—and to pay his cronies a pricely $7 thousand per acre for it.

Central Park is almost 850 acres, 2.5 miles long and .5 mile wide, with 58 miles of pathways. The city held a contest for park designs, which was won by Frederick Law Olmsted and Calvert Vaux. They planned a natural-looking landscape, which they wanted to call "Greensward." As a result, today's rocky ledges, meadows, and woods are only "man-made" nature, a tamed wilderness within sight of skyscrapers.

It took fifteen years to build and cost $14 million, as the designers evacuated squatters, moved rocks, drained swamps, created new lakes, and planted over 500,000 new trees and shrubs. They also created four sunken transverse roads that sent east-west traffic through the park without disrupting the view or the use of the land itself. (Olmsted later designed the Chicago World's Fair of 1893 as well as several other NYC parks.)

During the Great Depression in the 1930s, the Reservoir was emptied and the jobless (yesterday's homeless) built a "Hooverville" there. More recently, Parks Commissioner Robert Moses installed many asphalt playgrounds, a move that annoyed the environmentalists, who are also angry that the Metropolitan Museum of Art keeps wanting to encroach on the park. Central Park is used by everybody: VIPs jog there; people build ice brontosauruses, roller skate with their pets, and make love; there are free concerts and plays, ranging from Simon and Garfunkel to the New York Philharmonic, Gilbert and Sullivan to Shakespeare; and activities like boating, biking, riding horses, walking, bowling, ball playing or eating—you name it, you can do it in the park.

Mystery walkers should do this walk during regular business hours and not loiter in shady or hidden spots. Remember, too, that the hordes of early morning or evening dog walkers or joggers come to grief as regularly in real life as they do in mystery stories. Better not to walk alone, especially after dark. If you do, you have only yourself to blame if you find a body or turn into one yourself.

Still, there is great ambivalence about the place, even among the natives. In Amanda Cross's and Isabelle Holland's mystery stories, where characters wander in and out of the park continually, you may read how Kate Fansler's mother missed the days when she could play hide and seek in the Ramble. Fansler herself marches back and forth through the park by choice; her friends' children play there; her Theban School guard dogs exercise there; her nephew Leo plays baseball there; and, most significantly, Reed Amhearst makes his final, successful marriage proposal to Kate by the Boathouse in Central Park. Holland does place a mutilated body in the park, but the victim was not murdered there.

Go on a weekend, especially a Sunday, when the park is full of New Yorkers at play and no cars are allowed. In good weather it will be jammed and you will have to accept the *New Yorker*'s E. B. White's idea that in NYC eighteen inches is enough personal space to create privacy. But you can see and enjoy the sights while participating in this mass ritual that celebrates surviving another week in the Big Apple.

This walk does not go all the way from Central Park South at 59th Street to Central Park North at 110th Street. It goes from Grand Army Plaza at Fifth Avenue at 59th Street to the reservoir at 86th Street, then doubles back to Columbus Circle at Central Park South. Most mystery story sites do not venture north of the reservoir.

LENGTH OF WALK: About 2 miles

The length of the walk depends on how much you wander off the beaten paths. Watch it!

See map on page 228 for the boundaries of this walk and page 326 for a list of books and detectives mentioned.

PLACES OF INTEREST

Central Park
> *The Reservoir*, 86th Street transverse.
>
> *The Lake (and Loeb Boathouse)*, West 74th Street.
>
> *The Great Lawn (Cleopatra's Needle)*, 82nd Street.
>
> *The Ramble*, 75th Street.
>
> *Belvedere Lake and Castle*, Delacorte Theater, south of the Great Lawn at 80th Street.
>
> *The Sheep Meadow*, 68th Street.
>
> *The Mall*, 77th to 66th Streets.
>
> *The Central Park Zoo and Children's Zoo*, 65th Street.
>
> *Strawberry Fields*, East 72nd Street. Memorial to murdered Beatle John Lennon who lived at the Dakota. (See also Walk 10.)

Metropolitan Museum of Art, East 82nd Street and Fifth Avenue. (See Walk 8 for details.)

Ritz-Carlton Hotel, 112 Central Park South. Successor to the original Ritz Hotel on Madison Avenue between 46th and 47th Streets. Very expensive. Call 757-1900.

PLACES TO EAT

Tavern on the Green, Central Park West at 67th Street. Popular for birthdays, desserts. Ye Olde English outside/glassed interior. Outdoor tables in good weather. Drinks, preshow (Lincoln Center) food. Expensive. Call 873-3200.

Loeb Boathouse, East 72th Street. Refreshments, including drinks. Indoor/outdoor ambiance. Expensive. Open 11:00 A.M.– 11:00 P.M. Call 517-3623.

Metropolitan Museum of Art, East 82nd Street. Museum cafeteria and restaurant. Inexpensive Museum Dining Room, open to public on weekends. (See Walk 8.)

Mickey Mantle's, 42 Central Park South. Good for drinks, hamburgers, ribs, etc. Decor: baseball memorabilia, wooden tables. Expensive. Call 688-7777.

Rumplemayer's, St. Moritz Hotel, Central Park South. Ice cream!

Street Vendors, all over.

——————— CENTRAL PARK WALK ———————

Begin your walk at Central Park's Fifth Avenue entrance at Grand Army Plaza on 59th Street. This is the place where you can rent a horse and hansom to tour the park in style if you'd like. (One of the classic mysteries is Fergus W. Hume's *The Mystery of a Hansom Cab*, but its ambiance is strictly Victorian London.)

In S. S. Van Dine's *The Greene Murder Case*, as members of an old New York family continued to murder one another, the family doctor, Van Blon, took two of them for a ride one pleasant day. Amateur sleuth Philo Vance and his Watson, S. S. Van

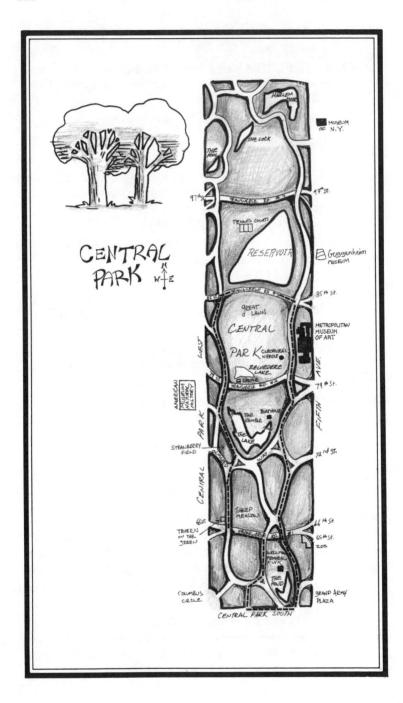

Dine, came along for the ride. The Daimler went north on Fifth Avenue to enter Central Park, and crossing the park, headed for Riverside Drive where it drove north. Its passengers admired the view of the Hudson River.

In thriller writer Helen MacInnes's *Neither Five Nor Three*, NYC career girl Rona Metford was in love with a guy who was really a Soviet spy. Scott Ettley needed her affection only to protect his cover. On a fine spring day Ettley took her for a romantic hansom cab ride through Central Park, but when his bosses told him Rona must be eliminated, Ettley coaxed her to walk in the park one evening so his Soviet confederates could mug her.

The Fifth Avenue entrance near the Plaza Hotel is the most popular corner for mysterious shadowers, muggers, and police stakeouts, so watch out. In Annette Meyers's *The Big Killing*, it was near the Plaza Hotel that Wall Street headhunter Leslie Wetzon realized she was being followed. Wetzon took off fast into Central Park, racing past nannies, joggers, senior citizens, and big black dogs. Across the park and out at Columbus Avenue, Wetzon finally trapped her shadow, who turned out to be Ann Buffolino, a childhood friend of the murdered Barry Stark.

In Ellery Queen's *The Roman Hat Mystery*, the NYPD staked out murdered Monte Field's valet near the Fifth Avenue entrance by the Plaza circle, where the valet had a rendezvous with Field's murderer. The valet sat inside Central Park on the nearest bench. Then, as the church bells tolled midnight, he got up, counted benches, and met the murderer at the seventh bench.

In Barbara Paul's wacky *Liars and Tyrants and People Who Turn Blue*, Shelby Kent, who had the strange ability to tell when people lied to her—she detected a red aura—was recruited to help the newly formed UN Militia. Sir John Dudley, in charge of both the militia and a UN investigation into some unexplained terrorist activity, took a walk in Central Park to clear the cobwebs out of his head. He sat on a bench thinking, until it began to get dark. Then he realized he was sitting on his elderly London derriere alone in perilous Central Park and scurried away.

In Amanda Cross's *The Theban Mysteries*, the Theban School's woman-hating security guard O'Hara took his guard dogs Rose and Lily to Central Park to run every morning. O'Hara was outraged when his dogs were accused of killing Mrs. Jablon, mother of Theban senior Angelica. Reed Amhearst finally tested the dogs himself. He hid from them in the school and let them find him to see what they would do.

In Frances and Richard Lockridge's *The Norths Meet Murder*, because he was reading a badly typed manuscript, editor Jerry West missed lunch, so he left his office for a walk in Central Park. This behavior left him with no alibi for the murder that took place in his Village apartment.

In Ellery Queen's *The French Powder Mystery*, Berniece French, the stepdaughter of the owner of French's Department Store, left the Astor Hotel (aka Waldorf Astoria) with her blond boyfriend. They drove around Central Park in a special cab and were later picked up in the park by another car. That was the last time Berniece was seen until her body was found.

In Isaac Asimov's *Murder at the ABA*, Central Park was only two blocks from writer Darius Just's apartment. Just and his new girlfriend, the ABA convention hotel's PR person, Sarah Voskovek, sat there in the gloaming when they were suddenly attacked. Just was a karate expert and fought off the attacker but banged his head on a tree and got a concussion.

Keeping a wary distance from benches, take the path to your right, heading past the Pond toward the Central Park Zoo and the smaller Children's Zoo. To your left is the Wollman Memorial Rink, which was redone by millionaire entrepreneur Donald Trump, who added a miniature golf course with models of the famous NYC skyscrapers.

In Marissa Piesman's *Personal Effects*, lawyer Nina Fischman, on the trail of the murderer of her childhood friend Susan, met Patrick, a sexy ex-lawyer with a dog named Daisy, whom they took to Central Park. Patrick commented they probably called it Trump Rink by now, indicating that he was not too impressed by "Trumping." In Mary Higgins Clark's *A Stranger Is Watching*, free-lancer Sharon Martin and her widowed suitor Steve Peterson were going to take his son Neil skating at the rink but Neil would not go.

The zoo is just south of the 66th Street transverse; the Children's Zoo is just north of it. They are separated by the archway with the Delacorte Clock. On your left is the 1870 Victorian building called the Dairy, once a milk bar, now a Visitors Information Center, and a charming, old-fashioned 1908 Carousel (or merry-go-round) under a canopy roof.

In Steve Allen's *Murder in Manhattan,* a day's shoot for a movie Steve is in took place there. In the makeup trailer parked nearby, the staff prepared Steve for his cameo part as decadent novelist Toots Gable (based on Truman Capote, author of *In Cold Blood*). Shooting their scene, Steve and Mimi, the director's wife, sat on the painted wooden horses stuck on brass poles, listening to the calliope music.

Explore the Central Park Zoo, which has been renovated to allow the animals to roam about in more natural surroundings. In Holland's *A Fatal Advent*, the Reverend Claire Aldington found the missing small boy soprano, whose mother had been murdered, hiding at the zoo. In Amanda Cross's *In the Last Analysis*, the small sons of murder suspect psychiatrist Dr. Emmanuel Bauer were taken to Central Park by their nanny to a babysitters' "colony" near the zoo. In Velda Johnson's *The Face in the Shadows*, Ellen Stacey and artist Len Vandering met at the zoo after all the bad guys had been caught. Steve Allen also met TV actor Zachary Holden by the sea lions' pool for a secret conference.

By far the nastiest episode at the zoo occurred in Lillian O'Donnell's *The Children's Zoo*. A gang of overprivileged punks staged an initiation rite there, slaughtering defenseless animals in cold blood and killing a guard. NYPD's Sergeant Norah Mulcahaney of Homicide responded to the first call and found herself involved in a series of senseless, brutal murders committed by rich kids from the Upper East Side. Fortunately, you can look at the birds and animals without seeing them strangled or stabbed.

Cross over the 66th Street transverse and go left on Olmstead Way until you come to a path called West Drive, which leads to the Tavern on the Green. Once the sheep's fold, the Tavern on the Green looks like a charming Old World inn, or a sort of brick British pub, with pointed, shingled roofs and a red awning. It has a greenhouse wing and outdoor tables and clusters of tiny lights, so the overall effect is a strange mixture of Japanese tea garden with glitter.

In Richard Barth's *The Condo Kill*, developer Jason Farrell invited senior activist Margaret Binton to eat at the Tavern and talk about their "mutual interests." Margaret had organized members of her senior citizen center to intimidate prospective tenants for his new building, in order to prevent him kicking out older tenants in another, scarcely occupied building he planned to tear down. While they lunched in Central Park, his strongman went into that almost empty building and killed one of the two remaining tenants.

As Margaret waited for Farrell, she saw mothers in Gucci belts and Calvin Klein jeans with young kids, businessmen flashing gold cuff links at each other, and elegant waiters. The last time she ate in the park she had been looking at the seals and eating from a brown paper bag. She and Farrell ate in the crystal room, done in enough gold to dazzle an archduke. By contrast, Crespi's Simona and her detective date lunched at "Chez Sabrett," a hot dog vendor with a red and yellow umbrella.

In Clark's *Loves Music, Loves to Dance*, Darcy Scott, trying to track her best friend Erin Kelley's killer, met a suspect from a personals ad here. Her date had lied about his age—he was fifty, not thirty—and he just wanted companionship when "in town" from Milwaukee. To get away, Darcy pretended to spot her husband and rushed out.

In Elizabeth Peters's *Naked Once More*, ex-librarian Jacqueline Kirby of the bronze hair, huge purse, and unexpected behavior, met her very conventional literary agent Chris here for lunch because *she* loved it. She arrived in an ankle-length cloak covered with sequins, which she had to tuck under her chair so it would not trip their waiter. They talked about the fascinating possibility that she might be chosen by the heirs of the dead Kathleen Darcy (Margaret Mitchell crossed with Mary Stewart and Jean Auel) to write the sequel to Darcy's incredibly best-selling novel, a one-of-a-kind phenomenon like *Gone with the Wind*. Jacqueline drank a martini, ate a salad, then had the chocolate cake known as the Deadly Delight.

After looking over or trying out the Tavern on the Green, take West Drive back toward Olmstead Way. This route takes you to the Sheep Meadow, a large open, grassy area where no frisbee games or loud radios are allowed.

In Piesman's *Personal Effects*, Nina Fischman and her date Patrick went there to throw a tennis ball for his dog Daisy because Nina had promised NYPD detective James Williams that she would not go "out of town" with any dates she met through personals ads.

In Trella Crespi's *The Trouble with a Small Raise*, NYPD detective Greenhouse called Simona and invited her to meet him in Central Park. This was not official business but a date. They sat in the Sheep Meadow—lots of space, no trees to block the sun—with the Manhattan population spread over the park like thick jam on toast.

In George Chesbro's *Bone*, social workers Anne Winchell and Barry Prindle, together with Dr. Ali Hakim, came to the Sheep Meadow. They were trying to persuade the homeless man called "Bone" to come in out of the rain. Bone had been squatting in the Meadow for two days without knowing where he was. As they talked to him, Bone suddenly "waked up" and began to speak, although he had no memory at all. His lack of memory convinced the NYPD that he had beheaded other homeless people.

After gazing at the Sheep Meadow keep going left, or east. You pass by the Bowling Greens, though some park habitués just use parkland. In Barth's *The Condo Kill*, the murdered tenant Angelo Varonetti bowled in a field, not on the courts near 69th Street, which were too crowded. When the developer's hit man had found him there, he dropped the heavy ball on Angelo's foot as a warning.

Toward your right on the eastern side of the park there are some tennis courts, although more of them are farther north beyond the reservoir. In Margaret Maron's *Death of a Butterfly*, NYPD Lieutenant Sigrid Harald parked near the tennis courts to look for murder suspect George Franklin. While waiting for him to finish a game, Sigrid watched a croquet game—the only sport she was good at, thanks to her southern grandmother—and ate a hot dog bought from a vendor.

In S. S. Van Dine's *The Canary Murder Case*, Philo Vance, his lawyer sidekick Van Dine, and his friend D.A. John F. X. Markham, drove from Vance's apartment in Murray Hill up Madison Avenue to Central Park. They took the 72nd Street entrance to reach the apartment of the murdered Canary (singer/showgirl/celebrity) at 184 W. 71st Street on the Upper West Side.

In William F. Love's *The Chartreuse Clue*, Roman Catholic Bishop Regan's bodyguard/chauffeur P.I. Davy Goldman had been to the scene of the crime at 501 W. 76th Street to check it out for the bishop. Then he drove through Central Park to pick up his girl, who lived at 225 E. 65th Street. The NYPD was not impressed by Davy's claim that to pick up his girl he took the longest way possible through Central Park "because it was a beautiful day." (Bishop Regan's residence was on West 37th Street.) In Maron's *One Coffee With*, NYPD Lieutenant Sigrid Harald also took 72nd Street, from the East to the West Side. She was on her way to inspect the brownstone of murdered Vanderlyn College art professor Riley Quinn.

Just north of the 72nd Street transverse and west of Olmstead Way is Strawberry Fields, a little landscaped memorial garden named for a 1967 song by Beatle John Lennon. Lennon was shot outside the Dakota on Central Park West. (See Walk 10.) There are no strawberries, but there are exotic plantings from twenty countries and a mosaic ground sculpture called "Imagine" given by his wife Yoko Ono.

In Charlotte MacLeod's *The Curse of the Giant Hogweed*, the hogweed was a strange plant with magical properties that could involve you in mythical adventures. In a 1990 letter to me, MacLeod explained that *Heracleum mantegazzianum* grows *anywhere*. This gargantuan relative of cow parsley and water hemlock takes over riverbanks and hedgerows, growing fifteen-foot stalks and bristles, with a dingy white flower with over 5,000 seeds. The hogweed would soon take over Central Park, but what a perfect way to eliminate muggers! It also seems to belong with the other foreign flora in John Lennon's Strawberry Fields and would allow the passersby to have an adventure à la Merlin or the Yellow Submarine.

Keep Strawberry Fields to your left as you walk along Olmsted Way on the edge of the Lake. You are looking for the footbridge over the Lake at its northwestern corner, which will take you into the Ramble. The Lake is really a lagoon, with reeds and water lilies and even some fishermen in good weather. You can rent a boat at the Loeb Boathouse on the eastern edge of the Lake. A number of mystery characters, like Stout's Archie Goodwin, were seen rowing here.

Trella Crespi's Simona Griffo was there on location to act as NYPD liaison after her agency's creative director, Fred Critelli, was murdered in his office. The NYPD wanted to talk to the number two art director, Dana Lehrman, but they had to deal with an entire set-up of a models' van, makeup, etc. and found everyone busy with shooting the ads for a client, "Merry Shirts." The photographer was aiming at the bridge where three female models stood, waving at a rowboat containing a male model in a tuxedo.

Because this kind of photo op is a fairly common weekday occurrence in Central Park, it is all the more intriguing to realize that in P. M. Carlson's *Murder Unrenovated*, actor Nick O'Connor sauntered across Central Park, followed by a lanky young woman in red beret, scarf, and trench coat. The spy accosted him by the footbridge in true Marlene Dietrich (or Evelyn Anthony, or Martha Albrand) style and asked, "Haben Sie Feuer?" When Nick O'Connor responded (à la Ian Fleming's James Bond), "Agent 42, I presume?" Maggie grabbed him, knocking him off balance, and they fell into the leaves under the bridge for some casual sex. They were observed only by two elderly couples and a golden retriever!

Cross the bridge and keep going to your right around the lake. On the paved pathways there are plenty of benches where people sit in good weather, reading books and newspapers. The park at this point is quite hilly and full of brambles and gnarled trees because you are now in the sinister Ramble. Go north on the paths through here, and better yet, like Nick, bring company.

In Amanda Cross's *A Trap for Fools*, intrepid Kate Fansler, who walked Central Park regularly, went home from a visit to the elegant East Side duplex of Columbia University benefactor Witherspoon, who had studied under murdered Professor Canfield Adams. Fansler took a southwesterly direction through the Ramble, wooded and bushy, and no longer as safe as it was in her mother's day. Fansler despised her mother's snobbish lament for the good old days, but felt it, too. (See Walks 8 and 10.)

On Christmas Day, in George Chesbro's *Second Horseman Out of Eden*, their friends in the NYPD took the Frederickson brothers, Garth and Mongo, "to see a present" left in the Ramble for them. It was the castrated and crucified body of the Reverend William Kenecky, a slimy TV evangelist and cult leader. Kenecky had been molesting little Vicky Brown, whose letter to Santa got the Fredericksons involved in the case.

In Isabelle Holland's *A Lover Scorned*, the naked, mutilated body of the Reverend Ida Blake was found in Central Park early one Saturday morning. This killing started a wave of serial killings of women priests that made the Reverend Claire Aldington's family and friends worry about her safety. But typically, the Reverend Claire went right on walking through Central Park alone.

Work your way north out of the Ramble to the 79th Street transverse. In Annette Meyers's *The Big Killing*, after the murder of broker Barry Stark at the Four Seasons, Leslie Wetzon was driven home by NYPD Sergeant Silvestri. Along the 79th Street transverse another car rammed them into the transverse wall and they were shot at.

Cross over the transverse carefully and find a path between the Shakespeare Garden, with the Japanese cherry blossoms, and Belvedere Castle and Lake with the Delacorte Theater. In Cross's *In the Last Analysis*, the suspect's wife Nicola had skipped her appointment with her shrink the day of the murder to wander about Central Park among the Japanese cherry blossoms (which cannot give her an alibi).

Stop to look at the view from tiny Belvedere Castle, a Victorian "fantasy" made to be a lookout point. Then turn to the left past the Delacorte Theater, where Shakespeare is performed, and go right to walk north toward the Reservoir, across the western edge of the Great Lawn, a vast green area with a cyclone fence around it.

In Carlson's *Murder Unrenovated*, there was a birthday celebration in 1972 for "Fred-Law" Olmsted, the principal creator of Central Park. There was a giant green birthday cake made of cheese and an actor dressed up to play Olmsted. Julia Northrup, a retired fifth-grade teacher who had written about Olmsted, went to the party with her stuffy son and daughter-in-law and grandson Greg. They heard the music of Scott Joplin and saw everybody from hippies to bag ladies to the NYC Establishment. (Julia's family wanted her to move out of the basement apartment in the brownstone Nick and Maggie O'Connor were buying in Brooklyn's Park Slope.)

Keep going north to the 85th Street transverse and cross it to reach the edge of the Reservoir. Unless you want to jog around it, follow the driveway, which is filled with runners, horses, people, and dogs. Head across the park toward East Drive.

In Cross's *In the Last Analysis*, when a patient did not show up for her appointment, Dr. Bauer went out and walked around and around the Reservoir. (Not an alibi.) Later, when Kate Fansler hired her niece Sally's fiancé Jerry to tail Dr. Bauer, Jerry saw him stop to help a silly fat lady find her lost dog nearby.

In Holland's *A Death at St. Anselm's*, vestryman and Wall Street lawyer Brett Cunningham told the Reverend Claire Aldington's son Jamey to run around the Reservoir twice (6 miles) with his dog Motley. Brett did it himself as often as he had time. By the time of *A Fatal Advent*, Jamey and Motley were also doing it.

In Elizabeth Daly's *The Book of the Lion*, a drunken Lost Generation writer Paul Bradlock was either mugged or had a brawl near the Reservoir. Bradlock's body was then left near some benches on Fifth Avenue. Henry Gamadge became involved in the murder when Bradlock's brother wanted to help the widow sell Bradlock's papers. It looked as if Bradlock had owned a copy of a missing Chaucer work, *The Book of the Lion*.

Turn right on East Drive to go south parallel to Fifth Avenue (or Museum Mile). If you haven't done so, cut over to Fifth

Avenue now to visit the Guggenheim Museum at 89th Street, housed in a fabulously modern Frank Lloyd Wright building. The museum's circular ramp ought to inspire some mystery writer à la Mary Roberts Rinehart's *The Circular Staircase*, or Dorothy L. Sayers's *Murder Must Advertise*, classic mysteries where circular stairs were killers.

As you walk south, you come to the back of the Metropolitan Museum of Art. You can go around and inside if you like. (See also Walk 8.) The Met is enormous and has places to eat, restrooms, and such, so it makes a good place to take a break. On your right near the statue of Alexander Hamilton is the spot where the real-life so-called yuppie murder took place several years ago, when a young man strangled his date.

The Egyptian wing and the Temple of Dendur are on the northeastern side of the Metropolitan. In Clark's *While My Pretty One Sleeps*, the Italian-born wife of retired NYPD Commissioner Myles Kearny was found near here with her throat cut. Kearny finally went to the museum, telling himself he had always wanted to see the Temple of Dendur, but really wanting to lay his wife Renata's ghost to rest. When his daughter Neeve went jogging in Central Park with publisher Jack Campbell, she also shied away from the museum, explaining to him why she hated the site.

Past the Metropolitan on East Drive you come to Cleopatra's Needle, an ancient obelisk that is the twin of the one on the Thames Embankment in London. Dating from 1600 B.C., it has nothing to do with Cleopatra, although the Romans took it to Alexandria from Heliopolis in 12 B.C. It was given to NYC by the Khedive of Egypt in 1881. In G. K. Chesterton's *The Man Who Was Thursday*, the spy "Thursday" landed by its twin, also called Cleopatra's Needle, on the Thames Embankment in the dead of night, on his way to meet "Sunday" in Leicester Square. (See *Mystery Reader's Walking Guide: London*, Covent Garden Walk.)

Cross over the 79th Street transverse and walk past the eastern edge of the Ramble until you come to Loeb's Boathouse on the Lake. You can get refreshments, rent a boat, or sit and watch the rowers. In Cross's *Poetic Justice*, Reed Amhearst and Kate

Fansler went to the park on a Saturday. Reed (always the perfect gentleman/lover in the style of Lord Peter Wimsey) asked if Kate wanted to rent a boat. She said no, she wanted to go get a beer at the Boathouse and sit on the hill and watch the bikers. She was filled with an un-Katelike nostalgia for the nineteenth-century days, when there were no cars or student uprisings. With her academic world coming to an end, Reed successfully interested her in Holy Matrimony (again following the Wimsey tradition). He even suggested that they be married on Thanksgiving Day so they would have no problem remembering to celebrate the date!

From the Boathouse go left to the Conservatory Pond where people sail model ships and then go back to East Drive. This area was the assembly point for a peace march to the UN led by Martin Luther King, Jr. in 1967. In Carlson's *Audition for Murder*, actors Nick and Lisette O'Connor came to NYC with students from upstate Hargate College (aka Cornell), where they had been doing a production of *Hamlet*. The march was held on a gloomy Saturday, with signs and chants like "Hey Hey, LBJ, How Many Kids Did You Kill Today?" They marched from Central Park to the UN, where Dr. King spoke. (See also Walk 7.)

Keep going past the Bandshell on your left and the Mall—a tree-lined avenue—on your right, until you come to the 66th Street transverse again. Take the path away from the Children's Zoo, then go south, leaving Central Park midway between Central Park West and Fifth Avenue.

Back on Central Park South, also known as 59th Street, look across the street at the row of handsome high rises and hotels where a surprising number of mysterious characters lived. In Velda Johnson's *The Face in the Shadows*, wealthy Howard Vandering's apartment was there. In John Lutz's *Shadowtown*, the soap opera producer Harry Overbeck had an apartment with a balcony twenty stories up. When NYPD detective "Ox" Oxman found out that Overbeck was covering up for the murderers, Overbeck jumped off his balcony.

In Donald E. Westlake's *God Save the Mark*, "easy mark" Fred Fitch's crooked Uncle Matt had died and left him

$300,000 and a classy co-op apartment on Central Park South. His uncle lived there with a brassy blond named Gertie Divine. When Fitch went to look over the apartment, he discovered that the rooms went on and on with a beautiful view of Central Park. In the closet off the maid's room Fitch also found a body.

Cross Central Park South at Seventh Avenue and walk toward Sixth Avenue. You are going past a group of classy hotels. The one to focus your attention on is the Ritz-Carlton, 112 Central Park South. Although it is not the original, which was on Madison Avenue at 46th Street, it's the best Ritz NYC now has to offer. (See Walk 6.)

The hotel itself is famous for its very expensive Jockey Club restaurant and its views of New York. It is very popular with upper-crust VIPs, so it will have to do for mysteries as well. In the Lockridges' *Murder Comes First*, Jerry North, a publisher when he and his wife Pam are not amateur sleuthing like Hammett's Nora and Nick Charles, was at the Ritz with an author during a murder. In Rex Stout's mysteries, Archie Goodwin's perennial girl, Lily Rowan, lived at the Ritz until she bought her penthouse on the Upper East Side. (See Walk 7.)

In Barnaby Ross's (aka Ellery Queen's) *The Tragedy of X*, Wall Street broker John De Witt, who had been tried for the murder of his partner Harvey Longstreet, celebrated his acquittal at the Ritz just before he, too, was murdered. De Witt got off because of the testimony of deaf actor Drury Lane, who also came to the victory party.

Go right past the Ritz on Central Park South, passing the Barbizon Hotel to Sixth Avenue. Cross Sixth Avenue to the St. Moritz Hotel. On the corner is the Café de la Paix, with its white iron railing and very Parisian tables and chairs. It was at the St. Moritz that Gray Grantham of the *Washington Post* secretly met Darby Shaw, the Tulane University student who had the key to the murder of two Supreme Court justices in John Grisham's *The Pelican Brief*.

Just beyond the Café de la Paix is Rumpelmayer's, a world-famous ice-cream parlor. Once upon a time it had a London twin, where Harriet Vane's future mother-in-law, the dowager Duchess of Denver, took her to tea in Dorothy L. Sayers's *Bus-*

man's Honeymoon. Stop in and have lunch, tea, or dinner, or just enjoy some elegant ice cream. The windows are delightfully decorated with children's toys, especially NYC's teddy bears.

In Amanda Cross's *The Players Come Again*, Kate Fansler was asked to write the biography of Gabrielle Foxx, the wife of Emmanuel Foxx, the greatest writer of the twentieth century. Accepting this assignment put Fansler in touch with the Foxx family and their memories about growing up in NYC. One occasion, recalled by the daughter of a maid, was a treat at Rumplemayer's when she lost her shabby purse.

In John Lutz's *Shadowtown*, Merv Egan, a "worn-out actor" and the discarded leading man/lover of star Lana Spence, told NYPD detective "Ox" Oxman that the last time he saw Lana was at Rumplemayer's. She was eating a chocolate sundae and he had kidded her about ruining her figure. He also called her the "Black Widow Spider."

This site was once the home of novelist and editor William Dean Howells, who pioneered the Genteel Tradition in American literature, and was influential in moving the center of publishing from Boston to NYC.

Next door to Rumplemayer's is the newer and trendier Mickey Mantle's, with wooden benches and tables without tablecloths, Little League menus for kids, an art gallery, baseball memorabilia on the walls, and chicken and hamburger and chili entrées. In Crabbe Evers's *Murderer's Row*, retired Chicago sports columnist Duffy House was asked by Baseball Commissioner Granville Chambliss to look into the murder of Yankee owner Rupert Huston, who had been shot at Yankee Stadium. House and Chambliss went to Mickey Mantle's to eat (although House preferred the Carnegie Deli) and they saw star Angie Dickinson there.

End the walk by treating yourself to food or drink at one of the places on Central Park South or patronize one of the street vendors that are sure to be nearby.

10

UPPER WEST SIDE WALK

BACKGROUND

Unlike the staid and proper Upper East Side, the Upper West Side has been home to successful social misfits: artists, actors, academics, and ethnic groups. With the recent arrival of Yuppies, however, the old neighborhood is slowly but inexorably becoming gentrified. This clash of cultures appears in contemporary mysteries, but the worst-case scenario is a real one: megabuilder Donald Trump wants to develop the empty Pennsylvania Railroad yards on the Hudson River between 60th and 72nd Street, just west of Lincoln Center.

Symbolic of the original settlement is the Dakota, at 1 W. 72nd Street and Central Park West, an apartment building a full block in size, built in 1884. Famous as the home of murdered Beatle John Lennon and his widow Yoko Ono, Lauren Bacall, and ex-Mayor John V. Lindsay, it was one of the first luxury apartment buildings in NYC. Originally it had seven floors of apartments, each with four to twenty rooms; three floors of servants' quarters; and a children's recreation room.

Its name came from the wisecrack that it was as far uptown as the Dakota territories were from civilization. But it started the movement of wealthy families from Midtown townhouses and mansions to apartments in that very "wilderness." Writer Edith Wharton thought these "bourgeois" places were hideous, but despite a liberated life-style, Wharton was quintessentially Old New York.

In mysteries of the 1920s and 1930s, this neighborhood was also the home of the very rich, whose estates along Riverside Drive overlooked the Hudson River. By the time the Broadway-7th Avenue subway reached the neighborhood in 1904 the area was becoming home to middle-class Jews and descendants of other immigrants, as well as well-to-do entertainers, artists, musicians, writers, and intellectuals. These groups were not welcome on the Upper East Side.

The Ansonia Hotel on Broadway between 73rd and 74th Streets was built in 1904 in "wedding cake" Beaux-Arts style. It was adored by performing artists because it had thick walls, allowing them to practice, and high ceilings, allowing them to paint and sculpt. It has been a haunt of writers for a century, and some famous fictional characters also lived here, from Theodore Dreiser's Sister Carrie, to J. D. Salinger's talented (and neurotic) Glass family, to Herman Wouk's Marjorie Morningstar. What is more important to mystery buffs is the fact that Edgar Allan Poe lived on W. 84th Street, a few blocks further up, while he wrote his haunted and much parodied poem "The Raven" (West 84th Street between Amsterdam and Central Park West has been renamed Edgar Allan Poe Street, but there are two markers because no one is quite sure where Poe actually lived).

As the Riverside mansions were torn down the area between Central Park and the Hudson River became seedy. Lincoln Center, built in 1962 with major support from the third John D. Rockefeller, revived the whole area. Then came the Baby Boomers, young rich professionals who demanded restaurants and boutiques, but who now march arm-in-arm with the area's retirees to demand an end to continued gentrification.

Upper Broadway is a wide thoroughfare with a string of island parks in the center, where you can sit and enjoy the street fairs, read the paper, or sign petitions against development. Designed to be NYC's Champs Élysée or Unter den Linden, today it is considerably grubbier. The Upper West Side is a true melting pot (or hodgepodge) of buildings, languages, swinging singles, upwardly mobile young families, retirees, Asians, Hispanics, and African-Americans, all of whom are represented in mysteries. Zabar's Delicatessen at Broadway and 80th Street, a gourmet deli that moved uptown in the 1930s, is probably the most enduring symbol of a neighborhood truly representative of Manhattan.

LENGTH OF WALK: 2.5 miles

This walk only goes to 84th Street to allow time for museums. See map on page 247 for the boundaries of this walk and page 330 for a list of books and detectives mentioned.

PLACES OF INTEREST

New York Convention and Visitors Bureau, 2 Columbus Circle. Mon.–Fri., 9:00 A.M.–6:00 P.M.; Sat.–Sun., 10:00 A.M.–6:00 P.M. Call 397-8222.

Lincoln Center for the Performing Arts, 140 W. 65th St. (Broadway and 64th Street). Guided tours daily, 10:00 A.M.–5:00 P.M. Call 877-1800. Center includes New York State Theater, Avery Fisher Hall, Alice Tully Hall, Vivian Beaumont Theater, Metropolitan Opera House, Guggenheim Bandshell, Juilliard School. Gift shop.

American Museum of Natural History, Central Park West at 79th Street. Open Mon.–Thurs., Sun., 10:00 A.M.–5:45 P.M.; Fri.–Sat., 10:00 A.M.–8:45 P.M. Admission fee. Call 769-5100. Restaurants, see Places to Eat. Restrooms. Gift shops.

Hayden Planetarium, Central Park West at 81st Street. Open daily except Thanksgiving and Christmas. Sky Show, special schedules. Admission fee. Call 769-5910.

The New-York Historical Society, 170 Central Park West. Open Tues.–Sun., 10:00 A.M.–5:00 P.M. Admission fee. Library. Restrooms. Call 873-3400.

The Jewish Museum (temporarily housed at the New-York Historical Society). Closed Saturday and Sunday. Call 399-3344.

Dakota (apartments), 72nd Street and Central Park West.

Riverside Drive and Park, W. 72nd Street to Dyckman Street.

Fordham University (Lincoln Center campus), 60th–62nd Streets, Columbus to Amsterdam Avenues. Bronx-based Roman Catholic university popular with returning scholar/midlife career change students.

John Jay College of Criminal Law, 59th Street and Amsterdam Avenue.

Murder, Ink, 271 W. 87th Street. First bookstore devoted entirely to mysteries. Original owner, Dilys Winn, author of *Murder, Ink* and *Murderess Ink*. Unpredictable hours. Call 362-8905.

PLACES TO EAT

American Museum of Natural History, Central Park West at 79th St. Atrium Restaurant and Food Express, lower level. Open daily. Reservations good idea. The Whale's Lair, cocktail lounge, Fri. evening and weekends.

Zabar's Delicatessen, 2245 Broadway (between 80th–81st Streets). Famous for Jewish delicacies, kitchenwares, eat in/take out.

The Ginger Man, 51 W. 64th Street. Saloon/Continental restaurant. Theater crowd. Expensive. Reservations. Call 399-2358.

Lincoln Square Coffee Shop, Columbus Avenue at 65th Street. Salads, home-baked bread and muffins. Call 799-4000.

———— UPPER WEST SIDE WALK ————

Begin your walk at Columbus Circle at 59th Street/Central Park South, Eighth Avenue and Broadway. Eighth Avenue becomes Central Park West one block north at 60th Street. This corner is a major transportation center, easy to reach by bus, subway, taxi, or on foot. On the south side of the Circle in an Islamic-style white marble building, originally an art museum, is the New York Convention and Visitors Bureau. It is open daily and you can get maps, brochures, and personal help with all kinds of things from tickets to places to stay or eat.

Columbus Circle was built in 1892 to celebrate the 400th

anniversary of Christopher Columbus's arrival (or encounter) in (with) the New World. Its development showed the increased political muscle of Italian-Americans as they began take over from the Irish pols. The Circle was meant to be a kind of Place de la Concorde, but the traffic is fierce and the statue of the Discoverer himself, above your head on an eighty-foot pedestal, is smallish. The nearby streets are dirty and the homeless sleep curled up in doorways everywhere.

To your left past the Convention Bureau is the old New York Coliseum and a group of dreary office buildings. In Stanley Ellin's short story, "The Nine to Five Man," Mr. Keesler commuted daily from Brooklyn to an office in the smallest, shabbiest building on Columbus Circle. Inside, an old man named Eddie ran the elevator (and provided an ongoing alibi for Keesler). Keesler had an office overlooking Central Park, where he unwrapped his mail and read *The New York Times*. He then went out and bought supplies in eight different drugstores, had lunch, and took the subway to Water Street. There, as a professional arsonist, Keesler set a fire for a warehouse owner who wanted to collect on his insurance. Back at the office, he left promptly at 5 P.M. to go home to Brooklyn.

In Mary Higgins Clark's *While My Pretty One Sleeps*, after meeting across the Hudson River in New Jersey with a hood who hired him to waste Neeve Kearny, Danny Adler was dropped off at Eighth Avenue. He walked toward Columbus Circle and bought a hot dog and a Coke from a street vendor to settle his nerves. He was not eager to "waste" the daughter of a former NYPD police commissioner and have 40,000 cops after him.

In S. S. Van Dine's *Benson Murder Case*, a street cleaner found the fishing rods last seen in a Cadillac parked in front of murder victim Benson's mansion near Columbus Circle. The rods (and car) belonged to a suspect called Pfyfe, whose mistress lived on the Upper West Side.

Take 60th Street out of Columbus Circle and go left to Columbus Avenue. Cross Columbus Avenue to the left (west) side and turn right to walk north. While the el raced up and down it, Columbus Avenue was a very commercial street; now it houses

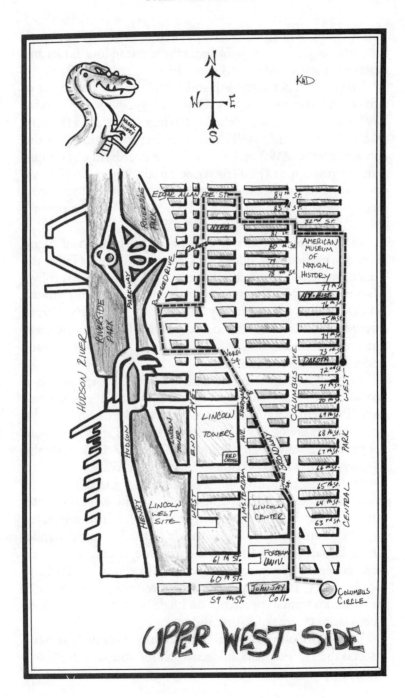

UPPER WEST SIDE

well-dressed, trendy singles who pay as much as $2,000 a month for a few rooms in a brownstone, whose entire four floors and basement their grandparents could have rented for $100.

To your left between 59th and 60th Streets at the corner of Amsterdam Avenue you will see John Jay College of Criminal Law, a branch of New York's City College system, and the alma mater of many of the NYPD's finest, in fact and fiction. It is also cohost with the MWA each year at Edgar awards time of symposium workshops at the New York Public Library, which are open (for a fee) to nonmembers, too. Some of the topics covered in 1992 were "Futuristics: New Crime," "Tomorrow's Spies," and "Writing the Best Seller Mystery."

In Margaret Maron's *One Coffee With*, Lieutenant Sigrid Harald's meticulous sidekick, Detective Tilden (Tillie the Toiler) went to night school there. In Haughton Murphy's *Murder for Lunch*, it was the alma mater of Reuben Frost's friend NYPD Detective Bautista. By the time of Murphy's *Murder Saves Face*, Bautista had retired from the NYPD to practice law, but Frost still asked him to help solve the murder of a young associate, Juliana Merriman.

In New Zealander Ngaio Marsh's *A Clutch of Constables*, Scotland Yard's Chief Superintendent Roderick Alleyn lectured to NYPD members at the Police College on the case of the Jampot. Chances are he did his lecturing here. His wife Troy spent her time on a zany canal trip near Ely on the Zodiak. (See also *Mystery Reader's Walking Guide: England*, Ely Walk.)

Occupying the whole block between 61st and 62nd Streets from Columbus to Amsterdam Avenues is the Lincoln Center campus of the Bronx's Fordham University, which celebrated its 150th anniversary at St. Patrick's Cathedral in September 1991. This campus, built at the same time as Lincoln Center, offers college- and graduate-level courses in education, law, and social services. It is also popular with "returning" students; it also hosts an annual conference on English mystery writer G. K. Chesterton, creator of Father Brown.

Between Columbus and Amsterdam Avenues on 62nd Street is the Professional Children's School, founded in 1914 to educate child actors of stage and later screen. Due west are the old Pennsylvania Railroad yards and abandoned piers, an area Donald Trump wants to develop.

Cross 62nd Street to the Lincoln Center for the Performing Arts, built in the 1960s with the support of John D. Rockefeller III. Its main entrance is at midblock where Broadway meets Columbus Avenue to form Lincoln Square. The whole of Lincoln Center, from 62nd to 65th Streets, is built on twelve acres, on the site of the slum where Leonard Bernstein's *West Side Story* was filmed. (See also Walk 5.)

As you walk up the steps to the courtyard, on your left is the New York State Theater, ahead is a fountain in front of the Metropolitan Opera House, and on the right is Avery Fisher Hall. All the buildings are white marble variations of classical and colonnaded facades. The Opera House's Chagall tapestries and crystal chandeliers, like the fountain, are spotlighted at night. The Center houses the New York Philharmonic, the Metropolitan Opera and the American Ballet Theatre, and the New York City Ballet and New York City Opera Company. At the Center are also the Vivian Beaumont Theater, the Library and Museum of Performing Arts, and across 65th Street is the Juilliard School of Music, and the Museum of American Folk Art.

In Margaret Maron's *Past Imperfect*, Jerry the Canary, who roosted in the rafters of subways (and saw the murderer who pushed NYPD staffer Lotte Fischer in front of a subway train) waited by the fountain in the Center's plaza as the shows let out. Jerry did birdcalls and begged enough to buy bed and breakfast for a week, but the NYPD did not catch him.

In Emma Lathen's *Death Shall Overcome*, the Sloan's John Putnam Thatcher had to attend the NAACP Benefit at the Center, with his daughter Laura. They met Ed Parry and his wife in the great lobby, then enjoyed/endured an orchestrated happening called *Roots*, based on a text by Richard Simpson, the black author who organized CASH's "March on Wall Street." There were white supremacist pickets outside and someone took a potshot at Parry inside.

In Clark's *While My Pretty One Sleeps*, Neeve Kearny and her father went to hear Pavarotti the Saturday after Nicky Sepetti, a mobster Kearny had "sent up," was released from prison.

Across Broadway from Lincoln Center at 51 W. 64th Street is
The Ginger Man, with old-fashioned dark woodwork and Tiffany lamp decor. The Ginger Man is a popular spot for post-
matinee drinks and nightcaps with Lincoln Center patrons. It is
also popular with the staff of ABC television who lunch there.
Clark's Kearnys went there after hearing Pavarotti.

Cross 65th Street at Lincoln Square. The world-famous
Juilliard School of Music is on your left. In Annette Meyers's
The Big Killing, Smith & Wetzon's client Laura Lee was a
Southern belle who came to NYC to study violin. Now she had
not only become a Wall Street broker, but also studied at Juil-
liard. Also at 65th Street and Columbus Avenue is the Museum
of American Folk Art, full of paintings, textiles, furniture, and
other exhibits. But don't confuse it with the American Craft
Museum across West 56th Street from the Museum of Modern
Art. (See Walk 6.)

In Meyers's *Tender Death*, Leslie Wetzon had met her older
friend Hazel Osborn at the Museum of American Folk Art.
Hazel was a retired social worker who had studied with Dr.
Bruno Bettelheim in Chicago and was now a "professional volunteer." Wetzon was augmenting her dancing income by making pillows and quilts for the museum shop where Hazel
worked one day a week.

At Lincoln Square you will also see the Lincoln Center Coffee Shop. In Orania Papazoglou's (aka Jane Haddam's) *Wicked,
Loving Murder*, Patience McKenna was trying to edit a special
section on writing romances at *Writing Magazine*. But soon after Patience got there one of owner-publisher Alida Brookfield's
nephews was murdered.

That weekend NYC was snowbound so Patience tramped
down West 72nd Street from her old-style but classy West Side
apartment, the Braedenvoorst (aka the Dakota or the Ansonia),
past brownstones with frosted windows, to Lincoln Square to
meet NYPD Lieutenant Luis Martinez at the Lincoln Center
Coffee Shop and talk about the crime. The Coffee Shop specializes in very strong coffee; it also has large plate glass windows
looking out at the city. Try it yourself.

To your right, across Columbus Avenue between 66th and

67th Streets, is ABC's headquarters. It is near the studio where the soap opera "All My Children" is shot. John Lutz's *Shadowtown* was about a similar TV soap opera, but its studio was located in Riverside Park. (Most mysteries use made-up names for TV stations so you can't pinpoint the scene of the crime.)

Walk up Broadway. At 67th Street pause to look right toward Central Park for a glimpse of the Hotel des Artistes, another studio building with large windows put up in 1918 by some artists who occupied half of the building and rented out the rest of the space. Among its tenants have been Isadora Duncan, Norman Rockwell, Rudolph Valentino, and Noel Coward—a classy lot. It was also the scene of a real-life crime in 1929. Dissolute Harry Crosby, the nephew of J. P. Morgan and founder of the Paris-based avant garde Black Sun Press, locked his door, made love to his mistress, and then shot her and himself.

Continue up Broadway, enjoying the charming side streets lined with old trees and brownstones. Some members of the Wolfe Pack think this may be the right locale for Nero Wolfe's brownstone, with the seven steps to the stoop and the orchid greenhouses on the roof. (If so, Nero Wolfe and Ellery Queen lived in the same neighborhood because the Queens' brownstone was due north at West 87th Street.)

To your left behind Lincoln Center near the Hudson River, there are more modern apartment buildings. In *A Trap for Fools*, Amanda Cross's African-American activist student Arabella's family lived at 140 Riverside Drive in a court building. Arabella fell (or was pushed) out of their tenth-story apartment window. Professor Kate Fansler went to the apartment afterward to meet Arabella's stepmother.

Continue up Broadway, looking at the specialty shops and people watching. It was on quiet West 69th Street that a former Radio City Music Hall Rockette, who worked in advertising, lived with her husband and two cocker spaniels called Pizza and Pepperoni. The block was so friendly its residents held an annual Halloween party, but one Saturday in 1991 when she took the dogs out, she was stabbed to death by a homeless, deranged killer who had served time for similar attacks.

Toward the river the buildings tend to be shabbier. Somewhere on West 70th Street in a brownstone converted into small apartments John Lutz put waitress Myra Deeber, a soap opera fanatic. Myra, who watched soaps all day, was a waitress by night. NYPD detective "Ox" Oxman used Myra as his expert on soaps when he was investigating the murders connected with the soap opera "Shadowtown."

Walk to 71st Street and look left. In Clark's *While My Pretty One Sleeps*, writer Ethel Lambston's ex-husband, his wife and daughters lived here near West End Avenue. Lambston was being slowly beggared by his obligation to pay Ethel $12,000 a year in alimony and her murder made his life much easier.

At 71st Street and Broadway you come to Sherman Square. This is an area where one square runs into another. The northern part of this intersection is called Verdi Square, where Broadway and Amsterdam, having crisscrossed, part company again. This is also where the islands that figured so prominently as home or office away from home in the Margaret Binton mysteries by Richard Barth appear in the middle of Broadway.

The neighborhood's annual West Side Fall Festival, sponsored by the Broadway Mall Association, is held here on one weekend. (There was another festival held near the Christmas holiday when the Wolfe Pack had its annual conference called the Black Orchid Weekend.) During the festival, Broadway from 66th to 71st Streets is closed to traffic. Stalls containing every kind of food imaginable, T-shirts, weaving, pottery, jewelry and second-hand books are set up. There are also many earnest people who may ask you to sign petitions to preserve the gardens, the neighborhood, the city, and the world.

At 72nd Street look to your left. Paul Engleman's P.I. Mark Renzler had his pad at 118 W. 72nd Street. Renzler used his living room as an office, but it was neither air-conditioned nor classy, so he was also glad to leave it to go check out a racetrack in New Jersey in *Who Shot Longshot Sam?* In 1969, the year of the first lunar landing and Woodstock, in Engleman's *Catch a Falling Angel*, Renzler was flown to Chicago to handle personnel problems for *Paradise* magazine publisher Arnold Long, a Hugh

Hefner-type entrepreneur. He wound up participating in the Days of Rage, a violent anti-Vietnam confrontation.

The famous Ansonia Hotel is on Broadway between 73rd and 74th Streets at Verdi Square. Another elegant Beaux-Arts apartment house, it was built in 1901, and featured two swimming pools, a lobby fountain with seals, and a small bear garden on the roof. Its famous inhabitants included Caruso, Toscanini, Stravinsky, Ezio Pinza and Lily Pons, as well as musical impresario Flo Ziegfield and baseball great Babe Ruth.

Turn left to walk west on 73rd Street across West End Avenue to Riverside Drive and Riverside Park. Landscaped in 1873 by Frederick Law Olmstead of Central Park fame, this area near the Hudson River was at first large estates, which gave way to palatial townhouses and apartment buildings of limestone and granite rather than the typical redbrick or brownstone. The atmosphere here was also changed when the elevated Henry Hudson Parkway was built in the 1930s.

Look to your left. In this vicinity a "mixed bag" of mystery characters lived. One was Martin Meyers's P.I., Patrick Hardy, chief consultant of Trouble Limited. Hardy, an ex-Marine, lived in a ground floor apartment at 7 Riverside Drive with his dog, Sherlock Holmes. In *Kiss and Kill*, Hardy preferred to spend his time on sex, gourmet food, old movies, and Proust. But he was hired to find the murderer of a dead stripper with Mob connections. Although he begrudged the time spent, Hardy did solve the case with the somewhat sarcastic help of NYPD Detective Sergeant Friday, who happened to be black.

In Ellery Queen's *The French Powder Mystery*, the French mansion was to the right between 73rd and 74th Streets on Riverside Drive. The night Mrs. French was murdered at the family department store, she caught a cab on Riverside Drive. Her daughter Berniece was also seen walking to 72nd Street, where she was picked up at 72nd and West End by a special cab. Berniece then disappeared and was later found murdered, too.

The Ives-Pope mansion was also on Riverside Drive in Queen's *The Roman Hat Mystery*. It was a huge, rambling stone house, set far back from the drive on respectable acreage, with gardens and a summer house. The NYPD police commissioner made the Queens go there to interview Frances Ives-Pope, a debutante engaged to Stephen Barry, who was an actor in the stage show *Gunplay*. Frances had been at the theater the night of the murder and been accosted by the murder victim, Monte Field.

In Queen's *The Greek Coffin Mystery*, the mansion of the mysterious millionaire James J. Knox, who had made a deal for a stolen da Vinci painting with the dead art dealer Georg Khalkis, was also in this area. Ellery Queen went to Riverside Drive to see Knox. He also arranged to plant Khalkis's secretary Joan Brett there as a spy.

In Dashiell Hammett's *The Thin Man*, the mansion once owned by missing inventor Clyde Winant was on Riverside Drive. After Winant's divorce, the family had moved away. Finally, in Dorothy L. Sayers's short story, "The Incredible Elopement of Lord Peter Wimsey," her most heartless villain, Standish Wetherall, was a wealthy American who lived in a "great white house in Riverside Drive, with peacocks and swimming-pool and gilded tower with roof-garden." Wetherall was the charmer who, out of insane jealousy, kept his lovely wife from taking her thyroid medication, so that she resembled an old crone and remained at his mercy.

The most fabulous, real-life, Riverside Drive residence was the one Charles Schwab built in 1904 at the corner of 73rd Street. It occupied an entire block. Schwab, like Frick, was a business associate of Andrew Carnegie. (See Walk 8.) The mansion, with its sixty-five rooms and a private chapel, was built like a French chateau. It seems a shame that in the 1940s the city fathers decided not to buy it for use as the mayor's official residence. As a result it was torn down and replaced by a redbrick apartment building also known as Schwab House.

But in S. S. Van Dine's *Benson Murder Case*, the Schwab residence was still very visible. Amateur sleuth Philo Vance stopped to contemplate it en route to questioning a suspect, but his faithful "Dr. Watson," S. S. Van Dine, who recorded these adventures, did not say what Vance thought of the mansion. Presumably it suited his elegant taste and love of splendor.

Many years later in Clark's *While My Pretty One Sleeps*,

Neeve Kearny lived in the brick Schwab House with her widower father, retired NYPD Commissioner Myles Kearny. One day mob hit man Danny Adler watched for Neeve outside Schwab House so he could "waste" her, but Adler was driven away by an affectionate poodle named Honey Bee, who jumped on him and kept him from shooting.

In the Amanda Cross mysteries there is no definite suggestion that Kate Fansler lived in an expensive apartment, but in *In the Last Analysis*, she did live in an old four-room apartment, overlooking the Hudson. Her large rooms had high ceilings, thick walls. The elegance was somewhat faded, but she did not have to put up with a windowless kitchen or Musak in the elevator. Kate may have gone on living there with Reed after their marriage—the evidence is inconclusive. But they continued living on the Upper West Side because Kate remained intrepid about walking through Central Park.

Keep going north on Riverside Drive, but glance to your right at the side streets, too. In this part of town, the sandstone known as "brownstone" was not the only material used to build the townhouses; some were brick, some granite, some limestone.

In Van Dine's *The Benson Murder Case*, there was a one-man garage at 74th Street near Amsterdam Avenue. It was here that the NYPD located the mysterious gray Cadillac with fishing rods sticking out the back. It had been parked in front of the murdered Alvin Benson's house. The car was owned by the playboy Leander Pfyfe. Pfyfe's mistress, the widowed Mrs. Paul Banning, had a small but rococo apartment at 28 W. 75th Street off West End Avenue. The strawberry blond had put up her jewels to help Pfyfe out of a tight corner.

Cross 75th Street and look to the right. In Ellery Queen's *The Roman Hat Mystery*, murdered lawyer Monte Field had a "monumental apartment" several blocks east between Columbus and Amsterdam Avenues at 113 W. 75th Street. A prostitute was found there the night Field was killed at the Roman Theater. Later, when Ellery was allowed to search the place, he found two important clues—books on handwriting and a secret cache of hats.

Go one more block up Riverside Drive to 76th Street. Turn right and walk along 76th Street to Broadway, crossing West End Avenue. In Marissa Piesman's *Unorthodox Practices*, Nina Fischman's mother Ida became suspicious when two elderly tenants—Mrs. Gross and Mrs. Kahn—died suddenly. Both lived in West End Avenue buildings being converted to expensive co-ops—and neither apartment had any cockroaches.

Cross Broadway and go east toward Amsterdam Avenue. The apartment of Barbara McCain was near the corner of Amsterdam and 76th Street in William Love's *The Chartreuse Clue*. A Benedictine monk and graduate student called Willy Fuller woke up in McCain's apartment to find her murdered. Fuller ran to Bishop Regan for help and Regan's "Archie Goodwin," P.I. Davy Goldman, went to check Fuller's story out. He met the murdered woman's friend Anne Shields, who lived in the next apartment, and together they eventually solved the murder.

Turn left to go up Broadway to 78th Street. Fred Fitch, who was everybody's patsy, went to visit a strange girl called Karen Smith, whom he had met in Union Square, farther east between Amsterdam and Columbus Avenues in Donald E. Westlake's *God Save the Mark*. (Fitch had just inherited $300,000, a large blond called Gertie, and a Central Park South co-op from his shyster Uncle Matt.) Fitch ended up hiding out at Karen's 78th Street apartment for several days; instead of true romance blossoming, both found the experience very embarrassing.

As you come to 79th Street and Broadway look about for an Irish bar that hasn't been gentrified. In Don Winslow's *A Cool Breeze on the Underground*, set in the year of America's bicentennial (1976), one called Meg's was a neighborhood bar serving beer, whiskey, and an occasional gin and tonic to the Irish population. That was the place where eleven-year-old West Side street kid Neal picked the pocket of P.I. Joe Graham. Graham chased Neil and caught him, then taught him the P.I. tricks of the trade. This was once a lower-income Irish neighborhood because in Amanda Cross's *The Players Come Again*, her narrator, Anne Gringold, "the perfect child of an upper servant," explained that during the winters her housekeeper mother did not "live in" but shared an apartment with Anne on the lower floor of a private house between Columbus and Amsterdam Avenues in the 80s.

Go to Broadway and 80th Street. Here you find world-famous Zabar's Delicatessen. An NYC landmark, it fills the place that Fortnum and Mason's does in London, both in mystery stories and real life. Zabar's moved from the Lower East Side in the 1930s to become an internationally known gourmet emporium, crowded and popular. Open 365 days a year, it specializes in all the true NYC foods (and yuppie loves), like smoked fish and fresh caviar, homemade pasta, whole grain bread, David's cookies, and whole bean coffee; in other words, the best of everything. In Piesman's *Unorthodox Practices*, Ida Fischman remembered Zabar's when it was a herring store, but she rolled with the punches.

In Annette Meyers's *The Big Killing*, Wall Street headhunter Leslie Wetzon, who had a date with a doctor she had met as the result of the murder of her client Barry Stark, went by Zabar's on her way home. Now there were limousines double-parked in front, but Wetzon could remember when Zabar's was just a small, neighborhood deli-grocery with pots, pans, and kettles hanging from the ceiling. It had tripled its size, adding prepared foods, salads and knishes, fresh cookies, a chocolate shop, more bread and rolls, and a second floor that undersold every housewares shop in the world. People came to NYC to see Zabar's, as if it were a landmark like the Statue of Liberty.

After checking Zabar's out thoroughly—or stopping for something to eat since you have walked about one mile—go one more block north on Broadway to 81st Street. To your left on Riverside Drive a Miss St. Clair, whom Alvin Benson had wined and dined the night of his murder, had an apartment in Van Dine's *The Benson Murder Case*.

Senior-citizen activist Margaret Binton's apartment was also on West 81st Street in Richard Barth's *A Ragged Plot*. Margaret had lived there with her husband Oscar until he died. The apartment had a Pullman kitchen, tiny bedroom, comfortable living room with worn orientals and antimacassars and lots of mystery books. She kept Thelma Winters there when Thelma's life was in danger because a developer wanted her apartment in *The Condo Kill*.

Walk up to 82nd Street. You can see the NYPD's 20th precinct just about where the "81st Precinct" was in the Margaret Binton stories. Her pals, Lieutenant Morley and Sergeant Schaeffer, worked there and kept an eye on Margaret, even going along with her wild ideas, like the time she decided that the city garden she was working in was the place where the loot from a diamond heist was buried.

At Broadway and 82nd Street look at the pedestrian bench on the island, often occupied by retirees and/or bagpersons. In Richard Barth's *The Condo Kill*, this was Margaret Binton's outside office. She held a meeting there with Angelo Varonetti (older Spencer Tracy look-alike) and her bingo-playing friend Thelma Winters. They were the last two residents in a building a developer was trying to empty to tear down.

Continue up Broadway to the Burger King at 83rd Street. In Meyers's *The Big Killing*, Leslie Wetzon went there daily to buy "her" streetperson, white-haired Sugar Joe, two coffees with three sugars each. On her way back to the bus stop on Broadway where Sugar Joe slept, Wetzon was mugged. She was rescued by Sugar Joe, who was stabbed to death by her attacker.

To the left on Riverside Drive and 83rd Street there was a small, graystone house visited by ex–Spanish Civil War hero Kit McKittrick in Dorothy B. Hughes's *The Fallen Sparrow*. The house had been cut up into apartments in which some sinister Nazi refugees lived on the second floor. Kit was asked there to dinner as part of a plot to recover the Babylon Goblets, which Kit had found (and hidden) in Spain.

Walk one more block north to West 84th Street and turn right toward Amsterdam Avenue. This walk does not quite reach the first bookstore to be devoted entirely to mysteries, Murder, Ink, located at 271 W. 87th Street. Begun by Dilys Winn, author of *Murder Ink*, its hours are unpredictable, so it is a good idea to call first. But Murder, Ink is well worth a visit.

Also located on 87th Street was the home of the Queens, father and son. (Since you have already gone a mile and have seen any number of excellent brownstones, the walk will not go that far north.)

In Ellery Queen's *The Roman Hat Mystery*, the Queens lived on the fourth (top) floor of a Victorian brownstone. It had thick-carpeted stairs and a huge oaken door. The foyer had a tapestry given them by a grateful duke. The high-ceilinged living room was lined on three sides with bristling bookscases, and over the fireplace there were shiny sabers, souvenirs of Inspector Queen's dueling days in Germany. There were lamps, easy chairs, low divans, footstools, and bright-colored leather cushions everywhere. "In a word, it was the most comfortable room two intellectual gentlemen of luxurious tastes could devise for their living quarters." Their man servant, Djuna, was a young Gypsy whom Inspector Queen had adopted when son Ellery was away at college.

North and west of the Queens' bachelor pad, at Riverside Park and 88th Street in John Lutz's *Shadowtown*, was the apartment of artist Jennifer Crane. NYPD Lieutenant E. L. "Ox" Oxman was living with her as she tried to sort out her life after being married to a wife beater. Her ex-husband, Zachary Denton, now worked for the TV soap opera "Shadowtown," which was shot in a huge Riverside Park warehouse converted to a studio.

Turn right on 84th Street toward Amsterdam Avenue. You are on "Edgar Allan Poe Street," which runs east to Central Park. There are two markers showing where Poe lived during the summer of 1844 while he wrote "The Raven" because the exact site is unknown. Remember that Washington Irving had described the whole Upper West Side at that time as a beautiful rural valley, and Poe lived in a dilapidated farmhouse on a hill.

Look for the markers, then turn right at Amsterdam Avenue and walk two blocks south. Between Amsterdam and Columbus Avenues at 156 W. 82nd Street in Rex Stout's *Too Many Clients*, Thomas Yeager had a love nest. His body was found in a vacant lot next to the building. One of a row of five-story brick houses, it was managed by Cesar Perez, who lived there with his wife and their gorgeous eighteen-year-old daughter Maria. Yeager's many girl friends took an elevator to the love nest, which was furnished in yellow satin, with blown-up photographs on the walls, and a huge bed.

Walk along 82nd Street east to Columbus Avenue. In Clark's *While My Pretty One Sleeps*, murdered free-lance reporter Ethel Lambston lived in the ground-floor apartment of a brownstone near Columbus Avenue. Before the murder Neeve Kearny had taken on the job of "dressing" Ethel with entire outfits. She had a delivery to make and became worried when Ethel disappeared. Ethel's sponger of a nephew took up residence in her apartment after her death. TseTse, a young actress who supported herself by cleaning for people like Ethel, not only helped Neeve hunt there for clues, but told off the nephew as well.

Somewhere on West 82nd Street in William Katz's *Open House* was the apartment of investment firm researcher Deborah Moore. She lived in a six-story redbrick affair built in 1935. The building did not have a doorman. That made it easy for the so-called RCA repairman, a serial killer, who had called ahead, to be let in and stab her to death with an ice pick.

A few blocks to your left at 238 Central Park West was the elegant apartment building lived in by Jason Farrell in Barth's *The Condo Kill*. Farrell was the shady developer/contractor who was trying to clear out the building at 621 W. 91st Street, where Margaret Binton's friends lived. Margaret, dressed like a sweet old lady, was let in Farrell's apartment by the doorman. She discovered that Farrell's place had fancy modern white furniture and rugs. Farrell was having his nails done when she gave him her ultimatum about leaving her friends alone.

Novelist Sinclair Lewis rented a duplex in the Eldorado Towers, an orange-colored Art Deco building at 300 Central Park West. Lewis, who called it "Intolerable Towers," wrote that he lived twenty-nine stories up in a cross between Elizabeth Arden's Beauty Salon on Fifth Avenue and the horse stables at Ringling Circus's winter headquarters in Sarasota, Florida, with a good view of the Orkney Isles. This was the same building where writer Herman Wouk placed the nouveau riche Jewish family of *Marjorie Morningstar*.

The area is therefore a highly appropriate milieu for Jerome

Charyn's "bumper" (enforcer) Sidney Holden, who buys an apartment there for himself and his love, the D.A.'s daughter-in-law, in *Paradise Man*. A realtor who laundered money for fur thieves (for whom Holden worked) found him six rooms on Central Park West for a mere $1.2 million.

Turn right on Columbus Avenue and walk south to 81st Street. Cross 81st Street and go left to enter the park on the north side by the Hayden Planetarium. This park is named for Margaret Mead, the famous anthropologist, who had an office in the old wing of the American Museum of Natural History for many years.

The Hayden Planetarium, connected with the American Museum of Natural History, has its own entrance on West 81st Street. In Carol Brennan's *Headhunt*, PR person Liz Wareham, who had been held up in her Upper West Side apartment by the kid brother of one of her clients, later met the kid here to discuss how he could track down the murderer of his brother's boss, King Carter. (Liz happened to be at the planetarium doing a photo shoot for another client.)

After visiting the planetarium, walk around the grounds to Central Park West, to the main entrance of the American Museum of Natural History. Like many of NYC's public buildings, its front is neoclassical and colonnaded, with high steps to sun yourself on and a large statue of NYC's native son—Mayor, Governor, and President—Teddy Roosevelt, who was instrumental in establishing the museum. Roosevelt was the world's first well-known environmentalist, famous for not shooting a bear cub (named Teddy).

Begun in 1872 (its south wing is Victorian, with gables and turrets), this is the largest museum of its kind in the world, and the best place to see dinosaurs (who came to a mysterious end) or get something to eat. In Barth's *The Condo Kill*, Margaret Binton met her Mafia contact, Donghia, at the Museum of Natural History after Angelo Varonetti was shot by Jason Farrell's hit man, Luther. They met in the museum café, where Donghia was having steak and eggs. He not only promised to use his West Coast connections to get some dirt on Farrell, but also suggested that she and Thelma Winters, the last tenant in the building under siege, hide out at his niece's place in the Catskills.

Take the time out to visit the museum and its restaurants, then continue south along Central Park West and cross 77th Street. All along here you pass elegant old apartment buildings. At Central Park West and 77th Street is the New-York Historical Society, which was recommended to me by mystery writers Annette and Martin Meyers as the best place to get information on old New York. (The Meyers have just published a historical saga called *The Dutchman*.)

The New-York Historical Society building was begun in1908 and is also neoclassical in design. Currently it is also home to the Jewish Museum (not open on Sat. or Mon.). This small museum has a largely Old New York collection, emphasizing the city's Dutch and English roots, and there is a family feel to its exhibits of portraits, Tiffany lamps, and furniture. Apropos Margaret Maron's Vanderlyn College, where Oscar Nauman headed the art department. John Vanderlyn was a famous New York painter, sponsored by Aaron Burr, making it obvious why Maron chose that name for her city college in *One Coffee With*.

In Steve Allen's *Murder in Manhattan*, Suzanne Tracy, beloved of TV actor Zach Holden, invited Steve to a meeting of FOP (Friends of Penguins) at the Museum of Natural History. Suzanne was a passionate animal rights activist who spit (or worse) on women she saw wearing furs.

More sedately, in Jonathan Gash's amusing *The Great California Game*, his British antiques expert Lovejoy (in NYC as an illegal alien en route home from Hong Kong) walked from 56th Street to the New-York Historical Society. There he saw few people, but a "staggering display of Regency furniture." Lovejoy had a meal nearby and then walked back to Columbus Circle at 59th Street, where he was picked up by two plainclothesmen and spent the night in jail.

When you come out of the New-York Historical Society, go right to 76th Street. You will see a sign saying that you are now in a Landmark Preservation District. The district, which runs from Central Park West to West 76th Street, includes a variety of handsome buildings, such as the massive neo-Gothic Unitarian-Universalist Church built in 1908. The pattern of buildings in the area is apartment buildings with large facades on Central Park West, and smaller, domestic-scale row houses on the side streets. Some of the elegant large facades have brass doctors' and lawyers' markers. An example is the apartment hotel called The Kenilworth, built in 1908 of festooned limestone, at 151 W. 75th Street.

Keep walking along to 74th Street and look to your right toward Columbus Avenue. In Rex Stout's *The Golden Spiders*, in the middle of a block between apartment houses with canopies and those without, Archie Goodwin found the apartment of the jeweler Gerster. Gerster's building did not have a canopy, but it did have a doorman. A pair of Golden Spider earrings had been displayed in his shop window on 46th Street. Gerster told Archie they had come from Paris and he had sold them to wealthy widow Laura Fromm, who was later murdered.

Continue to walk along Central Park West (where the city is doing massive repairs to the sewer pipes) to 73rd Street. At the northwest corner is the famous Dakota, built by the Singer Sewing Machine heir Edward Clark in 1884. It was the first apartment building of its kind and nicknamed the Dakota because it was so far uptown! It is now the home of many Beautiful People. The movie *Rosemary's Baby* was filmed there, and it was just outside on Central Park West that Beatle John Lennon was shot by a crazed fan. (See Walk 9 for Strawberry Fields.) Made of yellow-orange stone with romanesque windows and much Victorian "gingerbread" it is massively impressive.

In Carol Brennan's *Headhunt*, Liz Wareham ducked inside the "stone guardhouse" called the Dakota that she knew housed John Lennon, Lauren Bacall, and John Lindsay when she thought she was being followed. In Jack Finney's sci-fi mystery, *Time and Again*, time traveler Si Morley went to the Dakota. (In his introduction author Finney admitted that it really had not yet been built in 1882, the year that his mystery took place.)

In William Katz's *The Surprise Party*, which is a horror story about a young wife who unknowingly married a serial killer, the loving couple lived in a spacious five-room apartment with thick white carpet, modern white and steel furniture, and indirect track lighting, in a "brooding" half-century-old building with a view of Central Park. It sounds a lot like the Dakota or one of its neighbors.

In Maron's *One Coffee With*, murdered art professor Riley Quinn lived in an elegant brownstone around the corner from Central Park West on West 72nd Street (West 73rd is a better street for brownstones). Riley's expensive house had a basement areaway with an iron railing, six shallow steps to the stoop, a gleaming oak door, and beveled and leaded glass front windows with wrought iron bars to protect them. The front hall was paneled in walnut, with a Tiffany lamp and oriental rug, hung with large modern canvases. The house reminded Lieutenant Harald of the Brooklyn houses her aunts and uncles lived in. She found Riley's drunken widow in bed there with another Vanderlyn art professor.

End your walk at 72nd Street by crossing to Central Park to rest on a bench or get something to eat from one of the many street vendors. There is also a handy subway stop at West 72nd Street.

11

MORNINGSIDE HEIGHTS WALK

Cathedral of St. John the Divine
and Columbia University

BACKGROUND

The main features of this walk are two world-famous NYC institutions: the Cathedral of St. John the Divine (Episcopal) and Columbia University/Barnard College. Both were built in the late nineteenth century (the cathedral is still not complete), and both not only exist next door to Harlem but also are surrounded by the NYC poor, made up mostly of blacks and Puerto Ricans, but beginning to include Asians as well.

Student/community protests in the 1960s and 1970s stopped the expansion of Columbia University into Morningside Park, almost exactly at the time when NYC's other major private university, New York University, sold its Bronx campus and began to hold all classes downtown in Washington Square. (See Walk 3.)

In addition to these institutions, however, there are others in the area, such as the Jewish Theological Seminary of America at Broadway and 122nd Street, St. Luke's Hospital next to the cathedral, and the original City College (now University) of New York (or CUNY) at 131 Amsterdam Avenue, as well as landmarks like Grant's Tomb and Riverside Church on Riverside Drive.

From Morningside Drive behind the Cathedral and Columbia University, you can look down on the steep park called Morningside Heights and across into Harlem, New York's black community, known worldwide for its church services, soul food, and musical nightlife. Laid out by Frederick Olmstead in 1887, Morningside Park acts as a buffer zone between Harlem and its neighbors; but it is a refuge for muggers, panhandlers, and the homeless and is not safe after dark. For the ordinary mystery tourist the best way to see Harlem is to ride through the neighborhood on the bus en route to Audubon Terrace, Hamilton Grange, and the Cloisters. Another way is to take one of the many organized Harlem tours. (See Walk 10 for NYC Convention and Visitors Bureau.)

Historically, Harlem was named *Nieuw Haarlem* by its Dutch settlers, who farmed the area. As the land wore out, summer cottages began to appear. By the 1870s, when the railroad reached this far north and NYC had a population explosion, prospering German families from the Lower East Side began to move north and build brownstones.

When the development proved to be overbuilt, the half-empty apartments were rented to blacks, who were coming north for jobs, making Harlem by the 1920s NYC's largest black ghetto. This was the time of its golden age, when young white New Yorkers, like their London counterparts who went thrill-seeking in the East End, came to Harlem to enjoy jazz, soul food, and church music. These were the days of the Harlem Renaissance, when Josephine Baker, Lena Horne, Count Basie, Duke Ellington, and Cab Calloway played the Apollo Theater and the Cotton Club.

Harlem was also home to black writers and intellectuals like Countee Cullen and Langston Hughes, as well as W. E. B. Du Bois, who established the beginnings of a black literature known worldwide. Celebrities like singer Paul Robeson and Harlem's own Congressman Adam Clayton Powell, minister of the Abyssinian Baptist Church on 138th Street, were based there, too. The Great Depression ended the era; gradually the black middle class left, especially after the race riots of the 1960s. Today Harlem's population continues to decline.

East of Harlem between Central Park and the East River is the neighborhood known as Spanish Harlem or *El Barrio*. It was once an Italian neighborhood; now its inhabitants are largely Puerto Rican, West Indian, Cuban, and Haitian. They also resist gentrification, as NYU students discovered when they tried to "integrate" some of the brownstones in the 1980s.

The 1905 Elizabethan Gothic campus of NYC's City University lies between 131st and 141th Streets from Amsterdam to St. Nicholas Avenues. It had a free tuition policy until the 1970s, which allowed many of NYC's most famous sons and daughters to get an excellent education there.

Just north of Harlem is the Hamilton Heights Historic District, near 135th Street and the St. Nicholas subway station. It was named for Alexander Hamilton, whose country place was near there. You can see his Federal-style Hamilton Grange at 287 Convent Avenue and 142nd Street. Hamilton enjoyed it only briefly before he was killed in a duel with Aaron Burr at Weekhawken, New Jersey. (See Walks 1 and 5.)

At Audubon Terrace (155th Street and Broadway), there used to be a cluster of museums; many of them have moved, but the American Academy of Arts and Letters is still there. The neighborhood called Washington Heights begins at about 157th Street and goes past the George Washington Bridge, which crosses the Hudson River at 178th Street. The bridge is a steel structure built in 1931, offering a magnificent view of NYC. This neighborhood became a German-Jewish refuge during World War II.

At 160th Street and Edgecombe Avenue is the Morris-Jumel mansion, built by an English officer. He abandoned it during the American Revolution and it was taken over by George Washington as his headquarters. After the war Jumel bought it, then left it to his widow, who later married Aaron Burr.

Finally, north of Washington Heights and the George Washington Bridge is the Metropolitan Museum of Art's famous Cloisters. The entire collection of medieval buildings and art objects was established with money given by John D. Rockefeller, Jr. Fort Tryon Park, which contains the Cloisters, occupies the highest point in Manhattan. It was also designed by Frederick

Law Olmstead. Its surrounding neighborhood was once a Jew-
ish/Irish neighborhood, but now it is largely Hispanic. Within
walking distance of Fort Tryon Park is the Dyckman House at
Broadway and West 204th Street. It is the only eighteenth-
century Dutch Colonial farmhouse left on Manhattan.

LENGTH OF WALK: About 2 miles

On this walk, you are walking uphill the whole way.
It will go only to Riverside Church at W. 122nd Street; for
the other locations, listed as Possible Side Trips, you should take
a taxi, bus, or subway.

See map on page 272 for the boundaries of this walk and
page 334 for a list of the books and detectives mentioned.

PLACES OF INTEREST

Cathedral of St. John the Divine, Amsterdam and Cathedral
Parkway. Episcopalian. Begun in 1892, will be the world's
largest cathedral when completed. Gothic to Romanesque,
changed in midbuilding. Surrounded by the cathedral close
(cathedral office, housing for dean, bishop, staff). Community
outreach program/Cathedral School. Children's peace garden.
Open daily. Tours Mon.–Sat., Sun. after services. Cathedral
shop. Call 316-7540.

Morningside Park, Morningside Drive, 110th–123rd Streets. Very
hilly, dangerous terrain.

Columbia University, 114th–120th Streets between Amsterdam and
Broadway Avenues. Began in 1754 as King's College (charter
from George II) with eight students at Trinity Church. Changed
to Columbia College in 1784; moved to present site in 1897. An
Ivy League school that was a leader in the 1960s anti-Vietnam
War demonstrations. Admitted undergraduate women in 1983.
Also Teachers College (1887) and Barnard College (women,
founded in 1889). Upper and lower campuses designed by
McKim, Mead & White. Tours Mon.–Fri., except holidays, final
exams. See especially: Low Memorial Library, seated statue of
Alma Mater; Butler Library, facing Low Memorial Library; St.
Paul's Chapel, 1907 neo-Byzantine style. Call 280-2845.

Barnard College, across Broadway at 116th Street. Women's college founded 1889. Main building dates to World War I.

Riverside Park, 80th Street and Riverside Drive. Landscaped in 1873 by Olmstead and Vaux.

Union Theological Seminary, 120th and Reinhold Niebuhr Place. Protestant institution, 1910 Gothic quadrangle.

Riverside Church, Riverside Drive and West 122nd Street. French Gothic church paid for by John D. Rockefeller, Jr. A twenty-two-story tower with famous carillon, reached by elevator. Famous series of preachers.

Grant's Tomb, 122nd Street, in Riverside Park. Marble mausoleum like Napoleon's Tomb in Paris. (President/General) U. S. Grant and his wife buried here. Open Wed.–Sun., 9:00 A.M.–5:00 P.M. Call 666-1640.

POSSIBLE SIDE TRIPS

City University of NYC (CUNY). Formerly City College of NYC. Founded 1847. 1905 Gothic campus, Convent and St. Nicholas Avenues. Alma mater of many of NYC's immigrants/children. Tours Mon.–Thurs. Call 690-6977.

Harlem, 110th–155th Streets. Tours: Harlem Spirituals (gospel and jazz), call 302-2594; New York Big Apple Tours, call 691-7866; Gray Line Tours, call 397-2600.

Trinity Cemetery, 153rd–155th Streets, Riverside Drive to Amsterdam Avenue. Open only by special arrangement. Burial place of Astors, Van Burens, Audubon, and Clement Clarke Moore. (See Walk 4.)

Audubon Terrace, 155 Broadway. See American Academy of Arts and Letters. Open Tues.–Sat., 10:00 A.M.–5:00 P.M. Admission free.

Hamilton Grange, Convent Avenue and 141st Street. Federal-style country retreat of Alexander Hamilton. Open Wed.–Sun. Admission free. Call 283-5154.

Morris-Jumel Mansion, Edgecombe Avenue and 160th Street. 1765 Jumel Terrace. Open Tues.–Sun., 10:00 A.M.–4:00 P.M. Admission. Call 923-8008.

Fort Tryon Park. Contains the Cloisters, a branch of the Metropolitan Museum's medieval collection; chapel; chapter

house; and other treasures, such as Duc de Berry's *Book of Hours*
and the Unicorn tapestries. Collected by George Barnard, a
sculptor and architect enthusiast in early twentieth century.
Sold to John D. Rockefeller, Jr., who presented collection to
the Metropolitan and paid for site, building, etc. The Cloisters
has famous early music concerts and a view of Hudson River
and George Washington Bridge. Open daily except Mon.
Admission fee. Call 923-3700.

Dyckman House, 204th Street and Broadway. Dutch
eighteenth-century farmhouse (1748). Burned during the
Revolutionary War; rebuilt 1783. Open Tues.–Sun., 11:00
A.M.–5:00 P.M. Admission free.

PLACES TO EAT

As student turf, there are many good, cheap ethnic places to eat.

West End Cafe, 2911 Broadway. Hangout for 1950s Beats
(Kerouac, Ginsberg). Live jazz, cover charge. Inexpensive. Call
666-8750.

The Green Tree Hungarian Restaurant, corner of 111th Street and
Broadway. Middle European food. Inexpensive. Call 864-9106.

Hungarian Pastry Shop, next door to the Green Tree. Strong coffee
and rich poppy seed rolls.

The Terrace, French. At Columbia University, atop Butler Library
on College Walk (116th Street). Gorgeous view. Very
expensive. Lunch Tues.–Fri., noon to 3:00 P.M.; dinner
Tues.–Sat., 6:00–10:00 P.M.

W. & T. Pizzeria, Broadway at 112th Street.

—— MORNINGSIDE HEIGHTS WALK ——

Begin your walk at Cathedral Parkway, which is also 110th
Street and Central Park North. If you came by subway, when
you come out of the station at Broadway and 110th Street, you
will see a Burger King (a moderately civilized landmark like the
automat that it replaced) and many shops. Several shops are old
and junky enough to house a lamp with a genie, Aladdin style.

In Madeleine L'Engle's *The Young Unicorns*, the Austin children and their friend Josiah Davidson met such a genie in this neighborhood on their way home from school.

This far north, Broadway still has islands in its center with trees and benches and plantings. In Richard Barth's *A Ragged Plot*, at 102nd Street just west of Broadway, Margaret Binton found a vacant lot being gardened by Luiz Valdez, a Puerto Rican grounds keeper at Yankee Stadium who had a motley crew of kids helping him create a city garden. Luiz lived still farther north at West 128th Street, near CCNY.

Walk to your left along 110th Street to Riverside Drive and cross to look around Riverside Park. During the day there are lots of dogs being walked there. In Patricia Highsmith's *A Dog's Ransom*, dog owners Ed and Greta Reynolds had an apartment at about 109th and Broadway, with a dining area overlooking the Hudson River. Their adored black poodle Lisa was kidnapped (and murdered) when Ed, walking her at night in Riverside Park, let her loose. The murderer, a weird, disabled person named Kenneth Rowajinski, who liked to scare and hurt people, demanded a ransom for the (already dead) dog. Clarence Duhammel, a young NYPD cop, became emotionally involved with Lisa's owners when they brought the ransom note to the (mythical) 109th Precinct station and worked on the case for them.

Recross Riverside Drive and go left to walk up to 112th Street. Along the Drive there are big apartment buildings, but there are also older townhouses on the side streets. In L'Engle's *The Young Unicorns*, the Austins and blind young pianist Emily Gregory all lived in an old four-story mansion near 110th Street and Riverside Drive. The Austins walked their big dog Mr. Rochester in Riverside Park, and they could see the George Washington Bridge from their windows.

In Margaret Maron's *Death of a Butterfly*, Vanderlyn College art professor Oscar Nauman took NYPD Lieutenant Sigrid Harald to a French bakery and then to visit an old chum Dr. Jill Gill, the bug lady. Dr. Gill lived in a narrow brownstone near Riverside Drive. Her patio was filled with the butterflies she was raising. She gave Harald three black swallowtail caterpillars—

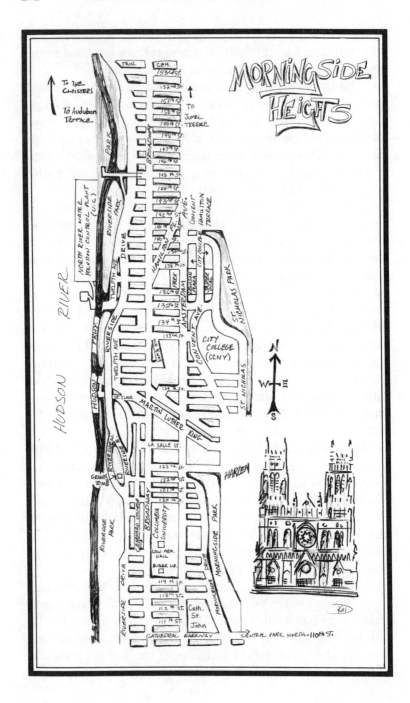

which lived on parsley, dill, and celery—but when Sigrid was called away to investigate Julie Redmond's murder, she ended up giving the caterpillars to her housemate Roman Tamegra, who wrote articles for kiddie magazines.

Turn right to take 112th Street past Broadway and keep going to Amsterdam Avenue. The neighborhood changes quite drastically along here, with the buildings getting much dingier and more decrepit. You'll notice that many of the people in this area are elderly and of various nationalities. Broadway and Amsterdam are still discount shopping areas, too, with small mom-and-pop stores.

At Amsterdam and 112th Street, you face the great west door of the unfinished (Episcopal) Cathedral of St. John the Divine, with its huge twin towers rising up overhead. Above the great front door is a famous huge rose window, which is done in deep blues and purples.

Cross Amsterdam Avenue to go inside one of the cathedral's side doors. Above the southern door, called the Portal of Paradise, you can see some work in progress, with statues and columns being carved and dressed. The workers are local people who are being taught by European master masons. Around the cathedral, from Amsterdam Avenue to Morningside Drive, is an area traditionally called the "close," which is surrounded by a high iron fence. Together with buildings for staff and housing for the dean, the close includes a park with the Peace Fountain to the south. To the east behind the cathedral there is a group of other buildings; on the north side by the 113th Street exit across the street from St. Luke's Hospital is the stone masons' yard.

The cathedral's interior is very dim even in bright daylight. Since it was begun in 1892, it has had three architects; the architecture changes from Gothic to Romanesque to Gothic again (where the choir begins). In the narthex are the famous Mortlake tapestries and some Russian Orthodox paintings of saints (called icons), along with votive candles; the whole cathedral is very eclectic, celebrating every kind of Christian tradition. Its stained glass windows are done in deep blues and red. There are chapels all around the nave and apse, although not all are in use. There are some tombs in the floor—European style—and marker stones for the famous Anglican cathedrals: St. Albans, Canterbury, St. David's, and St. Patrick's, and old abbeys such as Bury St. Edmunds. Here and there are pieces of modern art, poetry by prisoners, prayers for AIDS victims, and names of baptismal candidates.

The first service in 1899 was held in the crypt below the choir. The crypt is reached from one of the apse chapels, that of St. James, which is the first one on the right (south) side of the main altar. In L'Engle's *The Young Unicorns*, the bishop was engaging in skullduggery with street gangs in an abandoned subway station, which was reached from the cathedral crypt by way of that chapel.

The cathedral shop is around to your left on the north side. Oddly enough—since she is officially the cathedral librarian—there are no L'Engle mysteries for sale. You can walk through the shop—and use the restrooms—and go out through the stonecutters' yard on 113th Street. If you do, you will need to turn left and circle around the cathedral to enter the close on 110th Street.

Behind the cathedral is a colonial-style building—once an orphanage—now the Cathedral School for Boys and Girls of All Faiths. Cathedral House, Diocesan House, and Synod House are set around a quadrangle. Like Trinity Church on Wall Street (and Isabelle Holland's fictional St. Anselm's) the cathedral runs a soup kitchen and a shelter for the homeless. But its size and location make it a poor substitute for Holland's St. Anselm's.

In the garden where a peacock struts about, there is a huge sculpture above the Peace Fountain. It portrays a mighty St. Michael stomping on the Devil, who is a kind of crablike creature with nasty horns and claws. This statue represents the story of St. Michael's battle with the Devil in the *Book of Revelation*, written by St. John the Divine.

In L'Engle's *The Young Unicorns*, the cathedral had been completed (still not true). In her later mystery, *The Severed Wasp*, some of the same characters reappeared, grown up. Among them was the once boy chorister Josiah Davidson, now the dean and married to Susy Austin, a doctor at St. Luke's

Hospital. The cathedral in L'Engle's mystery was a very trendy place, totally unlike conservative St. Jude the Martyr's in Byfield and Tedeschi's *Solemn High Murder*.

All the "Episcopal" mysteries covered have references to the cathedral. In Isabelle Holland's *A Fatal Advent*, Canon Roberts, a former dean of St. Paul's Cathedral, London, knew the "people up there" (at St. John's). At the cathedral Roberts's special friend was an elderly cathedral canon who was probably the late Canon Edward West, an authority on church symbolism. West also appeared in L'Engle's mysteries as Canon "Tallis."

During their lunch at the Oyster Bar another envoy from the Archbishop of Canterbury, the Reverend Simon Bede, and Episcopal Center Director Jeremy Baxter also talked about the cathedral. Bede had gone there with a message from the archbishop and he told Baxter that Dean Oglethorpe was seething at the suggestion that instead of going ahead and building the tower on the cathedral they should use the money to install two enormous hundred-foot jets of water instead. In L'Engle's *The Young Unicorns* that idea also came up. Bede called the Right Reverend Martin Warrington, Bishop of New York, a sexy Santa Claus. Bishop Warrington came to St. Jude's to hold the funeral for its murdered rector Dunstan Owlsley. (See Walk 2.)

In Ellery Queen's *The Tragedy of X*, the wife of John De Witt was questioned about her alibi when her husband was murdered. She claimed that she drove by herself from West Englewood, New Jersey, to the city and went to the Cathedral of St. John, parked her car, and went in and sat a long time. She left the cathedral at about 10:30 P.M. and came back on the 42nd Street Ferry. The D.A. told her she could have taken the 125th Street (now Martin Luther King Drive) Ferry much more easily.

Somewhat surprisingly, in Emma Lathen's *Banking on Death*, young Sloan Guarantee Trust officer Ken Nicholas went with his Harvard classmates to the cathedral's Christmas Eve midnight service. They then did a whirlwind tour of NY nightspots (probably including some in nearby Harlem), leaving Nicholas terribly hung over on Christmas Day when his boss Thatcher called him.

Wander about the cathedral yourself or take a regular tour. Then go back outside. There are a number of places nearby on Broadway mentioned in L'Engle's *The Severed Wasp*. Among them are V. & T. Restaurant, at Amsterdam and 110th Street, where L'Engle's clerical cast of characters in *The Severed Wasp* went for pizza after an organ concert at the cathedral; the Hungarian Pastry Shop at Amsterdam and 11th Street; and The Green Tree, with homey Hungarian food, suggested by Dean Davidson.

You are also near the West End Cafe at 2911 Broadway, which was a Beats' hangout for writers such as Kerouac and Ginsberg in the 1950s. All the way up Broadway from 96th Street far past Columbia University are Chinese, Indian, Italian, you name it, restaurants, open most of the time.

Turn to your right when you come out of the cathedral and walk to 113th Street. Across the street you will see St. Luke's Hospital, where Dean Davidson's wife Susy (Austin) was a surgeon in L'Engle's *The Severed Wasp*. In Steve Allen's *Murder in Manhattan*, the day after Jayne came from California to hold Steve's hand because so many weird things were happening during the making of a movie, they were shooting in an old-fashioned apartment off Riverside Drive. When Jasper North, an English actor friend of Allen's, had a heart attack on the set, he was taken to St. Luke's Hospital. The Allens also went there and sat in the intensive care waiting room. After meeting NYPD Lieutenant Carlino, the three went out and got some lunch from a pushcart on the corner.

Walk right, past St. Luke's to Morningside Drive, which runs along Morningside Park and overlooks Harlem. This is your chance to view the park from afar if you don't have time to go there. In Amanda Cross's *The Theban Mysteries*, Morningside Heights Park had been partially leveled by bulldozers because Columbia University was going to build a gym there but was stopped by protestors. (This actually happened.) Go north up Morningside Drive to 116th Street and go left to Amsterdam Avenue.

The number of characters in NYC mysteries who have a "Columbia connection" is amazingly high. In Ellery Queen's

The Chinese Orange Mystery, Jo Temple, who was published by the Kirks' Mandarin Press, mentioned a Chinese artist named Yuen. She told Ellery that Yuen, the son of one of Canton's richest importers, was studying art at Columbia "as so many Chinese in this city do."

In Aaron Elkins's *The Dark Place*, Gideon Oliver, the anthropologist known to the media as "the Skeleton Detective," had been a pupil of Professor Abraham (Abe) I. Goldstein at the University of Wisconsin. Abe was an immigrant pushcart peddler metamorphosed into a world-renowned cultural anthropologist, "a spry little guy with a shock of frizzy white hair who looked so much like Artur Rubenstein he was asked for his autograph." In 1924, as a seventeen-year-old Russian immigrant speaking nothing but Yiddish, Abe had a pushcart business on the Lower East Side. A decade later—1934—he had a Ph.D. in anthropology from Columbia University. (The Gideon Oliver TV series starring the black actor confusingly transplanted Gideon Oliver himself from the University of Washington to Columbia University.)

In Don Winslow's *A Cool Breeze on the Underground*, Neal Carey, the Upper West Side slum kid adopted by P.I. Joe Graham, was working on his M.A. in eighteenth-century English literature at Columbia University. He was called away to find the runaway daughter of Senator John Chase, a presidential contender. Neal's girlfriend Diane was also going to graduate school at Barnard; they had met in a comparative lit class.

In Lisa Bennett's *Madison Avenue Murder*, NYPD detective Dante Cursio, who came to investigate the murder of an agency client, became emotionally involved with art director Peg Goodenough, the daughter of famous abstract artist Theo Goodenough. Cursio told Peg that he had an M.F.A. from Columbia University, but had found that he preferred police work to teaching art.

In *Murder in Manhattan*, when his old friend actor Jason North had his heart attack, which ended the day's shooting, Steve followed the third assistant director Trip Johnson to Columbia University's main quad. Steverino thought that Columbia was not a particularly attractive campus, dominated by the ponderous neoclassical Low Library and drab redbrick buildings—more like the edges of Moscow than NYC. Allen found the young director, whom he suspected was causing trouble, if not committing murder, sitting glumly on a bench with Low Library rising up behind him.

In Katherine Hall Page's *The Body in the Belfrey*, Faith Fairchild, recently of New York City, was stuck in New England as the wife of a clergyman. With her five-month-old son on her back, Faith hiked up the church hill to view the gorgeous fall scenery and wound up finding the body of a church member. She then rang the church bell. John Dunne, a state police officer who took charge of the murder, had gone to Columbia on a Regents scholarship. He told Faith that while at Columbia, he developed a taste for elegant clothes and New Orleans jazz, but then after he had come home from Vietnam, he became a cop like his old man.

In Charles A. Goodrum's *Dewey Decimated*, which is about Washington, D.C.'s Werner-Bok Library (aka the Library of Congress), PR person (Betty) Crighton Jones had gone to Columbia University. Having taken the PR job as a temporary deal, Crighton often took the shuttle back to her old haunts in New York, especially when coping with murder in the library's stacks.

In Meyers's *The Big Killing*, Wetzon's partner Xenia Smith had a Ph.D. in psychology from Columbia. In Meyers's *Tender Death*, Wetzon's senior citizen friend Hazel Osborn also had come to Columbia University to teach and work at one of the big neighborhood settlement houses.

In Pete Hamill's *The Deadly Piece*, reporter Sam Briscoe took Marta Torres to a salsa concert at Madison Square Garden. Marta was a Nuyorican, born on 108th Street and First Avenue in the heart of *El Barrio* (Spanish Harlem). She had gone from Washington Irving High School to Columbia to a fancy Protestant law firm, which she left to work for a NYC poverty program. In Edward Mackin's (aka Ralph MacInerny's) *The Nominative Case*, the upwardly mobile—and murdered—Dean Maggie Downs had transcended poverty and an Irish Catholic background to go to Columbia University, where she lost her faith but got her Ph.D.

In Dorothy Salisbury Davis's *The Lullaby of Murder*, Julie Hayes worked for gossip columnist Tony Alexander at *New York Daily*. She was sent to investigate the reopening of a 1920s ballroom on Amsterdam Avenue near Harlem that was going to run dance marathons. After interviewing the manager, Julie walked back through the campus of Columbia University to Broadway to catch the subway, thinking about the many buildings that had been torn down in NYC, while those at Columbia seemed eternal.

This benign, eternal existence, however, is not exactly the impression you have when reading the mysteries of Amanda Cross. At the same time, perhaps the most mysterious problem connected with Columbia University is whether it is indeed the place where Amanda Cross's professor, Kate Fansler, taught graduate courses in Victorian literature.

Beginning with *In the Last Analysis*, Cross said that Kate taught at "the university." In subsequent mysteries it appeared that her distinguished institution had an upper and lower campus; it was not only private, very well endowed, and stuffy, but also had an undergraduate, all-male college, and an extension school. Its classes were physically disrupted by its own students during the late 60s, and it was located somewhere near Central Park on the upper west side of Manhattan. Under these circumstances, it would be reasonable to conclude, as my Newberry Library class studying the New York mystery did to a woman, that it was appropriate, if not proved beyond a reasonable doubt, to compare the Columbia University campus with Kate Fansler's beloved but sexist institution. (This group decision was not in the least influenced by the fact that "Amanda Cross" is the pen name of Columbia English Professor Carolyn G. Heilbrun.) So this walk will explore Columbia University as a substitute for Cross's "the university." As in the case of Dorothy L. Sayers's mythical Shrewsbury College, the fit is not perfect, but it is quite snug.

In *The Theban Mysteries*, Kate Fansler was teaching a seminar on *Antigone* to the seniors at her old school, the Theban. These high school girls were also into "group therapy" with their drama teacher, which resulted in a mother's death. Checking

out the homes of the class, Fansler found one student lived only
a block or so from Columbia's President's House. Columbia's
President's House (once occupied by Dwight D. Eisenhower) is
on the northwest corner of Morningside Drive and 116th
Street. It is across Amsterdam Avenue from the Columbia Law
School, which is connected to the main campus by a pedestrian
overpass and features a striking statue by Lipschitz.

By the time of *No Word from Winifred*, Fansler's husband
Reed Amhearst was not only teaching at Columbia Law School,
but also had found academia to be the "good life." Reed even
managed to kid Kate into going to the annual Wall Street office
party of her stuffy lawyer brother Laurance to cultivate good
connections for his students. (Fansler also will go to any lengths
for a student.) This development indicated true love, for the
party invitation was addressed to Mr. and Mrs. Reed Amhearst
and they were served sushi. As a result of going, Fansler became
involved in finding the missing heir of two Oxford women writers and wound up attending her first MLA annual convention.
(See Walks 5 and 6.)

Columbia's main gate with statues of Science and Letters is
at Broadway and 116th Street across from the Barnard campus,
where you will exit. For now, cross Amsterdam Avenue and go
in the gate at 116th Street, which becomes College Walk. To
your left is massive Butler Library. It faces north or "up campus" toward the statue of Alma Mater, seated majestically before the wide steps in front of Low Memorial Library (now the
Administration Building) on the other side of redbricked College Walk.

The Terrace, an expensive French restaurant with a good
view of the city, is at the top of Butler Library. It is about the
only substitute for Cross's stodgy Faculty Club, with its very
old, very slow waiters, and questionable food. Kate was always
being taken there for what amounted to working lunches.

According to the student handbook, to go inside most university buildings you will need an I.D. or to be a part of a tour.
The tours start daily during term time in the information center
at Dodge Hall, which is across campus on College Walk at
Broadway. Dodge Hall is likely to be Cross's "Baldwin Hall,"

which housed the graduate English Department. In *In the Last Analysis*, both students and the NYPD were waiting for Kate Fansler on a bench outside her office door. In *No Word from Winifred*, Fansler's actress niece Leighton waited there and quizzed Kate's students about her. It is less likely that Kate's office was in Journalism, the building to the left next to modern Ferris Booth Hall on the corner of Broadway and 114th Street. (The Journalism School was founded in 1913 by NYC's Joseph Pulitzer, founder of the newspaper family and the prizes.)

After looking Dodge Hall over, turn right to walk back toward Alma Mater. It was somewhere about here that Fansler showed the poet-quoting instincts one would expect from an English professor (and a lover of Dorothy L. Sayers). In *In the Last Analysis*, Fansler met a professor outside her office and quoted T. S. Eliot's line about cruel April, only to have her fellow prof quote Edna St. Vincent Millay back. (Both poets liked NYC.)

It was at Columbia University in 1969 that the anti–Vietnam War student protests started when the students took over the Administration Building (Low Memorial Library). In *Poetic Justice*, Cross described the very scene. Fansler was walking across campus and met her old professor, Clemance, who asked her to serve on the committee for a thesis on W. H. Auden. While standing together they saw the tulips being trampled as the students took over the Administration Building and invaded the President's Office to rifle his files, read his mail, and "rescue" a Van Gogh.

Poetic Justice (like Auden's poems) expressed a very elegiac mood, which also led Kate to undertake matrimony, as a hedge against doom. This mystery is really Cross's American version of Sayers's *Gaudy Night*: a tribute to bright women, poetry, and civilization, complete with an ideal suitor to ward off—or with whom to suffer together—the attacks of the barbarians.

Take a good look at Alma Mater (the students tried in vain to blow her up during the demonstrations) and climb the steps to look around Low, a majestic building with a huge rotunda, which was designed by Charles McKim. (As is often the case with many NYC institutions, the campus architects were

McKim, Mead & White.) Once the library, Low now contains university offices, as well as a collection of university items, making it the likely place for Fansler to go to check out both the university records and the fellowship office as she tried to trace the career of her murdered grad student in *In the Last Analysis*.

Since Low is also built uphill, it is a possible setting for "Levy Hall" in *A Trap for Fools*, a later mystery. Canfield Adams, an unpleasant professor of Middle Eastern studies, was pushed to his death out an upper window there and Fansler, who had an unbreakable alibi, was asked to investigate the circumstances.

Come back down the steps and go to your left to look at Buell Hall, a brick house that is the oldest building on campus, predating the university itself. Behind it is Philosophy Hall, with the graduate student lounge; to your left is St. Paul's Chapel, a neo-Byzantine gem worth a look inside if it is open. It has a student art gallery and coffee house in the crypt (basement). Any building around campus that has elevators could be "Lowell Hall," where the elevators proved fatal in *Poetic Justice*.

In the same mystery, Columbia's School of General Studies (extension courses, returning scholars, and so on) was "University College." There the older students were so pleased by their education that they occupied their own building to keep it safe during the antiwar demonstrations. At the request of its dean, Frogmore, Kate supported their cause of preserving their school by letting four students into her class on Victorian Literature to show they were well prepared. In the process she met old friend, Polly Spencer, who had returned to school and gotten a degree to avoid babysitting her grandchildren.

Keep walking left on the brick pathway to a group of older buildings with pleasant ambiance, like Avery Hall with its charming, old-fashioned library, and Schermerhorn Hall. Then turn left to walk back across campus, past the steps leading up to the modern, rather ugly brick buildings that are terraced to the top of the hill. If you climb up, at the top turn left to Pupin Hall at the northwest corner of campus, where the Manhattan Project, which led to the development of the atomic bomb (and ended up in Chicago), began. Beyond Pupin there is a rampart with a good view of Riverside Park, Grant's Tomb, Riverside church with its famous tower, and Union Theological Seminary. Now retrace your steps to the lower campus to walk out the main entrance at 116th Street and Broadway.

In *The Theban Mysteries*, after inspecting some student apartments, Fansler walked back to Broadway and 116th Street and bought herself a hot dog complete with sauerkraut and mustard from a pushcart vendor. In *A Trap for Fools*, at the university bus stop at 116th Street, Fansler suddenly met the dean, whom she suspected of murder, but she was rescued by the appearance of the misogynist Butler, the university's security chief.

Across Broadway is Barnard College, a women's college founded in 1889. Its campus buildings date from the 1890s to 1960s. Cross over and look about, then turn to walk up Broadway to 120th Street (Reinhold Neibuhr Place). Go left to Riverside Drive where you will find Riverside Church.

This handsome French Gothic church was modeled after France's Chartres cathedral. Its tall tower and impressive carillon were donated by John D. Rockefeller, Jr. Despite the precedent in Dorothy L. Sayers's *The Nine Tailors*, you will be neither deafened nor killed if you climb past the seventy-four bells when they are ringing. There is an elevator, although you still have to walk up the last 140 steps. It's a great place from which to look at the George Washington Bridge.

In many ways Riverside Church's activist minister William Sloan Coffin sounds like a great model for Haughton Murphy's Dr. Clark in *Murder for Lunch*. Dr. Clark was resolutely "with it" and would "bury anybody," Christian, Catholic or whatever. Reuben Frost, the retired executive partner of the Wall Street law firm of Chase and Ward, contacted Clark when he had to arrange to bury murdered partner Graham Donovan. After the trendy funeral, a Jewish partner remarked that he had not realized that the Supreme Court had outlawed prayer in Christian churches.

You can also visit nearby Union Theological Seminary, where Reinhold Niebuhr and many other well-known Protestants taught, but no murders have occurred to date. You can also walk to Grant's Tomb along Riverside Drive at 122nd Street or simply stand on the corner at 120th Street and look at it. Designed like the ancient tomb of King Mausolus in Turkey and *Les Invalides*, Napoleon's tomb in Paris, its granite facade is grubby on the outside but well kept within. The answer to the classic question of who's buried in Grant's Tomb is that both General (later President) U. S. Grant, the victor in the Civil War, and his wife, Julia Dent Grant, are there.

After visiting Grant's Tomb, return along Riverside Drive to 116th Street and go left to Broadway where you can get a cab, bus, or subway, or have something to eat, ending your walk.

POSSIBLE SIDE TRIPS

There are a number of famous mystery sights you may want to visit north and east of this walk.

By Car. If you have a car, you can imitate S. S. Van Dine's Philo Vance and cover all of the side trips. In Van Dine's *The Greene Murder Case*, Philo Vance, followed by his faithful Van, went to the Greene family mansion and found the Greene sisters about to take a drive with Dr. Von Blon. They joined the party and drove through Central Park to Riverside Drive. According to Van Dine, the Hudson River lay like a sheet of blue glass below them, and the Jersey palisades were etched as plainly as a Degas drawing in the still clear air. They drove up Broadway all the way to Dyckman Street, then north through Yonkers, past Dobbs Ferry and nearly to Tarrytown, Washington Irving's old hometown on the Hudson River. They stopped at an isolated but scenic lookout, where they all got out to look up and down the river. Sibella Greene announced that this was the perfect site for a murder. Not so long afterwards, a member of the Greene family followed her suggestion.

On this side trip you can see the George Washington Bridge close up, or you can sidetrack to cross the Hudson at the bridge and look for Exit 3—a lookout on the New Jersey side. This was where hit man Danny Adler got his orders to "waste" Neeve Kearny in Clark's *While My Pretty One Sleeps*. It is also the place where Celia Blandings and Greco crossed the Hudson to visit Director Bassinetti of the Palisades Center in New Jersey in Clarins's *The Woman Who Knew Too Much*. They took the West Side Highway from Greenwich Village to the George Washington Bridge.

American Academy of Arts and Letters. The American Academy is at 155 Broadway at Audubon Terrace. In Amanda Cross's *Poetic Justice* Professor Kate Fansler took a cab north from the university to the American Academy of Arts and Sciences. She went hoping to see Auden's old Oxford College chum playwright Christopher Isherwood give Auden a medal, but neither one was there in person, which preserved Fansler's perfect record for never meeting Auden in real life. (For a number of years Auden lived in the East Village on St. Mark's Place. See Walk 2.)

Harlem, 110th Street to 162nd Street. Chester Himes's *The Real Cool Killers* was the story of two black NYPD Harlem precinct cops, Grave Digger and Coffin Ed, who solved a murder of a white man who had been preying on young black girls. They did it without causing "Whitey" (the NYC Establishment) to lose face, but in the process they also destroyed a street gang called the Moslems which was wreaking havoc on black youths, too. The description of Harlem life is spectacularly true to life.

The Cloisters, Fort Tryon Park. The Cloisters would be the perfect American habitat for Ellis Peters's twelfth-century monk Brother Cadfael who stars in her mystery series about Shrewsbury Abbey, located on the banks of the Severn River near Wales. (See *Mystery Reader's Walking Guide: England*, Shrewsbury Walk.) In *St. Peter's Fair*, Brother Cadfael dozed off in a Chapter meeting when he had been up all night seeking clues to a murder in a chapter house just like this one.

The opening scene of Velda Johnson's *The Face in the Shadows* took place at the Cloisters on a bright May day. Actress Ellen Stacey went there to enjoy the "oasis of medieval tranquility transplanted stone by ancient stone thirty-odd years ago from Europe to upper reaches of Manhattan Island."

Ellen went outside to look at New Jersey, hazy with spring green, and then down at the wind-ruffled Hudson. She could imagine the river unchanged from the time the *Half Moon*'s crew had sailed up it, marveling at its clarity, the teeming fish, and at the "faire, spicey odours drifting from the lush green banks." She was startled to find schoolgirl Cecily Vandering huddled on the terrace behind a tubbed evergreen, clearly durgged, because the pupils of her eyes were contracted to pinpoints.

Her school uniform was maroon with the monogram M.S. for Mainwaring School. It was one of the "curtesying Sisters"— an exclusive private school. None of the tourists looked like the girl's parents: they were senior citizens; a couple hand-in-hand in front of the tapestry of *The Hunt of the Unicorn*; three Japanese with cameras aimed at the courtyard fountain; a college girl sketching the medieval statues of the three kings; and, in the dim Romanesque chapel, an elderly woman who looked like a bag lady.

Ellen looked in girl's bag, found her name, address, and three packets of heroin, one empty. She got Cecily up and inside, and took her along the corridor once used by monks, and past the chapel. They climbed the stone stairs to the parking lot and an outdoor phone booth. There Ellen called Cecily's mother, who said to bring her home. Ellen took a cab to the well-to-do Upper East Side and found herself caught up in the problems of the wealthy Vandering family. (See Walk 8.)

SPECIAL HELPS

Authors, Books, and Sleuths by Walk

WALL STREET WALK: AUTHORS

Archer, Jeffrey	**Not a Penny More, Not a Penny Less**
Berry, Carole	**The Year of the Monkey**
Carlson, P. M.	**Murder Unrenovated; Rehearsal for Murder**
Christie, Agatha	**Murder on the Orient Express**
Clark, Mary Higgins	**While My Pretty One Sleeps**
Collins, Max Allan	**Stolen Away**
Cross, Amanda	**Poetic Justice; The Question of Max**
Dickens, Charles	——
Early, Jack	**Donato and Daughter**
Ellin, Stanley	**"The Nine to Five Man"**
Finney, Jack	**Time and Again**
Grisham, John	**The Pelican Brief**
Holland, Isabelle	**A Death at St. Anselm's; A Lover Scorned**
Irving, Washington	**A History of New-York from the Beginning of the World to the End of the Dutch Dynasty, by Diedrich Knickerbocker**
Lathen, Emma	**Ashes to Ashes; Banking on Death; By Hook or Crook; Death Shall Overcome**

Lockridge, Frances and Richard	The Norths Meet Murder
Mackin, Edward (aka Ralph McInerny)	The Nominative Case
Maling, Arthur	Lucky Stiff; Ripoff
Maron, Margaret	One Coffee With; Past Imperfect
Marshall, William	New York Detective
Masur, Hal	Tall, Dark and Deadly
McBain, Ed	Downtown
Meyers, Annette	The Big Killing
Murphy, Haughton (aka James Duffy)	Murder for Lunch
O'Donnell, Lillian	The Children's Zoo
Queen, Ellery	The Chinese Orange Mystery; The Greek Coffin Mystery; The Roman Hat Mystery
Rice, Craig	Having a Wonderful Crime
Rinehart, Mary Roberts	The Swimming Pool
Roosevelt, Elliott	Hyde Park Murder
Ross, Barnaby (aka Ellery Queen)	The Tragedy of X
Sayers, Dorothy L.	Clouds of Witness
Smith, J. C. S.	Nightcap
Stout, Rex	Fer-de-Lance; The Golden Spiders; The Red Band; Too Many Women
Van Dine, S. S.	The Benson Murder Case; The Canary Murder Case
Winslow, Don	A Cool Breeze on the Underground

WALL STREET WALK: BOOKS

Ashes to Ashes	Lathen, Emma
Banking on Death	Lathen, Emma
Benson Murder Case, The	Van Dine, S. S.

Big Killing, The	Meyers, Annette
By Hook or Crook	Lathen, Emma
Canary Murder Case, The	Van Dine, S. S.
Children's Zoo, The	O'Donnell, Lillian
Chinese Orange Mystery, The	Queen, Ellery
Clouds of Witness	Sayers, Dorothy L.
Cool Breeze on the Underground, A	Winslow, Don
Death at St. Anselm's, A	Holland, Isabelle
Death Shall Overcome	Lathen, Emma
Donato and Daughter	Early, Jack
Downtown	McBain, Ed
Fer-de-Lance	Stout, Rex
Golden Spiders, The	Stout, Rex
Greek Coffin Mystery, The	Queen, Ellery
Having a Wonderful Crime	Rice, Craig
History of New-York from the Beginning of the World to the End of the Dutch Dynasty, by Diedrich Knickerbocker, A	Irving, Washington
Hyde Park Murder	Roosevelt, Elliott
Lover Scorned, A	Holland, Isabelle
Lucky Stiff	Maling, Arthur
Murder for Lunch	Murphy, Haughton (aka James Duffy)
Murder on the Orient Express	Christie, Agatha
Murder Unrenovated	Carlson, P. M.
New York Detective	Marshall, William
Nightcap	Smith, J. C. S.
"Nine to Five Man, The"	Ellin, Stanley
Nominative Case, The	Mackin, Edward (aka Ralph McInerny)
Norths Meet Murder, The	Lockridge, Frances and Richard
Not a Penny More, Not a Penny Less	Archer, Jeffrey
One Coffee With	Maron, Margaret

Past Imperfect	Maron, Margaret
Pelican Brief, The	Grisham, John
Poetic Justice	Cross, Amanda
Question of Max, The	Cross, Amanda
Red Band, The	Stout, Rex
Rehearsal for Murder	Carlson, P. M.
Ripoff	Maling, Arthur
Roman Hat Mystery, The	Queen, Ellery
Stolen Away	Collins, Max Allan
Swimming Pool, The	Rinehart, Mary Roberts
Tall, Dark and Deadly	Masur, Hal
Time and Again	Finney, Jack
Too Many Women	Stout, Rex
Tragedy of X, The	Ross, Barnaby (aka Ellery Queen)
While My Pretty One Sleeps	Clark, Mary Higgins
Year of the Monkey, The	Berry, Carole

WALL STREET WALK: SLEUTHS

THE REVEREND CLAIRE ALDINGTON	Holland
MICHAEL J. BARNES	McBain
STEPHEN BRADLEY	Archer
NEAL CAREY	Winslow
NYPD LIEUTENANT DINA DONATO	Early
KATE FANSLER	Cross
REUBEN FROST	Murphy
AUGUST FRYE	Mackin
GRAY GRANTHAM	Grisham
NYPD LIEUTENANT SIGRID HARALD	Maron
NATE HELLER	Collins
BONNIE INDERMILL	Berry
SCOTT JORDAN	Masur
NEEVE KEARNY	Clark

DRURY LANE	Ross
JOHN J. MALONE	Rice
SIMON MARLEY	Finney
LOIS MAYNARD	Rinehart
NYPD SERGEANT NORAH MULCAHANEY	Maron
PAM AND JERRY NORTH	Lockridge
MAGGIE O'CONNOR	Carlson
ELLERY QUEEN	Queen
BROCK POTTER	Maling
HERCULE POIROT	Christie
ELEANOR ROOSEVELT	Roosevelt
JOHN PUTNAM THATCHER	Lathen
NYPD DETECTIVE VIRGIL TILLMAN	Marshall
PHILO VANCE	Van Dine
LESLIE WETZON	Meyers
LORD PETER WIMSEY	Sayers
NERO WOLFE	Stout

LOWER EAST SIDE WALK: AUTHORS

Adams, Henry	—
Aleichem, Sholom	—
Archer, Jeffrey	**Not a Penny More, Not a Penny Less**
Asch, Sholem	—
Auden, W. H.	**"Murder in the Guilty Vicarage"**
Barth, Richard	**A Ragged Plot**
Beats, The	**Allen Ginsberg, Frank O'Hara, Jack Kerouac, William Burroughs**
Berlin, Irving	—
Brooks, Van Wyck	—
Byfield, Barbara Ninde and Frank Tedeschi	**Solemn High Murder**

Byrne, Muriel St. Clare — The Lisle Letters
Chandler, Raymond — ——
Charyn, Jerome — Metropolis: New York as Myth, Marketplace and Magical Land
Clarins, Dana — The Woman Who Knew Too Much
Clark, Mary Higgins — While My Pretty One Sleeps
Cooper, James Fenimore — The Leatherstocking Tales
Crane, Stephen — Maggie: A Girl of the Streets
Cross, Amanda — No Word from Winifred; "Murder Without a Text"; Poetic Justice
cummings, e. e. — ——
Daly, Elizabeth — Murders in Volume 2
Dos Passos, John — ——
Doyle, Sir Arthur Conan — The Adventures of Sherlock Holmes
Early, Jack — Donato and Daughter
Foster, Stephen — ——
Holland, Isabelle — A Death at St. Anselm's
Hunter, Evan (aka Ed McBain) — The Blackboard Jungle
James, Henry — Turn of the Screw
Johnson, Velda — The Face in the Shadows
Kaufman, Bel — Up the Down Staircase
Lee, Manfred (aka Ellery Queen) — ——
Love, William F. — The Chartreuse Clue
Lutz, John — Shadowtown
Mailer, Norman — Tough Guys Don't Dance
Maron, Margaret — Baby Doll Games; Corpus Christmas; One Coffee With
Marshall, William — New York Detective
McBain, Ed — Downtown
Nusser, Richard — Walking After Midnight
O'Donnell, Lillian — The Children's Zoo
Papazoglou, Orania (aka Jane Haddam) — Wicked, Loving Murder
Paretsky, Sara (editor) — A Woman's Eye

Piesman, Marissa	**Personal Effects**
Queen, Ellery	**The Greek Coffin Mystery**
Riis, Jacob	**How the Other Half Lives**
Roosevelt, Elliott	**Hyde Park Murder**
Runyon, Damon	**Guys and Dolls**
Simenon, Georges	—
Singer, Isaac Bashevis	—
Steffins, Lincoln	—
Stout, Rex	**The Golden Spiders**
Uhnak, Dorothy	**The Bait**
White, E. B.	**Here Is New York**
Whitman, Walt	—

LOWER EAST SIDE WALK: BOOKS

Adventures of Sherlock Holmes, The	Doyle, Sir Arthur Conan
Baby Doll Games	Maron, Margaret
Bait, The	Uhnak, Dorothy
Blackboard Jungle, The	Hunter, Evan (aka Ed McBain)
Chartreuse Clue, The	Love, William F.
Children's Zoo, The	O'Donnell, Lillian
Corpus Christmas	Maron, Margaret
Death at St. Anselm's, A	Holland, Isabelle
Donato and Daughter	Early, Jack
Downtown	McBain, Ed
Face in the Shadows, The	Johnson, Velda
Golden Spiders, The	Stout, Rex
Greek Coffin Mystery, The	Queen, Ellery
Guys and Dolls	Runyon, Damon
Hyde Park Murder	Roosevelt, Elliott
Metropolis	Charyn, Jerome
"Murder in the Guilty Vicarage"	Auden, W. H.
Murders in Volume 2	Daly, Elizabeth
"Murder Without a Text"	Cross, Amanda
New York Detective	Marshall, William

Not a Penny More, Not a Penny Less	Archer, Jeffrey
No Word from Winifred	Cross, Amanda
One Coffee With	Maron, Margaret
Personal Effects	Piesman, Marissa
Poetic Justice	Cross, Amanda
Ragged Plot, A	Barth, Richard
Shadowtown	Lutz, John
Solemn High Murder	Byfield and Tedeschi
Tough Guys Don't Dance	Mailer, Norman
Up the Down Staircase	Kaufman, Bel
Walking After Midnight	Nusser, Richard
While My Pretty One Sleeps	Clark, Mary Higgins
Wicked, Loving Murder	Papazoglou, Orania (aka Jane Haddam)
Woman Who Knew Too Much, The	Clarins, Dana

LOWER EAST SIDE WALK: SLEUTHS

THE REVEREND CLAIRE ALDINGTON	Holland
BAKER STREET IRREGULARS	Doyle
MICHAEL J. BARNES	McBain
THE REVEREND SIMON BEDE	Byfield and Tedeschi
MARGARET BINTON	Barth
STEPHEN BRADLEY	Archer
MAX DARENOW	Nusser
DELANCEY STREET IRREGULARS	Love
NYPD LIEUTENANT DINA DONATO	Early
KATE FANSLER	Cross
NINA FISCHMAN	Piesman
HENRY GAMADGE	Daly
NYPD LIEUTENANT SIGRID HARALD	Maron

SHERLOCK HOLMES	Doyle
NEEVE KEARNY	Clark
PATIENCE MCKENNA	Papazoglou
TIM MADDEN	Mailer
JULES MAIGRET	Simenon
PHILIP MARLOWE	Chandler
NYPD SERGEANT NORAH MULCAHANEY	O'Donnell
NYPD DETECTIVE CHRISTIE OPARA	Uhnak
NYPD DETECTIVE "OX" OXMAN	Lutz
ELLERY QUEEN	Queen
BISHOP FRANCIS X. REGAN	Love
ELEANOR ROOSEVELT	Roosevelt
ELLEN STACEY	Johnson
V. I. WARSHAWSKI	Paretsky
NERO WOLFE	Stout

GREENWICH VILLAGE WALK: AUTHORS

Allen, Steve	**Murder in Manhattan**
Barth, Richard	**The Condo Kill**
Block, Lawrence	**The Sins of the Fathers**
Brennan, Carol	**Headhunt**
Browning, Robert	—
Byfield, Barbara Ninde and Frank Tedeschi	**Solemn High Murder**
Carlson, P. M.	**Audition for Murder; Murder Unrenovated; Rehearsal for Murder**
Carr, John Dickson	**The Mad Hatter Mystery**
Cather, Willa	**Death Comes for the Archbishop**
Chesterton, G. K.	**"The Sign of the Broken Sword"**

Clarins, Dana	The Woman Who Knew Too Much
Clark, Mary Higgins	Loves Music, Loves to Dance; While My Pretty One Sleeps
Crespi, Trella	The Trouble with a Small Raise
Daly, Elizabeth	Murders in Volume 2
Davis, Dorothy Salisbury	Lullaby of Murder
Day, Clarence	Life with Father
Dos Passos, John	Manhattan Transfer
Dreiser, Theodore	An American Tragedy
Early, Jack	Donato and Daughter
Eliot, T. S.	Murder in the Cathedral
Friedman, Mickey	"The Fabulous Nick"
Gash, Jonathan	The Great California Game
Green, Anna Katherine	The Leavenworth Case
Hammett, Dashiell	The Thin Man
Hart, Carolyn G.	Death on Demand
Highsmith, Patricia	A Dog's Ransom
Holland, Isabelle	The Flight of the Archangel; A Lover Scorned
James, Henry	The Turn of the Screw
James, P. D.	An Unsuitable Job for a Woman
Lathen, Emma	Banking on Death; Death Shall Overcome
Lee, Manfred (aka Ellery Queen)	—
L'Engle, Madeleine	A Severed Wasp
Lockridge, Frances and Richard	The Norths Meet Murder
Lockridge, Richard	Murder for Art's Sake
Lutz, John	Shadowtown
Mackin, Edward (aka Ralph McInerny)	The Nominative Case
Macleod, Charlotte (editor)	Christmas Stalkings
Maling, Arthur	Ripoff
Maron, Margaret	Baby Doll Games; Death of a Butterfly; Past Imperfect

Matteson, Stefanie	**Murder at Teatime**
McBain, Ed	**Downtown**
McKenney, Ruth	**My Sister Eileen**
Melville, Herman	**Billy Budd**
Millay, Edna St. Vincent	**"Renascence"**
O'Donnell, Lillian	**The Children's Zoo**
O'Neill, Eugene	**Morning Becomes Electra**
Penzler, Otto (with Lisa Drake)	**The Medical Center Murders**
Poe, Edgar Allan	**"The Purloined Letter"**
Queen, Ellery	**The Roman Hat Mystery**
Rice, Craig	**Having a Wonderful Crime**
Roosevelt, Elliott	**Hyde Park Murder**
Sayers, Dorothy L.	**Gaudy Night; Whose Body?**
Stein, Gertrude	**"The Lost Generation"**
Stout, Rex	**Fer-de-Lance; Gambit; Plot It Yourself; The Doorbell Rang; The Mother Hunt; Too Many Clients; "Died Like a Dog"**
Thomas, Dylan	**"A Child's Christmas in Wales"**
Twain, Mark	**Pudd'nhead Wilson**
Van Dine, S. S.	**The Benson Murder Case**
Van Doren, Carl and Mark (brothers)	——
Webster, John	**The Duchess of Malfi**
Welles, Orson	**"The War of the Worlds"**
West, Nathanael	**Miss Lonelyhearts**
Westlake, Donald	**Good Behavior**

GREENWICH VILLAGE WALK: BOOKS

Audition for Murder	Carlson, P. M.
Baby Doll Games	Maron, Margaret
Banking on Death	Lathen, Emma
Benson Murder Case, The	Van Dine, S. S.
Canary Murder Case, The	Van Dine, S. S.

Children's Zoo, The — O'Donnell, Lillian
Christmas Stalkings — Macleod, Charlotte (editor)
Condo Kill, The — Barth, Richard
Death of a Butterfly — Maron, Margaret
Death on Demand — Hart, Carolyn G.
Death Shall Overcome — Lathen, Emma
"Died Like a Dog" — Stout, Rex
Dog's Ransom, A — Highsmith, Patricia
Donato and Daughter — Early, Jack
Doorbell Rang, The — Stout, Rex
Downtown — McBain, Ed
"Fabulous Nick, The" — Friedman, Mickey
Fer-de-Lance — Stout, Rex
Flight of the Archangel, The — Holland, Isabelle
Gambit — Stout, Rex
Gaudy Night — Sayers, Dorothy L.
Good Behavior — Westlake, Donald
Great California Game, The — Gash, Jonathan
Having a Wonderful Crime — Rice, Craig
Headhunt — Brennan, Carol
Hyde Park Murder — Roosevelt, Elliott
Leavenworth Case, The — Green, Anna Katherine
Lover Scorned, A — Holland, Isabelle
Loves Music, Loves to Dance — Clark, Mary Higgins
Lullaby of Murder, The — Davis, Dorothy Salisbury
Medical Center Murders, The — Penzler, Otto (with Lisa Drake)
Mother Hunt, The — Stout, Rex
Murder at Teatime — Matteson, Stephanie
Murder for Art's Sake — Lockridge, Richard
Murder in Manhattan — Allen, Steve
Murder in the Cathedral — Eliot, T. S.
Murder Unrenovated — Carlson, P. M.
Murders in Volume 2 — Daly, Elizabeth
Nominative Case, The — Mackin, Edward (aka Ralph McInerny)

Norths Meet Murder, The — Lockridge, Frances and Richard
Past Imperfect — Maron, Margaret

Plot It Yourself	Stout, Rex
"Purloined Letter, The"	Poe, Edgar Allan
Rehearsal for Murder	Carlson, P. M.
Ripoff	Maling, Arthur
Roman Hat Mystery, The	Queen, Ellery
Severed Wasp, A	L'Engle, Madeleine
Shadowtown	Lutz, John
Sins of the Fathers, The	Block, Lawrence
Solemn High Murder	Byfield and Tedeschi
Thin Man, The	Hammett, Dashiell
Too Many Clients	Stout, Rex
Trouble with a Small Raise, The	Crespi, Trella
Turn of the Screw, The	James, Henry
Unsuitable Job for a Woman, An	James, P. D.
While My Pretty One Sleeps	Clark, Mary Higgins
Whose Body?	Sayers, Dorothy L.
Woman Who Knew Too Much, The	Clarins, Dana

GREENWICH VILLAGE WALK: SLEUTHS

THE REVEREND CLAIRE ALDINGTON	Holland
STEVE ALLEN	Allen
MICHAEL J. BARNES	McBain
THE REVEREND SIMON BEDE	Byfield and Tedeschi
MARGARET BINTON	Barth
CELIA BLANDINGS	Clarins
NICK AND NORA CHARLES	Hammett
NYPD LIEUTENANT DINA DONATO	Early
JOHN DORTMUNDER	Westlake
LISA DRAKE	Penzler
NYPD OFFICER CLARENCE DUHAMMELL	Highsmith

AUGUST FRYE	Mackin
HENRY GAMADGE	Daly
CHARLOTTE GRAHAM	Matteson
CORDELIA GRAY	James
SIMONA GRIFFO	Crespi
NYPD DETECTIVE MR. GRYCE	Green
NYPD LIEUTENANT SIGRID HARALD	Maron
JULIE HAYES	Davis
NEEVE KEARNY	Clark
ANNIE LAURANCE	Hart
LOVEJOY	Gash
JOHN J. MALONE	Rice
NYPD SERGEANT NORAH MULCAHANEY	O'Donnell
PAM AND JERRY NORTH	Lockridge
MAGGIE O'CONNOR	Carlson
NYPD DETECTIVE SERGEANT "OX" OXMAN	Lutz
BROCK POTTER	Maling
ELLERY QUEEN	Queen
ELEANOR ROOSEVELT	Roosevelt
SANTA CLAUS	Friedman
DARCY SCOTT	Clark
MATT SCUDDER	Block
JOHN PUTNAM THATCHER	Lathen
PHILO VANCE	Van Dine
HARRIET VANE	Sayers
KATHERINE VIGNERAS	L'Engle
LIZ WAREHAM	Brennan
NERO WOLFE	Stout

LOWER MIDTOWN WALK: AUTHORS

Ambler, Eric	**Coffin for Dimitrios**
Berry, Carole	**The Year of the Monkey**
Booth, John Wilkes	——

Burns, Charles E.	"Firecrackers"
Carlson, P. M.	Murder Unrenovated; Rehearsal for Murder
Charyn, Jerome	Paradise Man
Chesterton, G. K.	⸺
Christmas, Joyce	Suddenly in Her Sorbet
Clarins, Dana	The Woman Who Knew Too Much
Clark, Mary Higgins	Loves Music, Loves to Dance
Crespi, Trella	The Trouble with a Small Raise
Dentinger, Jane	Murder on Cue
Finney, Jack	Time and Again
Fleming, Ian	Gold Finger
Hammett, Dashiell	The Maltese Falcon; The Thin Man
Henry, O. (William S. Porter)	"The Ransom of Red Chief"
Holland, Isabelle	Flight of the Archangel; A Lover Scorned
Howells, William Dean	The Rise of Silas Lapham
Irving, Washington	A History of New-York from the Beginning of the World to the End of the Dutch Dynasty, by Diedrich Knickerbocker
Johnson, Velda	The Face in the Shadows
Lathen, Emma	Death Shall Overcome
Le Carre, John	The Spy Who Came In from the Cold
Lee, Gypsy Rose	The G-String Murders
Lockridge, Frances and Richard	The Norths Meet Murder
Lockridge, Richard	Murder for Art's Sake
Love, William F.	The Chartreuse Clue
Maling, Arthur	Lucky Devil
Maron, Margaret	Corpus Christmas; Death in Blue Folders; Past Imperfect

Marshall, William	New York Detective
Maugham, Somerset	Ashenden
Meyers, Annette	The Big Killing
Moore, Clement Clarke	"A Visit from St. Nicholas"
Morse, Samuel F. B.	——
Murphy, Haughton (aka James Duffy)	Murder Saves Face; Murder for Lunch
Nusser, Richard	Walking After Midnight
Oppenheim, E. Phillips	The Great Impersonation
Papazoglou, Orania (aka Jane Haddam)	Wicked, Loving Murder
Perelman, S. J.	——
Piesman, Marissa	Unorthodox Practices
Rice, Craig	Having a Wonderful Crime
Roosevelt, Elliott	Hyde Park Murder
Roosevelt, Theodore	——
Schermerhorn, Gene	Letters to Phil, Memories of a New York Boyhood
Stout, Rex	The Golden Spiders; Murder by the Book
Van Dine, S. S.	The Canary Murder Mystery
West, Nathanael	Miss Lonelyhearts
Wharton, Edith	——
Winslow, Don	A Cool Breeze on the Underground
Wolfe, Thomas	——

LOWER MIDTOWN WALK: BOOKS

Big Killing, The	Meyers, Annette
Canary Murder Case, The	Van Dine, S. S.
Chartreuse Clue, The	Love, William F.
Cool Breeze on the Underground, A	Winslow, Don
Corpus Christmas	Maron, Margaret
Death in Blue Folders	Maron, Margaret

Death Shall Overcome	Lathen, Emma
Face in the Shadows, The	Johnson, Velda
Flight of the Archangel	Holland, Isabelle
Golden Spiders, The	Stout, Rex
Great Impersonation, The	Oppenheim, E. Phillips
G-String Murders, The	Lee, Gypsy Rose
Having a Wonderful Crime	Rice, Craig
Hyde Park Murder	Roosevelt, Elliott
Lover Scorned, A	Holland, Isabelle
Loves Music, Loves to Dance	Clark, Mary Higgins
Lucky Devil	Maling, Arthur
Maltese Falcon, The	Hammett, Dashiell
Murder by the Book	Stout, Rex
Murder for Art's Sake	Lockridge, Richard
Murder for Lunch	Murphy, Haughton (aka James Duffy)
Murder on Cue	Dentinger, Jane
Murder Saves Face	Murphy, Haughton (aka James Duffy)
Murder Unrenovated	Carlson, P. M.
New York Detective	Marshall, William
Norths Meet Murder, The	Lockridge, Frances and Richard
Paradise Man	Charyn, Jerome
Past Imperfect	Maron, Margaret
Suddenly in Her Sorbet	Christmas, Joyce
Thin Man, The	Hammett, Dashiell
Time and Again	Finney, Jack
Trouble with a Small Raise, The	Crespi, Trella
Unorthodox Practices	Piesman, Marissa
"Visit from St. Nicholas, A"	Moore, Clement Clark
Walking After Midnight	Nusser, Richard
Wicked, Loving Murder	Papazoglou, Orania (aka Jane Haddam)
Woman Who Knew Too Much, The	Clarins, Dana
Year of the Monkey, The	Berry, Carole

Lower Midtown Walk: Sleuths

The Reverend Claire Aldington	Holland
Father Brown	Chesterton
Neal Carey	Winslow
Nick and Nora Charles	Hammett
Max Darenow	Nusser
Nina Fischman	Piesman
Reuben Frost	Murphy
Simona Griffo	Crespi
Sidney Holden	Charyn
Bonnie Indermill	Berry
Gypsy Rose Lee	Lee
John J. Malone	Rice
Patience McKenna	Papazoglou
Simon Morley	Finney
Pam and Jerry North	Lockridge
Maggie O'Connor	Carlson
Jocelyn O'Roarke	Dentinger
Brock Potter	Maling
Lady Margaret Priam	Christmas
Bishop Francis X. Regan	Love
Eleanor Roosevelt	Roosevelt
Darcy Scott	Clark
Sam Spade	Hammett
Ellen Stacey	Johnson
John Putnam Thatcher	Lathen
NYPD Detective Virgil Tillman	Marshall
Philo Vance	Van Dine
Leslie Wetzon	Meyers
Nero Wolfe	Stout

Midtown West Walk: Authors

Allen, Steve   **Murder in Manhattan**
Allingham, Margery   **The China Governess**

Armstrong, Charlotte	The Unsuspected
Asimov, Isaac	Murder at the ABA
Babson, Marion	Murder Sails at Midnight
Barth, Richard	A Ragged Plot
Bennett, Lisa	Seventh Avenue Murder
Bernstein, Leonard	West Side Story
Box, Edgar (aka Gore Vidal)	Death in the Fifth Position
Brennan, Carol	Headhunt
Byfield, Barbara Ninde and Frank Tedeschi	Solemn High Murder
Carlson, P. M.	Rehearsal for Murder
Chesbro, George	The Second Horseman Out of Eden; Bone
Christie, Agatha	—
Clarins, Dana	The Woman Who Knew Too Much
Clark, Mary Higgins	Loves Music, Loves to Dance; While My Pretty One Sleeps
Collins, Max Allan	Stolen Away
Cross, Amanda	In the Last Analysis; No Word from Winifred; The Question of Max; A Trap for Fools
Dale, Alzina Stone	Maker and Craftsman; The Outline of Sanity, A Life of G. K. Chesterton
Dannay, Frederic and Manfred Lee (aka Ellery Queen)	—
Davis, Dorothy Salisbury	A Gentle Murder; Lullaby of Murder
Dentinger, Jane	First Hit of the Season; Murder on Cue
Doyle, Sir Arthur Conan	—
Eliot, T. S.	Cats; Murder in the Cathedral
Evers, Crabbe (aka Bill Brashler)	Murderer's Row
Gash, Jonathan	The Great California Game

Hamill, Pete	The Deadly Piece
Hammett, Dashiell	The Thin Man
Hughes, Dorothy B.	—
Irving, Washington	A History of New-York from the Beginning of the World to the End of the Dutch Dynasty, by Diedrich Knickerbocker
Johnson, Velda	The Face in the Shadows
Lathen, Emma	Death Shall Overcome
Lockridge, Richard	Murder for Art's Sake
Love, William F.	The Chartreuse Clue
Lutz, John	Shadowtown
Maron, Margaret	Death in Blue Folders; Death of a Butterfly; Past Imperfect
McBain, Ed	87th Precinct mysteries
Moore, Clement Clarke	"A Visit from St. Nicholas"
Murphy, Haughton (aka James Duffy)	Murder for Lunch; Murder Saves Face; Murder Takes a Partner
O'Neill, Eugene	—
Papazoglou, Orania (aka Jane Haddam)	Wicked, Loving Murder
Pentecost, Hugh	The Substitute Victim
Penzler, Otto	The Mysterious Press
Peters, Elizabeth	Not for Love
Poe, Edgar Allan	"Murders in the Rue Morgue"
Queen, Ellery	The Greek Coffin Mystery; The Roman Hat Mystery; The French Powder Mystery
Quentin, Patrick	Puzzle for Players
Rinehart, Mary Roberts	The Circular Staircase; The Lamp in the Window
Ross, Barnaby (aka Ellery Queen)	The Tragedy of X

MIDTOWN WEST WALK: BOOKS

French Powder Mystery, The	Queen, Ellery
Gentle Murderer, A	Davis, Dorothy Salisbury
Golden Spiders, The	Stout, Rex
Great California Game, The	Gash, Jonathan
Greek Coffin Mystery, The	Queen, Ellery
Headhunt	Brennan, Carol
In the Last Analysis	Cross, Amanda
Lamp in the Window, The	Rinehart, Mary Roberts
Loves Music, Loves to Dance	Clark, Mary Higgins
Lullaby of Murder	Davis, Dorothy Salisbury
Maker and Craftsman	Dale, Alzina Stone
Method Three for Murder	Stout, Rex
Murder at the ABA	Asimov, Isaac
Murderer's Row	Evers, Crabbe (aka Bill Brashler)
Murder for Art's Sake	Lockridge, Richard
Murder for Lunch	Murphy, Haughton (aka James Duffy)
Murder in the Cathedral	Eliot, T. S.
Murder Must Advertise	Sayers, Dorothy L.
Murder on Cue	Dentinger, Jane
Murder Sails at Midnight	Babson, Marion
Murder Saves Face	Murphy, Haughton (aka James Duffy)
Murders in the Rue Morgue	Poe, Edgar Allan
Murder Takes a Partner	Murphy, Haughton (aka James Duffy)
Not for Love	Peters, Elizabeth
No Word from Winifred	Cross, Amanda
Outline of Sanity, The, A Life of G. K. Chesterton	Dale, Alzina Stone
Past Imperfect	Maron, Margaret
Please Pass the Guilt	Stout, Rex
Puzzle for Players	Quentin, Patrick
Question of Max, The	Cross, Amanda
Ragged Plot, A	Barth, Richard
Red Carnelian, The	Whitney, Phyllis
Rehearsal for Murder	Carlson, P. M.
Roman Hat Mystery, The	Queen, Ellery

Second Horseman Out of Eden	Chesbro, George
Seventh Avenue Murders	Bennett, Lisa
Shadowtown	Lutz, John
Solemn High Murder	Byfield, Barbara Ninde and Frank Tedeschi
Stolen Away	Collins, Max Allan
Substitute Victim, The	Pentecost, Hugh
Thin Man, The	Hammett, Dashiell
Too Many Clients	Stout, Rex
Tragedy of X, The	Ross, Barnaby (aka Ellery Queen)
Trap for Fools, A	Cross, Amanda
Unsuspected, The	Armstrong, Charlotte
While My Pretty One Sleeps	Clark, Mary Higgins
Wicked, Loving Murder	Papazoglou, Orania (aka Jane Haddam)
Woman Who Knew Too Much, The	Clarins, Dana

MIDTOWN WEST WALK: SLEUTHS

THE REVEREND SIMON BEDE	Byfield and Tedeschi
MARGARET BINTON	Barth
CELIA BLANDINGS	Clarins
SAM BRISCOE	Hamill
NICK AND NORA CHARLES	Hammett
FATHER DUFFY	Davis
DUPIN	Poe
KATE FANSLER	Cross
REUBEN FROST	Murphy
PEG GOODENOUGH	Bennett
NYPD LIEUTENANT SIGRID HARALD	Maron
JULIE HAYES	Davis
NATE HELLER	Collins
SHERLOCK HOLMES	Doyle

DUFFY HOUSE	Evers
FRANCIS HOWARD	Armstrong
DARIUS JUST	Asimov
JACQUELINE KIRBY	Peters
DRURY LANE	Ross
LOVEJOY	Gash
MACAVITY	Eliot
PATIENCE MCKENNA	Papazoglou
VALERIE MEADOWS	Babson
JOCELYN O'ROARKE	Dentinger
NYPD DETECTIVE "OX" OXMAN	Lutz
MAX POPPER	Wolk
ELLERY QUEEN	Queen
BISHOP REGAN	Love
PETER CUTLER SARGEANT III	Box
DARCY SCOTT	Clark
ELLEN STACEY	Johnson
JOHN SUGARMAN	Wolk
JOHN PUTNAM THATCHER	Lathen
PHILO VANCE	Van Dine
LIZ WAREHAM	Brennan
DORIE WEIGAND	Lockridge
LORD PETER WIMSEY	Sayers
NERO WOLFE	Stout

THE AVENUES WALK: AUTHORS

Allen, Steve	**Murder in Manhattan**
Bennett, Lisa	**Madison Avenue Murder**
Box, Edgar (aka Gore Vidal)	**Death in the Fifth Position**
Brennan, Carol	**Headhunt**
Byfield, Barbara Ninde and Frank Tedeschi	**Solemn High Murder**
Capote, Truman	**Breakfast at Tiffany's; In Cold Blood**

Carlson, P. M.	Murder Unrenovated; Rehearsal for Murder
Chaffets, Zev	Inherit the Mob
Charteris, Leslie	The Saint in New York
Charyn, Jerome	The Paradise Man
Chesbro, George	The Second Horseman Out of Eden; Bone
Christie, Agatha	At Bertram's Hotel
Clarins, Dana	The Woman Who Knew Too Much
Clark, Mary Higgins	A Stranger Is Watching; Loves Music, Loves to Dance; While My Pretty One Sleeps
Crespi, Trella	The Trouble with a Small Raise
Cross, Amanda	No Word from Winifred
Daly, Elizabeth	The Book of the Lion; The Book of the Crime
DeAndrea, William L.	The Lunatic Fringe
Dentinger, Jane	First Hit of the Season
Doctorow, E. L.	Ragtime
Early, Jack	Donato and Daughter
Eberhart, Mignon	Danger Money
Evers, Crabbe (aka Bill Brashler)	Murder at Wrigley Field
Gash, Jonathan	The Great California Game
Green, Anna Katherine	The Leavenworth Case
Hammett, Dashiell	The Thin Man
Hart, Carolyn G.	Death on Demand
Hillerman, Tony	The Thief of Time
Holland, Isabelle	A Fatal Advent; Flight of the Archangel; A Death at St. Anselm's
Hughes, Dorothy B.	The Fallen Sparrow
James, Henry	The American Scene
Johnson, Velda	The Face in the Shadows

Lathen, Emma	Ashes to Ashes; Death Shall Overcome; Banking on Death
Lockridge, Frances and Richard	Murder Comes First
Lockridge, Richard	Murder for Art's Sake
Maron, Margaret	Death in Blue Folders; Past Imperfect
Meyers, Annette	The Big Killing
Meyers, Martin	Hardy: Hung Up to Die; Kiss and Kill
Milne, A. A.	The Red House Mystery
Murphy, Haughton (aka James Duffy)	Murder Saves Face
O'Cork, Shannon	The Murder of Muriel Lake
Queen, Ellery	The Chinese Orange Mystery; The French Powder Mystery; The Greek Coffin Mystery
Rinehart, Mary Roberts	The Swimming Pool
Roosevelt, Elliott	Hyde Park Murder
Stout, Rex	The Golden Spiders; Too Many Clients; Too Many Women
Thurber, James	"The Macbeth Murder Mystery"
Van Dine, S. S.	The Benson Murder Case
Westlake, Donald	Good Behavior
Whitney, Phyllis	The Red Carnelian
Winslow, Don	A Cool Breeze on the Underground

THE AVENUES WALK: BOOKS

Ashes to Ashes	Lathen, Emma
At Bertram's Hotel	Christie, Agatha
Banking on Death	Lathen, Emma

Benson Murder Case, The	Van Dine, S. S.
Book of the Crime, The	Daly, Elizabeth
Book of the Lion, The	Daly, Elizabeth
Chinese Orange Mystery, The	Queen, Ellery
Cool Breeze on the Underground, A	Winslow, Don
Danger Money	Eberhart, Mignon
Death at St. Anselm's, A	Holland, Isabelle
Death in Blue Folders	Maron, Margaret
Death in the Fifth Position	Box, Edgar (aka Gore Vidal)
Death on Demand	Hart, Carolyn G.
Death Shall Overcome	Lathen, Emma
Donato and Daughter	Early, Jack
Face in the Shadows, The	Johnson, Velda
Fallen Sparrow, The	Hughes, Dorothy B.
Fatal Advent, A	Holland, Isabelle
First Hit of the Season	Dentinger, Jane
Flight of the Archangel	Holland, Isabelle
French Powder Mystery, The	Queen, Ellery
Golden Spiders, The	Stout, Rex
Good Behavior	Westlake, Donald
Great California Game, The	Gash, Jonathan
Greek Coffin Mystery, The	Queen, Ellery
Hardy: Hung Up to Die	Meyers, Martin
Headhunt	Brennan, Carol
Hyde Park Murder	Roosevelt, Elliott
In Cold Blood	Capote, Truman
Inherit the Mob	Chaffets, Zev
Kiss and Kill	Meyers, Martin
Leavenworth Case, The	Green, Anna Katherine
Loves Music, Loves to Dance	Clark, Mary Higgins
Lunatic Fringe, The	DeAndrea, William L.
"Macbeth Murder Mystery, The"	Thurber, James
Madison Avenue Murder	Bennett, Lisa
Murder at Wrigley Field	Evers, Crabbe (aka Bill Brashler)

Murder Comes First	Lockridge, Frances and Richard
Murder for Art's Sake	Lockridge, Richard
Murder in Manhattan	Allen, Steve
Murder of Muriel Lake, The	O'Cork, Shannon
Murder Saves Face	Murphy, Haughton (aka James Duffy)
Murder Unrenovated	Carlson, P. M.
No Word from Winifred	Cross, Amanda
Paradise Man, The	Charyn, Jerome
Past Imperfect	Maron, Margaret
Ragtime	Doctorow, E. L.
Red Carnelian, The	Whitney, Phyllis
Red House Mystery, The	Milne, A. A.
Rehearsal for Murder	Carlson, P. M.
Saint in New York, The	Charteris, Leslie
Second Horseman Out of Eden, The	Chesbro, George
Solemn High Murder	Byfield and Tedeschi
Stranger Is Watching, A	Clark, Mary Higgins
Swimming Pool, The	Rinehart, Mary Roberts
Thief of Time, The	Hillerman, Tony
Thin Man, The	Hammett, Dashiell
Too Many Clients	Stout, Rex
Too Many Women	Stout, Rex
Trouble with a Small Raise, The	Crespi, Trella
While My Pretty One Sleeps	Clark, Mary Higgins
Woman Who Knew Too Much, The	Clarins, Dana

THE AVENUES WALK: SLEUTHS

THE REVEREND CLAIRE ALDINGTON	Holland
STEVE ALLEN	Allen
SUSAN BEACH	Eberhart

THE REVEREND SIMON BEDE	Byfield and Tedeschi
CELIA BLANDINGS	Charins
NEAL CAREY	Winslow
NICK AND NORA CHARLES	Hammett
NYPD LIEUTENANT DINA DONATO	Early
JOHN DORTMUNDER	Westlake
KATE FANSLER	Cross
GARTH AND MONGO FREDERICKSON	Chesbro
REUBEN FROST	Murphy
HENRY GAMADGE	Daly
PEG GOODENOUGH	Bennett
WILLIAM (VELVEL) GORDON	Chaffets
SIMONA GRIFFO	Crespi
NYPD DETECTIVE MR. GRYCE	Green
NYPD LIEUTENANT SIGRID HARALD	Maron
PATRICK HARDY	Meyers
SIDNEY HOLDEN	Charyn
DUFFY HOUSE	Evers
NEEVE KEARNY	Clark
ANNIE LAURANCE	Hart
LIEUTENANT JOE LEAPHORN	Hillerman
LOVEJOY	Gash
MACBETH	Thurber
MISS MARPLE	Christie
SHARON MARTIN	Clark
LOIS MAYNARD	Rinehart
KIT MCKITTRICK	Hughes
NYPD OFFICER DENNIS PATRICK XAVIER MULDOON	DeAndrea
PAM AND JERRY NORTH	Lockridge
MAGGIE O'CONNOR	Carlson
JOCELYN O'ROARKE	Dentinger
ELLERY QUEEN	Queen
ELEANOR ROOSEVELT	Roosevelt
THE SAINT	Charteris

PETER CUTLER SARGEANT III	Box
DARCY SCOTT	Clark
NYPD SERGEANT TYRONE SCOTT	O'Cork
ELLEN STACEY	Johnson
JOHN PUTNAM THATCHER	Lathen
PHILO VANCE	Van Dine
LIZ WAREHAM	Brennan
LESLIE WETZON	Meyers
NERO WOLFE	Stout

MIDTOWN EAST WALK: AUTHORS

Allen, Steve	**Murder in Manhattan**
Bernstein, Leonard	**West Side Story**
Brennan, Carol	**Headhunt**
Byfield, Barbara Ninde and Frank Tedeschi	**Solemn High Murder**
Carlson, P. M.	**Audition for Murder**
Chaffets, Zev	**Inherit the Mob**
Charyn, Jerome	**The Education of Patrick Silver**
Chesbro, George	**Bone**
Chesterton, G. K.	**"In Defense of Detective Stories"**
Christie, Agatha	**Murder on the Orient Express**
Clarins, Dana	**The Woman Who Knew Too Much**
Clark, Mary Higgins	**Loves Music, Loves to Dance; A Stranger Is Watching; While My Pretty One Sleeps**
Collins, Max Allan	**Stolen Away**
Crespi, Trella	**The Trouble with a Small Raise**

Cross, Amanda	The Theban Mysteries
Dale, Alzina Stone and Barbara Sloan Hendershott	Mystery Reader's Walking Guide: London
Davis, Dorothy Salisbury	Lullaby of Murder
Eberhart, Mignon	Danger Money
Goldsborough, Robert	Death on Deadline
Gould, Chester	Dick Tracy
Grisham, John	The Pelican Brief
Hammett, Dashiell	The Thin Man
Hepburn, Katharine	Me
Highsmith, Patricia	A Dog's Ransom
Hillerman, Tony	The Thief of Time
Hitchcock, Alfred	North by Northwest
Holland, Isabelle	A Fatal Advent
Hughes, Dorothy B.	The Fallen Sparrow
Hunter, Evan (aka Ed McBain)	The Blackboard Jungle
Johnson, Velda	The Face in the Shadows
Lathen, Emma	Ashes to Ashes
Lockridge, Frances and Richard	Murder Comes First
MacLeod, Charlotte (ed.)	Christmas Stalkings
Marquand, John	—
Matteson, Stefanie	Murder at Teatime; Murder at the Spa
McBain, Ed	87th Precinct mysteries
Meyers, Annette	The Big Killing
O'Donnell, Lillian	The Children's Zoo
Paul, Barbara	Liars and Tyrants and People Who Turn Blue
Pentecost, Hugh	Beware Young Lovers
Penzler, Otto (with Lisa Drake)	The Medical Center Murders
Poe, Edgar Allan	—
Rinehart, Mary Roberts	—
Roosevelt, Elliott	—
Sayers, Dorothy L.	The Unpleasantness at the Bellona Club

Smith, Evelyn E.	"Miss Melville Rejoices"
Stout, Rex	Fer-de-Lance; Too Many Clients
Truman, Margaret	—
Van Dine, S. S.	The Canary Murder Case; The Greene Murder Case
White, E. B.	"Here Is New York"

MIDTOWN EAST WALK: BOOKS

Ashes to Ashes	Lathen, Emma
Audition for Murder	Carlson, P. M.
Beware Young Lovers	Pentecost, Hugh
Big Killing, The	Meyers, Annette
Blackboard Jungle, The	Hunter, Evan (aka Ed McBain)
Bone	Chesbro, George
Canary Murder Case, The	Van Dine, S. S.
Children's Zoo, The	O'Donnell, Lillian
Christmas Stalkings	MacLeod, Charlotte, ed.
Danger Money	Eberhart, Mignon
Death on Deadline	Goldsborough, Robert
Dog's Ransom, A	Highsmith, Patricia
Education of Patrick Silver, The	Charyn, Jerome
Face in the Shadows, The	Johnson, Velda
Fallen Sparrow, The	Hughes, Dorothy B.
Fatal Advent, A	Holland, Isabelle
Fer-de-Lance	Stout, Rex
Greene Murder Case, The	Van Dine, S. S.
"Here Is New York"	White, E. B.
"In Defense of Detective Stories"	Chesterton, G. K.
Inherit the Mob	Chaffets, Zev
Liars and Tyrants and People Who Turn Blue	Paul, Barbara
Loves Music, Loves to Dance	Clark, Mary Higgins

Lullaby of Murder	Davis, Dorothy Salisbury
Medical Center Murders, The	Penzler, Otto (with Lisa Drake)
"Miss Melville Rejoices"	Smith, Evelyn E.
Murder at Teatime	Matteson, Stefanie
Murder at the Spa	Matteson, Stefanie
Murder Comes First	Lockridge, Frances and Richard
Murder in Manhattan	Allen, Steve
Murder on the Orient Express	Christie, Agatha
Mystery Reader's Walking Guide: London	Dale and Hendershott
North by Northwest	Hitchcock, Alfred
Pelican Brief, The	Grisham, John
Solemn High Murder	Byfield and Tedeschi
Stolen Away	Collins, Max Allan
Stranger Is Watching, A	Clark, Mary Higgins
Theban Mysteries, The	Cross, Amanda
Thief of Time, The	Hillerman, Tony
Thin Man, The	Hammett, Dashiell
Too Many Clients	Stout, Rex
Trouble with a Small Raise, The	Crespi, Trella
Unpleasantness at the Bellona Club, The	Sayers, Dorothy
West Side Story	Bernstein, Leonard
While My Pretty One Sleeps	Clark, Mary Higgins
Woman Who Knew Too Much, The	Clarins, Dana

MIDTOWN EAST WALK: SLEUTHS

SUSAN BEACH	Eberhart
THE REVEREND SIMON BEDE	Byfield and Tedeschi
CELIA BLANDINGS	Clarins

BONE	Chesbro
PIERRE CHAMBRUN	Pentecost
NICK AND NORA CHARLES	Hammett
LISA DRAKE	Penzler
NYPD OFFICER CLARENCE DUHAMMELL	Highsmith
KATE FANSLER	Cross
WILLIAM GORDON	Chaffets
CHARLOTTE GRAHAM	Matteson
CARY GRANT (ROGER THORNHILL)	Hitchcock
SIMONA GRIFFO	Crespi
JULIE HAYES	Davis
NATE HELLER	Collins
NEEVE KEARNY	Clark
SHELBY KENT	Paul
NAVAJO LIEUTENANT JOE LEAPHORN	Hillerman
SHARON MARTIN	Clark
KIT MCKITTRICK	Hughes
MISS MELVILLE	Smith
MR. MOTO	Marquand
NYPD SERGEANT NORAH MULCAHANEY	O'Donnell
PAM AND JERRY NORTH	Lockridge
MAGGIE O'CONNOR	Carlson
HERCULE POIROT	Christie
DARCY SCOTT	Clark
PATRICK SILVER	Charyn
ELLEN STACEY	Johnson
SUPERMAN	
JOHN PUTNAM THATCHER	Lathen
DICK TRACY	Gould
PHILO VANCE	Van Dine
LIZ WAREHAM	Brennan
LESLIE WETZON	Meyers
NERO WOLFE	Stout

Upper East Side Walk: Authors

Allen, Steve	Murder in Manhattan
Allingham, Margery	The China Governess
Barth, Richard	The Condo Kill
Bennett, Lisa	Madison Avenue Murder
Box, Edgar (aka Gore Vidal)	Death in the Fifth Position
Brennan, Carol	Headhunt
Caspary, Vera	Laura
Christie, Agatha	The Secret of Chimneys
Christmas, Joyce	A Fete Worse Than Death
Clarins, Dana	The Woman Who Knew Too Much
Clark, Mary Higgins	Loves Music, Loves to Dance; While My Pretty One Sleeps
Crespi, Trella	The Trouble with a Small Raise
Cross, Amanda	In the Last Analysis; Poetic Justice; The Question of Max; A Trap for Fools
Dale, Alzina Stone and Barbara Sloan Hendershott	Mystery Reader's Walking Guide: London; Mystery Reader's Walking Guide: England
Daly, Elizabeth	The Book of the Crime; Murders in Volume 2; Somewhere in the House
Dentinger, Jane	First Hit of the Season
Doctorow, E. L.	Ragtime
Eberhart, Mignon	Woman on the Roof; Danger Money
Elkins, Aaron	A Glancing Light
Hammett, Dashiell	—
Hillerman, Tony	The Thief of Time
Holland, Isabelle	Flight of the Archangel; A Fatal Advent; A Death at St. Anselm's; A Lover Scorned

Hughes, Dorothy B.	The Fallen Sparrow
Johnson, Velda	The Face in the Shadows
Lathen, Emma	Banking on Death; Come to Dust
L'Engle, Madeleine	A Severed Wasp
Lockridge, Richard	Murder for Art's Sake
Love, William F.	The Chartreuse Clue
Lutz, John	Shadowtown
Maron, Margaret	Corpus Christmas; Death in Blue Folders; The Death of a Butterfly; One Coffee With
Marshall, William	New York Detective
Meyers, Annette	The Big Killing; Tender Death
Murphy, Haughton (aka James Duffy)	Murder Saves Face; Murder for Lunch
O'Cork, Shannon	The Murder of Muriel Lake
O'Donnell, Lillian	The Children's Zoo
Piesman, Marissa	Personal Effects
Rice, Craig	Having a Wonderful Crime
Rinehart, Mary Roberts	The Swimming Pool
Roosevelt, Elliott	Hyde Park Murder
Sanders, Lawrence	The First Deadly Sin
Stout, Rex	Some Buried Caesar; Too Many Clients; The Golden Spiders
Winslow, Don	A Cool Breeze on the Underground

UPPER EAST SIDE WALK: BOOKS

Banking on Death	Lathen, Emma
Big Killing, The	Meyers, Annette
Book of the Crime, The	Daly, Elizabeth
Chartreuse Clue, The	Love, William F.
Children's Zoo, The	O'Donnell, Lillian

China Governess, The	Allingham, Margery
Come to Dust	Lathen, Emma
Cool Breeze on the Underground, A	Winslow, Don
Corpus Christmas	Maron, Margaret
Danger Money	Eberhart, Mignon
Death at St. Anselm's, A	Holland, Isabelle
Death in Blue Folders	Maron, Margaret
Death in the Fifth Position	Box, Edgar (aka Gore Vidal)
Death of a Butterfly	Maron, Margaret
Face in the Shadows, The	Johnson, Velda
Fallen Sparrow, The	Hughes, Dorothy B.
Fatal Advent, A	Holland, Isabelle
Fete Worse Than Death, A	Christmas, Joyce
First Deadly Sin, The	Sanders, Lawrence
First Hit of the Season	Dentinger, Jane
Flight of the Archangel	Holland, Isabelle
Glancing Light, A	Elkins, Aaron
Golden Spiders, The	Stout, Rex
Having a Wonderful Crime	Rice, Craig
Headhunt	Brennan, Carol
Hyde Park Murder	Roosevelt, Elliott
In the Last Analysis	Cross, Amanda
Laura	Caspary, Vera
Lover Scorned, A	Holland, Isabelle
Loves Music, Loves to Dance	Clark, Mary Higgins
Madison Avenue Murder	Bennett, Lisa
Murder for Art's Sake	Lockridge, Richard
Murder for Lunch	Murphy, Haughton (aka James Duffy)
Murder in Manhattan	Allen, Steve
Murders in Volume 2	Daly, Elizabeth
Murder of Muriel Lake, The	O'Cork, Shannon
Murder Saves Face	Murphy, Haughton (aka James Duffy)
Mystery Reader's Walking Guide: England	Dale and Hendershott

Mystery Reader's Walking Guide: London	Dale and Hendershott
New York Detective	Marshall, William
One Coffee With	Maron, Margaret
Personal Effects	Piesman, Marissa
Poetic Justice	Cross, Amanda
Question of Max, The	Cross, Amanda
Ragtime	Doctorow, E. L.
Secret of Chimneys, The	Christie, Agatha
Severed Wasp, A	L'Engle, Madeleine
Shadowtown	Lutz, John
Some Buried Caesar	Stout, Rex
Somewhere in the House	Daly, Elizabeth
Swimming Pool, The	Rinehart, Mary Roberts
Tender Death	Meyers, Annette
Thief of Time, The	Hillerman, Tony
Too Many Clients	Stout, Rex
Trap for Fools, A	Cross, Amanda
Trouble with a Small Raise, The	Crespi, Trella
While My Pretty One Sleeps	Clark, Mary Higgins
Woman on the Roof	Eberhart, Mignon
Woman Who Knew Too Much, The	Clarins, Dana

UPPER EAST SIDE WALK: SLEUTHS

THE REVEREND CLAIRE ALDINGTON	Holland
SERGEANT BATTLE	Christie
SUSAN BEACH	Eberhart
MARGARET BINTON	Barth
CELIA BLANDINGS	Clarins
ALBERT CAMPION	Allingham
NEAL CAREY	Winslow
VINCE D'AMBROSIO	Clark

SUE DESART	Eberhart
KATE FANSLER	Cross
NINA FISCHMAN	Piesman
REUBEN FROST	Murphy
HENRY GAMADGE	Daly
SIMONA GRIFFO	Crespi
NYPD LIEUTENANT SIGRID HARALD	Maron
NEEVE KEARNY	Clark
NAVAJO LIEUTENANT JOE LEAPHORN	Hillerman
KIT MCKITTRICK	Hughes
NYPD LIEUTENANT MARK MCPHERSON	Caspary
JOHN J. MALONE	Rice
LOIS MAYNARD	Rinehart
NYPD SERGEANT NORAH MULCAHANEY	O'Donnell
CHRIS NORGREN	Elkins
PAM AND JERRY NORTH	Lockridge
JOCELYN O'ROARKE	Dentinger
NYPD LIEUTENANT "OX" OXMAN	Lutz
LADY MARGARET PRIAM	Christmas
BISHOP REGAN	Love
ELEANOR ROOSEVELT	Roosevelt
PETER CUTLER SARGEANT III	Box
NYPD SERGEANT TYRONE SCOTT	O'Cork
ELLEN STACEY	Johnson
JOHN PUTNAM THATCHER	Lathen
NYPD DETECTIVE VIRGIL TILLMAN	Marshall
KATHERINE VIGNERAS	L'Engle
LIZ WAREHAM	Brennan
LESLIE WETZON	Meyers
NERO WOLFE	Stout

CENTRAL PARK WALK: AUTHORS

Allen, Steve	Murder in Manhattan
Asimov, Isaac	Murder at the ABA
Barth, Richard	The Condo Kill
Capote, Truman	In Cold Blood
Carlson, P. M.	Murder Unrenovated; Audition for Murder
Chesbro, George	Bone; The Second Horseman Out of Eden
Chesterton, G. K.	The Man Who Was Thursday
Clark, Mary Higgins	Loves Music, Loves to Dance; While My Pretty One Sleeps; A Stranger Is Watching
Crespi, Trella	The Trouble with a Small Raise
Cross, Amanda	In the Last Analysis; The Players Come Again; Poetic Justice; The Theban Mysteries; A Trap for Fools
Dale, Alzina Stone and Barbara Sloan Hendershott	Mystery Reader's Walking Guide: London
Daly, Elizabeth	The Book of the Lion
Evers, Crabbe (aka Bill Brashler)	Murderer's Row
Fleming, Ian	—
Grisham, John	The Pelican Brief
Holland, Isabelle	A Death at St. Anselm's; A Fatal Advent; A Lover Scorned
Howells, William Dean	—
Hume, Fergus W.	The Mystery of a Hansom Cab
Johnson, Velda	The Face in the Shadows
Lockridge, Frances and Richard	Murder Comes First; The Norths Meet Murder

Love, William F.   The Chartreuse Clue
Lutz, John   Shadowtown
MacInnes, Helen   Neither Five Nor Three
MacLeod, Charlotte   The Curse of the Giant
                              Hogweed
Maron, Margaret   Death of a Butterfly; One
                              Coffee With
Meyers, Annette   The Big Killing
O'Donnell, Lillian   The Children's Zoo
Paul, Barbara   Liars and Tyrants and People
                              Who Turn Blue
Peters, Elizabeth   Naked Once More
Piesman, Marissa   Personal Effects
Queen, Ellery   The French Powder Mystery;
                              The Roman Hat Mystery
Rinehart, Mary Roberts   The Circular Staircase
Ross, Barnaby (aka Ellery   The Tragedy of X
  Queen)
Sayers, Dorothy L.   Busman's Honeymoon;
                              Murder Must Advertise
Stout, Rex   ——
Van Dine, S. S.   The Canary Murder Case;
                              The Greene Murder Case
Westlake, Donald   God Save the Mark

CENTRAL PARK WALK: BOOKS

Audition for Murder   Carlson, P. M.
Big Killing, The   Meyers, Annette
Book of the Lion, The   Daly, Elizabeth
Bone   Chesbro, George
Busman's Honeymoon   Sayers, Dorothy L.
Canary Murder Case, The   Van Dine, S. S.
Chartreuse Clue, The   Love, William F.
Children's Zoo, The   O'Donnell, Lillian
Circular Staircase, The   Rinehart, Mary Roberts
Condo Kill, The   Barth, Richard

Curse of the Giant Hogweed, The	MacLeod, Charlotte
Death at St. Anselm's, A	Holland, Isabelle
Death of a Butterfly	Maron, Margaret
Face in the Shadows, The	Johnson, Velda
Fatal Advent, A	Holland, Isabelle
French Powder Mystery, The	Queen, Ellery
God Save the Mark	Westlake, Donald
Greene Murder Case, The	Van Dine, S. S.
In Cold Blood	Capote, Truman
Liars and Tyrants and People Who Turn Blue	Paul, Barbara
Lover Scorned, A	Holland, Isabelle
Loves Music, Loves to Dance	Clark, Mary Higgins
Man Who Was Thursday, The	Chesterton, G. K.
Murder at the ABA	Asimov, Isaac
Murder Comes First	Lockridge, Frances and Richard
Murderer's Row	Evers, Crabbe (aka Bill Brashler)
Murder in Manhattan	Allen, Steve
Murder Unrenovated	Carlson, P. M.
Mystery of a Hansom Cab, The	Hume, Fergus W.
Mystery Reader's Walking Guide: London	Dale and Hendershott
Naked Once More	Peters, Elizabeth
Neither Five Nor Three	MacInnes, Helen
Norths Meet Murder, The	Lockridge, Frances and Richard
One Coffee With	Maron, Margaret
Pelican Brief, The	Grisham, John
Personal Effects	Piesman, Marissa
Players Come Again, The	Cross, Amanda
Poetic Justice	Cross, Amanda
Roman Hat Mystery, The	Queen, Ellery

Second Horseman Out of Eden, The	Chesbro, George
Shadowtown	Lutz, John
Stranger Is Watching, A	Clark, Mary Higgins
Theban Mysteries, The	Cross, Amanda
Tragedy of X, The	Ross, Barnaby (aka Ellery Queen)
Trap for Fools, A	Cross, Amanda
Trouble with a Small Raise, The	Crespi, Trella
While My Pretty One Sleeps	Clark, Mary Higgins

CENTRAL PARK WALK: SLEUTHS

THE REVEREND CLAIRE ALDINGTON	Holland
STEVE ALLEN	Allen
MARGARET BINTON	Barth
JAMES BOND	Fleming
BONE	Chesbro
VINCE D'AMBROSIO (FBI)	Clark
KATE FANSLER	Cross
NINA FISCHMAN	Piesman
MONGO AND GARTH FREDERICKSON	Chesbro
HENRY GAMADGE	Daly
KEVIN GILBERT, UN SECURITY	Paul
GRAY GRANTHAM	Grisham
SIMONA GRIFFO	Crespi
NYPD LIEUTENANT SIGRID HARALD	Maron
DUFFY HOUSE	Evers
DARIUS JUST	Asimov
NEEVE KEARNY	Clark
JACQUELINE KIRBY	Peters
DRURY LANE	Ross

NYPD SERGEANT NORAH MULCAHANEY	O'Donnell
PAM AND JERRY NORTH	Lockridge
MAGGIE O'CONNOR	Carlson
NYPD LIEUTENANT "OX" OXMAN	Lutz
ELLERY QUEEN	Queen
BISHOP FRANCIS X. REGAN	Love
PROFESSOR PETER SHANDY	MacLeod
ELLEN STACEY	Johnson
GABRIEL SYME ("THURSDAY")	Chesterton
PHILO VANCE	Van Dine
LESLIE WETZON	Meyers
LORD PETER WIMSEY	Sayers
NERO WOLFE	Stout

UPPER WEST SIDE WALK: AUTHORS

Allen, Steve	**Murder in Manhattan**
Barth, Richard	**The Condo Kill; A Ragged Plot**
Bernstein, Leonard	**West Side Story**
Brennan, Carol	**Headhunt**
Charyn, Jerome	**The Paradise Man**
Chesterton, G. K.	—
Clark, Mary Higgins	**While My Pretty One Sleeps**
Crosby, Harry	—
Cross, Amanda	**In the Last Analysis; The Players Come Again; A Trap for Fools**
Dale, Alzina Stone and Barbara Sloan Hendershott	**Mystery Reader's Walking Guide: England**
Dreiser, Theodore	**Sister Carrie**
Ellin, Stanley	**"The Nine to Five Man"**
Engleman, Paul	**Catch a Falling Angel; Who Shot Longshot Sam?**

Finney, Jack	Time and Again
Gash, Jonathan	The Great California Game
Hammett, Dashiell	The Thin Man
Hughes, Dorothy B.	The Fallen Sparrow
Katz, William	Open House; The Surprise Party
Lathen, Emma	Death Shall Overcome
Lennon, John	—
Lewis, Sinclair	—
Love, William F.	The Chartreuse Clue
Lutz, John	Shadowtown
Maron, Margaret	One Coffee With; Past Imperfect
Marsh, Ngaio	A Clutch of Constables
Meyers, Annette	The Big Killing; Tender Death
Meyers, Annette and Martin	The Dutchman
Meyers, Martin	Kiss and Kill
Murphy, Haughton (aka James Duffy)	Murder for Lunch; Murder Saves Face
Papazoglou, Orania (aka Jane Haddam)	Wicked, Loving Murder
Piesman, Marissa	Unorthodox Practices
Poe, Edgar Allan	"The Raven"
Queen, Ellery	The French Powder Mystery; The Roman Hat Mystery
Roosevelt, Teddy	—
Salinger, J. D.	—
Sayers, Dorothy L.	"The Incredible Elopement of Lord Peter Wimsey"
Stout, Rex	The Golden Spiders; Too Many Clients
Van Dine, S. S.	The Benson Murder Case
Westlake, Donald	God Save the Mark
Winn, Dilys	Murder Ink
Winslow, Don	A Cool Breeze on the Underground
Wouk, Herman	Marjorie Morningstar

UPPER WEST SIDE WALK: BOOKS

Benson Murder Case, The	Van Dine, S. S.
Big Killing, The	Meyers, Annette
Catch a Falling Angel	Engleman, Paul
Chartreuse Clue, The	Love, William F.
Clutch of Constables, A	Marsh, Ngaio
Condo Kill, The	Barth, Richard
Cool Breeze on the Underground, A	Winslow, Don
Death Shall Overcome	Lathen, Emma
Dutchman, The	Meyers, Annette and Martin
Fallen Sparrow, The	Hughes, Dorothy A.
French Powder Mystery, The	Queen, Ellery
God Save the Mark	Westlake, Donald
Golden Spiders, The	Stout, Rex
Great California Game, The	Gash, Jonathan
Headhunt	Brennan, Carol
"Incredible Elopement of Lord Peter Wimsey, The"	Sayers, Dorothy L.
In the Last Analysis	Cross, Amanda
Kiss and Kill	Meyers, Martin
Marjorie Morningstar	Wouk, Herman
Murder for Lunch	Murphy, Haughton (aka James Duffy)
Murder Ink	Winn, Dilys
Murder in Manhattan	Allen, Steve
Murder Saves Face	Murphy, Haughton (aka James Duffy)
Mystery Reader's Walking Guide: England	Dale and Hendershott
"Nine to Five Man, The"	Ellin, Stanley
One Coffee With	Maron, Margaret
Open House	Katz, William
Paradise Man, The	Charyn, Jerome
Past Imperfect	Maron, Margaret
Players Come Again, The	Cross, Amanda
Ragged Plot, A	Barth, Richard

"Raven, The"	Poe, Edgar Allan
Roman Hat Mystery, The	Queen, Ellery
Rosemary's Baby	—
Shadowtown	Lutz, John
Sister Carrie	Dreiser, Theodore
Surprise Party, The	Katz, William
Tender Death	Meyers, Annette
Thin Man, The	Hammett, Dashiell
Time and Again	Finney, Jack
Too Many Clients	Stout, Rex
Trap for Fools, A	Cross, Amanda
Unorthodox Practices	Piesman, Marissa
West Side Story	Bernstein, Leonard
While My Pretty One Sleeps	Clark, Mary Higgins
Who Shot Longshot Sam?	Engleman, Paul
Wicked, Loving Murder	Papazoglou, Orania (aka Jane Haddam)

UPPER WEST SIDE WALK: SLEUTHS

STEVEN ALLEN	Allen
SUPERINTENDENT RODERICK ALLEYN	Marsh
MARGARET BINTON	Barth
FATHER BROWN	Chesterton
NEAL CAREY	Winslow
NICK AND NORA CHARLES	Hammett
KATE FANSLER	Cross
FRED FITCH	Westlake
REUBEN FROST	Murphy
NYPD LIEUTENANT SIGRID HARALD	Maron
PATRICK HARDY	Meyers
SIDNEY HOLDEN	Charyn
NEEVE KEARNY	Clark
LOVEJOY	Gash
PATIENCE MCKENNA	Papazoglou

KIT MCKITTRICK	Hughes
SIMON MORLEY	Finney
NYPD LIEUTENANT "OX" OXMAN	Lutz
ELLERY QUEEN	Queen
BISHOP FRANCIS X. REGAN	Love
MARK RENZLER	Engleman
JOHN PUTNAM THATCHER	Lathen
PHILO VANCE	Van Dine
LIZ WAREHAM	Brennan
LESLIE WETZON	Meyers
LORD PETER WIMSEY	Sayers
NERO WOLFE	Stout

MORNINGSIDE HEIGHTS WALK: AUTHORS

Allen, Steve	**Murder in Manhattan**
Barth, Richard	**The Condo Kill; A Ragged Plot**
Bennett, Lisa	**Madison Avenue Murder**
Byfield, Barbara Ninde and Frank Tedeschi	**Solemn High Murder**
Clarins, Dana	**The Woman Who Knew Too Much**
Clark, Mary Higgins	**While My Pretty One Sleeps**
Cross, Amanda	**In the Last Analysis; Poetic Justice; A Trap for Fools; The Theban Mysteries**
Dale, Alzina Stone and Barbara Sloan Hendershott	**Mystery Reader's Walking Guide: England**
Davis, Dorothy Salisbury	**Lullaby of Murder**
Elkins, Aaron	**The Dark Place**
Goodrum, Charles A.	**Dewey Decimated**
Hammill, Pete	**The Deadly Place**
Highsmith, Patricia	**A Dog's Ransom**
Himes, Chester	**The Real Cool Killers**
Holland, Isabelle	**A Fatal Advent**

Johnson, Velda	**The Face in the Shadows**
Lathen, Emma	**Banking on Death**
L'Engle, Madeleine	**A Severed Wasp; The Young Unicorns**
Mackin, Edward (aka Ralph McInerny)	**The Nominative Case**
Maron, Margaret	**Death of a Butterfly, The**
Meyers, Annette	**The Big Killing; Tender Death**
Murphy, Haughton (aka James Duffy)	**Murder for Lunch**
Page, Katherine Hall	**The Body in the Belfrey**
Peters, Ellis	**St. Peter's Fair**
Queen, Ellery	**The Chinese Orange Mystery**
Ross, Barnaby (aka Ellery Queen)	**The Tragedy of X**
Van Dine, S. S.	**The Greene Murder Case**
Winslow, Don	**A Cool Breeze on the Underground**

MORNINGSIDE HEIGHTS WALK: BOOKS

Banking on Death	Lathen, Emma
Big Killing, The	Meyers, Annette
Body in the Belfrey, The	Page, Katherine Hall
Chinese Orange Mystery, The	Queen, Ellery
Condo Kill, The	Barth, Richard
Cool Breeze on the Underground, A	Winslow, Don
Dark Place, The	Elkins, Aaron
Deadly Piece, The	Hamill, Pete
Death of a Butterfly, The	Maron, Margaret
Dewey Decimated	Goodrum, Charles A.
Dog's Ransom, A	Highsmith, Patricia
Green Murder Case, The	Van Dine, S. S.
In the Last Analysis	Cross, Amanda

Lullaby of Murder	Davis, Dorothy Salisbury
Madison Avenue Murder	Bennett, Lisa
Murder for Lunch	Murphy, Haughton (aka James Duffy)
Murder in Manhattan	Allen, Steve
Mystery Reader's Walking Guide: England	Dale and Hendershott
Nominative Case, The	Mackin, Edward (aka Ralph McInerny)
Poetic Justice	Cross, Amanda
Ragged Plot, A	Barth, Richard
Real Cool Killers, The	Himes, Chester
Severed Wasp, A	L'Engle, Madeleine
Solemn High Murder	Byfield and Tedeschi
St. Peter's Fair	Peters, Ellis
Tender Death	Meyers, Annette
Theban Mysteries, The	Cross, Amanda
Tragedy of X, The	Ross, Barnaby (aka Ellery Queen)
Trap for Fools, A	Cross, Amanda
While My Pretty One Sleeps	Clark, Mary Higgins
Woman Who Knew Too Much, The	Clarins, Dana
Young Unicorns, The	L'Engle, Madeleine

MORNINGSIDE HEIGHTS WALK: SLEUTHS

STEVE ALLEN	Allen
THE REVEREND SIMON BEDE	Byfield and Tedeschi
MARGARET BINTON	Barth
CELIA BLANDINGS	Clarins
SAM BRISCOE	Hamill
BROTHER CADFAEL	Peters
NEAL CAREY	Winslow
KATE FANSLER	Cross
REUBEN FROST	Murphy
AUGUST FRY	Mackin

PEG GOODENOUGH	Bennett
GRAVE DIGGER AND COFFIN ED	Himes
NYPD LIEUTENANT SIGRID HARALD	Maron
JULIE HAYES	Davis
CRIGHTON JONES	Goodrum
NEEVE KEARNY	Clark
DRURY LANE	Ross
GIDEON OLIVER	Elkins
ELLERY QUEEN	Queen
FAITH SIBLEY	Page
CANON TALLIS	L'Engle
PHILO VANCE	Van Dine

BIBLIOGRAPHY

These are books that were especially useful in writing this guide.

Charyn, Jerome. *Metropolis: New York as Myth, Marketplace, and Magical Land*. New York: Avon, 1986.

Edmiston, Susan, and Linda D. Cirino. *Literary New York*. New York: Gibbs Smith Publisher, 1976, 1991.

Haycraft, Howard. *Murder for Pleasure*. New York: Carroll & Graf Publishers, 1941, 1984.

Irving, Washington. *A History of New-York by Diedrich Knickerbocker*. New York: The Continental Press, n.d.

Kane, Robert S. *New York at Its Best*. Lincolnwood, Ill.: Passport Books, 1989.

McCullough, David. *The Great Bridge*. New York: Simon & Schuster, 1972.

Schermerhorn, Gene. *Letters to Phil: Memories of a New York Boyhood, 1848–1856*. New York: New York Bound, 1982.

Simon, Kate. *Fifth Avenue: A Very Social History*. New York: Harcourt Brace Jovanovich, 1978.

Symons, Julian. *Mortal Consequences*. New York: Schoken Books, 1973.

_____. *The Tell-Tale Heart: The Life and Works of Edgar Allan Poe*. Middlesex: Penguin Books, 1978.

White, Norval, and Elliot Wilensky. *AIA Guide to New York City*. New York: Collier Books, 1978.

Winn, Dilys, ed. *Murder Ink*. New York: Workman Publishing, 1977.

_____, ed. *Murderess Ink*. New York: Bell Publishing, 1981.

Wright, Carol von Pressentin. *Blue Guide: New York*. New York: W. W. Norton & Co., 1983.

INDEX

TRAVEL AND CULTURE BOOKS

"World at Its Best" Travel Series
Britain, France, Germany, Hawaii,
Holland, Hong Kong, Italy, Spain,
Switzerland, London, New York, Paris,
Washington, D.C.

Passport's Travel Guides and References
IHT Guides to Business Travel in Asia &
Europe
New York on $1,000 a Day (Before
Lunch)
London on £1,000 a Day (Before Tea)
Mystery Reader's Walking Guides:
London, England, and New York
Chicago's Best-Kept Secrets
London's Best-Kept Secrets
New York's Best-Kept Secrets
Everything Japanese
Japan Today!
Japan at Night
Japan Made Easy
Discovering Cultural Japan
Living in Mexico
The Hispanic Way
Guide to Ethnic Chicago
Guide to Ethnic London
Guide to Ethnic New York
Passport's Trip Planner & Travel Diary
Chinese Etiquette and Ethics in Business
Korean Etiquette and Ethics in Business
Japanese Etiquette and Ethics in Business
How to Do Business with the Japanese
Japanese Cultural Encounters
The Japanese

Passport's Regional Guides of France
Auvergne, Provence, Loire Valley,
Dordogne, Languedoc, Brittany, South
West France, Normandy & North West
France, Paris, Rhône Valley & Savoy;
France for the Gourmet Traveler

Passport's Regional Guides of Indonesia
New Guinea, Java, Borneo, Bali, East of
Bali, Sumatra, Spice Islands,
Underwater Indonesia, Sulawesi

Up-Close Guides
Paris, London, Manhattan

Passport's "Ticket To . . ." Series
Italy, Germany, France, Spain

**Passport's Guides: Asia, Africa, Latin
America, Europe**
Japan, Korea, Malaysia, Singapore, Bali,
Burma, Australia, New Zealand, Egypt,
Kenya, Philippines, Portugal, Moscow,
Leningrad, The Georgian Republic,
Mexico

Passport's China Guides
All China; Beijing; Fujian; Guilin,
Canton & Guangdong; Hangzhou &
Zhejiang; Hong Kong; Macau; Nanjing
& Jiangsu; Shanghai; The Silk Road;
Taiwan; Tibet; Xi'an; The Yangzi
River; Yunnan

Passport's India Guides
All India; Bombay and Goa; Dehli, Agra
and Jaipur; Burma; Pakistan;
Kathmandu; Bhutan; Museums of
India; Hill Stations of India

Passport's Thai Guides
Bangkok, Phuket, Chiang Mai, Koh Sumi

On Your Own Series
Brazil, Israel

"Everything Under the Sun" Series
Spain, Barcelona, Toledo, Seville,
Marbella, Cordoba, Granada, Madrid,
Salamanca, Palma de Majorca

Passport's Travel Paks
Britain, France, Italy, Germany, Spain

Exploring Rural Europe Series
England & Wales; France; Greece;
Ireland; Italy; Spain; Austria;
Germany; Scotland

Nagel's Encyclopedia Guides
35 volumes on countries and regions
ranging from Albania to the U.S.S.R.

Passport Maps
Europe; Britain; France; Italy; Holland;
Belgium & Luxembourg; Scandinavia;
Spain & Portugal; Switzerland; Austria
& the Alps

Christmas in Series
France, Mexico, Spain, Germany, Italy

PASSPORT BOOKS
a division of *NTC Publishing Group*
Lincolnwood, Illinois USA